JOHN E. MEGLEY, II

D0903579

Quantitative Methods
for Managerial Decisions

Quantitative Methods for Managerial Decisions

C. M. PAIK

*Associate Professor, School of Government
and Business Administration
George Washington University*

McGRAW-HILL BOOK COMPANY

New York	St. Louis	San Francisco
Düsseldorf	Johannesburg	Kuala Lumpur
London	Mexico	Montreal
New Delhi	Panama	Rio de Janeiro
Singapore	Sydney	Toronto

QUANTITATIVE METHODS
FOR MANAGERIAL DECISIONS

2 3 4 5 6 7 8 9 0   DODO   7 9 8 7 6 5 4

Library of Congress Cataloging in Publication Data

Paik, C M 1931–
    Quantitative methods for managerial decisions.
    1. Decision-making—Mathematical models. I. Title.
HD69.D4P33   658.4′03′0151   72-7093
ISBN 0-07-048086-9

This book was set in Modern 8A by The Maple Press Company.
The editors were Richard F. Dojny and Joan Stern.
The production supervisor was Thomas J. Lo Pinto.
The drawings were done by Anco Technical Services.
The printer and binder was R. R. Donnelley & Sons Company.

To my family

Contents

Preface

Many books have been written in recent years on managerial applications of mathematical-quantitative methods. Yet selecting a text for the general introductory course in quantitative analysis in schools of business and government remains a frustrating experience. Some books are simply too rigorous and abstract for the average student in management. While rigor and abstractness are the fundamental attributes of mathematics, there is no justification for insisting on making mathematicians out of students with little mathematical aptitude or background. These books may be good in providing a solid foundation for those who wish to pursue a career in operations research, but they are not suitable for those who cannot afford to devote more than one or two semesters' work to the area. Then there are books that are too much of a how-to-do type, which emphasize the step-by-step application of mathematical solution techniques to a number of selected types of problem. For example, a book may describe the routine procedures for solving a linear-programming problem in detail, largely neglecting their logical-mathematical basis or economic interpretation. The student's ability or proficiency in following the procedures faithfully and solving a given problem represents neither a new level of mathematical sophistication nor an additional managerial-economic insight.

This book is intended primarily for use in the quantitative-methods course as a core requirement in master's degree programs in business and public administration and in upper-level undergraduate programs in management. Its specific aims are as follows.

1. The book attempts to give an appreciation of the mathematical methods as the "if so, then so" kind of logical reasoning. It minimizes mathematical manipulations per se but tries to demonstrate how these manipulations are really based on the general "if so, then so" mathematical reasoning. For this reason, the book does not even reproduce the probability and other tables necessary for drill type exercises.

2. The book attempts to put the mathematical-quantitative methods in the place they deserve in the broad perspective of management and decision making. The emphasis is on highlighting the relationship between the mathematical-quantitative aspect and the nonmathematical-quantitative aspect of managerial decision analysis.

3. As a way of providing motivation for studying abstract concepts and methods and also of providing general decision analytic insights, the "intuitive" explanation is integrated into the presentation of the formal, mathematical analysis. It is hoped that upon completion of the book, the student will be motivated to learn more rigorous mathematical methods for further technical proficiency.

4. The book provides an exposure to the language of mathematics and quantitative methods as a basis for more effective communication with operations researchers, systems analysts, etc., a breed now omnipresent in government and business.

The book does not require any previous college-level mathematical background. It is true that most graduate programs in administration today require some college-level mathematics for admission, but the writer's experience with graduate students at various institutions, including those with an undergraduate engineering background, indicates that a typical student in management, regardless of the specific number of courses in mathematics and statistics he has taken, has difficulty even with basic mathematics. In fact, many students appear to have built a psychological barrier against "things mathematical." The elementary mathematical concepts and methods explained in conjunction with their managerial application seem to help break down this barrier. Even so, it is unavoidable, given the diversity of students, that some may be already familiar with certain mathematical topics in the book. The following two features of the book are intended to alleviate the problem in such a case: (1) elementary mathematical notions are looked at from a fresh angle, new to most students, and (2) intellectual rigor and mental agility are required to tie together the "mathematics" part and the "economics" part of a given problem.

Because of the emphasis on intuitive understanding, each topic is introduced and discussed through concrete examples. But the ultimate justification for studying specific examples lies in that they allow a *generalization* beyond what is obvious in the examples. Thus for a given mathematical-quantitative concept, examples are chosen from diverse milieus so as to increase our ability to generalize particular experiences into seemingly dissimilar problem areas. In addition to examples, exercises are interspersed throughout the main body of exposition as a means of clinching the understanding of the ideas being discussed. There is no need to complete all the exercises if the reader sees clearly how they are to be answered.

Questions and problems at the end of each chapter provide means for reviewing the main concepts and methods covered in the chapter. The reader is urged to answer all of them. In fact, the discussion of these questions and problems may occupy the bulk of classroom time.

Many have contributed directly and indirectly to the writing of this book. They are too numerous to mention by name to express my deep gratitude and indebtedness.

C. M. PAIK

Quantitative Methods for Managerial Decisions

1
Decisions, Relations, and Mathematical Models

1-0 INTRODUCTION

The objective of this book is to provide an appreciation of the *scientific*, *mathematical*, and *quantitative methods* as "formal" aids to *managerial decision making*. In the current chapter a general understanding of these terms and of the relationships between them is attempted. It will enable the reader to view the topics of future chapters from a broad perspective and with a proper awareness of the limited role formal methods play in managerial decision making.

A major theme developed in this chapter is that (1) discovery, analysis, and testing of *relations* among a number of relevant factors (or variables) abstracted from a given problem situation are of critical importance to managerial decision making; (2) the scientific-mathematical-quantitative methods, with their origin independent of managerial decision-making context, provide the "formal," "rigorous," and "efficient" means of discovering, analyzing, and testing relations in general; (3) therefore, managerial decision making stands to gain from employment of these methods.

Recognition of the central role *relations* play both in decision analyses and in the scientific-mathematical-quantitative methods naturally leads us to a study of the ways in which relations can be depicted. The chapter presents a number of different ways of representing relations. For example, relations may be described verbally, or, more formally, in mathematical statements. Investigation of relations in terms of formal, mathematical statements, of course, is an observable feature distinguishing between scientific-mathematical-quantitative decision analyses and other kinds.

Whether in the real world of a decision situation or in the abstract world of mathematics, one encounters various types of relations. Some are simple; others more complex. Toward the end of the chapter some alternative bases for classifying relations are noted. The simplest of relations is *linear*, as differentiated from *nonlinear*. Or relations may be classified according to whether they are considered to exist with *certainty* or with a degree of *uncertainty*.

1-1 DECISIONS

Decision making is an extremely complex and baffling area of study. Under such names as problem solving, human behavior, theory of choice, theory of organization, policy formulation, or simply decision making, philosophers, psychologists, economists, sociologists, and political scientists alike have tried to understand the nature of the decision process. For the present discussion, however, it is simply proposed that a "deliberate" and "rational" decision (as opposed to an "impulsive" or "irrational" one) consists of some variation or refinement of the following interrelated steps:

Step 1 Discover and define the problem to be analyzed and solved and the objectives or values to be attained from the solution of the problem.

Step 2 Generate and list all seemingly practicable alternative courses of action, strategies, or policies that could be taken.

Step 3 For each of the alternative courses of action listed in step 2, predict and analyze both desirable and undesirable consequences, namely, *benefits*, or effectiveness, and *sacrifices*, or costs of resources consumed.

Step 4 Compare and evaluate the predicted benefits and sacrifices of alternative courses of action and choose that course of action which is most preferable in view of the decision maker's system of objectives as understood in step 1.

This description of the decision process sounds simple, but in most real-world decisions, the four steps are not independent of one another and each poses a formidable difficulty. Any executive, whether in government or in business, would readily testify to the importance and practical difficulty of the first step. What distinguishes a great executive from a mediocre one is his ability to perceive or create a "problem" even when the existing situation is, on the surface, satisfactory, to define or articulate vague and general anxiety into concrete and specific problems to solve, to expand and transform the scope and character of the problem from the form "initially posed" to a broader and more relevant form, and to establish the priority of a particular problem in relation to other problems.

This process of searching and defining the decision problem apparently cannot be carried out without the decision maker's initial understanding of what he wants to achieve in the given situation, i.e., objectives, but very often, the effort to define the problem necessitates clarification and modification of the objectives themselves. Thus, one must go back and forth between the definition of the problem and the definition of objectives. Whatever degree of interdependence there is between its two subprocesses, most critical in the first stage of the decision process are such elusive qualities as broad perspective, experience, innovative mind, and creativity of the decision maker.[1]

In the second stage of the decision process, namely, generating and listing alternative courses of action, the same sort of personal qualities of the decision maker or his staff analyst appear to be the most important. For example, in an analysis of the traffic problem of a metropolitan area, real alternatives to consider may eventually include the possibility of developing an underground mass-transit system or a water transportation system, of levying an entry tax, and even that of moving certain types of businesses out of downtown areas to the suburbs, as well as such more obvious ones as different car speeds, parking restrictions, various one-way traffic possibilities, and construction of more parking facilities. Broad perspective based on experience, ability to think through, and resourcefulness are the qualities necessary for perceiving alternative courses of action that are not initially evident.[2]

Deferring for the moment the discussion of the third decision step, we recognize that the fourth step also, evaluation of benefits and costs for the final selection of the most desirable course of action, is no easy task. Suppose that a firm is considering two alternative projects, A and

---

[1] For examples of chief executives exhibiting such qualities in business organizations, see T. Levitt, Marketing Myopia, *Harvard Business Review*, July-August, 1960.

[2] Addition of new alternatives to the list of initially proposed ones may change the character of the decision problem itself. There is obviously a close interaction between formulation of the problem and listing of alternatives. Perhaps it is better not to distinguish the two steps.

	Courses of action	
Predicted consequence	A	B
Benefit (revenue)	$1500	$2400
Sacrifice (costs)	1000	1800

Exhibit 1-1 Payoffs for A and B.

B, the desirable and undesirable consequences of which are predicted as in Exhibit 1-1.

The revenue from B is higher ($2400) than from A ($1500), but at the same time B costs more ($1800) than A ($1000). Which does the firm prefer, A or B? Two alternative ways of representing the desirability of the projects are at once obvious: (1) Since both benefits and sacrifices are measured on the common dollar scale, costs may be meaningfully deducted from benefits to obtain an indicator of desirability of each project. Thus,

Desirability of A = $1500 − $1000 = $500

Desirability of B = $2400 − $1800 = $600

The index of desirability of B, 600, is higher than that of A, 500; therefore, B is preferred to A. (2) Alternatively, the degree of desirability of each project may be indicated by the ratio of benefits to costs. Thus,

$$\text{Desirability of } A = \frac{\$1500}{\$1000} = 1.50$$

$$\text{Desirability of } B = \frac{\$2400}{\$1800} = 1.33$$

A yields the average benefit of $1.50 per dollar spent; B, $1.33. Contrary to the ranking under the first measure of desirability, A is now preferred to B. Which index of desirability is better? To answer the question, a number of factors must be taken into account, including consideration of other opportunities where the firm could invest the remaining $800 (the difference in outlay between A and B) if the lower-outlay project, A, is undertaken instead of B. Whatever the answer is, it suffices for our purpose here to recognize the difficulty involved.

In the above example, both benefits and costs are measured on a common scale, dollars. When they are not on a common scale, the difficulty of evaluating alternative acts becomes compounded. For example, in an analysis of alternative health programs that could be undertaken by the federal or state governments, benefits may be measured in deaths averted, or lives saved, and costs may be measured in dollars. If a proposed health program X is more effective in deaths averted but at the same time costlier than another proposed health program Y, which does or should the decision maker prefer, X or Y? The difficulty here, besides the one illustrated above, is that no objective trade-off or rate of exchange between the measures of benefits and costs is readily available. A \$1 cost sacrifice may be directly traded off for a \$1 benefit, but how many deaths averted are equivalent to a dollar sacrifice in resources? Ultimately the trade-off must be resolved through a subjective judgment of the decision maker.[1]

1-2 ROLE OF FORMAL METHODS

What can the scientific-mathematical-quantitative methods, in short, the formal methods, contribute to the first, second, and fourth steps of the decision process? To the extent that intuition, creativity, experience, tough-mindedness, and judgment of the decision maker are the most critical qualities, here only minimal (if any) direct tangible contribution may be expected. This, however, does not imply that there may not be any indirect, somewhat less obvious gains. Operations analysts or systems analysts, the practitioners of the formal analytical methods in business and nonbusiness organizations, claim that the benefits of these methods accrue in all steps of the decision process. The true essence of the formal methods as applied to practical decisions, they say, is the "scientific attitude" or "awareness" of the steps and methods followed in the analysis. The very effort of applying the formal methods explicitly and consciously would force the decision maker and his analysts to seek rigorously and creatively new options for achieving the same end and to question and reexamine the objectives themselves and the corresponding measures of effectiveness employed. Such certainly would be a major contribution.

But it is also true that the more direct and visible benefits of formal methods are reaped mostly in conjunction with the third step of the decision process, namely, prediction and analysis of the consequences of alternative courses of action. Only after the decision problem and objectives are defined and the measures of effectiveness and costs and the decision criterion selected, the specific, concrete scientific-mathematical-

---

[1] Some call this the *decision-criterion problem*. For a discussion of the problem in the context of governmental decisions, see C. J. Hitch and R. N. McKean, "The Economics of Defense in the Nuclear Age," pp. 158–181, Harvard, Cambridge, Mass., 1963. For a somewhat more advanced discussion in the context of business investment decisions, see F. Lutz and V. Lutz, "The Theory of Investment of the Firm," chap. 2, Princeton, Princeton, N.J., 1951.

quantitative methods and techniques become a direct and powerful tool for predicting and analyzing the patterns of variation in effectiveness and costs according to the variation in the course of action taken. The formal methods dealt with in this book are mainly in relation to the third step of the decision process.

1-3 RELATIONS

Crucial to the third stage of the decision is the association, or establishment of the relation, between alternative courses of action and expected consequences. Suppose a firm is considering four alternative plant sites, *A*, *B*, *C*, and *D*, for a proposed new plant. A prerequisite to the final selection of a site is to predict the consequences of each plant site; i.e., the firm must *relate* different plant sites to their corresponding consequences. The relationship between the two factors can be summarized conceptually in tabular form, as in Exhibit 1-2.

VARIOUS WAYS OF DEPICTING RELATIONS

To describe a particular plant site by its name every time the need arises to refer to it is unduly cumbersome. One may therefore use *symbols* or *shorthand notation* to identify the plant sites. For example, let

P_a = plant site *A*

P_b = plant site *B*

P_c = plant site *C*

P_d = plant site *D*

Likewise, let

O_a = consequences associated with P_a

O_b = consequences associated with P_b

O_c = consequences associated with P_c

O_d = consequences associated with P_d

Alternative sites	Plant site *A*	Plant site *B*	Plant site *C*	Plant site *D*
Consequences	Consequences *A*	Consequences *B*	Consequences *C*	Consequences *D*

Exhibit 1-2 Relation between sites and consequences.

Plant site	P_a	P_b	P_c	P_d
Consequence	O_a	O_b	O_c	O_d

Exhibit 1-3 Relation between set of P's and set of O's.

With the use of this compact notation, the table of the relationship between the set of alternatives and the set of consequences can be made simpler, as in Exhibit 1-3.

The relationship between two factors may be represented in forms other than tabular. An alternative way of describing the site-consequence relation is

$$[(P_a, O_a), (P_b, O_b), (P_c, O_c), (P_d, O_d)]$$

In this description, each plant site and the associated consequences are shown in parentheses. Four *ordered pairs* of the plant site and the consequences that make up the relation are given in four parentheses. Each pair is an *ordered* pair in the sense that the plant site is shown in the first position and the consequences in the second.

For visualization the same relation may be represented by a diagram as in Exhibit 1-4.

An interesting variation of the diagram of Exhibit 1-4 which would eventually prove very useful in mathematical analyses appears in Exhibit 1-5. Here four alternative plant sites are represented by four different points laid out on the horizontal axis P; four consequences are represented by four different points arranged on the vertical axis O. The association between the plant site and the consequences is denoted by broken arrows.

Once the elements, i.e., four plant sites, of the set of plant sites and the elements, i.e., four consequences, of the set of consequences are represented by the points on two axes as in Exhibit 1-5, a new possibility for

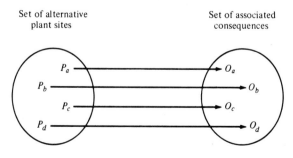

Set of alternative plant sites   Set of associated consequences

Exhibit 1-4 Relation between set of P's and set of O's.

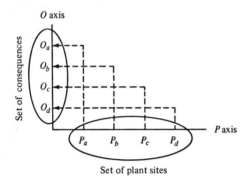

Exhibit 1-5 Relation between set of P's and set of O's.

Set of plant sites

visualizing the relation suggests itself: it can be agreed that four points, J, K, L, and M, in Exhibit 1-6, represent the relation between the plant sites and the consequences. Note that each of points J, K, L, M, in Exhibit 1-6 corresponds to each of the four ordered pairs given earlier. All points on the plane other than J, K, L, and M, such as Q, R, S, and T, are also subject to a useful interpretation. For example, R would represent the combination (P_c, O_b); T would represent the combination (P_a, O_c); but these ordered pairs are not constituents of the particular relation between the plant sites and the consequences of our concern. In another time, in another decision situation, however, the relevant relation might consist of $[(P_a, O_c), (P_b, O_d), (P_c, O_b), (P_d, O_a)]$; then, the points, Q, R, S, and T in Exhibit 1-6 would represent that particular relation.

The diagram which represents a particular relation between sets of objects as a particular set of *points* in space is called a *cartesian diagram*.

Still another way of looking at the relationship uses more compact notation as in the following.

Let an arbitrarily chosen subscript i stand for subscripts a, b, c, d. Then, the whole set of alternative plant sites $[P_a, P_b, P_c, P_d,]$ can be represented simply by one general symbol P_i. Likewise, one general symbol O_i can be employed to represent the entire set of consequences $[O_a, O_b, O_c,$

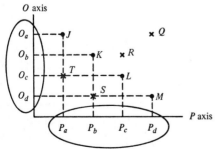

Exhibit 1-6 Cartesian diagram of relation between P's and O's.

O_d]. Now the presence of the relationship between the two factors can be represented as

$$P_i \rightarrow O_i$$

or

$$O_i = f(P_i)$$

or often simply $O = f(P)$ if it is understood that P and O (without subscripts) stand for the whole set of P's and for the whole set of O's, respectively.

Functions   The expression, $O = f(P)$ or $O_i = f(P_i)$ is read "O is related to or dependent on P" or "O is a function of P."[1]   However it is read, it simply denotes a certain pattern of relationship that exists between two sets of objects, O (consequences) and P (plant sites).

Variables P and O are called *variables* because they represent a set of *various* plant sites and a set of *various* consequences.   Further, in this particular instance, P may be called the *input variable* or *independent variable*, and O, the *output variable* or *dependent variable*, because in a sense the "direction" of the relationship is *from P to O* as indicated by the direction of the arrow in the diagrammatic representation.

Some operations analysts, particularly those with engineering orientation, might like to equate the relationship between independent and dependent variables to the input-output relationship in physical processes.   In all physical processes, something *goes into* the process and something *comes out* of the process.   Analogously, the relationship between plant sites and consequences may be viewed as in the imaginary "process" diagram of Exhibit 1-7.

[1] In mathematics, a function is defined as a special case of a relation.   For a more accurate definition of a function, see Prob. 5 at the end of the chapter.

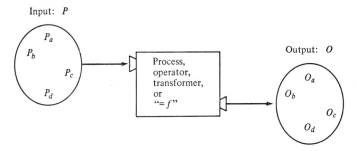

Exhibit 1-7   Process-diagram representation of a function.

When P_a (plant site A) is put into the "process," the corresponding consequence, O_a, comes out of it.   If P_b is put in, O_b comes out, and so on.   The specific nature of the "process," "operator," "transformer," or "$= f$" specifically determines the particular consequences associated with the particular plant sites.   The fact that when a particular plant site P_a is put in, a particular O_a comes out of the process is written $O_a = f(P_a)$. Likewise, $O_b = f(P_b)$, and so on.

1-4   RELATIONS IN MATHEMATICS AND OTHER SCIENCES

Although the concept of a relation between sets of objects and the different ways of depicting it have been introduced above specifically in reference to the set of *alternative* courses of action and the set of associated *consequences*, their applicability is much broader.   In decision analyses, besides (or before) the investigation of the relation between alternative acts and their ultimate consequences, it might be necessary, perhaps as an intermediate step, to determine and analyze such relations as the relation between the set of various speeds at which a machine is run and the set of different quantities of defective units the machine produces, the relation between the set of different levels of production volume and the set of varying average unit costs of production, and the relation between the set of alternative media of advertisement and the set of sizes of potential customers reached.

In scientific inquiries other than those of the decision-analytic context, too, it is readily seen that relations occupy a central place.   Thus, physicists may be concerned with the discovery and analysis of the relation between the passage of time, e.g., the set of seconds passed, and distance an object falls when dropped from an altitude, e.g., the set of feet the object falls; biologists may be interested in establishing the relation between the passage of time and the rate of growth of cells; psychologists may investigate the relation between the set of levels of children's intelligence and the set of levels of their achievement in school; economists may hypothesize the relation between the set of levels of an individual's income and the set of levels of his consumption (or saving).

The study of relations also constitutes the core of the discipline of mathematics.   In pure mathematics relations under investigation need not be between sets of objects from real-world phenomena, such as time, distance, rate of growth of cells, intelligence, achievement, or income. The relations pure mathematicians deal with are, as in Exercise 1-1 below, relations between sets of abstract symbols (such as English or Greek letters) and numbers (such as -100, 8, 5.6, $\sqrt{7}$, $\sqrt{-2}$) without any concern for whether these symbols and numbers stand for anything in the real world.

Exercise 1-1 Each of the five given sets,[1] A, B, X, Y, Z, consists of the elements as listed below:

$A = [k, l, m, n, o, p]$

$B = [p, q, r, s, t, u]$

$X = [0, 1, 2, 3, 4, 5]$

$Y = [-2, -1, 0, 1, 2, 3]$

$Z = [0, 2, 4]$

(a) Suppose that the sets A and B are related as follows:

Set A	k	l	m	n	o	p
Set B	u	s	q	p	r	t

(b) Suppose that the sets A and B are related as follows:

Set A	k	l	m	n	o	p
Set B	p	q	r	s	t	u

(c) Suppose that the sets A and X are related as follows:

Set A	k	l	m	n	o	p
Set X	0	2	4	5	3	1

[1] A set can be specified in two alternative ways. The first is to list all elements of the set, item by item, in brackets; the second is to state the "qualification" for the membership in the set rather than enumerating. Thus, the set A can be expressed: $A = [$letters from k through $p]$; the set X can be expressed: $X = [X: X$ is an integer from 0 through 5]. When the set is enumerated, the order in which the elements are written is immaterial. Thus, the set A could have been written $A = [m, n, p, k, o, l]$ instead of as above. But in an ordered pair (or a vector with two components), say (k, u), the order in which its components k and u appear is significant. That is, (k, u) and (u, k) are not the same ordered pair (vector). Note that in this book sets are given in brackets and ordered pairs (vectors) in parentheses.

(*d*) Suppose that the sets X and Y are related as follows:

Set X	0	1	2	3	4	5
Set Y	-2	-1	0	1	2	3

(*e*) Suppose that the sets X and Y are related as follows:

Set X	0	1	2	3	4	5
Set Y	3	2	1	0	-1	-2

(*f*) Suppose that the sets Y and Z are related as follows:

Set Y	-2	-1	0	1	2	3
Set Z	0	0	2	2	4	4

(*g*) Suppose that the sets Z and A are related as follows:

Set Z	0	2	4			
Set A	k	m	n	l	o	p

1. For (*a*) to (*g*) show the relation on the cartesian diagram.

Note Letters and numerals, as symbols, can be used in two different ways: (1) as means to identify different things; for example, a letter a may be used to identify a Smith; b, to identify a Jones; and a numeral 44, may identify a football player, Anderson; 3 may identify another football player, Brown; (2) as means of representing differences in some "quantity" or "order." For example, 5 is considered "more than" 3 or 4.8; -3 is "equal to" -3 but "less than" -1 or 10; and it may likewise be agreed in a given situation that a letter a is "less than" (or "more than") another letter, b; and b is "less than" (or "more than") e.

In both mathematics and applied sciences (including scientific decision analysis), numerals are used mostly in the second sense. Thus, the cartesian diagram is made much more useful by showing the elements of the number sets as points *in order* as

illustrated.   On the horizontal axis, points to the right represent higher numbers; on
the vertical axis, points to the top represent higher numbers.

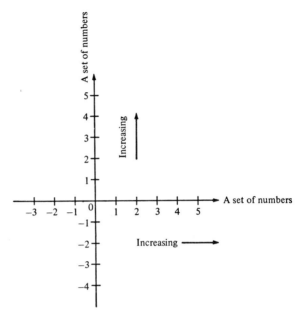

Use the ordered number scale as illustrated in drawing cartesian diagrams for
(c) to (g).   For (a) and (b), the order in which letters are represented as points on the
axes is inconsequential.

2. For each of (a) to (g) give the relation as a set of ordered pairs.   Locate the
points in the cartesian diagrams of part 1 which represent the elements of the set of
ordered pairs.

Note It is customary that in an ordered pair the element represented on the
horizontal axis be shown in the first position and the element represented on the
vertical axis in the second position.

3. For each of (d), (e), and (f), state *verbally* the particular relation, i.e., the
rule by which the corresponding element of the other set can be determined if an element of one set is known.

4. Translate the verbal statements of the relations obtained in part 3 into what
may be termed *mathematical statements* of the relations using such symbols as =, +,
and −.

MATHEMATICAL METHODS

If the relations mathematicians deal with are among objects which are
abstract, nonempirical, and inanimate and as such are of no interest to
decision analysts and other applied scientists inquiring into real-world
phenomena, what mathematics can offer to them is formal *methods* for
analyzing relations *in general*.   The essence of mathematics is the logically rigorous and efficient methods of investigating relations among any
kinds of objects—whether abstract or real.   Managerial decision analysts

can borrow these general methods from mathematics in investigating the relations of interest to them, just as other applied scientists—physicists, engineers, and economists—have so profitably done.

Mathematical methods may be defined in general as the analytical methods by which logically consistent conclusions are drawn from a particular given relation.[1]   In short, mathematical methods involve the kind of logical reasoning process which can be characterized as: If ——, then —— must be true.   We give two simple examples.   (1) If a relation between two sets of numbers X and Y is such that X_i's in set X are twice as large as the corresponding Y_i's in set Y, then, through application of a mathematical method, one can draw a logically air-tight conclusion that Y_i's must be half as large as the corresponding X_i's.   In symbols, if $X_i = 2Y_i$, then it must be that $Y_i = \frac{1}{2}X_i$.   (2) In another relation between X and Y, if the corresponding Y_i's are known to increase as X_i's increase in a certain specified way, application of a mathematical method (which will be studied in Chap. 3) would allow a logically inevitable conclusion of *how fast* Y_i is increasing at various values of X_i, namely, the rate of increase in Y_i per unit increase in X_i at various values of X_i.

To the extent that the above kind of reasoning is relevant in decision analyses, the mathematical methods can help decision making.

The following example illustrates how the concepts discussed so far apply to managerial decision analysis.

EXAMPLE 1-1

A firm produces and sells a chemical.   One of the decisions the firm must make for the next planning period is how many tons of the chemical it should produce and sell.   More formally, the different numbers of tons of the product that can feasibly be produced and sold is the set of alternative acts, i.e., the *decision variable.*

Upon definition of the alternative courses of action the next step in the decision is to predict the benefit (desirable consequences) and sacrifice (undesirable consequences) of each element of the set of alternative acts.   Suppose that the firm's management accepts receipts from sale, i.e., revenues, as the index of desirable consequences and costs of producing and selling as the index of undesirable consequences.

Let X = various numbers of tons of chemical produced and sold
      R = total revenues
      C = total costs
Then
$$R = f(X) \qquad \text{and} \qquad C = g(X)$$

---

[1] For an interesting discussion on the definition of mathematics, see Charles S. Peirce, "Essays in the Philosophy of Science," pp. 256–271, Liberal Arts, New York, 1957.

To establish the particular patterns of correspondence between the set of X's and the set of R's and between the set of X's and the set of C's (in short, to specify the relations f and g) is to predict the consequences of the alternative courses of action in this decision analysis.

Preliminary to determining the relation f, or $f(\cdot)$ as it is often written, suppose that the market for the chemical is such that the firm can sell more only by lowering the selling price. More formally, if we let p stand for the set of different prices per ton, p is related to, or is a function of, X, the tons sold by the firm in the market; that is, $p = h(X)$. Suppose further that on the basis of past experience with various prices the relation $h(\cdot)$ can be approximated by a formula (or mathematical statement) $p = 50 - X/200$.

Exercise 1-2 (a) Find a sufficient number of ordered pairs or combinations of (X, p) meeting the conditions of the relation to satisfy yourself that the relation is consistent with the earlier verbal statement that "the firm can sell more only by lowering the selling price." Present the ordered pairs in a table.

(b) Represent the ordered pairs of (X, p) obtained in part (a) as *points* in a cartesian diagram and link the points by drawing a line between them.

Note Ordered pairs used to identify points in the cartesian space are called *coordinates*. The first entry in an ordered pair is called the first coordinate; the second entry, the second coordinate.

Obviously there are an infinite number of points on the cartesian plane of part (b) representing an infinite number of possible combinations of (X, p)'s. Of all these points of the plane, locating and identifying only those which satisfy the statement of the relation $p = 50 - X/200$ is called *graphing* the relation.

(c) Arbitrarily pick any point on the line—not necessarily from the ones already calculated in part (a). Identify its coordinates and show that it satisfies the given mathematical statement of the relation.

(d) Arbitrarily pick any point which does not lie on the line and show that its coordinates do not meet the given condition of the relation $p = 50 - X/200$ and that therefore the point does not represent an element of the relation.

To proceed, it is recognized that the total revenue is calculated by multiplying the selling price per ton by the number of tons sold: $R = Xp$. Then, since the selling price per ton p can be determined by the formula $p = 50 - X/200$, $R = Xp$ becomes

$$R = X\left(50 - \frac{X}{200}\right) = 50X - \frac{X^2}{200}$$

Thus, if $X = 1000$ tons,

$$R = Xp = 1000(50 - \tfrac{1000}{200}) = 1000(45) = \$45{,}000$$

This procedure by which the relation between X and R is specified can be represented by the two-stage process diagram of Exhibit 1-8a.

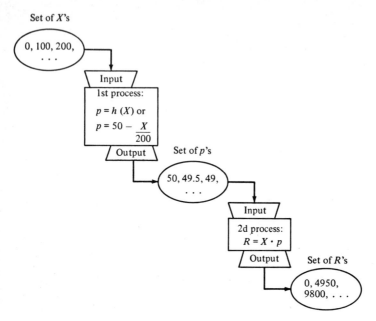

Exhibit 1-8a   Two-stage relation between X and R.

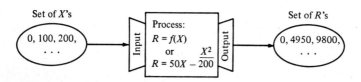

Exhibit 1-8b   One-combined-process conversion of X to R.

According to Exhibit 1-8a, an element of the set X, say 100, is fed into the first-stage process denoted by $p = h(X)$, which yields the corresponding element of the set p of 49.5.   Then this outcome of the first-stage process is fed into the second-stage process characterized by $R = Xp$, which yields the corresponding element of R of $4950.   The two-stage transformation of Exhibit 1-8a may be considered equivalent to the one-stage process conversion, as in Exhibit 1-8b.

Next, turning to the undesirable consequence, the costs of producing and selling, assume that the engineers and accountants of the company estimate that the fixed cost for the next planning period will be $10,000 and that the variable cost per ton will be $20.   Since the total cost consists of the fixed and variable costs, the cost function is specified as $C = g(X) = 10,000 + 20X$.

Further, inasmuch as negative production levels such as -10 tons or -300 tons are meaningless, X must be nonnegative; that is, $X \geq 0$. In addition, if the productive capacity of the firm is limited, say, to the maximum of 4000 tons, the additional restriction on X would be stated as $X \leq 4000$. Combined with the nonnegativity restriction, the restriction on the values of X becomes $0 \leq X \leq 4000$. But even if there is no limit on productive capacity, it is noted that from 5000 tons to 6000 tons there is a decrease in revenues of $5000, while total costs are still increasing, as seen from the following computation.

When $X = 5000$,

$$R = f(5000)$$

$$= (50 \times 5000) - \frac{(5000)^2}{200}$$

$$= 125,000$$

When $X = 6000$,

$$R = f(6000)$$

$$= (50 \times 6000) - \frac{(6000)^2}{200}$$

$$= 120,000$$

$$f(5000) - f(6000) = 125,000 - 120,000 = 5000$$

When $X = 5000$,

$$C = g(5000) = 10,000 + (20 \times 5000) = 110,000$$

When $X = 6000$,

$$C = g(6000) = 10,000 + (20 \times 6000) = 130,000$$

$$g(5000) - g(6000) = 110,000 - 130,000 = -20,000$$

Evidently, as X is increased beyond 6000 tons, R decreases and C increases; therefore, management need not consider the alternatives of producing any more than 6000 tons. Thus, the restriction on X is $0 \leq X \leq 6000$.

Exhibits 1-9a and 1-9b show in tabular form the relations

$$R = 50X - \frac{X^2}{200} \qquad 0 \leq X \leq 6000$$

$$C = 10,000 + 20X$$

Tons produced X	Revenue R	Tons produced X	Cost C
0	$ 0	0	$ 10,000
100	4,950	100	12,000
200	9,800	200	14,000
500	23,750	500	20,000
1,000	45,000	1,000	30,000
2,000	80,000	2,000	50,000
3,000	105,000	3,000	70,000
4,000	120,000	4,000	90,000
5,000	125,000	5,000	110,000
6,000	120,000	6,000	130,000

Exhibit 1-9a Relation between tons produced and revenues.

Exhibit 1-9b Relation between tons produced and costs.

Note that there are so many values the variable X can assume within the restriction that it is impossible to show all possible ordered pairs of (X, R) and (X, C) of the relations; consequently, only a few selected pairs are given.

Exercise 1-3 (a) Plot the data in Exhibits 1-9a and 1-9b as points on a cartesian diagram and link the points by a smooth curve, or line.

(b) Verify that any points on the curve or line satisfy the mathematical statements of the relations given above and that points not on the curve, or line, do not.

Now that alternative acts X have been related to their desirable and undesirable consequences R and C, the decision maker is in a position to make the final decision. To illustrate the final stage of the decision, compare the net desirability of two possible acts, $X = 4000$ and $X = 5000$. If the firm decides to produce 4000 tons, revenues R would be $120,000 and costs C, $90,000. If 5000 tons are produced, $R = \$125,000$ and $C = \$110,000$. Which combination of (R, C) is preferable: $(R, C) = (120,000, 90,000)$ or $(R, C) = (125,000, 110,000)$? If we denote the net desirability of a given combination of (R, C) by $d(R, C)$, is $d(120,000, 90,000)$ less than or greater than $d(125,000, 110,000)$? Since R represents *dollars gained* and C represents *dollars lost* by the firm, $R - C$, profit, would give a natural index of the net desirability: $d(R, C) = R - C$. The index of net desirability of the two acts under consideration is computed as follows.

When $X = 4000$, $(R, C) = (120,000, 90,000)$ and *profit* is

$d(120,000, 90,000) = 120,000 - 90,000 = 30,000$

When $X = 5000$, $(R, C) = (125,000, 110,000)$ and *profit* is

$d(125,000, 110,000) = 125,000 - 110,000 = 15,000$

The predicted profit of the act $X = 4000$, or \$30,000, is higher than that of the act $X = 5000$, or \$15,000. The firm would rather produce and sell 4000 tons than 5000 tons.

Formally, if we let π stand for profit, the fact that π is related to revenues R and costs C would be in general denoted by $\pi = d(R, D)$. π is a function of two variables; in other words, as both R and C vary, there is a corresponding variation in π. The particular relation can then be specified by the mathematical statement $\pi = R - C$. Since $R = 50X - X^2/200$ and $C = 10,000 + 20X$,

$$
\begin{aligned}
\pi &= R - C \\
&= \left(50X - \frac{X^2}{200}\right) - (10,000 + 20X) \\
&= 50X - 20X - \frac{X^2}{200} - 10,000 \\
&= 30X - \frac{X^2}{200} - 10,000
\end{aligned}
$$

In the above formula, π is related directly to X, rather than through the intervening variables, R and C. The relation between X and π can be represented graphically in two alternative ways, Exhibits 1-10a and 1-10b.

Exhibit 1-10a is merely the result of superimposing on top of each other the two graphs drawn in Exercise 1-3. The difference between the height of the revenue curve and the height of the cost line represents the magnitude of profit (or loss) at a given volume of output X. In the range where the revenue curve is higher than the cost line, the difference between the two represents profit; in the range where the cost line is higher than the revenue curve, the difference between the two represents loss, or negative profit. For example, when $X = 3000$, revenue is represented by the height of point Q_1, with the coordinates of (3000, 105,000); cost, by the height of point P_1, with the coordinates of (3000, 70,000); the profit of \$105,000 $-$ \$70,000 $=$ \$35,000 is represented by the distance $Q_1 P_1$. At $X = 6000$, the distance $Q_2 P_2$ represents the loss of \$130,000 $-$ \$120,000 $=$ \$10,000. When X is somewhere near 355 tons and 5970 tons, the heights of the revenue curve and of the cost line are the same, namely, $R = C$ or $\pi = 0$. These X values are called *break-even volumes*.

By computing ordered pairs (X, π)'s directly from the mathematical statement of the relation $\pi = 30X - X^2/200 - 10,000$, another form of profit graph can be constructed (Exhibit 1-10b).

In Exhibit 1-10b, the vertical axis represents profit in dollars. It

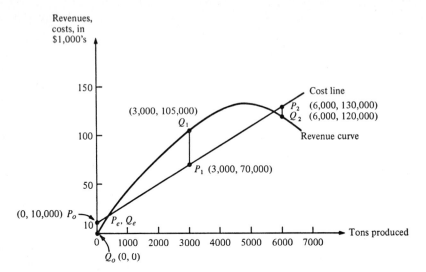

Exhibit 1-10a   Relations between X and R, C.

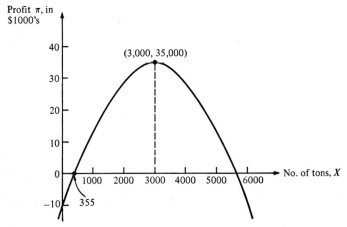

Exhibit 1-10b   Relation between X and π.

is extended downward beyond $0-profit point in order to accommodate the need to show losses, or negative profits. The heights—upward or downward depending on whether they represent profits or losses—of this new profit curve should, of course, be the same as the distance between the revenue curve and the cost line in Exhibit 1-10a. The reader can easily verify from both exhibits that profit is −$10,000 for 0 tons of production; profit is $0 for about 355 tons; the highest profit is $35,000, at $X = 3000$ tons.

Clearly, graphic representation through the use of cartesian diagrams or coordinate systems helps us understand the relation between alternative acts and corresponding profits. In particular, the graphs give some rough ideas of how fast or slow profits increase as X is increased. But, useful as graphs may often be for a quick visualization of how one factor (or set or variable) is related to another, like tables, they are cumbersome and impractical or impossible to construct on a two-dimensional plane when relations between more than two variables are under investigation. Mathematical statements, on the other hand, provide the most precise and versatile vehicle for examining relational patterns. For example, if a relation between X and R is specified mathematically as $R = 50X - X^2/200$, there is available a simple mathematical method by which the exact pattern of the variation of R corresponding to the variation of X can be determined without the help of tables or graphs.[1] Motivation in decision analyses and other scientific efforts for attempting to describe relations in mathematical statements is then twofold: (1) mathematical language is more accurate and efficient than common English (try to state *in words* the relation between X and R, for example), and (2) only when relations are translated into mathematical statements can we hope to manipulate them by mathematical methods so as to draw the necessary conclusions about the particular nature of the relation, e.g., the rate of variation.

Note on continuous and discrete variables Whereas in the above example both *fractions*, such as 0.5, 4.267, 109.0863 (tons), and *integers*, such as 1, 2, 16, 4673 (tons), are meaningful values of the variable X, in other examples, fractions may not be considered elements of the variable of concern. If the product of the firm is cars, instead of a chemical, for instance, fractions must be excluded as feasible values of X.

When a gap exists between two specified values of a variable, it is called *discrete* (within the specified interval). For instance, if the variable X refers to cars, the only meaningful values of X within the interval 1 to 3 are 1, 2, and 3, and consequently gaps exist between 1 and 2 and between 2 and 3. On the other hand, if X is *continuous* within 1 to 3, it can take on *any* value between 1 and 3 including 1.01, 1.2579, $\sqrt{2}$ ($= 1.4142135 \cdots$)*, 1.806, 2, 2.65, 2.8991, 3. Obviously, if continuous,

---

[1] The method will be discussed in Chap. 3.

* $\sqrt{2}$ is a peculiar number. Whereas all numbers shown here other than $\sqrt{2}$ can be *precisely* shown as fractions, an integer divided by an integer, e.g., $1.0065620913 = 10065620913/10000000000$, $\sqrt{2} = 1.4142135 \cdots$ cannot be *precisely* shown as a fraction because the dots at the end of 1.4142135 denote the fact that the number does not end at the last written decimal 5 but goes on and on without limit. Numbers that cannot be precisely shown as fractions are called *irrational numbers*. Integers and fractions together are called *rational numbers*. Rational and irrational numbers constitute *real numbers* (as contrasted to *imaginary numbers*).

the variable can assume an infinite number of values between any two specified numbers, for even such a short interval as between 1.1 and 1.2 may be divided into an infinite number of subintervals of infinitely small sizes. In the strictest sense of the term, no real-world variable may be considered a continuous variable. For example, although one can *conceptually* think of the difference between 5.654209876 tons and 5.654209877 tons, the difference of 0.000000001 ton may be indistinguishable in *practice*. But if it may be assumed, with no harm to analysis, that a ton of chemical is infinitely divisible, then the quantity of chemical may be treated as a continuous variable. Mathematics can be most helpful when variables are considered continuous; discrete variables are awkward to handle mathematically.

Exercise 1-4 A government agency has decided to start a manpower training program for the next planning period in order to reduce unemployment in a given target population group. Assuming that such matters as what constitutes the best curriculum, the optimal class size, and the optimal length of the training period, etc., have been decided, the only decision the agency must make currently is how many training units, i.e., class units, are to be established. Thus, the alternative courses of action in the decision problem can be characterized by the set of various numbers of class units that can be undertaken practically.

Once the alternative courses of action have been defined, the next step in the decision is to predict the benefit and sacrifice consequences of each element of the set of alternative acts. Suppose, for the purpose of a formal analysis, that the use of the estimated percentage reduction in unemployment as the quantitative index of benefit or (effectiveness) consequence and the use of the annual operating costs of the program as the measure of sacrifice (or cost) consequence are acceptable to the decision maker. His next task is to specify the *relations* between the set of alternative course of action, i.e., various possible numbers of class units, and the set of various estimated percentage reductions in unemployment and the set of possible levels of estimated annual operating costs. On the basis of an analysis of the results of the past programs of similar nature, of the demographic characteristics, and of the expectations for the future state of the labor market, suppose that the relations are estimated as follows:

$$E = 0.25X^2 + 10X \qquad 0 \le X \le 20$$
$$C = 50,000 + 10,000X \qquad X \text{ an integer}$$

where E = estimated percentage reduction in unemployment
     C = annual operating costs of program
     X = number of classes

(a) Show the relations in tabular form and in graphic form.

(b) State the remaining steps to the final decision on the problem and the additional information therefor.

(c) Identify the differences between this example and Example 1-1.

1-5 MATHEMATICAL STATEMENTS AND REVIEW OF ELEMENTARY METHODS

In the remaining chapters a number of mathematical methods which facilitate the analysis of relations in decision will be presented. As a

Table 1-1   Examples of open and closed statements

Verbal statement	*Mathematical statement*
Closed	
1. Seven is equal to seven	$7 = 7$
2. Seven is not equal to eight	$7 \neq 8$
3. Seven is not equal to seven	$7 \neq 7$
4. Seven is smaller than eight	$7 < 8$
5. Seven is greater than eight	$7 > 8$
6. Seven is not smaller than eight	$7 \nless 8$
7. Seven is either smaller than or equal to eight	$7 \leq 8$
Open	
8. X is equal to six	$X = 6$
9. X is smaller than six	$X < 6$
10. Nine is equal to X added to three	$9 = X + 3$
11. X take away five is greater than nine	$X - 5 > 9$
12. X multiplied by itself then multiplied by two is eight	$2X^2 = 8$
13. X multiplied by itself added to two is less than eleven	$X^2 + 2 < 11$

foundation for future topics, this section reviews some elementary mathematical methods.

Consider the list in Table 1-1 of verbal and mathematical statements of relations between two numbers or sets of numbers. Some are relations of equality; others, of inequality.

Closed statements and open statements   All of the first seven statements in Table 1-1 are either true or false. More specifically, 1, 2, 4, and 7 are true and 3, 5, and 6 are false.[1]   A statement that is either true or false in the form given is called a *closed statement.*   But some statements, as in examples in the second part of Table 1-1, are neither true nor false in the originally given form; they are called *open statements.* These statements (8 to 13) are neither true nor false *until X* is specified further.   Thus, statement 8, namely, $X = 6$, remains *open* until X is specified as 6, when it becomes *true* and closed, or until X is specified as any number other than 6, such as 5, 10, 4.2, -3, etc., when it becomes *false* and closed.

---

[1] That $7 \leq 8$ is a true statement often bothers students.   The definition of the symbol $\leq$ means *either or,* not *both and.*   Really it is a matter of defining the symbol; $\leq$ is *defined* such that $7 \leq 8$ is considered a true statement

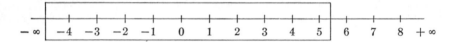

Exhibit 1-11 Solution of $X < 6$.

Solving an equation or statement of inequality Finding the values (elements) of X from a given set of numbers that would make a statement of equality or inequality true is called *solving the equation or the inequality*. When all values of X that make the statement true (or that satisfy the statement) are found, they form the *solution set* or *truth set*. Thus, the open statement of equality $2X^2 = 8$ has two solutions, 2 and -2, in other words, its solution set is a set of two elements, [2, -2]. The set of numbers within which the numbers (values) of X satisfying the statement are to be found is either explicitly given or implicitly understood in the context of the problem on hand. If not stated explicitly, it is assumed in this book to consist of all real numbers, which include all integers, e.g., -102, 9, 254, and all fractions, e.g., -9.235, $\frac{58}{11}$.

Next, for further illustration take statement 9, which says $X < 6$. Obviously, the solution set for the inequality consists of all numbers smaller than 6. Although there is no way of enumerating all solution elements (for they are infinitely many), they can be presented diagrammatically as in Exhibit 1-11. First, the set of all real numbers is represented as a straight line which extends infinitely in either direction from a point representing the number 0. Then the solution set of $X < 6$ is represented as the shaded portion of the real-number line. The number represented by any *point* in the shaded portion of the line is a solution, i.e., satisfies the statement $X < 6$. Numbers represented by points outside the shaded portion are not in the solution set.

Exercise 1-5 Find the solution sets of statements 10 to 13 in Table 1-1 and show them on the real-number line.

MATHEMATICAL METHODS FOR SOLVING STATEMENTS

For simple statements, it is possible to find the solution by trying out a few values of the unknown, but when the relational statements are more complex, the informal trial-and-error method may not work. One can then borrow more efficient procedures from mathematics.

Mathematical methods were earlier characterized as the process of deriving logically consistent conclusions from given statements, or that of developing an argument of the sort: If ——, then —— must be true. Though simple, the following illustrations of formal mathematical procedures for solving equations and inequalities demonstrate the basic nature of such methods.

Mathematical reasoning in solving $9 = X + 3$ If and when the values of X which satisfy the equality statement are found, the number on the left-hand side of the equality sign is the same as the number on the right-hand side.   *If* the left side, 9, is indeed the same as the right side, $X + 3$, deducting (or adding) any same number from (or to) both sides of the equality does not vitiate the equality.   Formally, if $9 = X + 3$ is true, it must also be true that

$$9 - 3 = (X + 3) - 3$$

or

$$6 = X$$

Therefore it is concluded that when $X = 6$, the original statement, $9 = X + 3$, is true and vice versa.

Mathematical reasoning in solving $x - 5 > 9$ If and when the solutions of the statement are found, the inequality statement will be true.   Then, adding any same number to both sides of the statement will leave the inequality unviolated.   If $X - 5 > 9$ is true, it follows that

$$(X - 5) + 5 > 9 + 5$$

is true; i.e.,

$$X > 14$$

is true.   Therefore, when $X > 14$, $X - 5 > 9$ is a true statement.

Mathematical reasoning in solving $2X^2 = 8$ If $2X^2$ is the same as 8, their halves are also the same.   That is, if $2X^2 = 8$ is true,

$$2X^2 \times \tfrac{1}{2} = 8 \times \tfrac{1}{2}$$

is also true; or

$$X^2 = 4$$

is true.   The number whose square is equal to 4 is either 2 or -2. Therefore, $X = 2$ or -2 satisfies the statement $X^2 = 4$ and, in turn, the statement $2X^2 = 8$.

Routine rule for finding solutions   The mathematical operations in the above illustrations may be summarized as a general rule:

Add to, subtract from, multiply, or divide by the same number both the left-hand and right-hand sides of equality or inequality as the case may be in a logically consistent manner so that the finally derived statement is in the form where the unknown alone, for example, x, is on only one side of equality or inequality, i.e., in the form

$$x = \text{\underline{\hspace{1cm}}} \qquad x < \text{\underline{\hspace{1cm}}} \qquad \text{or} \qquad x > \text{\underline{\hspace{1cm}}}$$

One caution in applying the above rule is that when both sides of an inequality are multiplied or divided by a (same) negative quantity, the direction of the inequality must be reversed to be logically consistent. For example, suppose a true statement, $2 < 5$. If we multiply both sides by the same positive number, say 10, logically consistent is the resulting statement, $(2 \times 10) < (5 \times 10)$, or $20 < 50$. But if we multiply both sides by a same negative number, say -10, the result is $(2 \times -10) < (5 \times -10)$ or $-20 < -50$, which is false. Only if the inequality sign is reversed from $<$ to $>$, is the resulting statement $-20 > -50$ true.

Thus, in order to find the values of x which make the statement $-2x < 5$ true, we reason as follows. If $-2x < 5$ is true, dividing both sides of the inequality by a negative number, -2 would require the reversal of the direction or sense of the inequality for the resulting statement to remain true. Namely, $-2x/-2 > 5/-2$, or $x > 5/-2$ is true.

Solving a system of statements　So far the discussion on solving statements has been in reference to a single statement of equality or inequality. As will be seen in future chapters, there arises the need in decision analyses to find solutions for a *system* of two or more statements, or values of the variables, which satisfy two or more statements *simultaneously*. For illustration, consider the following two statements:

$$x(2x + 3)(x - 2) = 0$$
$$x \leq 0$$

What are the values of x which satisfy both statements at the same time? The first statement is true if any of the three terms of the left side of the statement is zero, namely, if $x = 0$, $2x + 3 = 0$, or $x - 2 = 0$. Since $2x + 3 = 0$ if $x = -\frac{3}{2}$ and $x - 2 = 0$ if $x = 2$, the solution set of $x(2x + 3)(x - 2) = 0$ is $[0, -\frac{3}{2}, 2]$. Next the solution set for the second statement, $x \leq 0$, obviously contains zero and all negative numbers. The elements *common to both solution sets* are only two: $x = 0$ and $x = -\frac{3}{2}$ ($x = 2$ satisfies the first statement but not the second statement). Therefore, the solutions to the system of two statements are said to be $x = 0$ and $x = -\frac{3}{2}$.

Solving statements involving more than one variable　Unlike the examples of the above section, the statements of the relations between R and X, C and X, and p and X in Example 1-1 involve not one but two variables. The solutions to a statement with two or more variables are defined the same way as for one-variable statements, namely, as the values of the variables that make the statement true. For example, for $R = 50X - X^2/200$, the solutions constitute a set of ordered pairs, (X, R)'s, that satisfy the statement. Exhibit 1-9a gave a selected number of these ordered pairs in tabular form.

Exercise 1-6 (a) Find and show graphically the set of ordered pairs (x, y) that satisfy the following system of three statements simultaneously:

$$2x + y = 10$$
$$-2 \leq x \leq 5 \qquad x = \text{an integer}$$

(b) Give examples of (x, y)'s that are not solutions of the above system of statements.

1-6 RELATIONS BETWEEN MORE THAN TWO VARIABLES

To illustrate the basic concepts unfettered, the study of relations so far has been restricted to those between two variables at most, but real-world phenomena are rarely so simple as to involve only two variables. For the labor-training program described in Exercise 1-4, for example, the effect on unemployment of the number of class units cannot be viewed in isolation from the effect of such other factors as length of training sessions, level of government expenditures to increase labor mobility, e.g., payment for moving expenses, number of job openings in the community and vicinity, and levels of wages offered, etc. Effectiveness, then, may have to be considered related to more than one input variable. Formally, let

l = length of training sessions

m = government payment for moving expenses

n = number of job openings in the area

o = level of wages in the area

Then $E = \phi(X, l, m, n, o)$, where ϕ (Greek phi) stands for the yet unspecified relation between six variables.

Controllable and noncontrollable variables As defined earlier, E may be called output or the dependent variable and X, l, m, n, o input or independent variables. Further, of the five input variables, three (X, l, and m) are probably what the decision maker can control or vary according to his discretion; and they are therefore called *controllable* or *decision* variables. The other two (n and o) are outside the control of the decision-making agency, and called *noncontrollable variables*. Exhibit 1-12 gives the process-diagram representation of the relation. When specific values

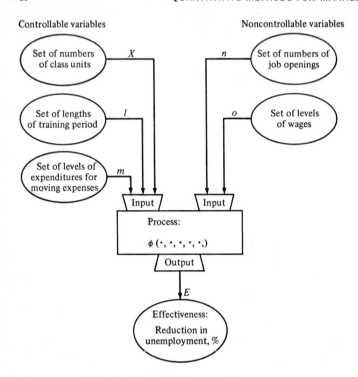

Exhibit 1-12   Relation $E = \phi(X, l, m, n, o)$.

of X, l, m, n, and o are fed intò the process, the particular process converts them into a particular value of E.

The relation between the six variables can be stated in a mathematical statement or formula and as *ordered sixes*, (X, l, m, n, o, E)'s, which satisfy the statement, but it cannot be shown graphically. All ordered sixes which satisfy the mathematical statement of the relation make up the solution set of the statement.

The following chapters deal with the mathematical statements of all kinds—statements of the relation between two single numbers, statements of the relation between more than two variables, and *systems* of statements of the relation between two or more variables. The above serves only as an introduction. In the remainder of this chapter some terminological matters will be resolved.

1-7   MODELS, SYSTEMS, AND SCIENTIFIC METHODS

In discussing scientific works and formal decision analyses, reference is often made to *models*, *systems*, and *scientific methods*. How are these terms related to one another and to what we have studied?

Hitch and McKean give a succinct definition of models:[1]

> Models are abstract representations of reality which help us to perceive significant relations in the real world, to manipulate them, and thereby predict others. They may take any numerous forms. Some are small-scale physical representations of reality, like model aircraft in a wind tunnel. Many are simply representations on paper—like mathematical models. Or finally, they may be simple sets of relationships that are sketched out in the mind and not formally put down on paper. . . . In systems analyses models of one type or another are required to trace the relations between inputs and outputs, resource and objectives, for each of the systems to be compared, so that we can predict the relevant consequences of choosing any system.

Clearly, models are nothing but abstract representations of relations in some real world entities or phenomena. The relations represented in mathematical statements such as $E = -0.25X^2 + 10X$ of the labor-training-program example are the mathematical models.

On the other hand, an acceptable definition of systems may be:[2]

> A system is a set of objects together with relationships between the objects and between their attributes.

Here again emphasis is on relationships. A mere collection of objects does not make a system; only when objects are tied together by relations do they become a whole, a system.[3] According to the definition, a mathematical statement such as $E = -0.25X^2 + 10X$ is no doubt a system; for the symbols E and X are the objects, and these objects are integrated by the arithmetic operations and the equality sign.

If $E = -0.25X^2 + 10X$ is a mathematical statement, a model, and also a system, as asserted above, what is the difference between these

---

[1] Hitch and McKean, *op. cit.*, p. 119. Also, for a more detailed discussion of various types of models, see Irwin Bross, "Design for Decision," pp. 161–182, Macmillan, New York, 1953.

[2] A. D. Hall and R. E. Fagen, Definition of System, reprinted in Walter Buckley (ed.), "Modern Systems Research for the Behavioral Scientists," p. 81, Aldine, Chicago, 1968.

[3] It is hard to think of any entity in this world that cannot be considered a system. Disorganized books and pencils strewn over a desk can be viewed as a system when mere distances between objects are taken as relations; even an atom is a system, made of protons, neutrons, electrons, related to one another. What is new with the term systems is the change in the way of looking at "old" things, with the emphasis on relations.

terms? As one delves deeper into the question, the distinction between the terms—particularly between models and systems—becomes hazier. But the terms may be so defined that a model is an abstract *representation* or *mirroring* of a reality, in a form different from the (original) reality itself, whereas a system is any components in relation whether it is a reality itself or the mirroring (model) of the reality. The relationship between the effectiveness and class units in the original social context is a system of reality; it can be reduced and represented or mirrored as a model in a mathematical statement, which in turn is a system. The sun and its planets with their relational patterns of distances and movements form a system in reality; this original system conception can be represented (or mirrored) as a system in another form, e.g., a physical model (a number of balls positioned in scaled, elliptical tracks), or as another system in another form, e.g., a mathematical model with a system of equality statements.

SCIENTIFIC METHODS AND QUANTITATIVE METHODS

Earlier in the chapter reference was made to "scientific inquiries"—both in decision-analytical and other contexts—without defining the terms. Tautologically, scientific inquiries may be defined as inquiries in which scientific methods are employed. One must now ask: What are scientific methods? We outline some of the observable attributes of the scientific methods or the revealed evidence that scientific methods are at work.

1. *Awareness of the method of analysis and inference by the researcher* If the researcher (or analyst) is *conscious* of the method by which he makes "if so, then so" kind of inference about the relations under investigation, the method is probably scientific. To many practicing scientists the most crucial to a scientific inquiry is the "scientific spirit, which is determined not to rest satisfied with existing opinions, but to press on the real truth of nature."
2. *Reproducibility of the result of the method* If the same conclusion can be expected to be reached by another scientist applying the same method in the same situation, the method is scientific. This feature probably results from attribute 1.
3. *Conscious interrelating of theory and empirical evidence* This attribute may be viewed as consisting of the following steps:
   a. (Initial) observation of empirical data on the relation of concern, e.g., repeated observations on the movements of the sun and the moon from the earth.
   b. Theorization, or formation of a hypothesis about the relation, e.g., specification of the dynamic law governing the positions and movements of the sun, of the moon, and of the earth at different times.

  c. Prediction on the basis of the hypothesis; e.g., from the relation hypothesized, draw a logically consistent conclusion that there will be observable a total eclipse of the sun at a specified time at a specified place.

  d. Testing of the prediction against new observations, e.g., the predicted eclipse is indeed observed (or not observed).

  e. Repeat steps *a* to *d* on the basis of new empirical evidence, thereby improving the theory.

This third attribute is much more concrete and specific than the first two. Application of a method with this attribute can come only from awareness of the method and increases the reproducibility of the analysis. Note that theorization or formation of a hypothesis about a relation is simply building a model.

4. *Use of quantitative measurements and mathematical models* Although no amount of quantitative measurements and mathematical models employed in a research makes it a scientific inquiry, many studies—especially in physical sciences—which may be justifiably labeled scientific make extensive use of mathematical models and quantitative measurements. The process of theory (or model) development as outlined in 3 need not *conceptually* presume use of quantitative measurements and mathematical statements, but *phenomenologically* speaking, according to Torgerson, "measurement is one of the things that enables these processes to be carried out. In large part, measurement enables the tool of mathematics to be applied to science."[1] More specifically, Torgerson quotes Hempel on the advantages of using measurements in science:[2]

"*a.* By means of ordering or metrical concepts, it is often possible to differentiate among instances which are lumped together in a given classification; in this sense a system of quantitative terms provides a greater descriptive flexibility and subtlety. (Thus, among objects which might all be classified as warm, some are warmer than others. The quantitative construct of *temperature* gives a much finer distinction.)

"*b.* A characterization of several items by means of a quantitative concept shows their relative position in the order represented by that concept. (Thus, an object with a temperature of seventy degrees is *warmer than* one of sixty degrees. Classificatory concepts only indicate that they are different.)

"*c.* Greater descriptive flexibility also makes for greater flexibility in the formation of general laws. (The law that an increase in the

[1] W. S. Torgerson, "Theory and Methods of Scaling," p. 1, Wiley, New York, 1958.
[2] *Ibid.*, p. 10.

temperature of a column of mercury is accompanied by an increase in the height of the column would be virtually impossible to state in terms of classificatory concepts.)

"*d.* The introduction of metrical terms makes possible an extensive application of the concepts and theories of higher mathematics: general laws can be expressed in the form of functional relationships between different quantities. (We may thus state precisely in mathematical terms the relation between the height of the column of mercury and its temperature.)"

Strictly speaking, there may be some conceptual differences between scientific, mathematical, and quantitative methods, but at the practical level of application to managerial decision making (for that matter, to other fields as well), mathematics would not be of much help without meaningful quantitative measurement of the decision, noncontrollable, and consequence variables; the awareness of the method (scientific spirit) would result in the maximum payoff only when quantitative-mathematical methods are employed. Perhaps no harm will be done if the three expressions are used interchangeably or referred to by a single expression as *formal methods*.

1-8   TYPES OF MODELS (RELATIONS) AND TRANSITION TO FUTURE CHAPTERS

To the extent that models are constructed for the purpose of prediction, i.e., for determining the value of one variable given the value of another variable, there is no hoping for anything like a perfect or errorless model. Even the most accurate of all models, the one representing the relation between the circumference and the length of a side of a square, $F = 4S$, where F stands for the circumference, S for the length of the side, is subject to an error that might be termed *measurement error*. Thus, given a square, suppose a side is measured as 4.251 in. Then, according to the model, the circumference of the square would be predicted to be $F = 4S = 4(4.251) = 17.004$ in. But when the circumference is actually measured, it may turn out to be, say, 17.010 in; another measurement may yield 17.001 in., and so on.

Errors or deviations from the prediction are compounded when one deals with such decision models as the cost function, $C = 10,000 + 20X$. The cost model predicts the cost of $C = 10,000 + 20(1000) = 30,000$ when 1000 tons is produced, but it is very unlikely that the actual cost would turn out to be $30,000. Besides the measurement error, the fact that the cost model was based on only a limited number of observations, e.g., past experiences, and the fact that many factors other than X (level of production) which have influence over costs were not included in the model—partly from ignorance, partly from design—give rise to additional uncertainty in the prediction. When such chances for error or uncertainty in the relation are not explicitly incorporated in the model, the model is said to be *deterministic;* when uncertainty is explicitly made part of the model, it is referred to as *probabilistic, statistical,* or *stochastic.* Discussions in Chaps. 2 to 5 largely ignore the element of uncertainty. Models from Chap. 6 on incorporate uncertainty explicitly.

An alternative basis for classifying models or relations is provided through the distinction between *linear* and *nonlinear.* A linear relation is one in which the variables are of the power of 1 and 0. For instance, if the relation is that of equality involving two variables, it can be reduced to the general form $y = a + bx$. Both y and bx are of the first degree; the constant a is considered to be of zero degree. $C = 50,000 + 10,000X$ (where C, X, 50,000, and 10,000 correspond to y, x, a, and b of the general form) and $C = 10,000 + 20X$ (where C, X, 10,000, and 20 correspond to y, x, a, and b of the general form) are examples of the linear model. The name linear derives from the fact that when graphed, the linear relation between two variables, $y = a + bx$, yields a straight line. As an extension of the two-variable case, the relation of more than two variables is called linear if only the first- or zeroth-power variables are involved, even though it can no longer be graphed as a straight line. For example, when a relation among four variables z, w, x, y is stated mathematically, $z = a + bw + cx + dy$, where a, b, c, d represent some specified constants, the relation is called linear.

All relations other than linear are, as expected, called nonlinear. Thus, $y = a + bx^3$, $y = a^x$, and $y = \sin x$ are all nonlinear relations between two variables x and y. The nonlinear relations used in the illustrations of this chapter, that is, $E = -0.25X^2 + 10X$ and $R = 50X - X^2/200$, are examples of a particular class of nonlinear relations named the *second-degree* or *quadratic relations.* In general, the quadratic relation between two variables x and y involving equality can be reduced to the form $y = a + bx + cx^2$. In quadratic relations, the variables are *at most* of the second degree.

Chapters 2, 4, and 5 deal mostly with linear models; Chap. 3 deals with nonlinear models.

QUESTIONS AND PROBLEMS

1. This chapter has given one person's conception of scientific methods, mathematical methods, quantitative methods, models, systems, relations, and decision making. Give, in your own words and conception, the definition, distinction, and interrelationships of the above terms.

2. Employing as many terms and concepts of this chapter as possible, analyze and plan the next vacation for yourself or your family.

3. A retail store must decide on the level of inventory of one of its staple items for the next planning year. Show how management should analyze and make the decision on the policies that would affect the level of inventory of the product for the next year. Use as many terms and concepts of this chapter as possible in the answer.

4. No precise distinction between a function and a relation has been given in this chapter (see footnote on page 9). Mathematics distinguishes the two. To explain the difference in reference to the relationship between only two sets of objects (or two variables), any kind of rule of correspondence (association) between the elements of the two given sets is called a *relation*, but a *function* is a special case of a relation where for each element of a given set, called the *domain* of the relation, there is only one corresponding element of the other given set, called the *range* of the relation. For illustration, suppose the following relations between two given sets of real numbers, X and Y:

Relation 1: $y = x + 3$
Relation 2: $y > x + 3$

where x represents an element of X and y represents the corresponding element of Y. In relation 1, for a specified value of x, there is only one corresponding value of y. Thus, for $x = 3$, the only corresponding y value is $y = x + 3 = 3 + 3 = 6$. Therefore, relation 1 is a function (or a functional relation), where X is the domain and Y the range. If, for $x = 3$, there were some corresponding y's other than 6, the relation could not be considered a function because an element of X, that is, 3, corresponds to more than one element of y. In relation 2, for $x = 3$ there are many values of y that satisfy the relation: $y = 6.2$, $y = 7$, $y = 10.02$, . . . all satisfy the inequality $y > x + 3 = 3 + 3 = 6$. Since for an element of X, the domain set, there is more than one corresponding y element in the relation, relation 2 cannot be considered a function. Verify that $y^2 = x$ is not a function when x is considered the domain but is a function when y is considered the domain.

5. Let the set $X = [a, b, c]$ and the set $Y = [p, q, r]$, and suppose the following relations between the two sets where the set X is considered the domain.

Relation $f_1 = [(a, p), (b, q), (c, r)]$

Relation $f_2 = [(c, r), (b, p), (a, q)]$

Relation $f_3 = [(c, p), (b, q), (a, r), (c, r)]$

Relation $f_4 = [(b, p), (a, r), (c, q), (a, p)]$

(a) Show the relations as the points on a cartesian diagram.
(b) Which of the relations are functions?
(c) If the set X is a group of babies and the set Y a group of mothers, show that only the functions are biologically feasible. (Nonfunctional relations are not.)

6. When x represents the domain and y the range in a function, y is named the *function of x*. Finding the corresponding y value for a given x value is also referred to as finding *the value of the function* for the given x value. For the following functions, find the values of the function at various given values of x.
(a) Let $y = f(x) = 2x - 1$.   Find $f(1), f(-\frac{1}{2}), f(0)$, and $f(\frac{1}{2})$.
(b) Let $y = f(x) = x$.   Find $f(0), f(100), f(0.5)$, and $f(-0.25)$.
(c) Let $y = f(x) = 4 + 0x$ or $y = 4$.   Find $f(3), f(0)$, and $f(-4)$.
(d) Let $y = f(x) = 9^x$.   Find $f(1), f(-2), f(\frac{1}{2}), f(0), f(3)$, and $f(-\frac{1}{2})$.
(e) Let $y = 1/(x + 1)$.   Find $f(99), f(1), f(0), f(-1)$, and $f(-100)$.

7. As numbers are added, subtracted, multiplied, and divided, occasions arise in formal analyses to add, subtract, multiply, and divide functions to form a new function. For example, suppose in a manufacturing firm, the cost of raw material per unit of the product produced is $3 and the cost of labor consists of a flat supervisory salary of $1000 for the given period and the variable labor cost of $2 per unit. If we let C_r and C_l represent the costs of raw material and of labor, respectively, and let x represent the number of units produced, then C_r and C_l are the functions of x as follows:

$$C_r = f(x) = 3x$$
$$C_l = g(x) = 1000 + 2x$$

The total cost of production C, then, is the sum of two functions, C_r and C_l; that is,

$$C = C_r + C_l = f(x) + g(x) = 3x + (1000 + 2x)$$
$$= 5x + 1000$$

(a) Let

$$f_1(x) = 2x + 10$$
$$f_2(x) = x$$
$$f_3(x) = (x + 5)^2$$

Find

$$G_1(x) = f_1(x) + f_2(x) + f_3(x)$$
$$G_2(x) = f_1(x) - f_2(x)$$
$$G_3(x) = f_1(x)f_2(x)$$
$$G_4(x) = \frac{f_1(x)}{f_2(x)}$$

(b) Find the values of the functions (G_i's) when $x = 0$, $x = 2$, $x = -5$, $x = -2$.

8. Often in our analyses we have to deal with a *composite* function, or a "function of a function." For example, suppose someone's savings S is a function of his income I as in $S = f(I) = 0.10I$. (This man saves 10 percent of his income.) The income in turn is a function of the number of hours x he works as in $I = g(x) = 6x$. (He is paid $6 an hour.) The savings is a function of the income function, and can be shown as a function of x as follows:

$$S = f(I) \qquad \text{or} \qquad S = 0.10I$$

Since

$$I = g(x) \qquad \text{or} \qquad I = 6x$$

by substitution,

$$S = f[g(x)] = H(x) \qquad \text{or} \qquad S = 0.10(6x) = 0.60x$$

(a) Let

$$t = f(u) = \frac{u + 3}{3} \qquad \text{and} \qquad x = g(t) = 2t$$

Find $x = h(u)$.

(b) When $u = 6$, $t = ?$ and $x = ?$ When $t = 4$, $u = ?$ and $x = ?$ When $x = 8$, $t = ?$ and $u = ?$

9. Use sufficient examples to show whether the following statements are true or false if a, b, x, and y are any real numbers.

(a) $a > a$ (b) $a \leq a$ (c) $a \gtrless b$

(d) $x > -x$ (e) $y \neq -(-y)$ (f) $\dfrac{xy}{y} = x$

(g) $-(a - b) = b - a$ (h) $x - y = 6 - x$

(i) $(x - y) - a = x - (y - a)$ (j) If $x = y$, then $ax = ay$

(k) If $x > y$, then, $ax > ay$ (l) If $x > y$, then, $x + a > y + b$

(m) If $x > y$ and $x > 0$, and $y > 0$, then $ax > by$

(n) $a(x + y) = ax + by$

(o) $(a + b)(x + y) = ax + ay + bx + by$

(p) $\dfrac{a/b}{c/d} = \dfrac{a}{b}\dfrac{d}{c}$

(q) $\dfrac{1}{a} + \dfrac{1}{b} = \dfrac{1}{a + b}$

10. Translate the following verbal statements of the relations into mathematical statements (or formulas) and then show whether the statement is true or not by checking a number of examples.

(a) The square of the sum of any two real numbers is equal to the square of the first number plus two times the product of the first and second numbers plus the square of the second number.

(b) The square of the difference of any two real numbers is equal to the square of the first number minus two times the product of the first and second numbers plus the square of the second number.

(c) The product of the sum and difference of any two real numbers is not equal to the difference of their squares.

11. Showing the process of reasoning explicitly, find the solution set for the following equations or inequalities. Then represent the solution set as points on the real-number line or the two-dimensional cartesian space.

(a) $-3x + 2 = 7$ (b) $-3x + 2 > 7$

(c) $4x + 6 = 9 + 2x$ (d) $\dfrac{x}{5} + 1 \leq 1.5x + 4$

(e) $5(2x + 1)(3 - x)(\frac{1}{3} + 2x) = 0$

(f) $x^2 > 0$ (g) $x^3 < 0$

(h) $2^x = 8$ (i) $2^x + 4 = 8$

(j) $2^x = \frac{1}{4}$ (k) $2^x = 1.4142$

(l) $2^x = 1$ (m) $(x + 2)(x - 3) > 0$

(n) $(x + 3)^2 = 16$ (o) $x^2 + 6x + 9 = 16$

(p) $2x + 3y = 60$ (q) $xy = 10$

12. Find the ordered pairs of (x, y) that satisfy the following systems of the relations. (In other words, solve the system of the statements.) Show them in the cartesian diagram.

(a) $x + y = 5$ (b) $x + y = 7$ (c) $y = 4 + x$
     $x > 2$ $x > y$ $2y = x$

13. B has 6 more marbles than A and 4 times the number of marbles C has. D has 1 fewer marble than C and one-third the marbles possessed by A. Find the number of marbles held by each.

Hint: Show the relations in mathematical statements and then reason deductively to solve these statements.

14. In reference to Example 1-1 answer the following questions. Show the process of mathematical reasoning explicitly.

(a) How many tons of the chemical can the firm produce at the cost of $95,000?

(b) How many tons of the chemical must be sold for the firm to receive a revenue of $105,000?

Hint: Desired, $R = 105,000$. Therefore, when the correct X value is found, the following equality statement must be satisfied:

$$105,000 = 50X - \frac{X^2}{200}$$

To solve this equation, first multiply both sides by the same quantity, -200:

$$-200(105,000) = -200(50X) + X^2$$

or

$$X^2 - 10,000X = -21,000,000$$

Then, add to, subtract from, multiply, divide both sides of the equality by the same quantities until the statement is reduced to the form

$$X^2 - 2aX + X^2 = (X - a)^2 = k$$

where a and k are some constants. From this form it is now easy to find the value of X which satisfies the statement. Refer to parts (n) and (o) of Prob. 11.

15. If the *total cost* for producing 1000 units is $20,000, the average cost per unit is calculated as $20,000/1000 = $20. Likewise, if the total cost is C for producing X units, the average unit cost is $C_u = C/X$. If the total-cost function is given as $C = 10,000 + 20X$, what is the average-unit-cost function? Plot the average-unit-cost function in a graph.

16. At the beginning of a period the level of the stock of a product is 1000 units. The rate of use of the item is 30 units a day. Thus the level of inventory is a function of the passage of time: $I = f(t)$, where I is the level of inventory and t the days passed. Answer the following, using as many mathematical statements as possible.

(a) Specify $I = f(t)$.

(b) What is the level of inventory at the end of 15 days?

(c) When would the inventory reach 50 units?

(d) When would the inventory be exhausted?

(e) Show the relation between I and t in a cartesian diagram.

17. Express in mathematical notation the fact that profits depend on fixed costs, variable costs, and revenues, in general and specifically.

18. If 10 gal of a chemical is added to 100 gal of water, how many gallons of the chemical or water should be added to the solution in order to make it a 15% solution? Use as much formal mathematics as possible.

2
Linear Models

2-0 INTRODUCTION

Of all types of relations, the linear relation is the simplest. Although strictly speaking, no real-world relations are linear, in many cases, nonlinear real relations can be reasonably approximated by linear models. Once they are so approximated, a considerable gain accrues to the analysis from the application of a branch of mathematics known as *linear algebra*. The linear programming discussed in Chaps. 4 and 5 is an instance where the assumption of linearity in the relations of concern has made it possible to apply the methods of linear algebra to practical affairs.

This chapter begins with an examination of the properties of the linear relation. Understanding of these properties enables one to discern real-world situations where the simplifying assumption of linearity will not critically alter the character of the relation. Specifically, the chapter first gives a number of situations where the relation of interest is linear between two or more variables. In the course of the discussion an effort will be made to distinguish the formal mathematical aspect from the economic interpretive aspect; in particular, the mathematical counterparts of the economic concepts of rate of substitution, opportunity cost, and trade-off will be made apparent.

When some facility in operating with single linear statements has been achieved, the discussion moves on to the situations where the chosen relations form a system of linear equality statements. The mathematical methods for solving a system of linear equations are then explained again in order to enhance the reader's understanding of the nature of the mathematical methods in general. In this connection, the economic concept of break-even will be tied in with the mathematical concept of a system of equations.

2-1 VARIOUS WAYS IN WHICH LINEAR RELATIONS ARE INDICATED

There are many ways in which the linear relation reveals itself initially to the analyst in a given decision or research situation. Some of these are described in the following.

FIXED-TERM–VARIABLE-TERM FORM OR $y = a + bx$

Consider the cost function, $C = 50,000 + 10,000X$, of the manpower training program in Exercise 1-1. This statement of the relation between C and X makes it obvious that if there is to be any variation in C as X varies, it must come from the second term of the right-hand side of the equation, $10,000X$, and not from the first term, $50,000$. In economics and accounting this constant amount, $50,000, is called fixed costs, i.e., those costs which, in a given period of operation, are incurred regardless of the level of activity. On the other hand, $10,000 in the $10,000X$ term is the variable cost per unit of activity, i.e., class unit.

In general, when all costs for a given activity (or production) can be neatly classified into two categories, fixed costs and variable costs,[1] the total costs (for a given period) are the sum of the two and can be expressed as a linear function of the form

$$y = a + bx$$

where y = total costs
a = fixed costs
b = variable costs per unit of x
x = level of activity

The following is another example where the relational situation is directly translatable into the general linear form of $y = a + bx$.

---

[1] Here variable costs per unit are considered to remain the same at all levels of activity. If not, the appropriate cost function is nonlinear. For an example, see Exercise 3-3.

EXAMPLE 2-1

| *Verbal statement* | *Mathematical statement* |

1. An object A travels from a starting point O straight ahead (on a straight line) at a constant speed of 2 ft/sec. The distance traveled is related to the passage of time.

1. $y = a_1 + b_1x$
where y = distance from point of origin O
x = travel time, sec
b_1 = speed, ft/sec
a_1 = position of A at $x = 0$ or when A begins its travel
Since $a_1 = 0$ and $b_1 = 2$,
$y = 0 + 2x = 2x$

2. Another object B begins traveling from the position 3 ft from O (A's starting point) at a constant speed of 1.5 ft/sec.

2. $y = a_2 + b_2x$
$= 3 + 1.5x$

The analogy of the initial distance of the object from point O and the speed of the object in this example to the fixed costs and the variable costs, respectively, in the earlier example, is evident.

Exercise 2-1 (*a*) Reason verbally, not mathematically, when A would catch up with B. (The mathematical method for solving the problem will be given later in the chapter.)

(*b*) Verify that when A's speed is 0.5, 1, 2, and 3 ft/sec, the distance of A from O at different times is expressed as $y = 0.5x$, $y = x$, $y = 2x$, and $y = 3x$, respectively, and that the line representing $y = bx$ in the cartesian diagram becomes steeper as b in bx becomes larger.

(*c*) Give the mathematical statements of the relation between the distance of B from O and the passage of time when B's initial position is -2.5, -1, 2, and 6.2 ft from O, and explain how their graphic representations would vary.

(*d*) Interpret -4, -3, and $-\frac{1}{2}$ in $y = -4 - 3x$ and $y = -\frac{1}{2}x$ in the context of time-distance phenomena.

Exercise 2-2 Given the general linear form of the relation between x and y, $y = a + bx$, nine combinations of positive, zero, and negative values of a and b are possible.

(*a*) Give specific numerical value examples for the nine possible combinations of a and b and graph the resulting relations between x and y.

(*b*) Generalize the nature of the relation between x and y for each combination of a and b. Specifically, include the answers to the following questions: (1) What is y when $x = 0$, or where does the line intercept the y axis? (2) What is x when $y = 0$, or where does the line intercept the x axis? (3) Does y increase or decrease as x increases?

Parameters Within the family of linear functions denoted by $y = a + bx$, a particular function is defined when the specific values of a and b are given. Inasmuch as a and b vary from one linear functional relation to another, they are variables, but to distinguish these variables from x and y, mathematicians call them (a and b) parametric variables or *parameters.* The notion of parameters applies to the cases of nonlinear relations as well. Thus, $y = a + bx + cx^2$ represents the whole class of the quadratic functional relations between x and y, and a specific function is defined when the parameters a, b, and c are specified. The parameter a in both the linear and quadratic functions is also referred to as the constant because the term does not vary (remains constant) as x varies; b and c are called the *coefficients* of the bx and cx^2 terms, respectively.

Rate of change   In investigating relations both in decision analyses and other formal research it is often necessary to find out the *rate of decrease or increase* in one factor (or variable) as another factor is varied.   Indeed, it could be asserted that most decisions in practical affairs were made on the "basis of incremental changes."   For example, an appropriate government agency in its budgetary decision would typically ask such questions as: What will be the *incremental* increase in benefits and costs if a new dam construction is added to the currently existing level of the water resources development program?   A business firm would be interested in knowing what incremental effect in sales there would be if the advertising expenditure were cut by $100,000.   The problem of determining the incremental changes for nonlinear relations will be the subject of discussion in the next chapter.   The present section discusses the rate of change for linear relations.

EXAMPLE 2-2

In Example 1-1, $R = f(X) = 50X - X^2/200$ and $C = g(X) = 10,000 + 20X$ were given as the revenue function and the cost function, respectively, of a chemical firm, where X is the number of tons of the product produced and sold.   Suppose that in the last period of operation the level of activity of the firm was 3100 tons, and now for the next period management is considering the alternative of producing and selling 3350 tons. How much increase in revenues and costs, and consequently profits, would there be as the result of the proposed increase in activity of 250 tons?   These changes are formally computed as follows.   Let

X_1 = last period's production = 3100 tons
X_2 = next period's production = 3350 tons
ΔX = change in production from last to next period

Then

$$\Delta X = X_2 - X_1 = 3350 - 3100 = 250$$

Similarly,

$$\Delta R = R_2 - R_1 = f(X_2) - f(X_1) = f(3350) - f(3100)$$

$$= \left[50(3350) - \frac{(3350)^2}{200} \right] - \left[50(3100) - \frac{(3100)^2}{200} \right]$$

$$= 111,387.5 - 106,950 = 4437.5$$

$$\Delta C = C_2 - C_1 = g(X_2) - g(X_1) = g(3350) - g(3100)$$

$$= [10,000 + 20(3350)] - [10,000 + 20(3100)]$$

$$= 20(3350 - 3100) = 5000$$

The resulting change in profits $\Delta\pi$ is

$$\Delta\pi = \Delta R - \Delta C = 4437.5 - 5000 = -562.5$$

The profit decreases by \$562.5; the firm would rather produce $X_1 = 3100$ tons than $X_2 = 3350$ tons.

The increase in revenue of $\Delta R = 4437.5$ and the increase in cost of $\Delta C = 5000$ are the increases attributable to the increase in X of $\Delta X = 250$ tons. In order to obtain the *rate of increase* of revenue and the *rate of increase* of cost *per ton* in X, ΔR and ΔC must be divided by ΔX as follows:

$$\text{Rate of increase in } R \text{ per ton} = \frac{\Delta R}{\Delta X} = \frac{4437.5}{250} = 17.75$$

$$\text{Rate of increase in } C \text{ per ton} = \frac{\Delta C}{\Delta X} = \frac{5000}{250} = 20$$

The choice of $\Delta X = 250$ in the above illustration was arbitrary; the same computations could have been carried out for any increment in production. To see what happens when the proposed change in production is different from 250 tons, the rates of change in R and C are recomputed for the case when $\Delta X' = 100$.

The last period's production is still $X_1 = 3100$ tons, but the next period's production X_3 is now assumed to be

$$X_3 = X_1 + \Delta X'$$

specifically,

$$X_3 = 3100 + 100 = 3200$$

$$\Delta R' = f(X_3) - f(X_1)$$

$$= \left[50(3200) - \frac{(3200)^2}{200} \right] - \left[50(3100) - \frac{(3100)^2}{200} \right]$$

$$= 108,800 - 106,950 = 1850$$

The rate of change in R per ton is

$$\frac{\Delta R'}{\Delta X'} = \frac{1850}{100} = 18.5$$

Likewise,

$$\Delta C' = g(X_3) - g(X_1) = [10,000 + 20(3200)] - [10,000 + 20(3100)]$$
$$= 20(3200 - 3100) = 2000$$

$$\frac{\Delta C'}{\Delta X'} = \frac{2000}{100} = 20$$

Exhibits 2-1a and 2-1b are the graphic representations of the rates of change.

Notes to Exhibit 2-1a   In reference to triangle AED:

Distance $AE = X_2 - X_1 = \Delta X = 250$

Distance $DE = $ distance $DX_2 - $ distance EX_2

$= R_2 - R_1 = \Delta R = 4437.5$

The rate of change per ton when $\Delta X = 250$ is

$$\frac{DE}{AE} = \frac{\Delta R}{\Delta X} = \frac{4437.5}{250} = 17.75$$

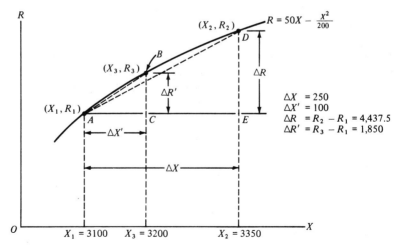

Exhibit 2-1a   Rate of change in revenue.

In reference to triangle ACB:

$$AC = X_3 - X_1 = \Delta X' = 100$$
$$BC = BX_3 - CX_3 = R_3 - R_1 = \Delta R' = 1850$$

The rate of change per ton when $\Delta X' = 100$ is

$$\frac{BC}{AC} = \frac{\Delta R'}{\Delta X'} = \frac{1850}{100} = 18.5$$

The rates of change $\Delta R/\Delta X$ and $\Delta R'/\Delta X'$ are seen as the ratios of the height to the base of the triangles, height/base—the increase in height, i.e., revenue, per unit increase in base, i.e., ton.

Furthermore, a comparison of the triangles AED and ACB reveals that the angle at the vertex A is larger for ACB than for AED. In general, the larger the rate of "height" increase per unit increase in "base," the larger the angle A. That is, the statement,

$$\frac{\text{Height}}{\text{Base}} \text{ for } ACB > \frac{\text{height}}{\text{base}} \text{ for } AED$$

$$\frac{\Delta R}{\Delta X} > \frac{\Delta R'}{\Delta X'} \quad \text{or} \quad 18.5 > 17.75$$

is geometrically represented by

Angle at A for $ACB >$ angle at A for AED

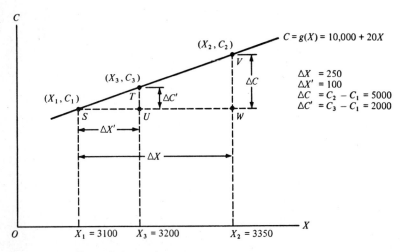

Exhibit 2-1b Rate of change in cost.

Notes to Exhibit 2-1b   In reference to triangle SWV:

$$SW = X_2 - X_1 = \Delta X = 250$$

$$VW = VX_2 - WX_2 = C_2 - C_1 = \Delta C = 5000$$

The rate of change per ton when $\Delta X = 250$ is

$$\frac{\text{Height}}{\text{Base}} = \frac{VW}{SW} = \frac{\Delta C}{\Delta X} = \frac{5000}{250} = 20$$

In reference to triangle SUT:

$$SU = X_3 - X_1 = \Delta X' = 100$$

$$TU = TX_3 - UX_3 = C_3 - C_1 = \Delta C' = 2000$$

The rate of change per ton when $\Delta X' = 100$ is

$$\frac{\text{Height}}{\text{Base}} = \frac{TU}{SU} = \frac{\Delta C'}{\Delta X'} = \frac{2000}{100} = 20$$

Since the ratios of height to base, $\Delta C/\Delta X$ and $\Delta C'/\Delta X'$, remain the same, the angle at S is also the same for both triangles.

In the above illustration, the rate of change in cost per ton, $\Delta C/\Delta X$, remains the same, 20, regardless of what the specific value of ΔX is, while the rate of change in revenue per ton, $\Delta R/\Delta X$, varies as ΔX is varied. In general, linear functions give the same rate of change no matter what ΔX is and no matter from what initial value of X the X is increased by ΔX. On the other hand, nonlinear functions yield varying rates of change for different values of ΔX and for different initial values of X from which the increment of ΔX occurs. More will be discussed on the rate of change of nonlinear relations in the next chapter. The following is the formal proof that the rate of change of the linear function does not vary and is the same as the variable-term parameter of the function.

Derivation of the rate of change for linear function   Given the general linear function $y = a + bx$, suppose that x_1 represents any arbitrarily chosen element of x. Then, the corresponding y value is $y_1 = a + bx_1$. Now suppose that x is increased from x_1 by any arbitrary units Δx, and denote the new resulting x value as x_2. Then,

$$x_1 + \Delta x = x_2 \qquad \text{or} \qquad x_2 - x_1 = \Delta x$$

The y value corresponding to x_2 is $y_2 = a + bx_2$. The change in y attributable to the change in x of Δx is

$$\Delta y = y_2 - y_1 = (a + bx_2) - (a + bx_1)$$
$$= bx_2 - bx_1 = b(x_2 - x_1) = b\,\Delta x$$

The rate of change per unit of x is

$$\frac{\Delta y}{\Delta x} = \frac{b \, \Delta x}{x} = b \qquad \text{provided } \Delta x \neq 0$$

The converse of the above is also true: If x and y are related in such a way that the rate of change, $\Delta y / \Delta x$, is constant or uniform at all levels of x, the relation between x and y is linear and consequently may be expressed as $y = a + bx$, where $b = \Delta y / \Delta x$. In some problems, the coefficient b in bx is initially revealed to the analyst as "variable costs per unit"; in others, it appears as "rate of change in y per unit of x." The reader should observe that in the speed-distance case of Example 2-1, the concept of *speed* is identical with the concept of *rate of change in distance traveled* per unit of time.

Exercise 2-3 (a) For the linear cost function, $C = 10,000 + 20X$, verify further that $\Delta C / \Delta X$ is always the same (20) by calculating it when X is increased from 1000 and from 1500 by ΔX of 0.2 and -4.

(b) For the nonlinear revenue function of $R = 50X - X^2/200$, verify that $\Delta R / \Delta X$ varies at different levels of X and for different values of ΔX by calculating $\Delta R / \Delta X$ when X is increased from 1000 and from 1500 by ΔX of 0.2 and -4.

Exercise 2-4 The capacity of a fuel tank is 100 gal. The fuel is consumed at a uniform hourly rate of 1.2 gal. The tank is full initially.

(a) State mathematically the relation between the level of remaining fuel and the passage of time.

(b) What is the fuel level after $4\frac{1}{4}$ hr? After 5 hr? What is the rate of change in fuel level per hour? Per second?

TWO-OBSERVATION FORM OR $y = a + [(y_2 - y_1)/(x_2 - x_1)]x$

In the above, examples of linear functional relations have been presented where the parameters a and b of the general form $y = a + bx$ are revealed directly. But even when they are not so revealed, if two of the (x, y) pairs that satisfy the relation are known and the relation is known to be linear, the parameters a and b can be determined.

EXAMPLE 2-3

Verbal statement	*Mathematical statement*
1. In 1971 the sales of a firm was 80,000 units, and the operating costs of the typing section were \$20,160. In 1965, a good year, the firm's sales were 100,000 units, and the operating costs of the typing section were \$22,700.	1. If y represents the annual operating costs of the typing section and x the sales in units, and if y_1 and y_2 stand for the typing costs of 1971 and 1965, respectively, and x_1 and x_2 for the sales of 1971 and 1965, respectively, then, $(x_1, y_1) = (80,000, 20,160)$ and $(x_2, y_2) = (100,000, 22,700)$.

2. The accounting department states that all costs of the typing section can be classified as either fixed or variable costs or, more formally, sales and typing costs are related linearly.

2. $y = a + bx$, where a is fixed costs and b is variable costs per unit. If and when the correct values of a and b are found, $y_1 = a + bx_1$ and $y_2 = a + bx_2$ are true. Namely, $20{,}160 = a + b(80{,}000)$ and $22{,}700 = a + b(100{,}000)$ are true.

Obviously, the problem of specifying the linear relation between the sales and the typing costs is identical with the mathematical problem of finding the values of a and b which satisfy the mathematical statements

$$20{,}160 = a + 80{,}000b$$
$$22{,}700 = a + 100{,}000b$$

simultaneously. The reader may be able to find the (a, b)'s satisfying the two equations by trial and error, but mathematics provides an efficient method for solving such systems of equations (as studied in a later section). Here the problem is solved alternatively by utilizing the conclusion in the preceding section that $b = \Delta y/\Delta x$ when the relation between x and y is linear as in $y = a + bx$.

When x is increased from $x_1 = 80{,}000$ to $x_2 = 100{,}000$, namely,

$$\Delta x = x_2 - x_1 = 20{,}000$$

the corresponding increase in y is from $y_1 = 20{,}160$ to $y_2 = 22{,}700$, namely, $\Delta y = y_2 - y_1 = 2540$. Therefore, the rate of change per unit increase in x is

$$\frac{\Delta y}{\Delta x} = \frac{y_2 - y_1}{x_2 - x_1} = \frac{2540}{20{,}000} = 0.127$$

Since $b = \Delta y/\Delta x$, the variable cost per unit is $b = 0.127$. The total variable cost when $x = 80{,}000$ units is $bx = 0.127(80{,}000) = \$10{,}160$. Now, the total cost when $x = 80{,}000$ is known to be $y = 20{,}160$. Accordingly,

$$y = 20{,}160 = a + bx = a + 0.127(80{,}000) = a + 10{,}160$$

From the above, the fixed cost a is determined:

$$a = 20{,}160 - 10{,}160 = 10{,}000$$

The resulting cost function is $y = 10{,}000 + 0.127x$.

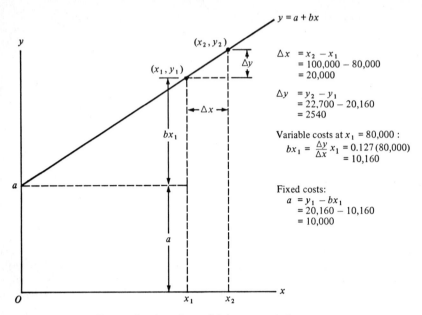

Exhibit 2-2   Determination of a and b in $y = a + bx$.

The reader may trace the above reasoning process geometrically in reference to the graphic representation of Exhibit 2-2.

Exercise 2-5 (a) For each pair of (x, y)'s specify the linear function.

(0,6) and (4,9)   (10,4) and (2,2)   (7,9) and (8,9)
(5, −2) and (5,10)   (−6,4) and (3, −5)   (−10, −4) and (−2, −2)

(b) Graph the functions obtained and identify the points representing the (x, y)'s given.

ACTIVITY-MIX FORM OR $k = mx + ny$

Frequently the linear relation between x and y originally reveals itself in a form directly translatable to the mathematical statement of the kind $k = mx + ny$, rather than $y = a + bx$.

EXAMPLE 2-4

Verbal statement	*Mathematical statement*
Two products, X and Y, are machined at a machine shop where 120 hr of machine time is available for the next period. Machining X requires 4 hr/unit; Y, 3 hr/unit. Management is interested in knowing the combinations of units of X and Y that can be machined from full utilization of the machine-time capacity.	The machine time required for machining x units of X is $4x$; for y units of Y it is $3y$. Consequently, for both X and Y, the total machine time required is $4x + 3y$. This must equal the total time available, that is, $120 = 4x + 3y$. Needless to say, x and y cannot be negative; namely, $x \geq 0$; $y \geq 0$.

Exercise 2-6   (*a*) Show in tabular form a selected number of combinations of x and y which satisfy this system of mathematical statements, namely,

$$120 = 4x + 3y \qquad x \geq 0$$
$$y \geq 0$$

(*b*) Graph the above.

(*c*) Calculate the rate of change in y per unit increase of x when x is increased from $x_1 = 20$ to $x_2 = 25$ and to $x_3 = 20.4$.   Show Δx and Δy on the graph.

As seen from the straight line graphed in Exercise 2-6, the equation $120 = 4x + 3y$ is a linear function. Consequently, it can be converted into the general linear form, $y = a + bx$, as follows. If $120 = 4x + 3y$ is true, then, $120 - 4x = 3y$ is true. If $120 - 4x = 3y$ is true, then, $y = (120 - 4x)/3$ must be true. Namely, $y = 40 - \frac{4}{3}x$ is true. The last equation is in the form $y = a + bx$, where $a = 40$ and $b = -\frac{4}{3}$. Inasmuch as $y = 40 - \frac{4}{3}x$ is the result of logically consistent mathematical operations on the originally given relational statement, $120 = 4x + 3y$, (x, y)'s which satisfy the latter should satisfy the former and vice versa. The reader may verify this fact by determining a few of (x, y)'s satisfying $y = 40 - \frac{4}{3}x$ and checking them against the table constructed in part (*a*) of Exercise 2-6.

Although the process of deriving the statement $y = 40 - \frac{4}{3}x$ from the statement $120 = 4x + 3y$ was strictly mathematical in that we did not worry about what it meant in terms of the real machine-time problem, once derived, $y = 40 - \frac{4}{3}x$ is subject to some meaningful interpretation. As shown in an earlier section, the coefficient $b = -\frac{4}{3}$ is of course the rate of change in y per unit increase in x, that is, $\Delta y/\Delta x$, which in the real-machine-problem context means that whenever 1 more unit of X is machined, the number of units of Y processed must be decreased by $\frac{4}{3}$ units. ($a = 40$ is the number of units of Y that can be machined if no X is processed, namely, $x = 0$.) A benefit of translating a real-world relation under investigation into a mathematical statement is obvious. Once translated, the original statement can be manipulated mathematically to obtain another statement which is logically equivalent to the original one. The analyst, then, would attempt to impute real-problem meanings to the derived statement. The interpretation might give an insight into the relation which was not apparent in the original form.

Rate of trade-off, rate of substitution, opportunity cost   In economic-analytical terminology, the coefficient $-\frac{4}{3}$, the rate of change, is often referred to as the *rate of trade-off* between X and Y in the sense that in order to have more of an activity, one must sacrifice some of the other activity given the limitation of resources. Alternatively, it could be called the *rate of substitution* of Y for 1 unit of X.

The apparent cost of resource (machine time) for processing a unit of X is 4 hr, but the "true" or ultimate cost may be deemed to consist of other opportunities forgone because of the channeling of the limited machine time to the X activity. Since $b = -\frac{4}{3}$ represents this opportunity in the Y activity lost, it may be considered the "true" or *opportunity cost* of 1 unit of X activity.

Exercise 2-7 (a) From $120 = 4x + 3y$, derive an equivalent function of the form $x = f(y) = a + by$, and interpret its parameters a and b in the machining-problem context.

(b) Verify by examples and graphs that (x, y)'s satisfying the function obtained in part (a) satisfy $120 = 4x + 3y$ and $y = 40 - \frac{4}{3}x$ and vice versa.

(c) Change the machine time available to 90, 180, and 240 hr and obtain the mathematical statements defining the relation between the number of units of X and the number of units of Y which can be machined by fully utilizing the available machine time. Graph the above and generalize about what happens to the line as the machine capacity is increased.

(d) State mathematically the relation between x and y when the machine time of 120 hr need not be fully utilized; i.e., idle machine time is acceptable. Display in graph form the combinations of (x, y) which satisfy the statement.

2-2 LINEAR RELATIONS INVOLVING MORE THAN TWO VARIABLES

In the above example, if the machine shop processes three products, X, Y, Z, instead of two, the situation entails a linear relation between three variables. Suppose that the third product Z requires 5 hr of machining per unit, the statement of the relation becomes $120 = 4x + 3y + 5z$, where the new variable z represents the number of units of Z produced. From this equation its mathematical equivalents of the forms $x = f(y, z)$, $y = g(x, z)$, and $z = h(x, y)$ can be derived.

To convert to the form, $x = f(y, z)$: If $120 = 4x + 3y + 5z$ is true, $4x = 120 - 3y - 5z$ must be true, and therefore $x = 30 - \frac{3}{4}y - \frac{5}{4}z$ must be also true. Likewise, the reader may verify the following derivations:

$$y = g(x, z) = 40 - \frac{4}{3}x - \frac{5}{3}z$$

and

$$z = h(x, y) = 24 - \frac{4}{5}x - \frac{3}{5}y*$$

From any of the four alternative forms of the statement of the relation the same set of combinations of x, y, z values, or *ordered triples*,

---

* When the functional relation in three variables, x, y, z, is expressed in the form $k = F(x, y, z)$, where k is a constant (for example, $120 = 4x + 3y + 5z$), it is said to be in an *implicit* form; when the same function is given in the form $x = f(y, z)$ (for example, $x = 30 - \frac{3}{4}y - \frac{5}{4}z$), $y = g(x, z)$ or $z = h(x, y)$, it is said to be in an *explicit* form.   The process of converting an implicit form into an explicit form, say, $y = g(x, z)$, is often referred to as *solving* for the variable y.

y	x									
	0	1	2	$\cdots$	10	11	$\cdots$	28	29	30
0	24	23.2	22.4	$\cdots$	16	15.2	$\cdots$	1.6	0.8	0
1	23.4	22.6	21.8	$\cdots$	15.4	14.6	$\cdots$	1	0.2	
2	22.8	22	21.2	$\cdots$	14.8	14	$\cdots$	0.4		
3	22.2	21.4	20.6	$\cdots$	14.2	13.4	$\cdots$			
$\cdots$	$\cdots$	$\cdots$	$\cdots$	$\cdots$	$\cdots$	$\cdots$	$\cdots$			
19	12.6	11.8	11	$\cdots$	4.6	3.8	$\cdots$			
20	12	11.2	10.4	$\cdots$	4	3.2	$\cdots$			
$\cdots$	$\cdots$	$\cdots$	$\cdots$	$\cdots$	$\cdots$	$\cdots$	$\cdots$			
38	1.2	0.4								
39	0.6									
40	0									

Exhibit 2-3 Table of the relation:

$$120 = 4x + 3y + 5z$$
$$x = 30 - \tfrac{3}{4}y - \tfrac{5}{4}z$$
$$y = 40 - \tfrac{4}{3}x - \tfrac{5}{3}z$$

or

$$z = 24 - \tfrac{4}{5}x - \tfrac{3}{5}y$$

and

$$x \geq 0 \qquad y \geq 0 \qquad z \geq 0$$

(x, y, z)'s, satisfying the relation can be determined. These ordered triples, which constitute the elements of the relation, are conveniently represented in tabular form as in Exhibit 2-3.

Notes to Exhibit 2-3

1. The column headings represent various values of x and the row headings various values of y; the entries in boxes represent various values of z. Thus, when $x = 10$ and $y = 3$, the corresponding value of z defined by the given relation is obtained by reading the entry in the box at the intersection of the $x = 10$ column and the $y = 3$ row, namely, $z = 14.2$.

Each box in the table therefore may be viewed as representing an ordered triple, (x, y, z), which is an element of the relation on hand.

2. The reader should locate the entries in the table which correspond to the ordered triples, $(0, 0, 24)$, $(0, 40, 0)$, $(30, 0, 0)$, $(10, 3, 14.2)$, and $(10, 20, 4)$ and satisfy himself that these combinations of x, y, z values meet the condition given by any of the four mathematical statements of the relation.

3. An ordered triple $(x, y, z) = (10, 3, 12)$ does not satisfy any of the four statements, as shown below:

$$4x + 3y + 5z = 4(10) + 3(3) + 5(12) = 109 \neq 120$$

$$x = 30 - \tfrac{3}{4}y - \tfrac{5}{4}z = 30 - \tfrac{3}{4}(3) - \tfrac{5}{4}(12) = 12.75 \neq 10$$

and so on. In other words, $(x, y, z) = (10, 3, 12)$ is not an element of the relation.

4. The boxes in the table marked with a cross represent the combinations of x, y, z, or ordered triples (x, y, z) that do not satisfy the relation. For example, the box at the intersection of the $x = 30$ column and the $y = 3$ row is marked with a cross. When $x = 30$ and $y = 3$, in order to satisfy the relation $120 = 4x + 3y + 5z$, z must be -1.8:

$$120 = 4(30) + 3(3) + 5z$$

$$5z = 120 - 120 - 9 = -9$$

$$z = -\tfrac{9}{5} = -1.8$$

This means that $(x, y, z) = (30, 3, -1.8)$ indeed is an element of the relation $120 = 4x + 3y + 5z$ (and its equivalents) only if z is allowed to be negative. Inasmuch as one of the statements defining the relation of concern is $z \geq 0$, this particular ordered triple must be excluded from the table.

Extending directly the convention of representing ordered pairs, (x, y)'s, as points on a two-dimensional space, one can graph the above relation between three variables by showing the ordered triples, (x, y, z)'s, which constitute the relation, as points in a three-dimensional space. Exhibit 2-4 is an attempt to visualize a three-dimensional graph on a two-dimensional plane. The reader should imagine a three-dimensional space defined by three perpendicularly intersecting axes, Ox, Oy, Oz. (Imagine a corner of a cubic room where two floor lines and a wall line intersect.) Then, various values of x, y, and z are represented as points on the Ox axis, Oy axis, and Oz axis, respectively. The reader should satisfy himself that it is reasonable to represent an ordered triple $(x, y, z) = (0, 0, 24)$ as point A, $(x, y, z) = (0, 40, 0)$ as point B, $(x, y, z) = (10, 3, 14.2)$ as point D, $(x, y, z) = (10, 3, 12)$ as point X,

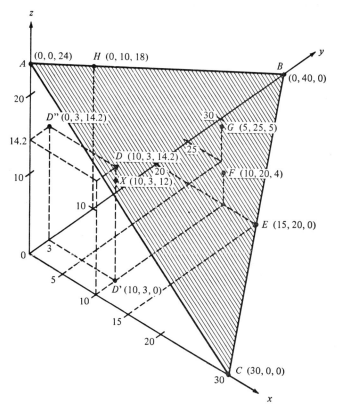

Exhibit 2-4 Graph of the relation:

$$120 - 4x + 3y + 5z$$
$$x = 30 - \tfrac{3}{4}y - \tfrac{5}{4}z$$
$$y = 40 - \tfrac{4}{3}x - \tfrac{5}{3}z$$

or

$$z = 24 - \tfrac{4}{5}x - \tfrac{3}{5}y$$

and

$$x \geq 0 \qquad y \geq 0 \qquad x \geq 0$$

and so on. In particular, the (x, y, z)'s corresponding to points A to H, in Exhibit 2-4 satisfy the relation $120 = 4x + 3y + 5z$ or its equivalent, while (x, y, z)'s corresponding to D', D'', and X are not elements of the relation. When all points representing the ordered triples of the relation are located and connected, they form a "straight" surface (with no curvature), ABC. Note that there are an infinite number of possible combinations of x, y, z, that are on the surface if fractions (and irrational numbers) as well as integers are allowed for the variables. The surface is straight because the relation is linear. A nonlinear function such as $z = a + bx + cy^2$, $z = a^x b^y$, would yield curved surfaces.

Exercise 2-8   (a) How would the graph change when the constant, 120, in the equation $120 = 4x + 3y + 5z$ is changed to 40, 150, 200?

(b) Interpret in the machining-problem context the constants and the coefficients of the variable terms in the statements $x = 30 - \frac{3}{4}y - \frac{5}{4}z$, $y = 40 - \frac{4}{3}x - \frac{5}{3}z$, and $z = 24 - \frac{4}{5}x - \frac{3}{5}y$.

(c) Find z values satisfying the relation when $x = 0$, $y = 10$; when $x = 15$, $y = 20$; when $x = 4$, $y = 0$. Find y values when $x = 0$, $z = 12$; when $x = 2$, $z = 10.4$.

(d) In the graph of Exhibit 2-4 locate points representing (5, 4, 20), (0, 10, 15), (20, 10, 2), (5, −5, 23), and (10, 20, 0) and test whether each is an element of the relation given.

(e) Calculate the rate of change in y per unit increase in x, $\Delta y/\Delta x$, when $\Delta x = x_2 - x_1$, that is, when x is increased from x_1 to x_2 for any given value of z.

(f) What happens to the relational statement when $z = 0$? Interpret the resulting statement.

LINEAR RELATIONS OF MANY VARIABLES

If in the above example, the shop produces more than three products, a linear relation of more than three variables emerges. This can be expressed as $z = a + bx + cy + dw + ev + \cdots$, where z, x, y, w, v, . . . are the variables, and a, b, c, d, e, . . . are the parameters defining the particular relation. Alternatively, it may be written

$$x_n = a_0 + a_1x_1 + a_2x_2 + a_3x_3 + \cdots + a_{n-1}x_{n-1}$$

Analogous to the two- and three-variable cases, the relation between n variables can be described in ways other than mathematical statements. For example, as the two- and three-variable relations are viewed as the sets of ordered pairs and ordered triples, the n-variable relation may be considered a set of ordered n-tuples such as $(x, y, w, v, \ldots, z)$ or $(x_1, x_2, x_3, \ldots, x_n)$. Although n-tuples can no longer be visualized in a two-dimensional diagram, a "point" in the n-dimensional space may be imagined to represent an ordered n-tuple.

A compact notation Σ   In complex decision analyses it often becomes necessary for many terms to be added together. For instance, in Example 1-1, the chemical firm may have many plants, instead of one. If the quantity of the chemical produced at plant 1 is represented by X_1 (tons) and the cost function of plant 1 by $C_1 = a_1 + b_1X_1$, and similarly if for plant 2, X_2 represents tons of the chemical produced and $C_2 = a_2 + b_2X_2$, the cost function, and if in general for plant i, X_i represents the output and $C_i = a_i + b_iX_i$, the cost function, then the total output of the firm in all its n plants would be $X = X_1 + X_2 + X_3 + \cdots + X_{n-1} + X_n$. To simplify the description of the above summation process, a more compact notation may be used:

$$X = \sum_{i=1}^{n} X_i$$

Likewise, the total cost of the firm is expressed as

$$C = C_1 + C_2 + C_3 + \cdots + C_i + \cdots + C_n$$

or

$$C = \sum_{i=1}^{n} C_i$$

Since for any plant i the cost is $C_i = a_i + b_i X_i$,

$$C = \sum_{i=1}^{n} C_i = \sum_{i=1}^{n} (a_i + b_i X_i) = (a_1 + b_1 X_1) + (a_2 + b_2 X_2)$$

$$+ \cdots + (a_i + b_i X_i) + \cdots + (a_n + b_n X_n)$$

$$= (a_1 + a_2 + \cdots + a_i + \cdots a_n)$$

$$+ (b_1 X_1 + b_1 X_1 + \cdots + b_i X_i + \cdots + b_n X_n)$$

$$= \sum_{i=1}^{n} a_i + \sum_{i=1}^{n} b_i X_i$$

In summary, the total cost is a function of n variables and is expressed as

$$C = f(X_1, X_2, X_3, \ldots, X_i, \ldots, X_n)$$

$$= \sum_{i=1}^{n} a_i + \sum_{i=1}^{n} b_i X_i$$

Exercise 2-9 Verify whether the following statements are true.

(a) $\sum_{i=3}^{6} i = 18$ (b) $\sum_{k=0}^{4} 2k = 2 \sum_{k=0}^{4} k = 20$ (c) $\sum_{j=1}^{n} kx_j = k \sum_{j=1}^{n} x_j$

(d) $\sum_{j=1}^{n} k_j x_j = k_j \sum_{j=1}^{n} x_j$ (e) $\sum_{i=1}^{3} i^2 - 14$

(f) $\sum_{i=0}^{5} x_i f_i = x_0 f_0 + x_1 f_1 + x_2 f_2 + x_3 f_3 + x_4 f_4 + x_5 f_5$

(g) $\sum_{i=1}^{n} (x_i + y_i + z_i) = \sum_{i=1}^{n} x_i + \sum_{i=1}^{n} y_i + \sum_{i=1}^{n} z_i$

(h) $\sum_{i=1}^{n} x_i y_i = \sum_{i=1}^{n} x_i \sum_{i=1}^{n} y_i$

2-3 SOLVING A SYSTEM OF LINEAR EQUALITIES

We have seen so far a number of hypothetical real-problem situations which are translatable into formal mathematical statements involving one or more variables and where in order to solve the original real problem, the corresponding mathematical statements have to be solved. This section studies situations where the inherent relations can be reduced to a *system* of linear equations and the necessary analysis calls for *solving* it.

EXAMPLE 2-5

For the same task two alternative methods of operation, A and B, are proposed for management's choice. Since the quality of the output of the operation is assumed the same for either method, the criterion for choosing between the two methods may be considered minimization of the total operating costs for a given planning period. Suppose that the total operating costs of either method consist of two elements, fixed costs and variable costs, as follows:

Costs	Method A	Method B
Fixed	$3000	$6000
Variable, per unit	$5	$3

Exhibit 2-5, the graphic representation of the two alternative cost functions, reveals that for the level of production $0 \le x < 1500$ the oper-

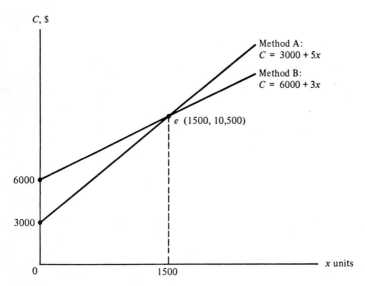

Exhibit 2-5 Relations:

$$C = 3000 + 5x$$
$$C = 6000 + 3x$$
$$x \ge 0.$$

ating costs of A are lower than those of B but for the level of production $1500 > x$ the costs of B are lower than those of A. When the level of production is exactly $x = 1500$, the two methods yield the same operating costs of \$10,500. The point e in the diagram represents the ordered pair $(x, C) = (1500, 10{,}500)$. This ordered pair is the only combination of x and C values which satisfies the two cost statements simultaneously. The decision rule for management is: If the expected production volume is less than 1500 units, select A; if the expected volume is more than 1500 units, select B; if the expected volume is exactly 1500, A and B are equally desirable.

Break-even volume   The production level of 1500 is special in that it is the volume where the preferential ranking of the two methods switches; it is called the *break-even volume*.   Graphically, the break-even point is where two lines intersect each other.   Mathematically, it is the particular ordered pair (x, C) which satisfies the two statements simultaneously. In other words, to find the break-even point is to *solve* the system of two equations.[1]

MATHEMATICAL METHODS FOR SOLVING A SYSTEM OF EQUATIONS

Without recourse to a graph, the above system of equations can be solved through the following mathematical reasoning process.   To solve:

$$C = 3000 + 5x \tag{1}$$
$$C = 6000 + 3x \tag{2}$$

Outline of substitution method

Step 1   If and only if the combinations of x and C values satisfying both equations at the same time are found, C of Eq. (1) and C of Eq. (2) will be equal; and therefore, Eq. (2), $C = 6000 + 3x$, can be substituted for C of Eq. (1); i.e., the equality statement,

$$6000 + 3x = 3000 + 5x$$

will be true.   If $6000 + 3x = 3000 + 5x$ is true, then,

$$5x - 3x = 6000 - 3000$$

is also true, and in turn, $2x = 3000$, or $x = 1500$ is true.

[1] When one of the equations in the system is the revenue function and the other the cost function, the solution of the system gives the more traditional definition of break-even volume.   See, for example, p. 19 and part (g) of Prob. 2-13.

Step 2 In order to satisfy Eqs. (1) and (2) when $x = 1500$, the C value must be

$$C = 3000 + 5x = 3000 + 5(1500) = 10{,}500$$
$$C = 6000 + 3x = 6000 + 3(1500) = 10{,}500$$

Therefore, the combination of $x = 1500$ and $C = 10{,}500$ is the only (x, y) which satisfies the two equations simultaneously, or the only solution to the system of equations. Alternatively, as described below, the substitution method can be applied so as to obtain the C value first and then the x value (instead of the x value first and then the C value as above).

Alternative substitution method

Step 1 From Eq. (1): if $C = 3000 + 5x$ is true, then,

$$5x = C - 3000$$

is true, and also

$$x = \frac{C - 3000}{5}$$

is true. If and only if the combinations of x and C values are found that satisfy both equations at the same time, x of Eq. (1) and x of Eq. (2) will be equal; and therefore, $x = (C - 3000)/5$, which was obtained from Eq. (1) can be substituted for x of Eq. (2); i.e., the equality statement

$$C = 6000 + 3x = 6000 + 3\,\frac{C - 3000}{5}$$

will be true. Or

$$C = 6000 + \tfrac{3}{5}C - 1800 = 4200 + \tfrac{3}{5}C$$

If $C = 4200 + \tfrac{3}{5}C$ is true, then $C - \tfrac{3}{5}C = 4200$ must be true; and also

$$\tfrac{2}{5}C = 4200$$
$$C = 4200(\tfrac{5}{2}) = 10{,}500$$

Step 2 In order to satisfy Eqs. (1) and (2), when $C = 10{,}500$, the x value must be as follows.
From $C = 3000 + 5x$:

$$10{,}500 = 3000 + 5x$$
$$5x = 10{,}500 - 3000$$
$$x = \frac{7500}{5} = 1500$$

From $C = 6000 + 3x$:

$$10,500 = 6000 + 3x$$
$$3x = 10,500 - 6000$$
$$x = 1500$$

Exercise 2-10 Show that the answer to part (a) of Exercise 2-1 is mathematically equivalent to solving a system of equations. Solve it by the substitution method.

EXAMPLE 2-6

Example 2-5 demonstrated how solving a system of equations enters into the break-even analysis. The present example illustrates a situation that necessitates solving a system of equations but cannot be characterized as involving break-even analysis.

Two metals, A and B, can be extracted from two types of ore, I and II; 1 lb of ore I yields 2 oz of A and 3 oz of B, and 1 lb of ore II yields 4 oz of A and 1.5 oz of B. (I is B-rich, and II is A-rich.) How many pounds of I and II are required to produce 50 oz of A and 30 oz of B?

Mathematical statement of the problem Let x_1 and x_2 represent the pounds of ore I and ore II processed by the firm, respectively. Then the number of ounces of A produced from x_1 lb of I is 2 oz multiplied by x_1, or $2x_1$; the number of ounces of A produced from x_2 lb of II is 4 oz multiplied by x_2, or $4x_2$; therefore, the total ounces of A from x_1 of I and x_2 of II is $2x_1 + 4x_2$. Likewise, the total ounces of B produced from x_1 of I and x_2 of II is $3x_1 + 1.5x_2$.

Since the firm wants to produce 50 oz of A and 30 oz of B,

$$2x_1 + 4x_2 = 50 \tag{1}$$
$$3x_1 + 1.5x_2 = 30 \tag{2}$$

The ordered pair (x_1, x_2) which satisfies Eqs. (1) and (2) is the solution of the problem.

Exercise 2-11 (a) Graph the ordered pairs (x_1, x_2) which satisfy Eq. (1).

(b) Do the same for Eq. (2).

(c) Locate on the graph the (x_1, x_2) which satisfies both equations simultaneously and read the specific values.

(d) Give a combination of x_1 and x_2 which does not meet the production requirement of either A or B and locate the point in the graph which represents that combination. Give a combination which meets the requirement of B but not of A and identify the corresponding point in the graph.

(e) Verify the result of part (c) by solving the system of equations by the substitution method.

Linear-combination method   A system of linear equalities can be solved by the substitution method as above, but there is another solution method, called the *linear-combination method*, although the kind of mathematical reasoning involved is essentially the same for both.

Application of the linear-combination method

$$2x_1 + 4x_2 = 50 \tag{1}$$

$$3x_1 + 1.5x_2 = 30 \tag{2}$$

Step 1   Any multiple of Eq. (1), that is, $k(2x_1 + 4x_2) = k(50)$, where k is any constant, for example, -10, -1.5, 3, 16, is *equivalent* to the original equation (1) in the sense that all ordered pairs, (x_1, x_2)'s, which satisfy one equation satisfy the other equation, and vice versa. For example, supposing that $k = -\frac{3}{2}$, if Eq. (1) is true, the result of multiplying both sides of the equation by k would leave the equality undisturbed; i.e., the derived statement

$$-\tfrac{3}{2}(2x_1 + 4x_2) = -\tfrac{3}{2}(50)$$

or

$$-3x_1 - 6x_2 = -75 \tag{1a}$$

would be true.   It follows therefore that solving the original system of equations (1) and (2) is equivalent to solving the derived system of equations (1a) and (2), namely,

$$-3x_1 - 6x_2 = -75 \tag{1a}$$

$$3x_1 + 1.5x_2 = 30 \tag{2}$$

Step 2   Inasmuch as the right-hand side of each equation is equal to its left-hand side (of course, only if and when x_1 and x_2 values satisfying the equation are found), adding the right-hand side and the left-hand side of Eq. (1a) to the right-hand side and the left-hand side of Eq. (2), respectively, would not violate the equality, i.e., the following would be a true statement:

Left side of (1a) + left side of (2)

= right side of (1a) + right side of (2)

More specifically,

$$(-3x_1 - 6x_2) + (3x_1 + 1.5x_2) = -75 + 30 \tag{3}$$

Equation (3) is called a *linear combination* of two equations (1) and (2). In general, a linear combination is defined as the sum of multiples of given equations.   To recapitulate, Eq. (3) is the result of multiplying Eq. (1) by a constant, $-\frac{3}{2}$, and Eq. (2) by a constant, 1, and adding them together.   Obviously, Eq. (3) is only one of many possible linear combinations that can be formed from Eqs. (1) and (2) by varying the constants by which they are multiplied.

Step 3   If Eq. (3), namely,

$$(-3x_1 - 6x_2) + (3x_1 + 1.5x_2) = -75 + 30$$

is true, the following is also true (and vice versa):

$$-3x_1 + 3x_1 - 6x_2 + 1.5x_2 = -45$$

$$0x_1 - 4.5x_2 = -45$$

$$x_2 = \frac{-45}{-4.5} = 10 \qquad\qquad (3a)$$

To summarize the reasoning process so far: if and only if the combinations of x_1 and x_2 values that satisfy Eqs. (1) and (2) simultaneously are found, they will satisfy Eq. (3), a linear combination of (1) and (2). [And conversely, all (x_1, x_2)'s satisfying Eq. (3), and only these, will satisfy Eqs. (1) and (2) simultaneously.] If Eq. (3) is true, then Eq. (3a), that is, $x_2 = 10$, is true, and vice versa. It follows that when the (x_1, x_2)'s satisfying Eqs. (1) and (2) are found, the x_2 value is 10.

     The reason that Eq. (1) was multiplied by a particular constant, $-\frac{3}{2}$, in the process of deriving Eq. (3) is clear. The constant $-\frac{3}{2}$ was chosen so that when the linear combination is formed, one of the variable terms (the term with x_1 in the above) disappears; i.e., its coefficient becomes zero. This will make it possible to determine the specific value of the other variable (x_2) directly from the resulting linear combination.

     Step 4   Now that $x_2 = 10$ has been found, this value of x_2 can be substituted for x_2 in Eq. (1) or (2) to obtain the corresponding value of x_1. But alternatively, the x_1 value satisfying the two equations simultaneously can be found by creating another linear combination of them just as was done for x_2 above. Now the linear combination must be formed so that the x_2 term will disappear:

$$1.5 \times \text{Eq. (1):} \qquad 1.5(2x_1 + 4x_2) = 1.5(50)$$
$$-4 \times \text{Eq. (2):} \qquad -4(3x_1 + 1.5x_2) = -4(30)$$

Adding the above two gives

$$1.5(2x_1 + 4x_2) - 4(3x_1 + 1.5x_2) = 1.5(50) - 4(30)$$

$$3x_1 + 6x_2 - 12x_1 - 6x_2 = 75 - 120$$

$$-9x_1 + 0x_2 = -45$$

$$x_1 = \frac{-45}{-9} = 5$$

Step 5 The reader may wish to check that $(x_1, x_2) = (5, 10)$ is the solution to the system of equations (1) and (2) by verifying whether the equations become true statements only at these values of the variables.

SOLVING SYSTEMS OF EQUATIONS OF THREE OR MORE VARIABLES

The substitution method or the linear-combination method explained above can be directly extended to solve systems of equations of more than two variables.   The two alternative methods are applied below to solve a system of three equations with three variables.

Find (x, y, z) that satisfy

$$2x + 4y + 6z = 20 \tag{1}$$
$$3x - \tfrac{1}{2}y + 2z = 10 \tag{2}$$
$$\tfrac{1}{3}x + 2y + 3z = 8 \tag{3}$$

Substitution method

Step 1 If Eq. (1), $2x + 4y + 6z = 20$, is true, then,

$$2x = 20 - 4y - 6z \qquad \text{and} \qquad x = 10 - 2y - 3z$$

are true.

Step 2 When the solution to the system is found, the x value must satisfy all three equations.   Therefore, when the x value which satisfies the first equation in its equivalent form, $x = 10 - 2y - 3z$, is substituted for x in Eqs. (2) and (3), the resulting equality statements should be true.   Substituting x in Eq. (2),

$$3x - \tfrac{1}{2}y + 2z = 10$$
$$3(10 - 2y - 3z) - \tfrac{1}{2}y + 2z = 10$$
$$30 - 6y - 9z - \tfrac{1}{2}y + 2z = 10$$
$$-\tfrac{13}{2}y - 7z = -20 \tag{2a}$$

Substituting x in Eq. (3),

$$\tfrac{1}{3}x + 2y + 3z = 8$$
$$\tfrac{1}{3}(10 - 2y - 3z) + 2y + 3z = 8$$
$$\tfrac{10}{3} - \tfrac{2}{3}y - z + 2y + 3z = 8$$
$$\tfrac{4}{3}y + 2z = \tfrac{14}{3} \tag{3a}$$

Step 3 From the above it follows logically that the y and z values which satisfy the derived equations (2a) and (3a) would satisfy the original system of the three equations, and vice versa.   Since Eqs. (2a) and

(3a) are equations of two variables, the reader can apply the substitution method again to solve them for y and z. Then, once the y and z values satisfying these equations are obtained, they can in turn be substituted in any of the original three equations to find the x value.

Linear-combination method   We review in general notation what is involved in solving a system of two linear equations by the linear-combination method.   Given the two linear equations of two variables

$$a_{11}x_1 + a_{12}x_2 = b_1 \tag{1}$$
$$a_{21}x_1 + a_{22}x_2 = b_2 \tag{2}$$

the basic idea is to find two linear combinations of the equations which would be ultimately simplified to the form of the following statements:

$$1x_1 + 0x_2 = C_1 \tag{1a}$$
$$0x_1 + 1x_2 = C_2 \tag{2a}$$

Since the coefficient of the x_2 term in Eq. (1a) is 0, Eq. (1a) is nothing but the statement $x_1 = C_1$; and likewise, Eq. (2a) is equivalent to $x_2 = C_2$. The linear combinations themselves give the solution.

Solving a system of three linear equations involves exactly the same process.   More specifically, in solving the following three equations of three variables

$$2x + 4y + 6z = 20 \tag{1}$$
$$3x - \tfrac{1}{2}y + 2z = 10 \tag{2}$$
$$\tfrac{1}{3}x + 2y + 3z = 8 \tag{3}$$

an attempt is made to form linear combinations of these equations such that eventually statements of the following form are obtained:

$$1x + 0y + 0z = C_1$$
$$0x + 1y + 0z = C_2$$
$$0x + 0y + 1z = C_3$$

Then the first statement gives the x value directly, that is, $x = C_1$; the second gives the y value, that is, $y = C_2$; the third gives the z value, that is, $z = C_3$, of the solution.   A step-by-step forming of linear combinations toward the final solution statements in reference to the above specific example follows.

Step 1   Multiply both sides of Eq. (1) by $\tfrac{1}{2}$ to form an equivalent equation (1a) and replace Eq. (1) by (1a) to obtain the new but equivalent system of equations

$$1x + 2y + 3z = 10 \tag{1a}$$
$$3x - \tfrac{1}{2}y + 2z = 10 \tag{2}$$
$$\tfrac{1}{3}x + 2y + 3z = 8 \tag{3}$$

Step 2   Replace Eq. (2) by a linear combination of (1a) and (2), i.e., Eq. (1a) times -3 plus Eq. (2), and replace Eq. (3) by a linear combination of (1a) and (3), i.e., Eq. (1a) plus Eq. (3) times -3. Equation (1a) times -3 plus Eq. (2) is

$$-3(1x + 2y + 3z) + (3x - \tfrac{1}{2}y + 2z) = -3(10) + 10$$
$$-3x - 6y - 9z + 3x - \tfrac{1}{2}y + 2z = -30 + 10$$
$$0x - \tfrac{13}{2}y - 7z = -20 \tag{2a}$$

Equation (1a) plus Eq. (3) times -3 is

$$(1x + 2y + 3z) + [-3(\tfrac{1}{3}x + 2y + 3z)] = 10 + [-3(8)]$$
$$1x + 2y + 3z - 1x - 6y - 9z = 10 - 24$$
$$0x - 4y - 6z = -14 \tag{3a}$$

Thus the newly derived system of equations equivalent to the original system is

$$1x + 2y + 3z = 10 \tag{1a}$$
$$0x - \tfrac{13}{2}y - 7z = -20 \tag{2a}$$
$$0x - 4y - 6z = -14 \tag{3a}$$

Step 3   Replace Eq. (1a) by a linear combination of Eqs. (1a) and (3a), i.e., Eq. (1a) plus Eq. (3a) times $\tfrac{1}{2}$.

$$(1x + 2y + 3z) + \tfrac{1}{2}(0x - 4y - 6z) = 10 + \tfrac{1}{2}(-14)$$
$$1x + 2y + 3z + 0x - 2y - 3z = 10 - 7$$
$$1x + 0y + 0z = 3 \tag{1b}$$

The newly derived system of equations to solve is

$$1x + 0y + 0z = 3 \tag{1b}$$
$$0x - \tfrac{13}{2}y - 7z = -20 \tag{2a}$$
$$0x - 4y - 6z = -14 \tag{3a}$$

Step 4 Replace (2a) by Eq. (3a) times $-\frac{7}{6}$ plus Eq. (2a); and replace (3a) by Eq. (2a) times $-\frac{8}{13}$ plus Eq. (3a). To replace Eq. (2a)

$$-\tfrac{7}{6}(0x - 4y - 6z) + (0x - \tfrac{13}{2}y - 7z) = -\tfrac{7}{6}(-14) + (-20)$$

$$0x + \tfrac{14}{3}y + 7z + 0x - \tfrac{13}{2}y - 7z = \tfrac{49}{3} - 20$$

$$0x - \tfrac{11}{6}y + 0z = -\tfrac{11}{3}$$

$$0x + 1y + 0z = -\tfrac{11}{3}(-\tfrac{6}{11})$$

$$0x + 1y + 0z = 2 \tag{2b}$$

To replace Eq. (3a)

$$-\tfrac{8}{13}(0x - \tfrac{13}{2}y - 7z) + (0x - 4y - 6z) = -\tfrac{8}{13}(-20) + (-14)$$

$$0x + 4y + \tfrac{56}{13}z + 0x - 4y - 6z = \tfrac{160}{13} - 14$$

$$0x + 0y - \tfrac{22}{13}z = -\tfrac{22}{13}$$

$$0x + 0y + 1z = 1 \tag{3b}$$

The new equivalent system of equations is

$$1x + 0y + 0z = 3 \tag{1b}$$

$$0x + 1y + 0z = 2 \tag{2b}$$

$$0x + 0y + 1z = 1 \tag{3b}$$

The x, y, z values which satisfy this system of equations are, of course, $x = 3$, $y = 2$, $z = 1$, and these same values satisfy its equivalent, the original system, as the reader may verify.

Further notes on the linear-combination method There are many alternative routes through which the original system of equations (1), (2), and (3) is converted, through linear combinations, to its logically equivalent system of equations (1b), (2b), and (3b). Some routes are more efficient than others in that the number of steps involved is fewer. Although a little practice will make the reader efficient quickly, there is no need to acquire such facility because what is important is an appreciation of the fundamental nature of the mathematical methods and because computer programs based on the linear-combination method are readily available for solving a system of linear equations of many variables.

Readers with some knowledge of algebra may notice that the linear-combination method is basically the same as what is called the *elimination method*, under which multiples of equations are added to (or subtracted from) other equations until the solution is found. For that matter, the mathematical nature of the substitution method is really the same as the linear-combination method. The crux of all these methods is the deductive reasoning of the "if so, then so" variety, the heart of the mathematical methods identified in Chap. 1.

Evidently the substitution method or the linear-combination method can be directly applied to solving a system of more than three variables. Suppose a system of n equations of n variables, $x_1, x_2, x_3, \ldots, x_{n-1}, x_n$, as follows:

$$a_{11}x_1 + a_{12}x_2 + a_{13}x_3 + \cdots + a_{1n}x_n = b_1$$
$$a_{21}x_1 + a_{22}x_2 + a_{23}x_3 + \cdots + a_{2n}x_n = b_2$$
$$\cdots \cdots \cdots \cdots \cdots \cdots \cdots \cdots \cdots \cdots \cdots \cdots$$
$$a_{n1}x_1 + a_{n2}x_2 + a_{n3}x_3 + \cdots + a_{nn}x_n = b_n$$

In order to find the values of $(x_1, x_2, x_3, \ldots, x_n)$ which satisfy the given system under the linear-combination method, the linear combinations of the given equations are formed successively to obtain the systems of equations that are *equivalent* to the originally given system until the *equivalent* system of equations assumes the following form:

$$1x_1 + 0x_2 + 0x_3 + \cdots + 0x_n = b_1'$$
$$0x_1 + 1x_2 + 0x_3 + \cdots + 0x_n = b_2'$$
$$0x_1 + 0x_2 + 1x_3 + \cdots + 0x_n = b_3'$$
$$\cdots \cdots \cdots \cdots \cdots \cdots \cdots \cdots \cdots \cdots \cdots \cdots$$
$$0x_1 + 0x_2 + 0x_3 + \cdots + 1x_n = b_n'$$

The answer, an ordered n-tuple, would be read from this last equivalent form as $(x_1, x_2, x_3, \ldots, x_n) = (b_1', b_2', b_3', \ldots, b_n')$.

Exercise 2-12   A firm produces three types of products, X_1, X_2, and X_3, which require three kinds of limited resources, as in the following table.

Resource	Requirement per unit			Total resources available
	X_1	X_2	X_3	
Labor hours	2	2.5	5	130
Material, lb	3	0.5	3	85
Machine hours	4	2	1	110

(a) Find the numbers of units of three products that the firm could produce utilizing all the limited resources—no more, no less—by applying the linear-combination method of solving a system of equations.

(b) Suppose that the last row of the table did not exist, i.e., machine hours were not required for producing any of the products. How many units of each product could be produced from fully utilizing the labor hours and the material?

(c) Suppose that the only resource required for producing any of the products is labor hours. How many units of each product could be produced using up the available labor time?

(d) Suppose that the firm produces only two products, X_1 and X_2. How many units of each can be produced if all three types of resources are to be fully utilized?

EXISTENCE OF SOLUTIONS

The methods of solving a system of equations have been illustrated only in cases where the number of variables and the number of equations in the system are the same. But as in parts (b), (c), and (d) of Exercise 2-12, a decision problem may necessitate an analysis of a system where the number of variables is more or less than the number of statements. The following are some of the general rules (or theorems) about the existence of solutions to a system of linear equations.

More variables than equations In general, if there are more variables than the number of equations in the given system, the system has many solutions (not one unique solution), namely, many combinations of the values of the variables satisfying all equations simultaneously. Without the formal proof, the reasonableness of the above assertion may be seen from observing some simple examples.

Suppose a system of equations has two variables, x_1 and x_2, and consists of only one equation, say, $3x_1 + 2.5x_2 = 120$. What values of x_1, x_2, satisfy this system of one equation with two variables? The reader knows already that there are infinitely many ordered pairs, (x_1, x_2)'s that are the solutions to the system.

Likewise, suppose a system of one or two equations with three variables, x_1, x_2, x_3. Part (b) of Exercise 2-12 is an example of the case of a three-variable, two-equation system, where it has already been observed that there are infinitely many ordered triples (x_1, x_2, x_3)'s which satisfy the two equations simultaneously. Part (c) of the same exercise illustrates the three-variable, one-equation case, which again yields infinitely many solutions.

Same numbers of variables and equations In general, if the number of variables, say n, and the number of equations, say m, are the same $(n = m)$, there exists a unique—one and only—solution, i.e., one and only ordered n-tuple. The validity of this theorem in the case of two-variable, two-equation systems was demonstrated in Example 2-6. Graphically, one equation defines a straight line, and the other equation defines another straight line. The two lines intersect each other at only one common point, (x_1, x_2), provided that the two lines are not parallel.

Likewise, part (*a*) of Exercise 2-12 illustrates the three-variable, three-equation case which yields a unique solution—one and only one ordered triple, (x_1, x_2, x_3), satisfying the system. Graphically, the reader may visualize that each of the three equations defines a plane in a three-dimensional space and the three planes would intersect only at one common point, (x_1, x_2, x_3), provided that no two of the planes are parallel to each other. (To help visualize this, think first of the points where only two of the planes meet. The points yield a straight line. Then, impose the remaining third plane and see that it would cut across the line—the intersection of the other two planes—at only one point.)

This theorem holds true only if the lines or planes representing equations are *not parallel* to one another. If any two (or more) of the equations in the system are graphed as lines or planes parallel to the another, there exists no unique solution to the system even when the number of equations is the same as the number of variables. When are lines or planes parallel? As already seen, two lines are parallel if the rate of change of one variable per unit change in the other variable is the same for both. As a review the reader may wish to verify that the following three examples of two-equation systems give rise to the same rate of change, $\Delta x_2/\Delta x_1$, and consequently parallel lines, or, in the last case, the same line:

$$3x_1 + 4x_2 = 4 \qquad\qquad\qquad\qquad (1)$$
$$3x_1 + 4x_2 = -9 \qquad\qquad\qquad\quad (2)$$

$$3x_1 + 4x_2 = 4 \qquad\qquad\qquad\qquad (3)$$
$$6x_1 + 8x_2 = 3 \qquad\qquad\qquad\qquad (4)$$

$$3x_1 + 4x_2 = 4 \qquad\qquad\qquad\qquad (5)$$
$$6x_1 + 8x_2 = 8 \qquad\qquad\qquad\qquad (6)$$

In general, given any two linear equations,

$$a_{11}x_1 + a_{12}x_2 = b_1$$
$$a_{21}x_1 + a_{22}x_2 = b_2$$

if $a_{11}/a_{21} = a_{12}/a_{22} \neq b_1/b_2$, then the lines are parallel. If $a_{11}/a_{21} = a_{12}/a_{22} = b_1/b_2$, then the lines are coincidental, the same line. Specifically, in the above system of equations (1) and (2), $a_{11}/a_{21} = a_{12}/a_{22} \neq b_1/b_2$. The two statements are logically *inconsistent* with each other, for whereas the left-hand sides of both equations are the same, the right-hand sides are different. How could the same $(3x_1 + 4x_2)$ be equal to 4 and -9 at the same time? In other words, no same (x_1, x_2) will satisfy both equations simultaneously. (Consequently, the two lines have no common point, and therefore they are parallel.)

The system of equations (3) and (4) is another case where

$$\frac{a_{11}}{a_{21}} = \frac{a_{12}}{a_{22}} \neq \frac{b_1}{b_2}$$

and the two statements are inconsistent and define two parallel lines. The inconsistency can be seen more readily when one of the two equations is converted to its equivalent form as follows. Multiply Eq. (4) by $\frac{1}{2}$:

$$\tfrac{1}{2}(6x_1 + 8x_2) = \tfrac{1}{2}(3)$$

or

$$3x_1 + 4x_2 = \tfrac{3}{2} \tag{4a}$$

The resulting equivalent system of equations is

$$3x_1 + 4x_2 = 4 \tag{3}$$
$$3x_1 + 4x_2 = \tfrac{3}{2} \tag{4a}$$

Equations (3) and (4a) are logically inconsistent, and consequently so are (3) and (4) themselves. Again, no solution to Eqs. (3) and (4) exists.

In the last system of equations (5) and (6), $a_{11}/a_{21} = a_{12}/a_{22} = b_1/b_2$. Multiplying Eq. (6) by $\frac{1}{2}$ gives the following equivalent system:

$$3x_1 + 4x_2 = 4 \tag{5}$$
$$3x_1 + 4x_2 = 4 \tag{6a}$$

It is clear that Eqs. (5) and (6) are two equations in appearance only; the system of equations is not of two but only one; i.e., the case is not that of $n = m$ but that where the number of variables is more than the number of equations (two versus one). Thus, infinitely many ordered pairs (x_1, x_2)'s satisfy the system.

Next, taking up the case of three variables, three equations, suppose the following general system of linear equations:

$$a_{11}x_1 + a_{12}x_2 + a_{13}x_3 = b_1 \tag{1}$$
$$a_{21}x_1 + a_{22}x_2 + a_{23}x_3 = b_2 \tag{2}$$
$$a_{31}x_1 + a_{32}x_2 + a_{33}x_3 = b_3 \tag{3}$$

As in the two-variable case, when the ratios of the coefficients of the variable terms—but not the ratio of the constant terms (b_j's)—of any two of Eqs. (1), (2), and (3) are the same, the corresponding two planes are parallel. Take, for example, Eqs. (2) and (3). If

$$\frac{a_{21}}{a_{31}} = \frac{a_{22}}{a_{32}} = \frac{a_{23}}{a_{33}} \neq \frac{b_2}{b_3}$$

the two equations are inconsistent; no ordered triples (x_1, x_2, x_3)'s could satisfy both statements simultaneously; the two planes corresponding to them would never meet; i.e., they are parallel; consequently, there is no solution to the given system of three equations.   If it so happened that $a_{21}/a_{31} = a_{22}/a_{32} = a_{23}/a_{33} = b_2/b_3$, the two equations [Eqs. (2) and (3)] would be equivalent; in effect, no more than one equation; therefore, the original system of equations [Eqs. (1) to (3)] would be equivalent to the system of only two independent (nonequivalent) equations [Eq. (1) and either (2) or (3)].   This means that since there are more variables than equations, there would be infinitely many solutions to the system.

To summarize the condition for existence of a unique solution of a system of equations where the number of variables is the same as the number of equations: a unique solution does not exist if the ratios of the coefficients of the variable terms of any two equations in the system are the same.   Although this statement is always true, it is not the complete condition.   The more complete condition must be stated as follows: in order for a system of linear equations with the same numbers of variables and equations to have a unique solution, none of the equations in the system should be a linear combination of two or more of the other equations.   When none of the equations in the system can be formed from a linear combination of other equations, the system is called *linearly independent;* the system is bona fide, and has a unique solution.   If one or more equations in the system are linear combinations of other equations in the system, then the system is *linearly dependent* and is equivalent to a system *less* the equations which are the linear combinations of others.   Consequently, the system possesses more than one unique solution.

Fewer variables than equations   In general, if there are fewer variables than the number of equations (that are linearly independent), the system does not have a solution (an ordered n-tuple) which satisfies all the equations simultaneously.   To see the reasonableness of the above assertion, consider the following example of a two-variable, three-equation system:

$$a_{11}x_1 + a_{12}x_2 = b_1 \tag{1}$$

$$a_{21}x_1 + a_{22}x_2 = b_2 \tag{2}$$

$$a_{31}x_1 + a_{32}x_2 = b_3 \tag{3}$$

Graphically, the above system would in general yield three straight lines as in the accompanying sketch.   There are no points where all three lines meet; i.e., no (x_1, x_2)'s which satisfy all three statements at the same time.   Of course, points A, B, and C, represent (x_1, x_2)'s which satisfy

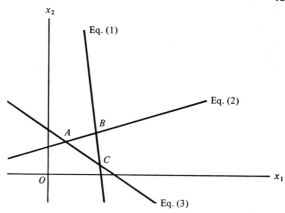

two (only) of the three equations simultaneously.   Part (*d*) of Exercise
2-12 illustrates such a case.

2-4   TRANSITION TO FUTURE CHAPTERS

This chapter has examined the nature of the linear relation and some
examples of the real-world situations which can be represented by a statement of linear equality or a system of linear equalities.   We have seen
how the decision analysis required in such real-world situations necessitates solving the system of equations involved, and consequently, bor-
rowing mathematical methods for solving systems of equations.

Although this chapter has dealt with only the situations which can
be modeled strictly by the statements of linear *equations*, there are situations which require as their models systems of linear *inequalities*.   Chapters 4 and 5 will discuss such situations.   In Chap. 3 we examine the
properties of nonlinear relationships and examples of real-world situations
that can be modeled by nonlinear relationships.

QUESTIONS AND PROBLEMS

1. Explain the meaning of the following statements:
   (*a*) *y* is a linear function of *x*.
   (*b*) *y* is an increasing linear function of *x*.
   (*c*) *y* is a decreasing linear function of *x*.
   (*d*) *z* is a linear function of *w*, *x*, *y*, and the coefficients of the variables are all
positive.
2. Given a function $y = f(x)$, explain the concept of the rate of change.
3. Explain the concepts of rate of substitution, tradeoff, and opportunity cost.
Illustrate how they would reveal themselves in mathematical statements of relations.

4. What is meant by solutions of an equation, by solutions of an inequality (statement), and by solutions of a system of equations?

5. Explain the nature of the mathematical method involved in solving a system of linear equations.

6. Explain both the nonmathematical (economic) and mathematical aspects of the break-even analysis.

7. Imagine four sections of a hilly road which can be pictured as in the diagrams (a) to (d). Parts (a) and (b) are straight uphills; (c) and (d) are straight downhills.

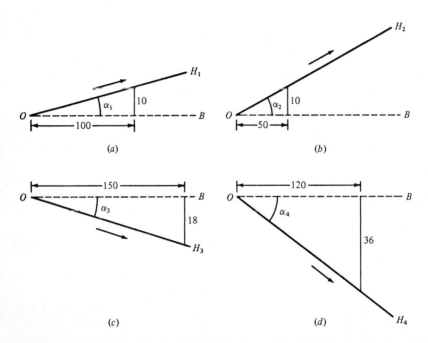

(a) (b)

(c) (d)

Intuitively, we would agree that hill OH_2 is steeper than hill OH_1, or the *slope* of OH_2 is steeper than that of OH_1; and that the downhill OH_4 is steeper than the downhill OH_3. Road engineers represent the steepness of a hill or a slope in two alternative ways: (1) by the angles, α_1, α_2, α_3, α_4 (note that $\alpha_2 > \alpha_1$ and that conventionally α_3 and α_4 would be shown as negative angles such as $-20°$ or $-60°$ in order to denote the fact that they represent downhills) and (2) by calculating the height climbed (or descended) per unit distance, e.g., 1 ft or 1 yd, "traveled" on the base line OB. Thus, the steepness of each of the four slopes (or gradients) would be expressed as in the following:

Gradient of OH_1: $\frac{10}{100} = 0.1$

Gradient of OH_2: $\frac{10}{50} = 0.2$

Gradient of OH_3: $-\frac{18}{150} = -0.12$

Gradient of OH_4: $-\frac{36}{120} = -0.3$

For the purpose of calculating the slopes of OH_3 and OH_4, the height *descended* is represented by a *negative* number (of feet).

(a) Calculate the corresponding height ascended or descended for each of the four hills when the base traveled is 4, 100, 200, or x ft. Is a negative value of x meaningful?

(b) Show each of the four hills on a graph of xy plane, where the y axis measures the height of the points on a hill from a base level, e.g., sea level, and the x axis measures the corresponding distance traveled on the base line, assuming that the starting point of the hill O is at $(x, y) = (0, 0)$, at $(x, y) = (0, 80)$, and at $(x, y) = (10, 50)$, respectively. For each of the assumptions for the position of O, determine the mathematical statement of the relation between the height y and the distance on the base line x in the form $y = a + bx$ for each hill.

(c) Show that b in $y = a + bx$ is the same as $\Delta y/\Delta x$ and is the slope of the hill. Interpret a in the road-engineering context.

8. A city government is allotted a budget of $\$B$ million for the purpose of constructing additional subway routes and/or additional limited-access highways in order to ease the traffic congestion in the city. The cost engineers estimate that the subway construction costs $\$4$ million per mile and the freeway construction $\$2.5$ million per mile.

(a) Express the relation between the budget allotted and the number of miles of subway and freeway added in the mathematical statement. What is the trade-off between the freeway and subway construction? (Use formal mathematics in answering the question.)

(b) Graph the above relation assuming that $B = 60$; $B = 100$; $B = 120$; $B = 200$.

(c) For the city government to decide on the allocation of the fund to the subway and freeway constructions, it must also know the benefit of each to the city. If we let E stand for the benefit expected and x, y, stand for miles of subway and miles of freeway constructed, respectively, then, $E = f(x, y)$. How would you measure E? What kind of a relation would the above represent?

9. Within the past 2 years, a municipal bus transit company was allowed to raise its bus fare from 20 to 25, 28 and 33 cents successively. The average daily fare receipts under different fares are given in the table.

Fare per ride p	Daily receipts R	Number of daily rides q
$0.20	$ 8,400	
.25	9,750	
.28	10,416	
.33	11,286	

(a) Fill in the third column, number of daily (fare-paying) rides. Specify the function $q = f(p, R)$.

(b) Specify the demand function $q = g(p)$, assuming it is a linear function, namely, $g(p) = a + bp$, and graph it. What is $\Delta q/\Delta p$ at various levels of fare?

(c) Specify the revenue function $R = h(p)$ and graph it. What is $\Delta R/\Delta p$ at various levels of fare?

10. A manufacturing firm produces two types of products, I and II. The input requirements for 1 unit of each of the two products and the costs of the inputs are given below:

Input	Product I	II	Cost
Labor, hr	$\frac{1}{2}$	$\frac{3}{4}$	$4/hr
Raw material, units	3	2	$1/unit

In addition to the above variable costs, the firm must carry a fixed cost of $2000/week.

(a) Express the total weekly production cost of the firm C as a function of the number of units of I produced, x_1, and the number of units of II produced, x_2, $C = f(x_1, x_2)$.

(b) Graph the above function in a perspective three-dimensional cartesian space, in the mode of Exhibit 2-4.

(c) Determine the cost functions when x_2 is assumed to be at 100, 200, 250, . . . , and graph them on Cx_1 plane. Find the lines in the graph of part (b) corresponding to the lines obtained in part (c).

(d) Determine the relations between C and x_2 assuming that x_1 is at 50, 100, 200, . . . , and graph them on the Cx_2 plane. Find the lines in part (b) corresponding to the lines of part (d).

(e) Determine the relations between x_1 and x_2 assuming that C is 2000, 3000, 3600, . . . , and graph them on the x_1x_2 plane. Find the lines of (e) in the graph of (b).

Note: The lines obtained in parts (c) to (e) are called *contour lines*, a term borrowed from geography, because in a sense, they represent different levels of height.

(f) For parts (c) to (e), what is the rate of change? How would you interpret the rate of change?

11. Give the values of the variables that satisfy the following systems of equality and inequality statements:

(a) $5x + 6 = 10$
    $x \leq 0$

(b) $2.5x + 3y = 30$

(c) $120 = 2x_1 + x_2 - 3x_3$

(d) $y = 2x + 3$
    $y < x$

(e) $1x_1 + 0x_2 + 0x_3 = 5$
    $0x_1 + 2x_2 + 0x_3 = 4$
    $0x_1 + 0x_2 + 1x_3 = -6$

(f) $x_1 + x_2 + x_3 = 1$
    $1 - x_1 - x_2 = x_3$
    $1 - x_2 - x_3 = x_1$
    $1 - x_1 - x_3 = x_2$

(g) $4a + b = 6$
    $a - b = 3$

(h) $4a + b = 6$
    $a = 3 - \frac{1}{4}b$

(i) $5x_1 + 2x_2 = 10$
    $k(5x_1 + 2x_2) = 10k$

(j) $5x_1 + 2x_2 = 10$
    $k(5x_1 + 2x_2) = 10k + 3$

where k is a constant, e.g., -3, 4.6, in both (i) and (j)

(k) $2x_1 + x_2 = 4$
    $-x_1 + 3x_2 = 6$
    $\frac{1}{2}(2x_1 + x_2) + 2(-x_1 + 3x_2) = \frac{1}{2}(4) + 2(6)$

(l) $a_{11}x_1 + a_{12}x_2 = b_1$
    $a_{21}x_1 + a_{22}x_2 = b_2$

12. Satisfy yourself that the following statement is valid. Given two points in a three-dimensional space, many straight planes that pass both points can be defined, but given three (different) points in a three-dimensional space, a unique straight plane is defined. Of course, specifying the particular plane (in a three-dimensional space) is mathematically equivalent to specifying the parameters a, b, c of the general linear function $z = a + bx + cy$, where x, y, z are the variables. Suppose three points in a three-dimensional cartesian space, the xyz space, are given as $(x_1, y_1, z_1) = (0, 0, 0)$, $(x_2, y_2, z_2) = (2, 3, 6)$, and $(x_3, y_3, z_3) = (4, 2, 8)$. Find the parameters, a, b, c, of the plane $z = a + bx + cy$ which pass through these three points.

    Hint: Solve a system of three equations.

13. Let x = number of units of product produced and sold by a given firm
    p = selling price of product per unit
    v = variable cost of producing and selling 1 unit of product
    F = fixed costs of firm for given planning period
    R = total revenue (or sales) of firm for period
    C = total costs of firm for period
    π = profit (or net income) of firm for period
    (*a*) Specify the function $R = f_1(x, p)$.
    (*b*) Specify the function $C = f_2(F, v, x)$.
    (*c*) Specify the function $\pi = f_3(R, C)$.
    (*d*) Specify the function $\pi = f_4(x)$.
    (*e*) Find the value of x from the function determined in part (*d*) when $\pi = 0$, and interpret the x value obtained in terms of the economics of the firm.

    (*f*) Find the value of x from the function determined in part (*d*) when $\pi = 0.1R$, that is, the profit is 10 percent of the total revenue, and interpret the x value.

    (*g*) Find the values of x which satisfy the following system of three equality statements:

$$R = f_1(x, p)$$

$$C = f_2(F, v, x)$$

$$R = C$$

    (*h*) Repeat parts (*a*) to (*g*) assuming that $p = \$5$, $v = \$3$, $F = \$3000$. Graph the functions, R, C, π, on the same graph.

14. As illustrated in the diagram, Jones begins bicycling from his starting point O toward the destination D at 10 mi/hr. At the same starting time, Smith begins walking toward the same destination D at 4 mi/hr, but his starting point P is 10 mi ahead of Jones's starting point O.

```
|←——10——→|
     mi
————————————————————————————→ D

O              P
Jones          Smith
starts         starts
here           here
```

    (*a*) Give the mathematical statement of the relation between the passage of time and the distance from O for Jones, and the same for Smith. Graph the two statements of the relation between time and distance.

(b) Repeat (a) measuring the distance for both Jones and Smith from P (instead of O).

(c) When would Jones catch up with Smith both in time and distance? Answer the question from an intuitive, verbal reasoning and also from a formal, mathematical reasoning, making use of the relational statements of part (a) or (b).

15. An oil refinery can use three types of crude oil, I, II, III, to produce three types of product, gasoline, fuel oil, and lamp oil, according to the following table.

	Amount produced by 1 barrel of crude oil, gal		
Product	*Type I*	*Type II*	*Type III*
Gasoline	10	12	10
Fuel oil	6	9	12
Lamp oil	4	2	4

(a) Suppose the refinery wants to produce exactly 1380 gal of gasoline and 900 gal of fuel oil (regardless of how many gallons of lamp oil are produced at the same time) from using only type I and type II crude oils. If it is technically feasible, how many barrels of I and II oils are required?

(b) Could the refinery produce exactly 1380 gal of gasoline and 900 gal of fuel oil (regardless of what happens to lamp-oil production) by using all three types of crude oil in some proportion? If so, how many barrels of each crude oil? Pose and solve the questions in mathematical statements.

(c) Could the refinery produce exactly 1380 gal of gasoline and 900 gal of fuel oil using only one type of crude oil? If so, how many barrels? Pose and solve the questions in mathematical statements.

(d) Could the refinery produce exactly 1010 gal of gasoline, 810 gal of fuel oil, and 320 gal of lamp oil from using a combination of I, II, III crude oils? If so, how many barrels of each? Pose and solve the questions in mathematical statements. How about using a combination of any two of the three crude oils?

(e) Check the above answers with the general rules about the existence of solutions to systems of equations given in Sec. 2-3.

16. In Prob. 15, the amount of lamp oil produced from a barrel of type I, II, and III crude oil was given as 4, 2, and 4 gal, respectively. Now suppose that they are 5.5, 5.25, 1; that is, the last row of the refinery production coefficients is changed. Further, change the production requirements for gasoline, fuel oil, and lamp oil to 1010, 810, and 402.5 gal, instead of 1010, 810, 320 as in part (d) of Prob. 15. What combination of types I, II, and III crude oil would produce the required outputs?

Hint: The new production coefficients of lamp oil produced per barrel of types I, II, and III crude oil, 5.5, 5.25, 1 gal, are obtained by adding $-\frac{3}{4}$ times the coefficients of fuel oil (second row figures in Prob. 15) to the coefficients of gasoline (first-row figures in Prob. 15). Likewise, the new quantity of lamp oil required of 402.5 gal is obtained by adding $-\frac{3}{4}$ times that of fuel oil to that of gasoline. In other words, the third equation is a linear combination of the other two equations.

17. Refer to part (d) of Prob. 15. The production requirements of 1010, 810, and 320 gal for gasoline, fuel oil, and lamp oil, respectively, were rather arbitrarily chosen numbers. In general, suppose the requirements were b_1, b_2, b_3 gal for gasoline, fuel oil, and lamp oil, respectively. Solve the production problem under this supposition.

18. The cost summaries for the machine repair and maintenance department, the electric power generating department, and the steam generating department of a paper company for a typical period of planning are as tabulated.

Machine repair and maintenance department	
For itself	$ 10,000
For electric power department	30,000
For steam power department	30,000
For paper-pulp manufacturing department	50,000
Total	$120,000

Electric power department	
For itself	$10,000
For machine repair and maintenance department	20,000
For steam power department	10,000
For paper-pulp manufacturing department	40,000
Total	$80,000

Steam power department	
For itself	$ 0
For machine repair and maintenance department	0
For electric power department	10,000
For paper-pulp manufacturing department	50,000
Total	$60,000

(a) Present the data on the cost interdependency among the service departments in a grid-form table, where columns and rows identify various departments.

(b) Calculate and present in a grid-form table the cost inputs from other departments that are required for carrying out the level of activity of a given department measured by 1 dollar's worth cost of operation in the department.

(c) Suppose that the paper company expects an increase in sales of paper in the next period, and consequently the paper-pulp manufacturing department expects an increase in the services required of the service departments, namely, an increase of $7500 from the machine repair and maintenance department, an increase of $2000 from the electric department, and an increase of $11,000 from the steam department. Determine the costs of operations expected of the three service departments during the next period.

19. A firm produces n products machined by m machines. The machining time required for processing one unit of the jth product at the ith machine is in general denoted by a_{ij}. For example, if the fifth product requires 3.2 hr of the third machine, then $j = 5$ and $i = 3$; therefore $a_{ij} = a_{35} = 3.2$. The machine times required at all machines for all products may be conveniently given in table form. x_j stands for the number of units produced of the jth product.

Machine	Product					
	1	2	3		j	n
1	a_{11}	a_{12}	a_{13}	$\cdots$	a_{1j} $\cdots$	a_{1n}
2	a_{21}	a_{22}	a_{23}	$\cdots$	a_{2j} $\cdots$	a_{2n}
3	a_{31}	a_{32}	a_{33}	$\cdots$	a_{3j} $\cdots$	a_{3n}
i	a_{i1}	a_{i2}	a_{i3}	$\cdots$	a_{ij} $\cdots$	a_{in}
m	a_{m1}	a_{m2}	a_{m3}	$\cdots$	a_{mj} $\cdots$	a_{mn}

(a) Interpret (verbally) $a_{23}x_3$, $a_{m2}x_2$, $a_{3j}x_j$, $a_{ij}x_j$, a_{mn}.

(b) Interpret $\displaystyle\sum_{j=1}^{n} a_{2j}x_j$, $\displaystyle\sum_{j=3}^{5} a_{3j}x_j$, $\displaystyle\sum_{j=1}^{n} a_{ij}x_j$.

(c) Interpret $\displaystyle\sum_{i=1}^{m} a_{i2}x_2$, $\displaystyle\sum_{i=1}^{m} a_{ij}x_j$.

(d) Interpret $\displaystyle\sum_{i=1}^{m} \left(\sum_{j=1}^{n} a_{ij}x_j \right)$, $\displaystyle\sum_{j=1}^{n} \left(\sum_{i=1}^{m} a_{ij}x_j \right)$.

3
Nonlinear Models, Rates of Change, and Derivatives

3-0 INTRODUCTION

In contrast to Chaps. 1 and 2, where most illustrations involved linear relations, the focus of the present chapter is on nonlinear relations, but the reader should be aware of the similarity of the analysis here to that in the preceding chapters in order to appreciate the nature of the "if so, then so" kind of logical reasoning of mathematical methods as a *general* tool of analysis applicable to any type of relation in any type of problem. The chapter first presents and analyzes a number of hypothetical examples of the problem situations which call for nonlinear models and then introduces the mathematical concept of the derivative function (or calculus) as a continuation of the discussion of the rate of change and incremental analysis begun in Chap. 2.

3-1 EXAMPLES OF NONLINEAR RELATIONS

Quadratic functions As noted previously, when a function between x and y takes (or may be converted equivalently into) the general form

$y = a + bx$, it is called a linear function; when it takes the general form
$y = a + bx + cx^2$, it is called a quadratic function. Thus, in reference
to Examples 1-1 and 2-2, the cost function of the firm, $C = 10,000 + 20X$,
is a linear function; the revenue function, $R = 50X - X^2/200$, and the
profit function, $\pi = -X^2/200 + 30X - 10,000$, are quadratic functions.
For the revenue function, the parameters, a, b, and c are 0, 50, and $-\frac{1}{200}$,
respectively.

Solving a quadratic equation   There exist many (X, C)'s, (X, R)'s and
(X, π)'s which satisfy the statements cited above, but for a specified value
of X, there are only one value of C, only one value of R, and only one
value of π that satisfy the equality statements.   Finding the values of
C, R, and π from the three equations is called solving the equations for
C, R, and π, respectively.   Conversely, for specified values of C, R, and
π, the values of X which satisfy the three equations can be found; stated
alternatively, the equations can be solved for X.   To illustrate, suppose
the firm wishes to know how many tons of the chemical it should sell in
order to attain the revenue of $R = \$45,000$.   Then

$$R = 50X - \frac{X^2}{200}$$

$$45,000 = 50X - \frac{X^2}{200} \tag{1}$$

or

$$-\frac{X^2}{200} + 50X - 45,000 = 0 \tag{1a}$$

Solving the equality statement (1), or its equivalent (1a), for X gives
$X = 9000$ and $X = 1000$ as follows.   Multiply both sides of Eq. (1a) by
a same number, -200:

$$-200\left(-\frac{X^2}{200} + 50X - 45,000\right) = 0$$

$$X^2 - 10,000X + 9,000,000 = 0 \tag{2}$$

Now add to both sides of Eq. (2) a same number, 16,000,000:

$$X^2 - 10,000X + 9,000,000 + 16,000,000 = 16,000,000$$

$$X^2 - 10,000 + 25,000,000 = 16,000,000$$

or

$$X^2 - 2(5,000)X + (5,000)^2 = 16,000,000 \tag{3}$$

Since for any two numbers, M and N, $(M + N)^2 = M^2 + 2MN + N^2$ is always true, Eq. (3) may be written equivalently as

$$(X - 5{,}000)^2 = 16{,}000{,}000 \tag{3a}$$

If $(X - 5{,}000)^2$ is equal to $16{,}000{,}000$, their square roots must also be equal to each other, namely,

$$X - 5000 = \pm\sqrt{16{,}000{,}000}$$

or

$$X - 5000 = \pm 4000$$

Therefore,

$$X = 5000 \pm 4000$$

Both $X = 9000$ and $X = 1000$ satisfy Eq. (1) and therefore would yield the revenue of $45,000.

General formula for solving a quadratic equation The same kind of logical reasoning process can be applied to solving any quadratic equation of the form $a + bx + cx^2 = 0$. Given

$$a + bx + cx^2 = 0 \tag{1}$$

Multiply both sides of Eq. (1) by a same number, $1/c$:

$$\frac{1}{c}(a + bx + cx^2) = 0$$

$$\frac{a}{c} + \frac{b}{c}x + x^2 = 0 \tag{2}$$

or

$$x^2 + 2\frac{b}{2c}x + \frac{a}{c} = 0 \tag{2a}$$

Add to both sides of (2a) a same number, $(b/2c)^2$:

$$x^2 + 2\frac{b}{2c}x + \left(\frac{b}{2c}\right)^2 + \frac{a}{c} = \left(\frac{b}{2c}\right)^2$$

or

$$x^2 + 2\frac{b}{2c}x + \left(\frac{b}{2c}\right)^2 = \left(\frac{b}{2c}\right)^2 - \frac{a}{c}$$

or

$$\left(x + \frac{b}{2c}\right)^2 = \frac{b^2}{4c^2} - \frac{a}{c}$$

or

$$\left(x + \frac{b}{2c}\right)^2 = \frac{b^2 - 4ac}{4c^2} \tag{3}$$

Take the square root of both sides of (3):

$$x + \frac{b}{2c} = \pm \sqrt{\frac{b^2 - 4ac}{4c^2}}$$

or

$$x + \frac{b}{2c} = \pm \frac{\sqrt{b^2 - 4ac}}{2c}$$

Therefore,

$$x = -\frac{b}{2c} \pm \frac{\sqrt{b^2 - 4ac}}{2c}$$

or

$$x = \frac{-b \pm \sqrt{b^2 - 4ac}}{2c}$$

The reason for deriving the general formula is obvious. Whenever a quadratic equation must be solved in practice, the general formula can be mechanically applied instead of a prolonged mathematical reasoning that would otherwise be necessary.

Exercise 3-1 (a) In reference to the revenue function of the chemical firm, verify the validity of the general solution formula derived above by using it to find the solution for X when $R = 45{,}000$ and checking the result with that of the earlier lengthy logical reasoning.

(b) Find the levels of output which would yield \$0 profit and \$30,000 profit (1) without and (2) with the general formula.

Exercise 3-2 (a) Show on the cartesian diagram the points representing all (x, y)'s that satisfy each of the following functions, and explain verbally how y varies as x increases:

$$y = 2x^2 - x - 6 \tag{1}$$
$$y = 2x^2 - x \tag{2}$$
$$y = 2x^2 - x + 3 \tag{3}$$
$$y = -2x^2 - x - 6 \tag{4}$$
$$y = -2x^2 + x + 3 \tag{5}$$
$$y = \tfrac{1}{4}x^2 + 2x - 3 \tag{6}$$
$$y = \tfrac{1}{4}x^2 - 2x - 3 \tag{7}$$

(b) What would happen to the shape of the curves of a quadratic function, $y = a + bx + cx^2$, as the coefficient c of the x^2 term is varied?

(c) Find the values of x that satisfy each of the above when $y = 0$ and when $y = 3$.

nth-degree polynomial functions   When a relation between x and y is represented by a mathematical statement in the general form

$$y = a_0 + a_1x + a_2x^2 + a_3x^3 + \cdots + a_{n-1}x^{n-1} + a_nx^n$$

or $y = \displaystyle\sum_{i=0}^{n} a_ix^i$, y is called a polynomial function of x.   Note that the linear function and the quadratic function are two special cases of the polynomials, where $n = 1$ and $n = 2$, respectively.   The polynomial of the third degree ($n = 3$) is often called the cubic function; that of the fourth degree ($n = 4$), the quartic function, and so on.   The polynomials of a degree higher than $n = 1$ are in general nonlinear.   Unlike the linear and quadratic cases, solving for x (given a value of y) is much more difficult for higher-degree functions and is not studied in this book.   But it should be emphasized that complex as a polynomial may appear, it is nothing but a formal statement of the pattern of a particular relation between variables, namely, specification of $y = f(x)$.

Exercise 3-3   The fixed costs of a manufacturer of a product for a given period are expected to be FC $=$ \$20,000.   The variable costs in thousands of dollars are assumed to take the form VC $= x^3/3 - 4x^2 + 30x$, where x is the number of units in thousands of the product produced and sold.[1]
    (*a*) Express the total costs T (in thousands of dollars) as a function of x.
    (*b*) Express the relation between x and T in tabular form (for selected x values) and in graphic form.
    (*c*) What happens to the total costs, variable costs, and fixed costs as the level of production and sales increases?   Give examples of technological and economic factors that cause the kind of total-cost variations as in the present case.
    (*d*) How many units of the product can be manufactured at the total cost of \$53,000?   (1) Formulate the problem mathematically and (2) read the solution from the graph.   (3) Determine the average cost per unit and average variable cost per unit at this level of production.
    (*e*) Express the average-unit-cost function mathematically.

Exponential and logarithmic functions   Besides linear, quadratic, and higher-power polynomial functions, there are many other classes of function, the properties of which mathematicians have studied over centuries.   Exponential and logarithmic functions are two of these which are often found useful in modeling certain real-world relations.   The following is a simple example of a situation which gives rise to an exponential function.

---

[1] Here variable costs are used in the sense different from the definition given in Sec. 2-1, where total variable costs were linear; i.e., the variable cost per unit was fixed. Here, total variable costs are nonlinear; i.e., the variable cost per unit varies.

EXAMPLE 3-1

If a sum of money, say $1000, is invested in a savings account compounded annually at a rate, say, of 6 percent per annum, the value of the money at the end of a given number of years is computed as follows.

Value at end of 1st year

$$V_1 = 1000 + 1000(0.06) = 1000(1 + 0.06) = 1000(1.06) = 1060$$

Value at end of 2d year

$$V_2 = 1060 + 1060(0.06) = 1060(1 + 0.06)$$

Since $1060 = 1000(1 + 0.06) = 1000(1.06)$,

$$V_2 = 1000(1 + 0.06)(1 + 0.06) = 1000(1 + 0.06)^2$$
$$= 1000(1.06)^2 = 1123.6$$

Value at end of 3d year

$$V_3 = 1123.6 + 1123.6(0.06) = 1123.6(1 + 0.06)$$

Since $1123.6 = 1000(1 + 0.06)^2 = 1000(1.06)^2$,

$$V_3 = 1000(1 + 0.06)^2(1 + 0.06) = 1000(1 + 0.06)^3$$
$$= 1000(1.06)^3 = 1191.02$$

From the pattern discernible in the computation, the compounded value in general at the end of xth year is inferred as

$$V = 1000(1 + 0.06)^x = 1000(1.06)^x$$

The above equality statement, of course, is the specification of a functional relation between two variables, x and V, that is, $V = f(x)$. In general, when a function between two variables, x and y, is in the form $y = ab^x$, it is called an *exponential function*. In this compounded-value formula, two parameters are specified, $a = 1000$ and $b = 1.06$.

Concept of present value   Suppose a decision maker is to choose between the option of receiving $1000 *now* and the option of receiving $1060 *one year hence*. If the 6 percent per annum savings deposit represents the best investment opportunity open to the decision maker, he would naturally be indifferent between the two options, for if he took the first option, he would put the $1000 received in the savings account, and after one year, his wealth would be the same as if he took the second option. In other words, the utility of $1000 now is the same as the utility of $1060 one year from now. In symbols, $U(1000 \text{ now}) = U(1060 \text{ one year hence})$. If a utility index of 1000 is assigned to the option of receiving $1000 now, the same utility index of 1000 must be assigned to the option of receiving $1060 one year hence. Alternatively, the value or worth of $1060 one year from now is the same as the value or worth of $1000 now; or the *present value* of $1060 one year hence is $1000. Furthermore, it follows that for the same decision maker with the same set of investment opportunities open to him, the present value of any amount larger than $1060 received one year hence is higher than $1000 (now) and that if the set of investment opportunities available to the decision maker is represented by a rate higher than 6 percent per annum, the present value of $1060 one year hence is less than $1000 (because if $1000 received now is invested to make more than 6 percent a year, its value at the end of one year is more than $1060).

If the present value of $1060 one year from now is $1000, the present value of $1 one year from now is

$$\text{PV(\$1, one year hence)} = \frac{1000}{1060}$$

$$= \frac{\cancel{1000}}{\cancel{1000}(1 + 0.06)}$$

$$= \frac{1}{1 + 0.06}$$

If the present value of $1123.60 two years from now is $1000, the present value of $1 two years from now is

$$\text{PV(\$1, two years hence)} = \frac{1000}{1123.60}$$

$$= \frac{\cancel{1000}}{\cancel{1000}(1 + 0.06)^2}$$

$$= \frac{1}{(1 + 0.06)^2}$$

Likewise in general, if the present value of $V = 1000(1 + 0.06)^x$ x years from now is $1000, the present value of $1 x years hence is

$$\text{PV(\$1, } x \text{ years hence)} = \frac{1000}{V}$$

$$= \frac{\cancel{1000}}{\cancel{1000}(1 + 0.06)^x}$$

$$= \frac{1}{(1 + 0.06)^x}$$

or

$$PV(\$1, x \text{ years hence}) = \frac{1}{1.06^x}$$

Since in mathematics $1/a^m = a^{-m}$, for example, $1/2^5 = 2^{-5}$, the above formula for calculating the present value of a dollar received at the end of x number of years can also be written

$$PV(\$1, x \text{ years hence}) = (1.06)^{-x}$$

In general, the formula for the present value of $\$A$ is

$$PV(\$A, x \text{ years hence}) = \frac{A}{(1 + 0.06)^x} = A(1.06)^{-x}$$

Exercise 3-4 (a) Graph the compounded-value function $V = (1 + 0.06)^x$ for both positive and negative integers of x, and interpret negative x values and associated V values.

(b) Could V values be mathematically determined when x values are fractions?

(c) Repeat parts (a) and (b) for the present-value function $PV = (1 + 0.06)^{-x}$.

Solving exponential equations What amount of money should be invested now to provide $1262.48 by the end of 4 years if the investment yields 6 percent per annum? Mathematically the problem is obviously to solve the equation $1262.48 = A(1 + 0.06)^4$ for A. The reader is already equipped to find the value of A which satisfies the statement since the task is that of solving a linear equation.

At what rate of return or interest would an investment of $1000 yield $1210 by the end of 2 years? The mathematical formulation of the problem is to find the value of i in the equation, $1210 = 1000(1 + i)^2$. Again, the reader is equipped to find mathematically the value of i satisfying the equality statement, a quadratic equation.

If the question is at what rate of return would an investment of $1000 yield $1210 by the end of 3 years, 4 years, etc., the problem is to solve higher-order polynomial equations such as, $1210 = 1000(1 + i)^3$, $1210 = 1000(1 + i)^4$. As observed earlier, solving higher-order polynomial equations is difficult, but using logarithms (to be defined shortly) facilitates the solution process.

How many years does it take for an investment of $1000 to accumulate to $1594 at the interest rate of 6 percent a year compounded annually? The mathematical formulation of the problem is to solve an exponential equation, $1594 = 1000(1 + 0.06)^x$. The answer can be read from the graph of Exercise 3-4. Even if the graph were not available, the solution could be found through trial and error, namely, by trying a number of possible x values until that value of x is found which satisfies the equation. But again, using logarithms provides a formal way of solving it.

Logarithms and logarithmic functions Besides its usefulness in solving certain higher-degree polynomial and exponential functions, the logarithm serves many other purposes in mathematical analysis. For the various uses of logarithms, the reader is referred to any standard algebra text. Here the discussion is limited largely to an introduction of the logarithmic notation.

Common languages such as English are often too ambiguous, inaccurate, and cumbersome to serve as a vehicle for rigorous analyses. Mathematicians therefore devise a more exact language—notation—of their own. A number of mathematical signs such as $=$, $+$, $>$, $\leq$, Σ have already been introduced. The following definition of the logarithm is to be understood in the same, notational, sense. When mathematicians wish to refer to the power to which, say, 10 must be raised to obtain 1000, they write $\log_{10} 1000$. Since 10 must be raised to the power of 3, or alternatively, 10 must be multiplied by itself 3 times, to obtain 1000, $\log_{10} 1000 = 3$. Note that $\log_{10} 1000 = 3$ necessarily implies $10^3 = 1000$. To give another example, since $2^4 = 16$, if we wish to refer to the power, i.e., 4, to which the base number 2 must be raised to yield 16, we write $\log_2 16$. In general, given any number y which can be stated in the exponent form a^x, that is, $y = a^x$, its logarithm to the base a is $\log_a y = \log_a a^x = x$.

Inasmuch as x varies, as y is varied, x may be considered a function of y, in particular, a logarithmic function. The reader should satisfy himself that Exhibits 3-1 and 3-2 are the tabular representation of two logarithmic functions, $x = \log_{10} y$ and $x = \log_2 y$, respectively.

It can be proved that for any given positive number y its logarithm can be found for any positive base. For example, for a given y value, $y = 23$, its logarithms $\log_{23} 23$, $\log_{100} 23$, $\log_{2.718} 23$, $\log_5 23$, $\log_3 23$, $\log_{0.5} 23$ are all defined. But in mathematical analyses, the most commonly used bases of the logarithms are 10 and $e \approx 2.718$. Logarithms with base 10 are called *common* logarithms, and in notation the base is often omitted; that is, $\log_{10} y$ is written $\log y$. Logarithms with base e are called *natural* logarithms and written either $\log_e y$ or $\ln y$. (e is a number like $\pi \approx 3.14$ which is indispensable for theoretical analyses in mathematics.)

Inverse functions It is readily seen that there exists an intimate connection between exponential functions and logarithmic functions. By definition, if $y = a^x$ (an exponential function), then it must be that $x = \log_a y$ (a logarithmic function). This connection between the exponential and

Independent variable y	*y to the base 10;* $y = 10^x$	*Dependent variable x;* $\log_{10} y = x$
$0.00001 = \dfrac{1}{100,000}$	10^{-5}	$\log 0.00001 = -5$
$0.0001 = \dfrac{1}{10,000}$	10^{-4}	$\log 0.0001 = -4$
$0.01 = \dfrac{1}{100}$	10^{-2}	$\log 0.01 = -2$
$0.316 \approx \dfrac{1}{\sqrt{10}}$	$10^{-\frac{1}{2}}$	$\log 0.316 = -0.5$
1	10^0	$\log 1 = 0$
$3.1623 \approx \sqrt{10}$	$10^{\frac{1}{2}}$	$\log 3.1623 = 0.5$
10	10^1	$\log 10 = 1$
$31.623 \approx \sqrt{10^3}$	$10^{1.5} = 10^{\frac{3}{2}}$	$\log 31.623 = 1.5$
100	10^2	$\log 100 = 2$
1000	10^3	$\log 1000 = 3$

Exhibit 3-1   Tabular representation of $x = \log_{10} y$ (for selected values of y).

logarithmic functions is the same kind as is present between a linear function $y = a + bx$ and another derived from it, $x = -a/b + y/b$, because here too if $y = a + bx$, then $x = -a/b + y/b$. In general, given a function $y = f(x)$, if a function $x = g(y)$ can be derived, then the function $g(\cdot)$ is called an *inverse function* of $f(\cdot)$. Thus, $x = \log_a y$ is the inverse function of $y = a^x$; $x = -a/b + y/b$ is the inverse function of $y = a + bx$ (and vice versa).

Independent variable y	*y to the base 2;* $y = 2^x$	*Dependent variable x;* $\log_2 y = x$
$0.015625 = \frac{1}{64}$	2^{-6}	-6
$0.03125 = \frac{1}{32}$	2^{-5}	-5
$0.5 = \frac{1}{2}$	2^{-1}	-1
$0.707 \approx \dfrac{1}{\sqrt{2}}$	$2^{-\frac{1}{2}}$	-0.5
1	2^0	0
$1.414 \approx \sqrt{2}$	$2^{\frac{1}{2}}$	0.5
2	2^1	1
4	2^2	2
8	2^3	3
16	2^4	4

Exhibit 3-2   Tabular representation of $x = \log_2 y$.

Exercise 3-5   (a) Find the inverse function $x = g(y)$ of the linear function $y = f(x) = 6 + 2x$.

(b) Find the inverse function $x = g(y)$ of $y = f(x) = 3^x$.

(c) Find the inverse function $x = g(y)$ of $y = f(x) = (\frac{1}{2})^x$.

(d) For parts (a) to (c), graph $x = g(y)$ (with the independent variable y shown on the horizontal axis and the dependent variable x on the vertical axis), and graph $y = f(x)$ (with the independent variable x on the horizontal axis and the dependent variable y on the vertical axis).   Verify that the inverse functions are symmetrical to the line $y = x$.

Other nonlinear functions   Besides polynomial, exponential, and logarithmic functions, many other classes of functions are used in theoretical and practical analyses. [For example, $y = \sin x$, $y = \cos x$, $y = (ax^2 + b)/(cx^4 - dx^3) + e$.]   The reader is again reminded that no matter how complex and alien they may look, they merely specify the particular pattern of the relation between variables.

3-2   RATES OF CHANGE AND DERIVATIVES

It was observed in Chap. 2 that decisions on many occasions are based on incremental analyses.   For instance, in deciding on how much to spend on advertising for the next year, instead of comparing the *total* expected advertising expenditure with the total expected sale, the *incremental,* or additional, advertising expenditure planned (additional to the last period) might be contrasted to the *incremental* expected sale.   In other words, the decision on the advertising expenditure would depend critically on the expected *rate of change* (more probably an increase than a decrease) in sales per dollar increase in advertising.

According to Chap. 2, if (total) sales y is related to (total) advertising x linearly, i.e., in the form $y = a + bx$, the rate of change in sales per dollar increase in advertising $\Delta y/\Delta x$ is always b, but if y is a nonlinear function of x, that is, $y = f(x)$ in general, $\Delta y/\Delta x$ varies depending on the level of x from which the increment of Δx is planned.   Since for the different values of x there exist the corresponding values of $\Delta y/\Delta x$, the rate of change itself is a function of x, that is, $\Delta y/\Delta x = g(x)$.   This section studies how mathematics can help in incremental decision analyses by providing formal means by which the particular pattern of this rate-of-change function, $\Delta y/\Delta x = g(x)$ can be derived from a given totals function, $y = f(x)$.

EXAMPLE 3-2

Starting from point O, if an object travels at a constant speed of, say, 3 ft/sec, the distance traveled from O is a linear function of seconds

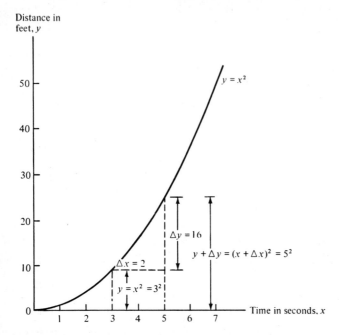

Exhibit 3-3 Graph of $y = x^2$, $x \geq 0$.

passed, that is, $y = 3x$, where y is the distance of travel in feet and x the passage of time in seconds. But suppose for the current illustration that the distance traveled is a nonlinear function of time, $y = x^2$, which is graphed as in Exhibit 3-3.

The graph makes it obvious that the distance traveled y increases at an increasing rate as the time x increases. This is so because speed is ever-increasing as time passes; i.e., the object is accelerating. Furthermore, the way the curve is drawn smoothly from point to point indicates that the object is accelerating smoothly—without sudden spurts. It follows then that the speed of the object is changing, i.e., increasing, smoothly from one moment to the next, and, at least at the conceptual level, the object never travels a finite duration of time at any one given speed. Under such circumstances, how can the speed of the object be measured at a given point of time such as $x = 3$? One practical way of measuring the speed at a given point of time would be to approximate it by getting an average speed in the vicinity of the given time point. More specifically, observe and measure the distance the object travels during a "small" duration of time beginning from the given time and divide the distance by that small time duration. In symbols, find the increment in distance Δy (feet) attributable to the travel during the small

Table 3-1   Computation of average speed

At $x = 3$ and for $\Delta x = 2$	At $x = x$ and for $\Delta x = \Delta x$
1. Distance at $x = 3$ $y = x^2 = 3^2 = 9$	1. Distance at $x = x$ $y = x^2$
2. Distance after $\Delta x = 2$ sec $y + \Delta y = (x + \Delta x)^2$ $= (3 + 2)^2 = 25$	2. Distance after $\Delta x = \Delta x$ $y + \Delta y = (x + \Delta x)^2$
3. Distance attributable to $\Delta x = 2$ $(y + \Delta y) - y$ $= (3 + 2)^2 - 3^2 = 16$	3. Distance attributable to $\Delta x = \Delta x$ $(y + \Delta y) - y = (x + \Delta x)^2 - x^2$ $\Delta y = x^2 + 2x\,\Delta x$ $+ (\Delta x)^2 - x^2$ $= 2x\,\Delta x + (\Delta x)^2$
4. Average speed during $\Delta x = 2$ $\dfrac{\Delta y}{\Delta x} = \dfrac{16}{2} = 8$ ft/sec	4. Average speed during $\Delta x = \Delta x$ $\dfrac{\Delta y}{\Delta x} = \dfrac{2x\,\Delta x + (\Delta x)^2}{\Delta x}$ $= 2x + \Delta x \qquad$ ft/sec

time increment Δx (seconds), and compute the average speed per second as $\Delta y/\Delta x$. This procedure is followed in Table 3-1 to obtain an approximate average speed at a given point of time. The left-hand side calculates the average speed in the neighborhood of a specific time point, $x = 3$, for a specified Δx of 2 sec; the right-hand side gives in general the average-speed computation near any time point x and for any Δx.

The reader may verify that the average speed of 8 ft/sec for the case where $x = 3$ and $\Delta x = 2$ can be obtained from the general formula $\Delta y/\Delta x = 2x + \Delta x$ and compute the average speed, $\Delta y/\Delta x$, at various time points, x's (given $\Delta x = 2$ sec) to ascertain that it is an increasing linear function of x. In addition, the reader is urged to check back to the graph of Exhibit 3-3 to see how Δx and Δy are shown geometrically.

In the above illustration, the choice of $\Delta x = 2$ was rather arbitrary. Δx could well have been 3, 10, $\frac{1}{2}$, $\frac{1}{10}$ sec, etc. Exhibit 3-4 demonstrates how $\Delta y/\Delta x$ varies as Δx is varied.

The variation in the average speed according to the variation in Δx is shown geometrically in Exhibit 3-5, which is a blowup of a portion of the graph of Exhibit 3-3.

The distances AG, AE, AC in Exhibit 3-5 represent three different values of Δx, namely, $\Delta x = 2$, $\Delta x = 1$, and $\Delta x = 0.5$, respectively. Since $x = 3$, the three corresponding $x + \Delta x$ values are $3 + 2 = 5$, $3 + 1 = 4$, and $3 + 0.5 = 3.5$, respectively. When $\Delta x = 2$, Δy is computed as

$$\Delta y = (x + \Delta x)^2 - x^2 = (3 + 2)^2 - 3^2 = 16$$

Value of Δx		Value of $\Delta x/\Delta y$		
4		$\dfrac{(x + \Delta x)^2 - x^2}{\Delta x} =$		$\dfrac{(3 + 4)^2 - 3^2}{4} = 10$
	or	$2x + \Delta x$	$=$	$2 \times 3 + 4 = 10$
3		$2x + \Delta x$	$=$	$2 \times 3 + 3 = 9$
2		$2x + \Delta x$	$=$	$2 \times 3 + 2 = 8$
1		$2x + \Delta x$	$=$	$2 \times 3 + 1 = 7$
0.5		$2x + \Delta x$	$=$	$2 \times 3 + 0.5 = 6.5$
0.1		$2x + \Delta x$	$=$	$2 \times 3 + 0.1 = 6.1$
0.02		$2x + \Delta x$	$=$	$2 \times 3 + 0.02 = 6.02$

Exhibit 3-4 Average speed at $x = 3$ for various values of Δx.

This is shown as the distance FG in the diagram. Likewise, when $\Delta x = 1$, $\Delta y = (x + \Delta x)^2 - x^2 = (3 + 1)^2 - 3^2 = 7$, which is shown as DE. Then the three alternative average speeds for three alternative values of Δx are:

$$\text{For } \Delta x = 2: \quad \frac{\Delta y}{\Delta x} = \frac{FG}{AG} = \frac{16}{2} = 8$$

the magnitude of which is represented by the slope of the line L_1 or the angle FAG.

$$\text{For } \Delta x = 1: \quad \frac{\Delta y}{\Delta x} = \frac{DE}{AE} = \frac{7}{1} = 7$$

the slope of the line L_2 or the angle DAE.

$$\text{For } \Delta x = \tfrac{1}{2}: \quad \frac{\Delta y}{\Delta x} = \frac{BC}{AC} = \frac{3.25}{0.5} = 6.5$$

the slope of the line L_3 or the angle BAC.

Instantaneous rate of change or speed Which is the better approximation of the speed right at the instant $x = 3$, the average speed $\Delta y/\Delta x$ with a larger Δx or that with a smaller Δx? Since a larger Δx means that the object must travel for a longer duration at "speeds" different from that at $x = 3$ than a smaller Δx, the answer is obviously that the smaller the Δx, the better $\Delta y/\Delta x$ approximates the speed at the instant $x = 3$. As far as Exhibit 3-4 goes, therefore, $\Delta y/\Delta x$ when $\Delta x = 0.02$, that is, 6.02 ft/sec, is the best approximation of the speed at $x = 3$. But $\Delta y/\Delta x$ could have been computed for a Δx value smaller than 0.02. At the conceptual level, indeed Δx can be made smaller and smaller ad infinitum. In notation, this process of making Δx smaller and smaller

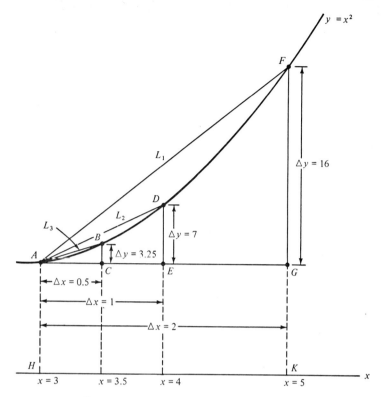

Exhibit 3-5   Geometry of $\Delta y / \Delta x$, as Δx varies.

but never reaching 0 itself is denoted by $\Delta x \to 0$.   What would happen to $\Delta y / \Delta x$ when $\Delta x \to 0$?   From an examination of the way $\Delta y / \Delta x$ changes as Δx is lowered from 4 to 0.02 in steps (Exhibit 3-4) it may be guessed that the average speed would get smaller and smaller approaching 6 ft/ sec ad infinitum, but never reaching 6 itself.   This limiting process is expressed as

$$\lim_{\Delta x \to 0} \frac{\Delta y}{\Delta x} = 6$$

Remember that Δx never becomes 0; if it did, the average speed computation, $\Delta y / \Delta x$, would be meaningless because $\Delta x = 0$ means that the object has not traveled for any duration, and mathematically, Δy divided by $\Delta x = 0$ would also be meaningless.   Accordingly, $\Delta y / \Delta x$ never becomes 6 itself; it approaches 6 closer and closer with no end.   This limit of the average speed, 6 ft/sec, is called the *instantaneous speed* at $x = 3$, or the *instantaneous rate of change* in y per unit change in x at $x = 3$.

As to the geometric representation of the instantaneous rate of change, observe that in Exhibit 3-5 the lines L_i become flatter and flatter as $\Delta x \to 0$ and in the end would approach closer and closer the line *tangent* to the curve $y = x$ at $x = 3$, that is, the line which touches the curve only at one point, $(x, y) = (3, 9)$. The slope of this tangent line is considered the instantaneous rate of change at $x = 3$. The diagram of Exhibit 3-6 further demonstrates the nature of the limiting line for $\Delta y / \Delta x$.

Since the tangent line L is straight, it can be described mathematically in the form $y = a + bx$. The slope or rate of change of the line has already been seen to be 6, namely, $b = 6$, and therefore $y = a + 6x$. The slope 6 of the line means that if the object maintained its instantaneous speed attained at $x = 3$ and traveled at that speed for 1 sec (AN in the diagram), it would go 6 ft (MN); in 2 sec (AQ), 12 ft (QP). But actually the object accelerates; consequently, after 1 sec from $x = 3$ it will be at point D (not M) on the curve $y = x^2$; after 2 sec, it will be at point S (not P).

The other parameter of the tangent line, a, can be determined as follows. Since the line passes point A, whose coordinates are $(x, y) = (3, 9)$, the equality statement, $y = a + 6x$, must be true when these x, y values are substituted in it. Namely, $9 = a + 6(3)$. The value of a which satisfies the last equality is $a = 9$. Line L is now completely specified as $y = 9 + 6x$.

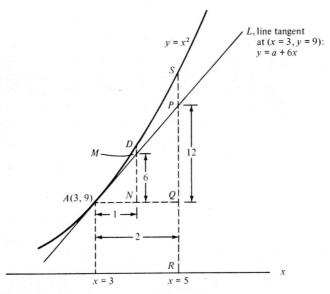

Exhibit 3-6   Geometry of $\displaystyle \lim_{\Delta x \to 0} \frac{\Delta y}{\Delta x} = \frac{dy}{dx}$ at $x = 3$.

Derivative functions In the above, $\lim\limits_{\Delta x \to 0} (\Delta y/\Delta x)$ was determined at a particular value of x, $x = 3$. In general, the formula for $\lim\limits_{\Delta x \to 0} (\Delta y/\Delta x)$ at any given value of x for $y = x^2$ is obtained as follows:

$$\Delta y = (y + \Delta y) - y$$
$$= (x + \Delta x)^2 - x^2$$

Therefore,

$$\frac{\Delta y}{\Delta x} = \frac{(x + \Delta x)^2 - x^2}{\Delta x} = \frac{x^2 + 2x\,\Delta x + (\Delta x)^2 - x^2}{\Delta x}$$

$$= \frac{2x\,\Delta x + (\Delta x)^2}{\Delta x} = 2x + \Delta x$$

Then

$$\lim_{\Delta x \to 0} \frac{\Delta y}{\Delta x} = \lim_{\Delta x \to 0} (2x + \Delta x)$$

Now as Δx approaches 0, $2x + \Delta x$ approaches $2x$ closer and closer. Therefore,

$$\lim_{\Delta x \to 0} \frac{\Delta y}{\Delta x} = \lim_{\Delta x \to 0} (2x + \Delta x) = 2x$$

$\lim\limits_{\Delta x \to 0} (\Delta y/\Delta x) = 2x$ means that for different values of x there are corresponding values of $\lim\limits_{\Delta x \to 0} (\Delta y/\Delta x)$; that is, the instantaneous rate of change is a function of x. This function $\lim\limits_{\Delta x \to 0} (\Delta y/\Delta x) = 2x$ is called the *derivative* of the original function $y = x^2$ and commonly written dy/dx. The value of the derivative function at $x = 3$ is verified as

$$\frac{dy}{dx} = 2x = 2(3) = 6 \text{ ft/sec}$$

The derivative of a function $y = f(x)$, in general, is defined as

$$\frac{dy}{dx} = \lim_{\Delta x \to 0} \frac{\Delta y}{\Delta x} = \lim_{\Delta x \to 0} \frac{(y + \Delta y) - \Delta y}{\Delta x} = \lim_{\Delta x \to 0} \frac{f(x + \Delta x) - f(x)}{\Delta x}$$

Alternatively, the derivative is often denoted by $f'(x)$ or $df(x)/dx$; the process of finding the derivative is often called *differentiation* (of the original function). A function for which the derivative exists is called a *differentiable function*, and because of the limiting process involved, that is, $\Delta x \to 0$, a necessary condition for a function to be differentiable is that it be continuous.

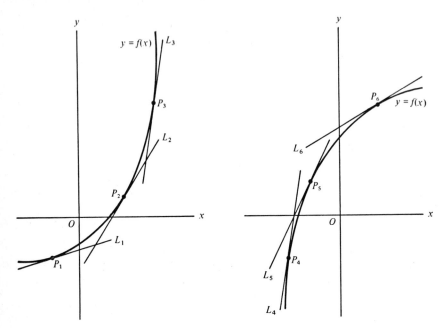

Exhibit 3-7a $y = f(x)$ is increasing at increasing rates.

Exhibit 3-7b $y = f(x)$ is increasing at decreasing rates.

Derivative function and positive and negative rates of change In the above time-distance example, $dy/dx = 6$ meant that the change in y per unit increase in x at $x = 3$ is an *increase* of 6 ft/sec. In other words, the function $y = x^2$ *is increasing* at $x = 3$ at that rate. In general, at a given value of x, *if and only if* $dy/dx > 0$, the original function $y = f(x)$ *is increasing* at that value of x. This seems reasonable when the definition of the derivative itself is examined: $dy/dx > 0$ means that

$$\lim_{\Delta x \to 0} \frac{f(x + \Delta x) - f(x)}{\Delta x} > 0$$

When $\Delta x > 0$, namely, when $(x + \Delta x)$ is larger than x,

$$\lim_{\Delta x \to 0} \frac{f(x + \Delta x) - f(x)}{\Delta x} > 0$$

only if $f(x + \Delta x) - f(x) > 0$, that is, only if $f(x + \Delta x) > f(x)$. The last condition $[f(x + \Delta x) > f(x)]$ means that the function must be increasing from x to $x + \Delta x$.

Conversely, if and only if $dy/dx < 0$, the original function $y = f(x)$ is decreasing at that value of x. $dy/dx < 0$ means that $f(x + \Delta x) < f(x)$ when $\Delta x > 0$; that is, the value of y is larger at x than at $x + \Delta x$.

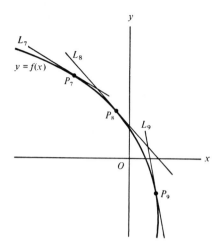

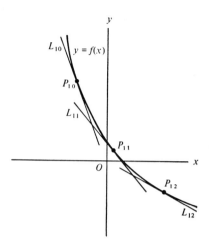

Exhibit 3-8a $y = f(x)$ is decreasing at increasing rates.

Exhibit 3-8b $y = f(x)$ is decreasing at decreasing rates.

Exhibits 3-7a and 3-7b and 3-8a and 3-8b demonstrate the relation between the pattern of variation of the original function and its derivative. If $y = f(x)$ is an increasing function, the tangent lines representing dy/dx at various points have positive slopes (Exhibit 3-7); if $y = f(x)$ is a decreasing function, the dy/dx lines have negative slopes (Exhibit 3-8).

Notes on Exhibits 3-7 and 3-8

1. In both Exhibits 3-7a and 3-7b of the original function $y = f(x)$ is increasing through all values of x; therefore, $dy/dx > 0$ at all values of x. Consequently, the slopes of all the tangent lines, L_1 to L_6, are positive.

2. But in Exhibit 3-7a, $y = f(x)$ increases at an *increasing rate;* namely,

$$\frac{dy}{dx} \text{ at } P_1 < \frac{dy}{dx} \text{ at } P_2 < \frac{dy}{dx} \text{ at } P_3$$

therefore,

Slope of $L_1 <$ slope of $L_2 <$ slope of L_3

Conversely, in Exhibit 3-7b, $y = f(x)$ increases at a *decreasing* rate; namely,

$$\frac{dy}{dx} \text{ at } P_4 > \frac{dy}{dx} \text{ at } P_5 > \frac{dy}{dx} \text{ at } P_6$$

therefore,

Slope of L_4 > slope of L_5 > slope of L_6

3. In both Exhibits 3-8a and 3-8b, $y = f(x)$ is decreasing through all values of x; therefore, $dy/dx < 0$ at all values of x. Consequently, the slopes of all the tangent lines, L_7 to L_{12}, are negative.

4. But in Exhibit 3-8a, $y = f(x)$ decreases faster and faster as x increases. Thus,

$$\frac{dy}{dx} \text{ at } P_7 > \frac{dy}{dx} \text{ at } P_8 > \frac{dy}{dx} \text{ at } P_9$$

If the negative sign of dy/dx is ignored,[1]

$$\left|\frac{dy}{dx}\right| \text{ at } P_7 < \left|\frac{dy}{dx}\right| \text{ at } P_8 < \left|\frac{dy}{dx}\right| \text{ at } P_9$$

Geometrically,

Magnitude of slope of L_7 < magnitude of slope of L_8
< magnitude of slope of L_9

Conversely, in Exhibit 3-8b, $y = f(x)$ decreases slower and slower as x increases. Thus,

$$\frac{dy}{dx} \text{ at } P_{10} < \frac{dy}{dx} \text{ at } P_{11} < \frac{dy}{dx} \text{ at } P_{12}$$

In terms of absolute values,

$$\left|\frac{dy}{dx}\right| \text{ at } P_{10} > \left|\frac{dy}{dx}\right| \text{ at } P_{11} > \left|\frac{dy}{dx}\right| \text{ at } P_{12}$$

Accordingly,

Magnitude of slope of L_{10} > magnitude of slope of L_{11}
> magnitude of slope of L_{12}

Exercise 3-6 (a) Graph the function $y = f(x) = 2x^2$.
(b) Find and graph its derivative function, $y' = f'(x) = dy/dx = \lim_{\Delta x \to 0} (\Delta y/\Delta x)$.

(c) Verify that when x is a positive number, say $x = 3$, and $\Delta x = 0.1, f(x + \Delta x) - f(x) > 0$, and consequently, the rate of change

$$\frac{f(x + \Delta x) - f(x)}{\Delta x} > 0$$

---

[1] Given a negative number, say -4, its *absolute value* refers only to its *magnitude*, namely, 4. The absolute value of -4 is written $|-4| = 4$.

(d) Verify that when x is a negative number, say $x = -2$, and $\Delta x = 0.1$, $f(x + \Delta x) - f(x) < 0$, and consequently, the rate of change

$$\frac{f(x + \Delta x) - f(x)}{\Delta x} < 0$$

(e) Verify that for $x > 0$, $y = f(x) = 2x^2$ increases as x increases, and dy/dx is positive and increases as x increases.

(f) Verify that for $x < 0$, y is positive but decreases as x increases, and dy/dx is negative and increases as x increases.

Derivative function and maxima and minima of the function   If $dy/dx > 0$ means that $y = f(x)$ is increasing and $dy/dx < 0$ means that it is decreasing, $dy/dx = 0$ must mean that the function $y = f(x)$ is neither increasing nor decreasing, namely, stationary. In general, there are three possible ways in which $y = f(x)$ may render its derivative dy/dx stationary or zero.   Exhibits 3-9a to 3-9c illustrate these three cases.

It is evident from Exhibit 3-9 that in order to determine where a function $y = f(x)$ reaches a peak (a maximum value) or a bottom (a minimum value) without its graph, the following steps are to be carried out.

Step 1   Given $y = f(x)$, obtain its derivative function, $dy/dx = f'(x)$; for example, if $y = f(x) = x^2$, its derivative is $dy/dx = f'(x) = 2x$, as determined earlier.

Step 2   Find the values of x where $dy/dx = f'(x)$ is zero.   For example, $dy/dx = f'(x) = 2x = 0$. $2x$ is zero only when $x = 0$.

Step 3   Step 2 gives all values of x where the minima, maxima, or inflections occur.   Therefore, in order to determine which one of the three possibilities is the case, the change in the values of dy/dx in the neighborhood of these x values must be investigated.   For example,

$$\frac{dy}{dx} = 2x = 0 \qquad \text{when } x = 0$$

as in step 2.   When $x = -0.1$, a value slightly smaller than zero,

$$\frac{dy}{dx} = 2x = 2(-0.1) = -0.2 < 0$$

When $x = 0.1$, a value slightly larger than zero,

$$\frac{dy}{dx} = 2x = 2(0.1) = 0.2 > 0$$

Since dy/dx changes from negative to positive through $x = 0$, $x = 0$ is where $y = x^2$ is a minimum.

There are many real-world problem analyses where it is necessary to find the maximum or minimum of a given function.   The general steps

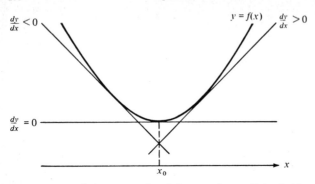

Exhibit 3-9a $dy/dx = 0$. A minimum of $y = f(x)$: dy/dx changes from negative to positive through that value of x where $dy/dx = 0$.

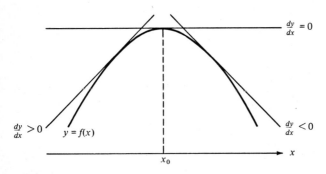

Exhibit 3-9b $dy/dx = 0$. A maximum of $y = f(x)$: dy/dx changes from positive to negative through that value of x where $dy/dx = 0$.

for locating maxima and minima will be applied in the next section to some hypothetical managerial decision problems, but first a number of general rules for determining the derivatives are presented.

RULES OF DIFFERENTIATION[1]

Rule 1   If $y = f(x) = ax^n$, where a and n are any real number,

$$\frac{dy}{dx} = f'(x) = anx^{n-1}$$

[1] There are many more rules than given here.   For other rules of differentiation, see any standard calculus text.

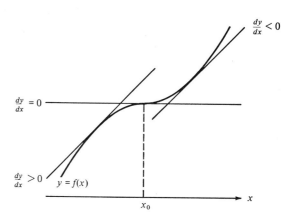

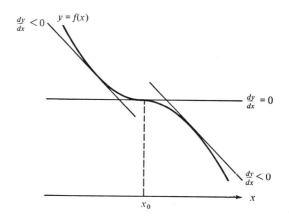

Exhibit 3-9c $dy/dx = 0$. An inflection of $y = f(x)$: dy/dx has the same sign through that value of x where $dy/dx = 0$.

For example, if $y = f(x) = 3x^4$,

$$\frac{dy}{dx} = 3(4x^{4-1}) = 12x^3$$

If $y = f(x) = -2\sqrt{x} = -2x^{\frac{1}{2}}$,

$$\frac{dy}{dx} = -2(\tfrac{1}{2}x^{\frac{1}{2}-1}) = -1x^{-\frac{1}{2}} = -x^{-\frac{1}{2}} = -\frac{1}{\sqrt{x}}$$

If $y = f(x) = 2/x = 2x^{-1}$,

$$\frac{dy}{dx} = 2(-1)(x^{-1-1}) = -2x^{-2}$$

If $y = f(x) = 6$, $y = 6 = 6x^0$; therefore,

$$\frac{dy}{dx} = 6(0)(x^{0-1}) = 0$$

From this result, another special rule is derived:

    Rule 1a   If $y = f(x) = k$, where k is any constant, then $dy/dx = 0$.

    Rule 2   If $y = f(x) = g(x) + h(x)$, then

$$\frac{dy}{dx} = f'(x) = g'(x) + h'(x)$$

For example, let

$$g(x) = \left(0.5x^2 + \frac{1}{x^2}\right)$$

$$h(x) = (-10 + x^3)$$

$$f(x) = g(x) + h(x)$$

$$= \left(0.5x^2 + \frac{1}{x^2}\right) + (-10 + x^3)$$

Then

$$\frac{df(x)}{dx} = \frac{dg(x)}{dx} + \frac{dh(x)}{dx}$$

$$= [0.5(2)(x^{2-1}) - 2x^{-2-1}] + 0 + 3x^{3-1}$$

$$= x - 2x^{-3} + 3x^2 = x - \frac{2}{x^3} + 3x^2$$

    Rule 3   If $y = f(x) = g(x)h(x)$, then

$$\frac{dy}{dx} = f'(x) = g'(x)h(x) + g(x)h'(x)$$

For example, let

$$g(x) = 0.5x^2 + \frac{1}{x^2}$$

$$h(x) = -10 + x^3$$

$$f(x) = g(x)h(x) = \left(0.5x^2 + \frac{1}{x^2}\right)(-10 + x^3)$$

Then

$$\frac{df(x)}{dx} = g'(x)h(x) + g(x)h'(x)$$

$$= \left(x - \frac{2}{x^3}\right)(-10 + x^3) + \left(0.5x^2 + \frac{1}{x^2}\right)(3x^2)$$

Or let

$$g(x) = \sqrt{x} + x^3$$

$$h(x) = \frac{1}{x^2} = x^{-2}$$

$$f(x) = g(x)h(x) = \frac{\sqrt{x} + x^3}{x^2} = (\sqrt{x} + x^3)(x^{-2})$$

Then

$$\frac{df(x)}{dx} = g'(x)h(x) + g(x)h'(x)$$

$$= (\tfrac{1}{2}x^{\frac{1}{2}-1} + 3x^2)(x^{-2}) + (\sqrt{x} + x^3)(-2x^{-2-1})$$

$$= \frac{1/(2\sqrt{x}) + 3x^2}{x^2} + \frac{-2(\sqrt{x} + x^3)}{x^3}$$

Rule 4 If $y = f(u)$ and u is, in turn, a function of x, $u = g(x)$, then $y = h(x)$. The derivative of y with respect to x is

$$\frac{dy}{dx} = \frac{dh(x)}{dx} = \frac{dy}{du}\frac{du}{dx}$$

For example, let

$$y = h(x) = (x^2 + 5)^3$$

and (in turn) let

$$u = g(x) = x^2 + 5$$

and accordingly,

$$y = f(u) = u^3$$

Then

$$\frac{dy}{dx} = h'(x) = \frac{dy}{du}\frac{du}{dx} = 3u^2(2x)$$

$$= 3(x^2 + 5)^2(2x)$$

Rule 5a If $y = f(x) = \ln x$,

$$\frac{dy}{dx} = \frac{1}{x}$$

Rule 5b   If $y = f(x) = \log_a x$,

$$\frac{dy}{dx} = \frac{1}{x} \log_a e$$

Rule 6a   If $y = f(x) = e^x$,

$$\frac{dy}{dx} = e^x$$

Rule 6b   If $y = f(x) = a^x$,

$$\frac{dy}{dx} = a^x \ln a$$

3-3   USE OF DERIVATIVES IN LOCATING MAXIMA AND MINIMA

The time-distance phenomenon of Example 3-2 that served to introduce the concept of the derivative and the instantaneous rate of change can readily be converted into an example in an entirely different context by considering x as the number of units of a product produced and y as the corresponding total costs of production in $y = f(x) = x^2$. Then, the rate of change in y per unit increase in x is interpreted as the increase in total costs per unit increase in x at various levels of x, namely, the *marginal cost* of production.   In Example 3-3 below the concepts of the derivative are applied to an economic/managerial problem.

EXAMPLE 3-3

A producer of a chemical must decide how many tons of the chemical to produce and sell in the next period in order to maximize profit.   As in Examples 1-2 and 2-2, assume the following relations between the total revenue R, the total costs C, and the number of tons produced and sold X:

$$R = f(X) = 50X - \frac{X^2}{200}$$

$$C = g(X) = 10,000 + 20X$$

The net profit of the firm is

$$\pi = h(X) = R - C = -\frac{X^2}{200} + 30X - 10,000$$

The decision problem can be approached from two alternative angles, *incremental approach* and *total approach*.   The two are the same in effect and yield the same solution, but on the surface they appear distinct.

Incremental analysis The process of decision making in small steps, or increments, is as follows.

Step 1 Suppose arbitrarily that the firm's current production level is at $X = 100$ tons, a sufficiently low level of activity. Then, ask the question: Does it pay for the firm to increase its production from the current level by a small increment ΔX to $X + \Delta X = 100 + \Delta X$?

Step 2 The answer to the above question depends on whether the increase in revenue attributable to ΔX is larger than the corresponding increase in costs. Only if $\Delta R > \Delta C$, should the firm decide to increase its production to $X + \Delta X$. For an illustration, ΔR and ΔC are computed below for $X = 100$ and $\Delta X = 10$:

$$\Delta R = f(X + \Delta X) - f(X)$$

$$= 50(X + \Delta X) - \frac{(X + \Delta X)^2}{200} - \left(50X - \frac{X^2}{200}\right)$$

$$= 50X + 50\,\Delta X - \frac{X^2 + 2X\,\Delta X + (\Delta X)^2}{200} - 50X + \frac{X^2}{200}$$

$$= 50\,\Delta X - \frac{2X\,\Delta X + (\Delta X)^2}{200}$$

For $X = 100$ tons and $\Delta X = 10$ tons,

$$\Delta R = 500 - \frac{2000 + 100}{200} = \$489.50$$

$$\Delta C = g(X + \Delta X) - g(X)$$

$$= 10{,}000 + 20(X + \Delta X) - (10{,}000 + 20X) = 20\,\Delta X$$

For $X = 100$ tons and $\Delta X = 10$ tons,

$$\Delta C = \$200$$

Since $\Delta R = \$489.50 > \Delta C = \$200$, the firm would prefer the 110-ton level of production to the current level of $X = 100$ tons.

Step 3 Now that the firm is at $X = 110$, should it increase its production further from 110 to $110 + \Delta X$? ΔR now is computed as

$$\Delta R = 50\Delta X - \frac{2X\,\Delta X + (\Delta X)^2}{200} = 500 - \frac{2200 + 100}{200} = \$488.50$$

and

$$\Delta C = 20\Delta X = \$200$$

Since $\Delta R = \$488.50 > \Delta C = \$200$, the firm should increase its production from 110 to 120 tons.

Step 4 Now does it pay for the firm to increase its production from $X = 120$ to $X + \Delta X = 120 + 10$? As the incremental decisions—the decisions on 10 tons at a time—are repeated as above, somewhere ΔR becomes less than ΔC and therefore it will not pay for the firm to move from X to $X + \Delta X$. Then that level of X constitutes the optimal solution of the firm.

Note that in the above analysis the choice of $\Delta X = 10$ was arbitrary and that the accuracy of analysis would be improved if ΔX were made smaller. In fact, a great saving in computation would result from applying the concept of derivative if the revenue and cost functions were assumed continuous and ΔX were considered as approaching zero, or $\Delta X \to 0$.

Exactly the same reasoning as the above incremental analysis underlies the economists' decision rule that a firm will produce and sell as long as its *marginal revenue* is larger than its *marginal cost* or, alternatively, a firm will increase its production until the marginal revenue becomes equal to the marginal cost. Verbally the definition of the marginal revenue is given as the increase in total revenue per unit increase in output and the marginal cost as the increase in total cost per unit increase in output. In mathematical notation, the marginal revenue and the marginal cost are

$$\text{Marginal revenue} = \frac{dR}{dX} = \lim_{\Delta X \to 0} \frac{\Delta R}{\Delta X}$$

$$\text{Marginal cost} = \frac{dC}{dX} = \lim_{\Delta X \to 0} \frac{\Delta C}{\Delta X}$$

The economists' decision rule on the output decision then is mathematically the same as finding the value of X where $dR/dX = dC/dX$ or $dR/dX - dC/dX = 0$. As long as the rate of increase in R per unit increase in X, (dR/dX), is larger than the rate of increase in C per unit increase in X, (dC/dX), increasing X would improve the firm's profit. But once X reaches the value where $dR/dX = dC/dX$, a further increase in X would reduce profit because beyond that level of X, $dR/dX < dC/dX$. Since

$$\frac{dR}{dX} = \lim_{\Delta X \to 0} \frac{\Delta R}{\Delta X} = 50 - \frac{X}{100}$$

$$\frac{dC}{dX} = \lim_{\Delta \to 0} \frac{\Delta C}{\Delta X} = 20$$

to find the value of X where $dR/dX = dC/dX$, one must find the value of X which satisfies

$$50 - \frac{X}{100} = 20$$

$$\frac{X}{100} = 50 - 20$$

$$X = 3000 \text{ tons}$$

Total analysis The above incremental approach may look somewhat contrived, though it undoubtedly gives an insight into the nature of the decision problem, particularly in light of the fact that a more straight-forward approach may be "to find the volume which maximizes the total profits of the firm." That is, the decision problem is viewed simply as that of finding the value of X which maximizes

$$\pi = R - C = -\frac{X^2}{200} + 30X - 10{,}000$$

Applying what was learned in the preceding section about the conditions for a maximum of a function, namely, (1) that $d\pi/dX$ is zero at the value of X where profit is a maximum and (2) that through that value of X, $d\pi/dX$ changes its sign from positive to negative, the problem is solved as below.

Step 1

$$\frac{d\pi}{dX} = -\frac{X}{100} + 30$$

Since $d\pi/dX = 0$ if a maximum,

$$-\frac{X}{100} + 30 = 0$$

$$\frac{X}{100} = 30$$

$$X = 3000$$

Step 2 To check whether $X = 3000$ satisfies the second condition of a maximum, $d\pi/dX$ is computed for $X = 2990$ and for $X = 3010$. When $X = 2990$,

$$\frac{d\pi}{dX} = -\frac{2990}{100} + 30 > 0$$

When $X = 3010$,

$$\frac{d\pi}{dX} = -\frac{3010}{100} + 30 < 0$$

Therefore, $X = 3000$ is a maximum-profit volume.

The result of the total analysis is, as expected, the same as that of the incremental analysis. The two seemingly different approaches are really the same. The essence of the total analysis is to find X which makes $d\pi/dX = 0$. But since $d\pi/dX = dR/dX - dC/dX$, the condition $d\pi/dX = 0$ is the same as the condition $dR/dX - dC/dX = 0$ or $dR/dX = dC/dX$, which is the incremental condition.

3-4 NONLINEAR RELATIONS OF MORE THAN TWO VARIABLES

The concepts and methods involving the derivative function are readily adaptable to the analysis of relations of more than two variables. Although the following example concerns a three-variable case, $z = f(x, y)$, whatever conclusions drawn here may be extended to cases with more than three variables.

EXAMPLE 3-4

Suppose that a retailer's profit π (in thousands of dollars) in a given period is a function of two decision variables, advertising expenditure x and investment in inventory y (both variables in thousands of dollars), namely,

$$\pi = f(x, y) = 100 - 2x^2 + 12x + xy - 1.5y^2 + 19y$$

Note that even when $x = y = 0$, π is still $100,000. The xy term in the equation signifies that advertising and availability of inventory reinforce each other in increasing sales and profit. Since the x^2 and y^2 terms have negative coefficients, π would eventually begin decreasing as x and y are increased higher and higher.

As in the linear relation between three variables in Sec. 2-2, the nonlinear function can be represented in a grid tabular form and in a three-dimensional perspective graph as in Exhibit 2-4. Since the function here is nonlinear, its graph would not be a (straight) plane as in Exhibit 2-4 but a bowl-shaped curved surface, as visualized in Exhibit 3-10. Points which make up the curved surface represent the ordered triples (x, y, π) that satisfy the statement $\pi = f(x, y)$.

How does π change as x and y are increased? For a specified value of x, π is a function of y alone, and therefore all the concepts studied in the bivariate (two-variable) case, such as those concerning maxima,

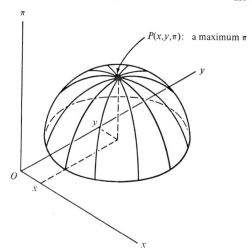

Exhibit 3-10 $\pi = f(x, y)$.

minima, and rates of change, apply here directly. Thus when $x = 3$, $\pi = 100 - 2(3)^2 + 12(3) + 3y - 1.5y^2 + 19y$ or $\pi = 118 + 22y - 1.5y^2$; accordingly, $d\pi/dy = 22 - 3y$. Geometrically, specification of $x = 3$ is represented by the *sectioning* (cutting) of the $\pi = f(x, y)$ surface along $x = 3$ plane as in Exhibit 3-11. Sectioning reduces the surface to a curve $\pi = 118 + 22y - 1.5y^2$ on a two-dimensional plane ($y\pi$ plane). For y values less than $7\frac{1}{3}$, $d\pi/dy > 0$; therefore, π increases as y increases. For $y > 7\frac{1}{3}$, $d\pi/dy < 0$; therefore, π decreases as y increases. For $y = 7\frac{1}{3}$, $d\pi/dy = 0$, and further, $d\pi/dy$ changes from positive to negative at that value of y. Therefore, π, the profit, is a maximum when y, the inventory investment, is $7\frac{1}{3}$.

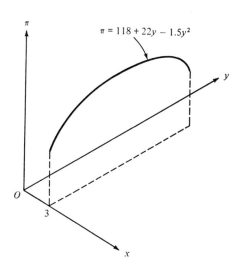

Exhibit 3-11 $\pi = 100 - 2x^2 + 12x + xy - 1.5y^2 + 19y$ when $x = 3$, or $\pi = 118 + 22y - 1.5y^2$.

Partial derivatives   In general, the derivative of $\pi = f(x, y)$ with respect to y for any specified value of $x = x$ is called the *partial derivative* of π with respect to y and written

$$\frac{\partial \pi}{\partial y} = \frac{\partial f}{\partial y} = f'_y$$

(∂ is Greek delta.) In order to obtain $\partial \pi / \partial y$, x's in the function $\pi = f(x, y)$ are treated as though they were *constants*, and the function is differentiated with respect to y. Thus, given

$$\pi = f(x, y) = 100 - 2x^2 + 12x + xy - 1.5y^2 + 19y$$

for a given value of $x = x$,

$$\frac{\partial \pi}{\partial y} = f'_y = 0 - 0 + 0 + x - 3y + 19 = x - 3y + 19$$

(Note that since $2x^2$ is considered a constant, its derivative is zero; the derivative of xy is x; and so on.) From the above partial-derivative formula, it can be verified that when $x = 3$,

$$\frac{\partial \pi}{\partial y} = 3 - 3y + 19 = 22 - 3y$$

as obtained earlier.

Likewise, for a specified value of $y = y$, the partial derivative of π with respect to x can be obtained:

$$\frac{\partial \pi}{\partial x} = f'_x = -4x + 12 + y$$

When would $\pi = f(x, y)$ be a maximum or a minimum? If $\pi = f(x, y)$ is represented by a surface, as in Exhibit 3-10, it has a maximum, a peak P at a given value of x and a given value of y. How are such x, y values found? The fact that point P (x, y, π) is a maximum implies that if the surface is sectioned (through that point) in all directions, all the resulting two-dimensional curves individually peak, i.e., have the maximum, at the point, or *at least* that if the surface is sectioned in two fundamental directions, namely, along $x = x$ and $y = y$, the resulting two curves individually have a maximum at the point, as illustrated in Exhibit 3-12. This means that the minimum necessary conditions for a maximum are that the rates of change in π in the two fundamental directions be zero, namely, $\partial \pi / \partial x = 0$ and $\partial \pi / \partial y = 0$. Thus, for $\pi = f(x, y) = 100 - 2x^2 + 12x + xy - 1.5y^2 + 19y$ to be a maximum,

$$\frac{\partial \pi}{\partial x} = -4x + 12 + y$$

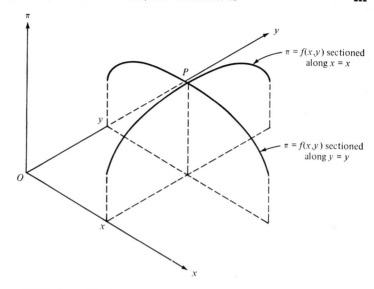

Exhibit 3-12   Maximum of $\pi = f(x, y)$.

must be zero, *and also*

$$\frac{\partial \pi}{\partial y} = x - 3y + 19$$

must be zero.   The (x, y) that satisfies the two conditions

$$-4x + 12 + y = 0 \tag{1}$$
$$x - 3y + 19 = 0 \tag{2}$$

is obtained $(x, y) = (5, 8)$ according to the procedure of Chap. 2
Multiply Eq. (2) by 4 and add to Eq. (1):

$$-11y + 88 = 0$$
$$y = \tfrac{88}{11} = 8$$

Substitute $y = 8$ in Eq. (1):

$$-4x + 12 + 8 = 0$$
$$x = \tfrac{20}{4} = 5$$

Analogous to the two-variable case, $\partial \pi / \partial x = 0$ and $\partial \pi / \partial y = 0$ are the *necessary*, but not *necessary and sufficient*, conditions.   For π to be a maximum at the given point (x, y), in addition to $\partial \pi / \partial x = 0$ and $\partial \pi / \partial y = 0$, $\partial \pi / \partial x$ must change from positive to negative through that value of x and $\partial \pi / \partial y$ must change from positive to negative through that value of y. The reader may verify that these conditions hold for the above example, and as a result it may be concluded that the profit of the firm would be maximized at $x = 5$ (advertising expenditure of \$5000) and $y = 8$ (inventory investment of \$8000).

Converse to the case of maximum, if at a given (x, y), $\partial\pi/\partial x = 0$ and $\partial\pi/\partial y = 0$ and also $\partial\pi/\partial x$ and $\partial\pi/\partial y$ change from negative to positive through the (x, y), then this (x, y) yields a *minimum* π. If $\partial\pi/\partial x = 0$ and $\partial\pi/\partial y = 0$ but $\partial\pi/\partial x$ and $\partial\pi/\partial y$ do not change signs, then the point is neither maximum nor minimum.

3-5 CONCLUSION

After studying linear relations in Chap. 2, we turned our attention in Chap. 3 to nonlinear relations. An objective of this chapter has been to emphasize the notion that even the most complex nonlinear functions are merely ways of specifying the pattern of variation of one variable in relation to another variable, just as was the case with simple linear relations.

Inasmuch as investigation of relations in general may be approached from an incremental point of view as well as from a total point of view, this chapter studied some basic concepts of the derivative, the mathematicians' tool for incremental analysis. Further, the chapter illustrated how the mathematical concepts of the derivative function facilitate finding a maximum or minimum of a function when the function is differentiable.

QUESTIONS AND PROBLEMS

1. Explain the concepts of rate of change, instantaneous rate of change, and the derivative function.

2. Give examples of nonlinear functions and explain the kind of relational pattern involved for each.

3. What is an inverse function?

4. Evaluate (or find the numerical value of) the following:

    (a) e^{-2} (b) $27^{\frac{2}{3}}$ (c) $9^{-\frac{1}{2}}$ (d) $5^{-2}3^{-3}$

    (e) $4(2^0)$ (f) $(\frac{3}{5})^{-1}$ (g) $(\frac{5}{4})^2$ (h) $\log_e e^{\frac{2}{3}}$

    (i) $\log_{10} 1000$ (j) $\log_{13} 1$ (k) $\log_{10} 0.01$

    (l) If $f(x) = \dfrac{x^2 - 2}{x + 1}$, what is (i) $\lim\limits_{x \to -3} f(x)$ and (ii) $\lim\limits_{x \to -1} f(x)$?

    (m) If $f(x) = \dfrac{2x}{x^2}$, what is (i) $\lim\limits_{x \to 0} f(x)$ and (ii) $\lim\limits_{x \to \infty} f(x)$?

    (n) $\lim\limits_{y \to 0} \dfrac{(1 + y)^2 - 1}{y}$ (o) $\lim\limits_{a \to -\infty} \dfrac{1,000,000}{a^2}$

5. (a) Graph $xy = 4$.

    (b) Is the function continuous? If not, where is it discontinuous?

6. For an exponential function $y = ab^x$, the parameters a and b could be negative, positive, fractions, integers, etc. Sketch the graph of y for the possible combinations of the values of a and b as laid out in a grid-form table as shown.

	$a < 0$	$0 < a < 1$	$a = 1$	$a > 1$
$b < 0$				
$1 > b > 0$				
$b = 1$				
$b > 1$				

7. On savings deposits, M bank pays an interest of 6 percent compounded annually and N bank pays 4 percent per annum compounded quarterly.

(a) If you had \$1000 to invest in a savings account for 2 years, which bank would you prefer?

(b) Derive, for each bank, the formula by which the compounded value at the end of xth year can be computed for an original deposit of \$$A$.

8. (a) If you invest \$1000 a year at the end of each year for 3 years in a savings account which pays 5 percent compounded annually, how much would you have in the account at the end of 3 years (assuming no withdrawals)?

(b) Derive the mathematical formula that would give the compounded value at the end of nth year if \$$A$ a year is invested at the end of each year for n years in a savings account which pays i percent compounded annually.

(c) A company will need \$100,000 at the end of 3 years to repay an obligation. How much should the company set aside at the end of each year in a sinking fund which earns 8 percent a year in order to have \$100,000 as needed?

9. (a) Specify circumstances under which you as an individual would accept an offer whereby you receive \$250 a year for 5 years by paying \$1000 now. (Formulate the problem mathematically.)

(b) Would the problem similar to part (a) arise in business and government decisions?

10. Assume that the yield of corn (in thousands of bushels) from a tract of land is $y = 3x^2/2$, where x is tons of fertilizer applied.

(a) Compute $\Delta y/\Delta x$ when $x = 4$, and $\Delta x = 2$, $\Delta x = 0.1$, and $\Delta x = -0.5$.

(b) Interpret (or explain the economic meaning of) the $\Delta y/\Delta x$'s in part (a).

(c) What is $\lim_{\Delta x \to 0} (\Delta y/\Delta x)$ when $x = 4$?

(d) What happens to the derivative function of y as x is increased from zero?

(e) Interpret part (d).

11. (a) If $y = \sqrt{x}$, $(x \geq 0)$, find dy/dx.

(b) If $x = y^2/\sqrt{1 - y}$, $(y < 1)$, find dx/dy.

(c) If $u = (2v + 1)/v^2$, $(v \neq 0)$, find du/dv.

(d) If $y = (x^2 + 4)^{\frac{1}{3}}(1 - x)$, find dy/dx.

    (e) If $f(x, y) = (x^2 + y^2)^{\frac{1}{2}}$, find $\partial f/\partial x$ and $\partial f/\partial y$.
    (f) If $w = u^2v^2 + v - 4uv + 4$, find $\partial w/\partial u$ and $\partial w/\partial v$.
    (g) If $y = e^{2x^2} + 3$, find dy/dx.
    (h) If $u = \log (v^2 + 2v)$, find du/dv.

12. In a given range of x values, a function $y = f(x)$ may vary as in one of the 11 patterns illustrated. For each, state what happens to dy/dx as x is increased.

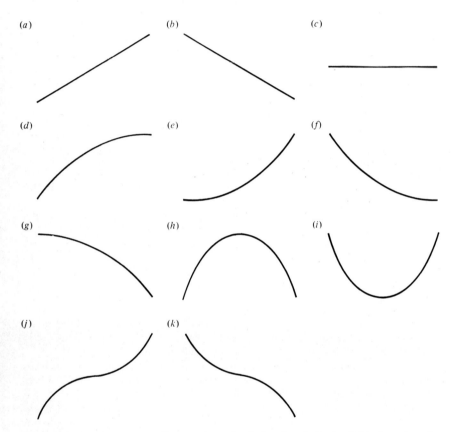

13. *Higher-order derivatives*   Inasmuch as the derivative dy/dx itself is a function of x, the derivative of dy/dx can be obtained, which gives the rates of change of dy/dx. The derivative of a derivative, called the *second-order derivative*, is written

$$\frac{d}{dx}\frac{dy}{dx} \qquad \frac{d^2y}{dx^2} \qquad f''(x) \qquad y''$$

and for partial derivatives

$$\frac{\partial}{\partial x}\frac{\partial y}{\partial x} \quad \text{or} \quad \frac{\partial^2 y}{\partial x^2}, \qquad \frac{\partial}{\partial y}\frac{\partial y}{\partial x} \quad \text{or} \quad \frac{\partial^2 y}{\partial y\,\partial x}$$

    (a) For each of the curves in Prob. 12 state what happens to d^2y/dx^2.

14. In Exercise 3-3, the total cost of a firm in $1000s was given as a cubic function of x, units in thousands:

$$T = \text{VC} + \text{FC} = \frac{x^3}{3} - 4x^2 + 30x + 20$$

One of the requirements of the exercise was to graph the function.

(a) Verify the graph in Exercise 3-3 by evaluating dT/dx and d^2T/dx^2.

(b) Determine mathematically the volume x which yields the minimum average unit cost.

15. The sales volume (in units) of a product Q is given as a function of its price per unit p as

$$Q = 10{,}000e^{-0.25p}$$

where $e \approx 2.718$. The cost of producing and selling consists of fixed costs of $6000 and variable costs per unit of $1.

(a) Express the total revenue R as a function of p.

(b) Express the total cost C as a function of p.

(c) Compute the profit when $p = \$4, \$8, \$p$.

(d) Find the price which would yield the maximum profit?

(e) How would you find the break-even volume?   (Just set up the problem.)

16. By cutting out the shaded portions of a square cardboard 20 in each side and folding along the dotted lines (as in the diagram) an open-top box is made.   At what value of x would the volume of the box be the maximum?

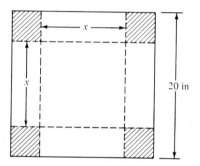

17. A machine can be set at various speeds to machine a product, x units/hr.   When it is set too fast or too slow, however, the number of defective units increases, and accordingly the cost of reworking the defectives increases.   Suppose that the cost of reworking defectives per hour C_r is the minimum, $30 per hour, when the machine is set to process 160 units/hr, and that the increase in C_r is directly proportional to the square of the deviation in speed from 160 units/hr.   When the machine is set at 140 or 180 units/hr, the cost of reworking defectives per hour is determined to be $5 higher than when it is set at 160 units/hr.   In addition to the cost of reworking defective units, the cost of operating the machine includes $150 per hour regardless of the speed of the machine.

(a) Express the cost of reworking defective units per hour as a function of speed x.

(b) At what speed would the cost of reworking defective units be $75 per hour?

(c) Express the average unit cost of producing the product as a function of speed.

(d) When would the average unit cost of the product be minimum?

18. A firm manufactures two products, I and II.   The total costs of production consist of the common fixed costs of \$2800 and the variable costs of \$4 and \$6 per unit for I and II, respectively.   The respective demands for I and II are

$$x_1 = p_2 - 3p_1 + 200$$
$$x_2 = 0.5p_1 - 4p_2 + 150$$

where p_1 = price per unit of I
$\quad\quad\ p_2$ = price per unit of II

(a) Interpret the coefficients of p_1 and p_2 in the demand functions.

(b) Give the total revenue R as a function of p_1 and p_2.

(c) Give the total cost of the firm C as a function of p_1 and p_2.

(d) Find $\partial R/\partial p_1$ and $\partial C/\partial p_2$ when $p_1 = 10$ and $p_2 = 15$, and interpret.

(e) Find the prices that maximize the profit.   How much is the profit?   How many units of sale?

19. *The least-squares method*   Suppose that the costs of production in the past three periods have been observed as tabulated.

Period	Units produced, x	Total cost, y
First	3	\$ 6
Second	9	8
Third	11	14

(a) Find the quadratic cost curve $y = a + bx + cx^2$ which passes through all three observed (x, y)'s.

(b) Find the linear cost function $y = a + bx$ which would minimize the sum of the squares of deviations of the three observed (x, y)'s from the line, namely, minimize $\Sigma d_i{}^2 = d_1{}^2 + d_2{}^2 + d_3{}^3$ in the diagram.   *Hint:* $d_1 = 6 - [a + b(3)]$.   When a line is fitted to observed data according to the above criterion, i.e., minimization of $\Sigma d_i{}^2$, it is called the *least-squares line*.

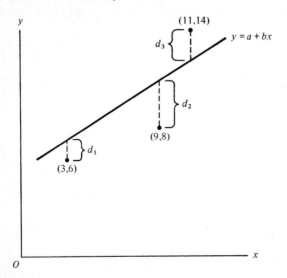

20. In 1952, the demand for use of the Lincoln Tunnel, which connects New Jersey with midtown Manhattan, considerably exceeded its capacity. The Port of New York Authority undertook a series of studies to understand better what goes on in a traffic flow so that they could increase the flow through the tunnel. After a long study, they found that speed S (in miles per hour) and density D (in vehicles per mile) were closely related by the functional relationship $S = 42 - 0.3D$. The traffic flow is measured by V (in vehicles per hour), and $V = SD$. The problem was then reduced to finding the maximum attainable V by controlling the speed of the flow S. The relationship between S and D was taken as a fixed behavioral relationship within which the Authority had to work.[1]

(*a*) Formulate the Authority's decision problem mathematically.

(*b*) Find the first-degree derivative of V with respect to S.

(*c*) Find the value of dV/dS at $S = 15$, and interpret.

(*d*) Find the optimal speed, namely, the speed which would maximize the traffic flow.

(*e*) Find V'', and interpret.

[1] C. R. Carr and C. W. Howe, "Quantitative Decision Procedures in Management and Economics," p. 72, McGraw-Hill, New York, 1964.

4
Linear Programming:
Introduction and Formulation

Decision making may be defined as the human endeavor to allocate *limited resources* (or means) to various types of *activities* in order to achieve certain *objectives* (or ends). Thus, with respect to *government decisions*, the government has at its disposal such limited resources as natural and human resources, tax revenues, etc., to allocate to such varied activities as education, health, conservation, urban development, housing, transportation, etc., in order to maximize the "welfare" of the society. With respect to *business decisions*, management allocates such limited resources as capital, manpower, productive capacity, etc., to such varied activities as production of different products, research and development, employee education, community service, etc., for the purpose of "surviving and growing," and profit making.

General mathematical model of a decision The above definition of decision making can be translated into a general mathematical model as follows.

Let X_1, X_2, X_3, . . . , X_n represent the designations (names) of various activities, for example, in the governmental-decision context, X_1 = education program, X_2 = housing program.

Let x_1, x_2, x_3, . . . , x_n represent the *levels* of the above designated activities undertaken, for example, x_1 = number of schools built and operated, x_2 = number of houses built.

Let e represent the level of attainment of the objective, for example, for government, the degree of social welfare attained if measurable; for business, often profit.[1]

Let C_1, C_2, C_3, . . . , C_m represent the designations of various limited resources, for example, capital funds, tax revenues, skilled labor.

Let k_1, k_2, k_3, . . . , k_m represent the limit, or capacity, of the above limited resources, for example, k_2 = number of machine hours available, k_5 = number of skilled workers available.

Then the level of attainment of the objective varies according to the variations in the levels of various activities; that is, e is a function of x_1, x_2, x_3, . . . , x_n,

$$e = f(x_1, x_2, x_3, \ldots, x_n)$$

which, under most circumstances, would be an increasing function in the sense that as any x_j is increased, holding others at the same level, e would increase.

Also, the level of consumption of each of the limited resources varies as the levels of various activities are varied.   Formally,

Level of consumption of $C_1 = g_1(x_1, x_2, x_3, \ldots, x_n)$

Level of consumption of $C_2 = g_2(x_1, x_2, x_3, \ldots, x_n)$

. . . .

Level of consumption of $C_m = g_m(x_1, x_2, x_3, \ldots, x_n)$

which are again likely to be increasing functions.   Within the framework of these definitions, decision making can be characterized as an effort to find the values of x_1, x_2, x_3 . . . , x_n, which maximize

$$e = f(x_1, x_2, x_3, \ldots, x_n)$$

subject to

$$g_1(x_1, x_2, x_3, \ldots, x_n) \leq k_1$$
$$g_2(x_1, x_2, x_3, \ldots, x_n) \leq k_2 \qquad x_1, x_2, x_3, \ldots, x_n \geq 0$$
. . . .
$$g_m(x_1, x_2, x_3, \ldots, x_n) \leq k_m$$

---

[1] Here a single objective of the decision maker is assumed.   For multiple objectives e represents a sort of superutility which measures and combines the utility of "oranges" and that of "apples" or the utility of educational programs and that of beautification programs on a same scale.

Inequalities under the heading of "subject to" are interpreted as follows. The first statement, $g_1(x_1, x_2, \ldots, x_n)$, represents the level of consumption of the resource C_1 at a given set of levels of $x_1, x_2, \ldots, x_n$. Since the decision maker has only k_1 of the resource C_1, the level of consumption cannot exceed the available k_1. Likewise, for any resource C_i, $g_i(x_1, x_2, \ldots, x_n) \leq k_i$. In addition, inasmuch as negative levels of activities are ruled out, the level of any activity must be either zero or positive; hence, $x_1, x_2, \ldots, x_n \geq 0$. The function to be maximized, $e = f(x_1, x_2, \ldots, x_n)$, is called the *objective function*. The inequality statements are called *constraints* or *side conditions*.

If the objective function is an increasing function, it appears that the decision maker can maximize it by increasing the levels of all activities, $x_1, x_2, x_3, \ldots, x_n$, indefinitely; but obviously this is not possible because increases in x_j's can be accomplished only through increases in consumption of resources, $g_i(x_1, x_2, \ldots, x_n)$. The decision maker must therefore find the particular mix, or ordered n-tuple, $(x_1, x_2, x_3, \ldots, x_n)$, which satisfies all the inequality statements and also maximizes e.

Linear programming   Formulation of a decision problem into the mathematical form as above is called *mathematical programming*. *Linear programming* is a subclass of general mathematical programming in which both the objective function and the constraints are linear relations. The counterpart of linear programming is, as expected, *nonlinear programming*, where either the objective function or all or some of the constraints (or both) are nonlinear relations. The general model of linear-programming problems is as follows.

Find the values of the decision variables $x_1, x_2, \ldots, x_n$ which maximize

$$e = v_1 x_1 + v_2 x_2 + v_3 x_3 + \cdots + v_n x_n$$

subject to (or satisfying)

$$a_{11}x_1 + a_{12}x_2 + a_{13}x_3 + \cdots + a_{1n}x_n \leq k_1$$
$$a_{21}x_1 + a_{22}x_2 + a_{23}x_3 + \cdots + a_{2n}x_n \leq k_2$$
$$\cdots \cdots \cdots \cdots \cdots \cdots \cdots \cdots \cdots \cdots \cdots$$
$$a_{m1}x_1 + a_{m2}x_2 + a_{m3}x_3 + \cdots + a_{mn}x_n \leq k_m$$

$$x_1, x_2, x_3, \ldots, x_n \geq 0$$

This system of linear inequalities is in the same form as the general system of linear equations discussed in Chap. 2 except that one involves inequality signs and the other equality signs. The method of solving systems of linear equations given in Chap. 2 is readily adaptable to solving the system of linear inequalities and consequently to solving the entire linear-programming problem. Methods of solution for nonlinear-programming problems are naturally more difficult, and this book elects not to discuss them.

As in other topics in the book, there are two aspects to a linear-programming problem, economics and mathematics. In this chapter an attempt is made to ascertain what kinds of real-world economic problems lend themselves to mathematical linear-programming formulation. Specifically, in this chapter, the verbal description of economic situations is first translated into linear-programming models, and then the decision problems are solved through graphic analyses. To enhance intuitive understanding, the graphic analyses will be tied closely with the economic reasoning underlying them. This, it is hoped, will lay the foundation and motivation for studying the formal solution method in Chap. 5.

Although the general mathematical model of linear programming presented earlier involved maximization of a linear objective function and the chapter begins its discussion with an example calling for maximization of an objective function, there are situations which require minimization of an objective function. Toward the end of the chapter an example of a minimization problem is given to demonstrate that it is essentially no different from the maximization case.

4-1 MAXIMIZATION PROBLEM

Typically a firm must decide how much of its limited resources, e.g., funds, manpower, facilities, is to be channeled to production (and sale) of different products. One of the main objectives of the firm in such a resource-allocation decision is attainment of profit. A hypothetical example where the firm can produce two types of products will be discussed.

EXAMPLE 4-1 PRODUCT-MIX DECISION

A firm can produce one or both of two products, I and II, in any mix. The selling price per unit of I is $12; that of II is $9. The out-of-pocket costs of producing a unit of I are $7; those of II, $6. Thus, the contribution to the firm's profit per unit of I is $5 (= 12 − 7); that of II is $3.

Besides the above costs, production of both products requires consumption of a special raw material the supply of which is limited to 36,000 lb. One unit of I requires 4 lb of this raw material, and one unit of II requires 3 lb.

In addition, production of 1 unit of I takes 4 hr of machining time and 2 hr of assembly-line time; that of II takes 10 hr of machining time and 2.5 hr of assembly-line time. 60,000 hr of machine time and 20,000 hr of assembly-line time are available for the next period, and no addition to either capacity is planned.

The gist of the decision is to find the numbers of units of I and II which can be produced within the given limited resources and which will at the same time maximize the profit.

Mathematical formulation   The relationships relevant to the decision can be formulated in a mathematical model as follows.

Let x_1 and x_2 represent the numbers of units of products I and II produced, respectively. If x_1 units of I are produced, the profit contribution from product I would be $5 per unit times x_1, or $5x_1$. If x_2 units of II are produced, the profit contribution from II would be $3 per unit times x_2, or $3x_2$. Therefore, the total contribution to the firm's profit π from both is

$$\pi = 5x_1 + 3x_2$$

The raw material required for producing x_1 units of I and x_2 units of II is 4 lb times x_1 plus 3 lb times x_2, or $4x_1 + 3x_2$. Likewise, the machining time required for producing x_1 units of I and x_2 units of II is $4x_1 + 10x_2$; the assembly-line time required for producing x_1 units of I and x_2 units of II is $2x_1 + 2.5x_2$. Since the resource requirements for producing x_1 units of I and x_2 units of II cannot exceed the available capacities, x_1 and x_2 must satisfy the inequality statements

$$4x_1 + 3x_2 \leq 36{,}000 \qquad \text{for raw material}$$
$$4x_1 + 10x_2 \leq 60{,}000 \qquad \text{for machine time}$$
$$2x_1 + 2.5x_2 \leq 20{,}000 \qquad \text{for assembly-line time}$$

In addition

$$x_1 \geq 0 \qquad x_2 \geq 0$$

because the number of units of I or II must be either zero, i.e., no production, or some positive level.

Feasible solutions and optimal solutions   Combinations of x_1 and x_2 that the firm *could produce* (technically) *within the given resources* are called *feasible solutions*. Mathematically, the feasible solutions are the ordered pairs (x_1, x_2) which satisfy the inequality statements listed above. Evidently there are many feasible solutions. Of all the feasible solutions, the particular combination of x_1 and x_2 which will yield the maximum profit, the highest attained value of the objective function, $\pi = 5x_1 + 3x_2$, is called the *optimal solution*.

Exercise 4-1   (a) Check whether the following levels of production, (x_1, x_2), are feasible or not:

(0, 0)	(8000, 1100)	(9000, 0)	$(8999, \frac{4}{3})$
(15,000, 16,000)	(5000, 4000)	$(5001, 3999\frac{1}{5})$	(0, 7200)
(7500, 2000)	(−50, 2000)		

(*b*) Which of the feasible solutions of part (*a*) yields the highest profit, i.e., maximizes the objective function?   The lowest profit?

(*c*) Give any two combinations of x_1 and x_2 which would use up the raw material available.   Give any two combinations of x_1 and x_2 which would leave some raw material unused.   Give any two (x_1, x_2)'s which would leave exactly 12,000 lb of raw material unused.

(*d*) Find (x_1, x_2)'s which would use up any two of the three limited resources (irrespective of the third resource).   Formulate the problem mathematically.

(*e*) Give any two (x_1, x_2)'s which would yield exactly \$30,000 profit; exactly \$12,000 profit; exactly \$60,000; determine whether they are feasible or not.

(*f*) Determine the rate of substitution between x_1 and x_2, that is, $\Delta x_2/\Delta x_1$, for each of the resource constraint inequalities, and interpret it.

(*g*) Determine the rate of change between x_1 and x_2 for the objective function and interpret it.

(*h*) Suppose the only resource limitation of the firm is 36,000 lb of raw material; in other words, the other two resources are plentiful.   What combination(s) of x_1 and x_2 will produce the highest profit?   Support your answer through verbal reasoning.

GRAPHIC REPRESENTATION AND INTERPRETATION

Even though one must eventually discard the crutch of diagrammatic visualization (it is cumbersome or useless when the situation is even slightly more complicated than the above example), this section analyzes and solves the problem graphically so as to sharpen the reader's understanding of the nature of the problem and lay the foundation for an understanding of the nongraphic method.

Constraints   The points in the shaded portion of the diagram of Exhibit 4-1*a*, namely, the "northeast quarter" or the first quadrant of the $x_1 x_2$ plane, represent the ordered (x_1, x_2)'s satisfying the nonnegativity restriction on x_1 and x_2, that is, $x_1 \geq 0$, $x_2 \geq 0$.

Next, in reference to the raw-material constraint, the combinations of x_1 and x_2 that would use up all the raw material in stock *exactly*—no more, no less—are the ordered pairs (x_1, x_2) which satisfy the equality part of the constraint, that is, $4x_1 + 3x_2 = 36{,}000$, and are represented by the points lying on the line segment $R_1 R_2$ (and no other points) in Exhibit 4-1*b*.

It is easy to see that any point below the line, such as F_1 and F_2, represents a combination of x_1 and x_2 which would consume *less than* 36,000 lb of the raw material or would satisfy the inequality part of the constraint, that is, $4x_1 + 3x_2 < 36{,}000$.   For example, F_1 represents $(x_1, x_2) = (1503, 4000)$, and this ordered pair is verified to satisfy the inequality statement:

$$4(1503) + 3(4000) = 6012 + 12{,}000 = 18{,}012 < 36{,}000$$

Point N_2, or $(x_1, x_2) = (10{,}500, -2000)$, satisfies the equality statement $4x_1 + 3x_2 = 36{,}000$.   [$4(10{,}500) + 3(-2000) = 36{,}000$.]   But x_2

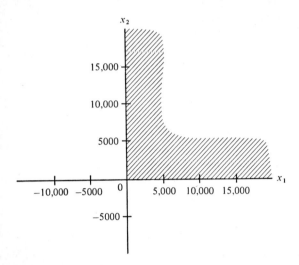

Exhibit 4-1a Definition of the $x_1 x_2$ plane; x_1, $x_2 \geq 0$.

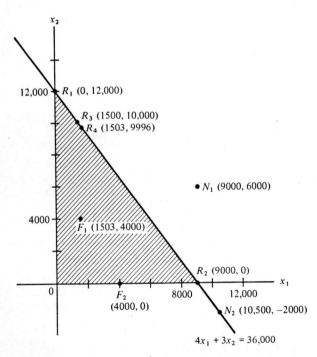

Exhibit 4-1b $(x_1,\ x_2)$'s satisfying $4x_1 + 3x_2 \leq 36,000$, x_1, $x_2 \geq 0$.

$= -2000$ is a negative number, in violation of the nonnegativity condition, $x_2 \geq 0$, and therefore, the particular (x_1, x_2) is not a feasible solution. Obviously, then, the (x_1, x_2)'s which satisfy the following system of statements simultaneously are represented by the points lying within the shaded triangle (including the points on the boundary lines):

$$4x_1 + 3x_2 \leq 36,000 \qquad x_1, x_2 \geq 0$$

Of course, a point like N_1, $(x_1, x_2) = (9000, 6000)$, does not satisfy the statement $4x_1 + 3x_2 \leq 36,000$ while satisfying the statements, $x_1, x_2 \geq 0$, and therefore it represents a nonfeasible production.

Similarly, the points which satisfy each of the other two resource constraints can be located. Exhibit 4-2 shows the result of combining all constraints in one single graph. Any point lying within the shaded polygon $OPQRS$ (including the boundary lines), represents a combination of x_1 and x_2 which satisfies the requirement for nonnegativity of the variables and the constraints of limited resources.

Exercise 4-2 (*a*) Show that points A, B, C, O, P, Q, R, S in Exhibit 4-2 represent feasible production for the firm and that D, E, F, G, H represent nonfeasible production.

(*b*) For each of the feasible solutions A, B, C, O, P, Q, R, S, determine the levels of *idle* capacities that would be left unused *after* production.

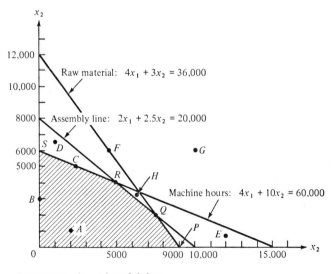

Exhibit 4-2 (x_1, x_2) satisfying

$$4x_1 + 3x_2 \leq 36,000$$
$$4x_1 + 10x_2 \leq 60,000 \qquad x_1, x_2 \geq 0$$
$$2x_1 + 2.5x_2 \leq 20,000$$

The objective function and its maximization   Within the area of feasible solutions, the polygon $OPQRS$, which point represents the mix of x_1 and x_2 that would yield the maximum profit? If both variables are continuous, e.g., if the products are chemicals and fractions of 1 unit, say, $\frac{3}{4}$ ton of a product can be produced, then infinitely many combinations of x_1 and x_2 represent feasible solutions. Even if the variables can assume only integers (the products are not divisible), still there is an extremely large number of combinations of x_1 and x_2 that are within the feasible region. The next task is to find the particular feasible solution, i.e., a point, that gives the highest profit.

This task is aided greatly by a theorem:[1] *If there exists a maximum-profit solution to the problem, it will be found among the combinations of x_1 and x_2 values represented by the vertices (extreme corners) of the feasible solution polygon.* According to this theorem, one of the vertices (O, P, Q, R, S) will turn out to be the maximum-profit solution. Without a formal mathematical proof, the reasonableness of this important proposition is demonstrated as follows.

The objective function $\pi = 5x_1 + 3x_2$ is nothing but a formula for computing the profit for any given production mix. In graphic terms, for any point on the x_1x_2 plane the corresponding profit can be computed by applying the formula. For instance, for the point representing $(x_1, x_2) = (1200, 3000)$, the profit is

$$\pi = 5x_1 + 3x_2 = 5(1200) + 3(3000) = \$15,000$$

The firm's wish to maximize profit, then, can be translated on the diagram into the desire to be at a point as far out in the northeast direction as the limited resources allow.

Now suppose that one wishes to identify all the combinations of x_1 and x_2 other than (1200, 3000) that would yield the same profit of \$15,000. Any ordered pair (x_1, x_2) which satisfies the statement

$$\pi = 15,000 = 5x_1 + 3x_2$$

represents the mix of production resulting in a profit of \$15,000. All points that yield \$15,000 profit form a straight line, as shown in Exhibit 4-3.

Similarly, the combinations of x_1 and x_2 which yield any other levels of profit, in particular, \$0, \$30,000, \$45,000, \$60,000, \$90,000, can be found. The (x_1, x_2)'s which yield these specified amounts of profit are given as dotted lines in Exhibit 4-4.

---

[1] A theorem is a proposition which can be proved true from given assumptions (or other propositions). Mathematicians employ "if so, then so" reasoning to prove theorems.

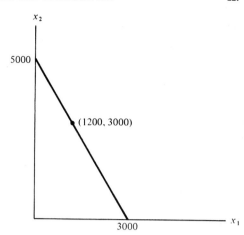

Exhibit 4-3 (x_1, x_2)'s satisfying $15,000 = 5x_1 + 3x_2$; $x_1, x_2 \geq 0$.

Notes on profit lines in Exhibit 4-4

1. Since all points lying on a given line represent production mixes yielding the same amount of profit, each line is called an *equal-profit line* or *isoprofit line.*

2. Since the coefficients of the variables, 5 and 3, are the same for all equal-profit statements, the profit lines are parallel to one another.

3. An infinite number of equal-profit lines can be drawn by varying the amount of profit π.

4. The farther *out* in the northeast direction the profit line is, the higher the profit level it represents. Since there is only one mix, $(x_1, x_2) = (0, 0)$, which would yield $\pi = \$0$, the line for $\pi = 0 = 5x_1 + 3x_2$ is represented simply as a point, namely, O.

5. Each and every point on the x_1x_2 plane is on one and only one equal-profit line. This is an alternative way of stating that any given combination of x_1 and x_2 yields a *specific* amount of profit.

Maximum-profit solution   Now that both the objective function and the area of feasible solutions have been defined on the x_1x_2 plane, the next step is to locate the (x_1, x_2) which maximizes profit without violating the given constraints. This can be achieved by superimposing the graph of isoprofit lines on the graph of the feasible-solution polygon of Exhibit 4-2 to complete Exhibit 4-4. Since the farther the profit line is from the origin $(0, 0)$, the higher the profit is, the point on the profit line located farthest from the origin which at the same time remains within the boundaries of the feasible-solution polygon $OPQRS$ represents the maximum-profit solution. Such a point is shown to be P, for which $(x_1, x_2) = (9000, 0)$. With this production mix, the profit of the firm

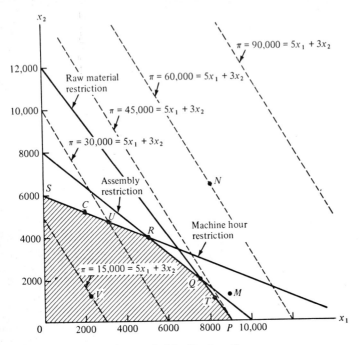

Exhibit 4-4   Constraints and objective function.

would be $\pi = 5x_1 + 3x_2 = 5(9000) + 3(0) = \$45,000$, the maximum. No other (x_1, x_2) would give a higher profit. For example, M and N are on a profit line higher than the \$45,000 line but are not feasible solutions. T, U, V, and Q, R, S represent feasible solutions, but the profit lines drawn through them represent profits lower than \$45,000.

There is an alternative way of looking at this maximization process. Though obviously unprofitable, suppose that the firm considers $(x_1, x_2) = (0, 0)$ as a feasible course of action for the next period's production. Graphically, this means that the firm would be at point O. Since O is on an equal-profit line, $\pi = 0 = 5x_1 + 3x_2$, the firm in its desire to maximize its profit would move to higher and higher profit lines, i.e., from $\pi = 0$ to points on the $\pi = 10,000$ line, on the $\pi = 15,000$ line, on the $\pi = 30,000$ line, and so on.

The firm can continue this process until a further move would mean stepping out of the feasible polygon, i.e., running out of one (or more) of the limited resources. Inasmuch as the vertices of the feasible solution area are the points farthest out in the northeast direction, the highest profit line the firm can attain, i.e., the line from which a further move means leaving the feasible area, would pass one of the vertices. In this example, P happens to be that vertex. (If the firm is at T, it is on a profit line lower than the profit line for P. Consequently, it would move to P. But once the firm is at P, it cannot move to a higher profit unless it can go beyond the capacity limitations.)

In this example, as the firm moves from the $0 profit level to higher and higher profit lines, it steps out of the feasible solution area initially at P. However, if the slope of the equal-profit lines were different from the one given, the point at which the profit line departs the feasible-production polygon initially might be different from P; that is, the maximum profit (x_1, x_2) might occur at a vertex other than P. This can be seen easily by using a ruler to represent the equal-profit lines of varying slopes as follows.

On Exhibit 4-4 set a ruler so that the angle by which it cuts the horizontal axis is different from the angle formed by the current-profit lines $\pi = 5x_1 + 3x_2$. Then, maintaining the same angle, move the ruler gradually from the origin O toward the northeast direction, scanning the feasible-solution region, and determine the point at which the ruler moves out of the feasible region initially.

The reader should verify that if the angle of the ruler is steeper than the current-profit lines, the ruler still loses its contact with the feasible area initially at P, but if the angle is flatter than the current-profit lines, the point of initial departure from the feasible area is at vertices other than P. Specifically, if the slope of the ruler is somewhere between the slope of the raw-material restriction line and the slope of the assembly-line restriction line, the last contact point with the feasible-solution area as the ruler is moved from the origin toward the northeast direction is Q. If the ruler is made still flatter, say somewhere between the slope of the machine-hour restriction line and the slope of the assembly-line restriction line, the point of initial departure is at the vertex R. If the slope of the ruler is made flatter than the slope of the machine-hour constraint, the point of last contact is at the vertex S.

Finally, as a special case, suppose the slope of the ruler coincides exactly with the slope of one of the resource constraint lines, say the slope of the machine-hour restriction line. Then, as the ruler is moved from lower to higher profits, it loses contact with the feasible-solution region initially at all points on the line segment RS, including R, U, C, S. This means that all points between R and S represent the same maximum profit mixes of x_1 and x_2 for the firm. It follows then that as far as economics is concerned, the firm does not care which one of the many alternative mixes of x_1 and x_2 is selected. Thus, even when such a special case arises, the proposition that the maximum-profit production mix is found among the vertices of the feasible-solution area is still valid, for R and S are two of the vertices themselves, and if either one yields the highest profit, the firm need not worry about whether there are other feasible points representing the same level of profit.

Exercise 4-3   (a) Give an example of the per unit profit contributions of I and II that would yield the maximum-profit production mix at Q, R, and S, respectively.

(b) Give an example of the per unit profit contributions of I and II that would yield the same maximum-profit solution both at Q and R. Are there any other points which yield the same maximum profit?

(c) Compare the pair of per unit profit contributions of the two products which yielded the maximum profit at P with the pair of per unit profit contributions of the two products which yielded the maximum profit at S, and explain why at P only the first product is produced (with no production of the second) while at S only the second product is produced (with none of the first).

4-2 MINIMIZATION PROBLEM

Some of the basic concepts of linear programming have been discussed in reference to an example in which the objective function is *maximized*. In the following example *minimization* instead of maximization of the objective function is called for. The primary purpose of this section is to show that the same concepts apply to both minimization and maximization problems.

EXAMPLE 4-2

A group of patients require a diet that will supply them *at least* 2000 calories and *at least* 600 units of vitamin D per person per day. The dietician recommends that the requirement be met from two foods, I and II. Each unit of I supplies 40 calories and 8 units of vitamin D; each unit of II supplies 20 calories and 12 units of vitamin D. The cost of 1 unit of I is 4 cents and that of 1 unit of II is 5 cents. Find the mix of I and II foods that minimizes the cost while meeting the dietary requirements.

Mathematical formulation Let x_1 and x_2 stand for the numbers of units of foods I and II purchased, respectively. Then, calories supplied from x_1 units of I and x_2 units of II are $40x_1 + 20x_2$. Likewise, the total vitamin D supplied from x_1 units of I and x_2 units of II is $8x_1 + 12x_2$. A minimum daily requirement of calories 2000 means that the total calories supplied must be either equal to or in excess of 2000 calories. Mathematically, the statement is

$$40x_1 + 20x_2 \geq 2000$$

Likewise, the minimum vitamin D requirement is expressed as an inequality statement: $8x_1 + 12x_2 \geq 600$.

In addition to these two restrictions, x_1 and x_2 cannot be negative; that is, $x_1, x_2 \geq 0$. The objective of the decision maker is to minimize the total cost of the foods. Since x_1 units of the first food cost $4x_1$ cents and x_2 units of the second cost $5x_2$ cents, the total cost C is

$$C = 4x_1 + 5x_2$$

To recapitulate: the model of the decision problem is to find (x_1, x_2) which would *minimize*

$$C = 4x_1 + 5x_2$$

subject to

$$40x_1 + 20x_2 \geq 2000$$
$$8x_1 + 12x_2 \geq 600 \qquad x_1, x_2 \geq 0$$

The present linear-programming formulation is different from Example 4-1 in two respects: (1) here the objective function is to be minimized, not maximized, and (2) the inequality sign here is that of greater than instead of less than.

Graphic solution   The shaded area in Exhibit 4-5 represents the combina; tions of x_1 and x_2 that satisfy the nonnegativity restrictions on the vari-

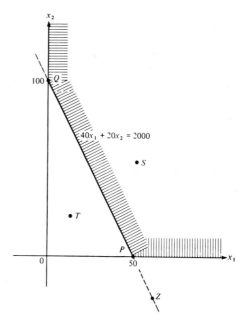

Exhibit 4-5 (x_1, x_2)'s satisfying $40x_1 + 20x_2 \geq 2000$; $x_1, x_2 \geq 0$.

ables and the dietary requirement for calories. Note that the points on the line PQ represent (x_1, x_2)'s that satisfy the *equality* statement,

$$40x_1 + 20x_2 = 2000$$

namely, the combinations of foods that yield exactly 2000 calories. Consequently, the points on the northeast side of the line PQ such as S represent the combinations of x_1 and x_2 that yield more than 2000 calories, that is, (x_1, x_2)'s satisfying the inequality statement, $40x_1 + 20x_2 > 2000$. Note also that a point such as T that lies on the other side (southwest side) of the line PQ yields less than 2000 calories. Point Z satisfies the statement $40x_1 + 20x_2 = 2000$ but violates $x_2 \geq 0$.

Similarly, the points which represent (x_1, x_2)'s satisfying the vitamin D constraint can be defined on a cartesian diagram. The result of superimposing the graphs of the nonnegativity requirements and both dietary requirements is given in Exhibit 4-6. The reader should verify that all points lying on the line UV, such as U, V, W, Y, represent the combinations of two foods which yield *exactly* 600 units of vitamin D, or (x_1, x_2)'s that satisfy $8x_1 + 12x_2 = 600$. The points on the northeast side of the line such as S and X represent (x_1, x_2)'s that satisfy the inequality $8x_1 + 12x_2 > 600$.

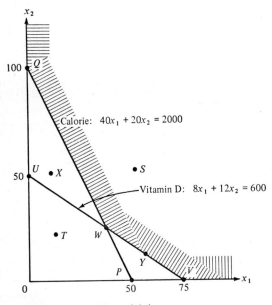

Exhibit 4-6 (x_1, x_2)'s satisfying

$$40x_1 + 20x_2 \geq 2000$$
$$8x_1 + 12x_2 \geq 600$$
$$x_1, x_2 \geq 0$$

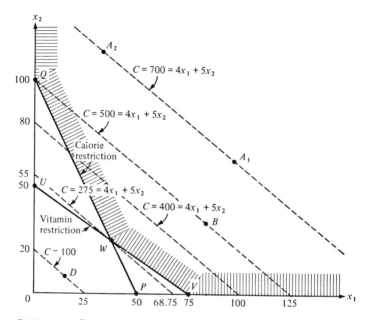

Exhibit 4-7 Constraints and equal-cost lines.

The feasible area common to all constraints is shown in Exhibit 4-6 as the shaded area bounded by the vertical axis (point Q and up), the broken lines QWV, and the horizontal axis (point V and out). Only points within this region represent feasible diets. Which of the (x_1, x_2)'s that lie within the feasible-solution region represent the least-cost diet? In order to answer the question, the equal-cost lines are superimposed on Exhibit 4-6 to obtain Exhibit 4-7.

In reference to Exhibit 4-7, the reader should satisfy himself that points A_1 and A_2 on the $C = 700$ line represent feasible diets (diets that meet the nutritional requirements) but the cost of these diets is 700 cents; that B and Q on the $C = 400$ line represent feasible diets with a cost of 500 cents, lower than 700 cents but still too costly; that as the hospital management moves down in the southwest direction to lower and lower cost lines, it would step out of the feasible region initially at point W, which is on the $C = 275$ line. Thus, W represents an (x_1, x_2) which meets the dietary requirements and yet entails the minimum food cost. Although point D represents a lower-cost diet ($C = 100$), it is nonfeasible.

Again as in the earlier case of a maximization problem, a variation in the cost coefficients of the two foods would alter the slope of the objective function, namely, of the equal-cost lines. When this happens, the equal-cost lines may leave the feasible region initially at an extreme corner point, a vertex of the feasible region other than W, specifically, either at V or W. It is reasonable to expect that the proposition on the existence of an optimum solution given in connection with the earlier maximization example applies to the minimization problem. If there exists a minimum-cost solution to the problem, it will be found among the combinations of x_1 and x_2 values represented by the vertices (extreme corners) of the feasibility region.

Exercise 4-4 (a) For each of Q, V, and W determine the levels of *excess* nutrients supplied.

(b) Give an example of the per unit costs of foods I and II that would yield the minimum-cost diet at Q and V instead of W.

(c) As a special case, Q and W may represent diets of the same cost. Give the per unit costs of foods I and II that would give rise to such a situation.

4-3 WEANING FROM THE GRAPHIC METHOD

As demonstrated above, linear-programming problems involving two types of activities, i.e., two decision variables, can be solved by the use of graphs; but when more than two types of activity are involved, the graphic method becomes too awkward or inoperable. Even for only two variables the graphic method is inefficient and often inaccurate. Ultimately, therefore, a more efficient nongraphic method of solution must be found if the concept of linear programming is to be useful in practical application.

The *simplex method* is one such formal method which is readily programmable for computation by digital computers. The remainder of this chapter presents the mathematical basis for the simplex method for solving linear-programming problems in general.

EVALUATION OF ALL VERTICES OF FEASIBLE REGION

The graphic analysis has made use of the important proposition that an optimal solution, if it exists, is to be found among the vertices of the feasible-solution area. Can these extreme corners be identified without the aid of the graph? The following demonstrates how the (x_1, x_2)'s represented by the vertices of the feasible-solution area, i.e., points P, Q, R, and S of Exhibit 4-2, can be specified without reading them off the graph.

Coordinates of vertex P Point P is where the lines $x_2 = 0$ and $4x_1 + 3x_2 = 36,000$ meet; therefore, its coordinates are (x_1, x_2) satisfying

$$4x_1 + 3x_2 = 36,000$$

and

$$x_2 = 0$$

simultaneously. Substituting the second statement into the first,

$$4x_1 + 3(0) = 36,000$$
$$x_1 = 9000$$

(x_1, x_2) for P is $(9000, 0)$.

Coordinates of vertex Q These are (x_1, x_2) satisfying

$$4x_1 + 3x_2 = 36,000$$

and

$$2x_1 + 2.5x_2 = 20,000$$

simultaneously. Either by the substitution method or the linear-combination method, the coordinates of Q are determined to be $(7500, 2000)$.

Coordinates of vertex R These are (x_1, x_2) satisfying

$$2x_1 + 2.5x_2 = 20,000$$

and

$$4x_1 + 10x_2 = 60,000$$

simultaneously. The coordinates of R are $(x_1, x_2) = (5000, 4000)$.

Coordinates of vertex S These are (x_1, x_2) satisfying

$$4x_1 + 10x_2 = 60,000$$

and

$$x_1 = 0$$

simultaneously. The coordinates of S are $(x_1, x_2) = (0, 6000)$.

Computation of profit For each vertex, the attainment of the objective function is calculated:

P: $\quad 5x_1 + 3x_2 = 5(9000) + 3(0) = \$45,000$
Q: $\quad 5x_1 + 3x_2 = 5(7500) + 3(2000) = \$43,500$
R: $\quad 5x_1 + 3x_2 = 5(5000) + 3(4000) = \$37,000$
S: $\quad 5x_1 + 3x_2 = 5(0) + 3(6000) = \$18,000$

Since P gives the highest profit, the firm would produce 9000 units of I and no units of II.

Likewise, for the diet problem of Example 4-2, the cost of each vertex of the feasible region can be determined without recourse to the graphic method. The reader should satisfy himself which system of

Table 4-1   Cost evaluation of vertices

Vertex	Coordinates	Cost $= 4x_1 + 5x_2$
V	$(x_1, x_2) = (75, 0)$	$4(75) + 5(0) = 300$
W	$(x_1, x_2) = (37\frac{1}{2}, 25)$	$4(37\frac{1}{2}) + 5(25) = 275$
Q	$(x_1, x_2) = (0, 100)$	$4(0) + 5(100) = 500$

equations must be solved to identify the coordinates of each vertex given in Table 4-1. The least-cost solution is represented by vertex W, the same result as that arrived at by the graphic method.

AN ALTERNATIVE WAY OF FINDING VERTICES OF THE FEASIBLE REGION

The alert reader may have noticed that in the above determination of the extreme corners of the feasible region the crutch of graphic visualization has not been discarded completely. In the product-mix case, for instance, *only on the basis of the knowledge from the graph* that P *was* one of the vertices and formed by the intersection of two lines

$$4x_1 + 3x_2 = 36,000$$

and

$$x_2 = 0$$

was it decided that its coordinates were the (x_1, x_2) that satisfied the two particular equations simultaneously. Given the original mathematical constraint statements reproduced below, but no graphs, could the vertices be found mathematically?

$$4x_1 + 3x_2 \leq 36,000$$
$$4x_1 + 10x_2 \leq 60,000 \qquad x_1, x_2 \geq 0$$
$$2x_1 + 2.5x_2 \leq 20,000$$

From the preceding section, it seems reasonable to speculate that the vertices could be identified by first converting the inequality constraints into the corresponding five equality statements as follows and then finding (x_1, x_2)'s that satisfy any two of the five equations at the same time:

$$4x_1 + 3x_2 = 36,000 \qquad\qquad (1)$$
$$4x_1 + 10x_2 = 60,000 \qquad\qquad (2)$$
$$2x_1 + 2.5x_2 = 20,000 \qquad\qquad (3)$$
$$x_1 = 0 \qquad\qquad (4)$$
$$x_2 = 0 \qquad\qquad (5)$$

This procedure was carried out *partially* when the coordinates of P, Q, R, S were determined in the preceding section.   Thus, the (x_1, x_2) which satisfied Eqs. (1) and (5) at the same time was seen to give vertex P; the (x_1, x_2) which satisfied Eqs. (1) and (3), vertex Q; the (x_1, x_2) which satisfied Eqs. (2) and (3), vertex R; and the (x_1, x_2) which satisfied Eqs. (2) and (5), vertex S.   But what about the (x_1, x_2)'s that satisfy Eqs. (1) and (2) simultaneously, Eqs. (1) and (4) simultaneously, Eqs. (2) and (5) simultaneously, and Eqs. (3) and (5) simultaneously?   According to the graph of Exhibit 4-2, these (x_1, x_2)'s are not even feasible solutions.   Obviously, the suggested procedure is not discriminating enough. Although it yields *all* vertices of the feasible region, in addition to them it yields some nonfeasible solutions.   If no graph were available, one could not tell which particular pair of equations would give a vertex of the feasible region and which would not.

In order to identify all the vertices, and the vertices *only* (of the feasible region), an entirely nongraphic procedure must be followed.

Conversion of inequality resource constraints to equivalent equality resource constraints   The conversion of inequalities to equalities as in the above cannot be regarded as an equivalent conversion because finding the values of the variables satisfying one is not the same as finding the values of the variables satisfying the other.   For instance, the raw-material constraint statement of inequality, $4x_1 + 3x_2 \leq 36{,}000$, is not equivalent to the equation $4x_1 + 3x_2 = 36{,}000$.   The (x_1, x_2)'s that satisfy the equation are only those production mixes which use up *exactly* 36,000 lb of the material, while the inequality statement allows the (x_1, x_2)'s that fall short of using up the entire amount of 36,000 lb. In particular, $(x_1, x_2) = (15, 26)$ satisfies the inequality statement but not the equation.

On the other hand, if the original raw-material inequality statement is converted into a new form of equality statement,

$$4x_1 + 3x_2 + x_3 = 36{,}000$$

where the new variable, x_3, is nonnegative, that is, $x_3 \geq 0$, then the conversion is equivalent in the sense that all the combinations of x_1 and x_2 that satisfy one statement (and no other combinations) satisfy the other statement as well, and vice versa.   The reader should check the validity of this assertion by finding some random examples of (x_1, x_2)'s that satisfy the inequality statement and showing that indeed they satisfy the equality statement as well and conversely, by finding examples of (x_1, x_2, x_3)'s that satisfy the equality statement and showing that the values of x_1 and x_2 in these (x_1, x_2, x_3)'s satisfy the original inequality statement.   Note that the two statements are equivalent only if $x_3 \geq 0$.

The conversion of the inequality statement into an equivalent equality statement is *mathematically* necessary because inequalities are more difficult to deal with mathematically. But in the product-mix case, the derived equivalent equation bears a special economic meaning. The original statement, $4x_1 + 3x_2 \leq 36,000$, is a mathematical translation of the (verbal) statement that the raw material used in the production of x_1 units of product I and x_2 units of product II is either equal to or less than the total material available of 36,000 lb. When the raw material used in production is less than the total available 36,000 lb, some units of the material must be left unused. Let this unused portion of the material be represented by x_3. Then x_3 is a variable because when the level of production, that is, x_1 and x_2, is varied, x_3 varies accordingly. Since whatever is unused for production of x_1 and x_2 is x_3, the raw material used plus x_3 always equals 36,000 lb. To translate this into a mathematical statement

Raw material used in production of x_1 and x_2	plus	remaining pounds unused	equals	Total pounds available
$4x_1 + 3x_2$	$+$	x_3	$=$	36,000

If x_1 and x_2 are such that their production uses up exactly the total available 36,000 lb, then $x_3 = 0$ and no raw material remains unused. x_3, therefore, is either some positive number or 0, but never negative. In symbols, $x_3 \geq 0$.

Slack variables   The variables, such as x_3 above, which are used to convert inequality statements into equivalent equality statements are called *slack variables*. Slack variables, the introduction of which into the analysis is mathematically motivated, are often amenable to some useful economic interpretation as above.

Exercise 4-5   Convert the following inequality statements into equivalent equality statements, using in each case the slack variable z such that $z \geq 0$. Demonstrate the equivalence through some examples of the solutions of the statements.

(a) $2x + \frac{1}{3}y \leq 12$ (b) $x_1 + 5x_2 \geq 6$ (c) $x \geq 6$

(d) $y \geq 0$ (e) $w - u \geq -3$ (f) $-y \leq 100$

(g) $-x \leq -2$

Through applying the similar equivalent conversion to the other two resource constraints, the original set of inequality constraints for the production-mix example is converted into the following set of equivalent equations and nonegativity restrictions:

$$4x_1 + 3x_2 + x_3   = 36{,}000$$
$$4x_1 + 10x_2 + x_4 = 60{,}000 \qquad x_1, x_2, x_3, x_4, x_5 \geq 0$$
$$2x_1 + 2.5x_2   + x_5 = 20{,}000$$

The slack variables, x_4 and x_5, can be interpreted as the machine hours and assembly-line hours remaining unused (or idle), respectively, after production of x_1 units and x_2 units of the two products.

Before proceeding, the reader is reminded that the feasible production mixes of x_1 and x_2 can be found either as solutions to the original system of inequalities or, alternatively, as solutions to the equivalent system of equalities and nonnegativity statements. Actually, solving the derived equivalent system is nothing more than explicitly computing the resources remaining unused upon producing a given feasible combination of x_1 and x_2 that satisfies the original system. Thus if

$$(x_1, x_2) = (100, 50)$$

is a feasible solution satisfying the original system of constraints, then in order to satisfy the converted equivalent system of constraints, x_3, x_4, and x_5 must be determined as follows.

Since $4x_1 + 3x_2 + x_3 = 36{,}000$,

$$\begin{aligned} x_3 &= 36{,}000 - 4x_1 - 3x_2 \\ &= 36{,}000 - 4(100) - 3(50) \\ &= 35{,}450 \text{ pounds} \end{aligned}$$

Since $4x_1 + 10x_2 + x_4 = 60{,}000$,

$$\begin{aligned} x_4 &= 60{,}000 - 4x_1 - 10x_2 \\ &= 60{,}000 - 4(100) - 10(50) \\ &= 59{,}100 \text{ machine hours} \end{aligned}$$

Since $2x_1 + 2.5x_2 + x_5 = 20{,}000$,

$$\begin{aligned} x_5 &= 20{,}000 - 2x_1 - 2.5x_2 \\ &= 20{,}000 - 2(100) - 2.5(50) \\ &= 19{,}675 \text{ assembly hours} \end{aligned}$$

In summary, the example of a feasible solution may be presented in two alternative ways:

1. $x_1 = 100$ units and $x_2 = 50$ units; that is, $(x_1, x_2) = (100, 50)$.
2. Or in a more detailed form:

$$x_1 = 100 \qquad x_2 = 50 \qquad x_3 = 35{,}450 \qquad x_4 = 59{,}100$$
$$x_5 = 19{,}675$$

That is,

$$(x_1, x_2, x_3, x_4, x_5) = (100, 50, 35{,}450, 59{,}100, 19{,}675)$$

To give an example of a nonfeasible solution, $(x_1, x_2) = (10{,}000, 0)$ is shown to be nonfeasible in terms of the original system of constraints as follows:

Raw material: $\quad 4x_1 + 3x_2 = 4(10{,}000) + 3(0) = 40{,}000$
$$\not\leq 36{,}000$$

Machine hours: $\quad 4x_1 + 10x_2 = 4(10{,}000) + 10(0) = 40{,}000$
$$\leq 60{,}000$$

Assembly hours: $\quad 2x_1 + 2.5x_2 = 2(10{,}000) + 2.5(0) = 20{,}000$
$$\leq 20{,}000$$

$x_1 = 10{,}000 \geq 0 \qquad x_2 = 0 \geq 0$

The solution violates the constraint of the raw material though satisfying all others. The same solution, $(x_1, x_2) = (10{,}000, 0)$, is again found nonfeasible in terms of the converted equivalent system as follows:

Raw material: $\quad 4x_1 + 3x_2 + x_3 = 36{,}000$
$x_3 = 36{,}000 - 4x_1 - 3x_2$
$\quad = 36{,}000 - 4(10{,}000) - 3(0)$
$\quad = -4000$

Machine hours: $\quad 4x_1 + 10x_2 + x_4 = 60{,}000$
$x_4 = 60{,}000 - 4x_1 - 10x_2$
$\quad = 60{,}000 - 4(10{,}000) - 10(0)$
$\quad = 20{,}000$

Assembly hours: $\quad 2x_1 + 2.5x_2 + x_5 = 20{,}000$
$x_5 = 20{,}000 - 2x_1 - 2.5x_2$
$\quad = 20{,}000 - 2(10{,}000) - 2.5(0)$
$\quad = 0$

$x_1 = 10{,}000 \geq 0 \qquad x_2 = 0 \geq 0 \qquad x_3 = -4000 \not\geq 0$
$x_4 = 20{,}000 \geq 0 \qquad x_5 = 0 \geq 0$

Thus $(x_1, x_2) = (10{,}000, 0)$ or

$$(x_1, x_2, x_3, x_4, x_5) = (10{,}000, 0, -4000, 20{,}000, 0)$$

satisfies the three resource constraint equalities, but $x_3 = -4000$ violates the nonnegativity constraints of the variables; therefore the solution is nonfeasible. (The firm cannot produce 10,000 units of product I because the raw material is in short supply by 4000 lb.)

Returning to the initial reason for converting the original system of constraints (inequalities) into its equivalent system of equations, we obtain the solutions that correspond to the vertices of the feasible-solution region (and only the vertices) as follows.

Basic feasible solutions Find the solutions to the converted equivalent-system of resource and nonnegativity constraints (alternatively, the values of x_1, x_2, x_3, x_4, and x_5 satisfying all the equality statements and nonnegativity conditions simultaneously) in which three variables (out of the total five) are nonzeros and the remaining two variables are zeros.

Such solutions represent the vertices of the feasible solution area, and are called the basic feasible solutions. If there is an optimal solution, it is found among the basic feasible solutions.

According to this fundamental theorem of linear programming, an ordered quintuple $(x_1, x_2, x_3, x_4, x_5) = (100, 50, 35{,}450, 59{,}100, 19{,}675)$, though a feasible solution, is not a basic feasible solution and therefore would not be represented by a vertex of the feasible-solution polygon because all five variables have nonzero values. This particular solution would be represented in the graph of Exhibit 4-2 as a point well inside the boundaries of the feasibility region—clearly not a vertex.

On the other hand, another feasible solution

$x_1 = 0$

$x_2 = 6000$

$x_3 = 36{,}000 - 4x_1 - 3x_2 = 36{,}000 - 4(0) - 3(6000) = 18{,}000$

$x_4 = 60{,}000 - 4x_1 - 10x_2 = 60{,}000 - 4(0) - 10(6000) = 0$

$x_5 = 20{,}000 - 2x_1 - 2.5x_2 = 20{,}000 - 2(0) - 2.5(6000) = 5000$

should be adjudged a basic feasible solution, a vertex solution, because three variables, x_2, x_3, x_5, are nonzeros and the remaining two, x_1, x_4, are zeros. In Exhibit 4-2, this solution is represented by vertex S. Likewise, the reader may verify that each of the other vertices, P, Q, and R of Exhibit 4-2, represents a basic feasible solution. (This can be seen readily from the fact that the vertices are where two resource lines meet, which means that two of the resources are completely used up; i.e., two of the slack variables are zeros, and the remaining three variables are positive nonzeros. For example, point Q is the intersection of the raw-material and assembly-line-hour lines, which means that there remains neither unused raw material nor unused assembly-line capacity, namely, $x_3 = 0$, $x_5 = 0$. Further, since Q is inside the machine-hour line, x_4 is some positive nonzero value; and obviously, x_1 and x_2 are nonzeros.)

In addition, the reader should satisfy himself that all points in the feasible region other than the vertices represent *nonbasic feasible solutions*, the feasible solutions where more than three variables carry nonzero (positive) values, and that a point formed by the intersection of two resource lines other than the vertices of the feasible-solution polygon lies outside the remaining resource line, thus representing a nonfeasible solution, which in turn means that one of the slack variables is a negative number, in violation of the nonnegativity constraint on the variables.[1]

Finally, the origin O in Exhibit 4-2 requires a special comment: $(x_1, x_2) = (0, 0)$, of course, represents a feasible production, trivial as it is. More specifically, the origin represents the following combination of the variables:

$$x_1 = 0$$

$$x_2 = 0$$

$$x_3 = 36{,}000 - 4x_1 - 3x_2 = 36{,}000 - 4(0) - 3(0)$$
$$= 36{,}000$$

$$x_4 = 60{,}000 - 4x_1 - 10x_2 = 60{,}000 - 4(0) - 10(0)$$
$$= 60{,}000$$

$$x_5 = 20{,}000 - 2x_1 - 2.5x_2 = 20{,}000 - 2(0) - 2.5(0)$$
$$= 20{,}000$$

The obvious economic interpretation of the solution is that no production of either product takes place, and consequently all resources remain idle in totality. This solution has three nonzero positive variables, x_3, x_4, x_5, and two zero variables, x_1, x_2, thus indicating a basic feasible solution. Indeed, as seen in Exhibit 4-2, the origin O is geometrically a vertex of the feasible-solution polygon. Although in the discussion so far, the

---

[1] We could define a *basic solution* (distinct from a *basic feasible solution*) as an ordered quintuple $(x_1, x_2, x_3, x_4, x_5)$ which satisfies the three resource equality statements (but not necessarily the nonnegativity conditions for the variables) where three variables are nonzeros (not necessarily positive) and the remaining two are zeros. Then a point formed by two intersecting resource lines other than the vertices of the feasible region, e.g., the point where the raw-material line and the machine-hour line meet, may be called a *basic solution* because two of the slack variables are zeros, for example, $x_3 = 0$, $x_4 = 0$, and the remaining three variables, x_1, x_2, x_5, are nonzeros. This ordered quintuple satisfies the three resource equations but violates the nonnegativity condition, $x_5 \not\geq 0$. This solution, therefore, is *not* a *basic feasible solution*.

vertex solution represented by the origin has been ignored for the good reason that it is such an obviously unprofitable production mix, not much harm is done even if it is included as one of the vertices, basic feasible solutions, among which the maximum-profit solution is to be found. Searching for one best solution among O, P, Q, R, S involves only an insignificant amount of additional computation compared to the task of searching for one best solution among P, Q, R, S (excluding O), and either would yield the same result.

MATHEMATICAL METHOD FOR FINDING BASIC FEASIBLE SOLUTIONS

Now that the reasonableness of the proposition that the maximum-profit solution is to be found only among the basic feasible solutions has been established, we explain a strictly nongraphic method by which the basic feasible solutions for the production-mix example are identified. At this point the reader may wish to review the material discussed in Sec. 2-3, for the method here is simply that of solving a system of linear equations where there are more variables than the number of equations.

Step 1: Originally given Maximize

$$\pi = 5x_1 + 3x_2$$

Subject to

$$4x_1 + 3x_2 \leq 36,000$$
$$4x_1 + 10x_2 \leq 60,000 \qquad x_1, x_2 \geq 0$$
$$2x_1 + 2.5x_2 \leq 20,000$$

Step 2: Conversion to an equivalent formulation Maximize

$$\pi = 5x_1 + 3x_2$$

Subject to

$$4x_1 + 3x_2 + x_3 \qquad\qquad = 36,000$$
$$4x_1 + 10x_2 \qquad + x_4 \qquad = 60,000 \qquad x_1, x_2, x_3, x_4, x_5 \geq 0$$
$$2x_1 + 2.5x_2 \qquad\qquad + x_5 = 20,000$$

Or alternatively, maximize

$$\pi = 5x_1 + 3x_2 + 0x_3 + 0x_4 + 0x_5$$

subject to

$$4x_1 + 3x_2 + 1x_3 + 0x_4 + 0x_5 = 36,000$$
$$4x_1 + 10x_2 + 0x_3 + 1x_4 + 0x_5 = 60,000 \qquad x_1, x_2, x_3, x_4, x_5 \geq 0$$
$$2x_1 + 2.5x_2 + 0x_3 + 0x_4 + 1x_5 = 20,000$$

The two alternative formulations are completely identical because, for any given equation, adding zeros to either side of the equation does not violate the equality. For example, in reference to the objective function, adding $0x_3 + 0x_4 + 0x_5$ does not alter it because $0x_3 + 0x_4 + 0x_5$ is always zero regardless of the values of x_3, x_4, and x_5. (The zero coefficients of x_3, x_4, and x_5 may be interpreted as profit contribution per unit of unused limited resources. Unused resources do not bring in any profit; hence, zero profit coefficients for x_3, x_4, and x_5.)

Step 3: Identification of basic feasible solutions   According to Sec. 2-3, in general there are infinitely many solutions to a system of equations where the number of variables is more than the number of equations. Thus the system of equations (with five variables in three equations)

$$4x_1 + 3x_2 + 1x_3 + 0x_4 + 0x_5 = 36,000 \tag{1}$$

$$4x_1 + 10x_2 + 0x_3 + 1x_4 + 0x_5 = 60,000 \tag{2}$$

$$2x_1 + 2.5x_2 + 0x_3 + 0x_4 + 1x_5 = 20,000 \tag{3}$$

has infinitely many solutions. Of these infinitely many solutions, if the solutions that contain a negative value for at least one variable are discarded, only the feasible solutions remain (represented by the points within the feasible region). Of these feasible solutions, in turn, only those where two of the five variables are zeros and the other three are nonzero values are the *basic* feasible solutions (represented by the extreme corner points of the feasible region). Therefore, if the above system of three equations is solved for any three of the variables after setting the remaining two variables at zero, and if the values of the three nonzero variables in that solution are nonnegative, it will be a basic feasible solution. This process is carried out below to identify all the basic feasible solutions. Observe that there are in all ten different ways in which two out of five variables can be selected to be set at zero:

Case 1: $[x_1, x_2]$ Case 2: $[x_1, x_3]$

Case 3: $[x_1, x_4]$ Case 4: $[x_1, x_5]$

Case 5: $[x_2, x_3]$ Case 6: $[x_2, x_4]$

Case 7: $[x_2, x_5]$ Case 8: $[x_3, x_4]$

Case 9: $[x_3, x_5]$ Case 10: $[x_4, x_5]$

Case 1: The solution where $x_1 = 0$, $x_2 = 0$ *and* x_3, x_4, x_5 *are nonzero*
1.   Equivalent to Eq. (1) to (3) are

$$1x_3 + 0x_4 + 0x_5 = 36,000 - 4x_1 - 3x_2 \tag{1a}$$

$$0x_3 + 1x_4 + 0x_5 = 60,000 - 4x_1 - 10x_2 \tag{2a}$$

$$0x_3 + 0x_4 + 1x_5 = 20,000 - 2x_1 - 2.5x_2 \tag{3a}$$

2. Since $x_1 = 0$ and $x_2 = 0$, substituting these in Eqs. (1a) to (3a) gives

$$1x_3 + 0x_4 + 0x_5 = 36,000$$
$$0x_3 + 1x_4 + 0x_5 = 60,000$$
$$0x_3 + 0x_4 + 1x_5 = 20,000$$

or

$$x_3 = 36,000$$
$$x_4 = 60,000$$
$$x_5 = 20,000$$

3. $x_1 = 0$, $x_2 = 0$, $x_3 = 36,000$, $x_4 = 60,000$, $x_5 = 20,000$ is a basic feasible solution because two variables are zeros and three are positive nonzeros. This solution is represented by point O in Exhibit 4-2.

Case 2: *The solution where $x_1 = 0$, $x_3 = 0$ and x_2, x_4, x_5 are nonzero*
1. Equivalent to Eqs. (1) to (3) are

$$3x_2 + 0x_4 + 0x_5 = 36,000 - 4x_1 - 1x_3 \tag{1b}$$
$$10x_2 + 1x_4 + 0x_5 = 60,000 - 4x_1 - 0x_3 \tag{2b}$$
$$2.5x_2 + 0x_4 + 1x_5 = 20,000 - 2x_1 - 0x_3 \tag{3b}$$

2. Since $x_1 = x_3 = 0$, substituting these in Eqs. (1b) to (3b), gives

$$3x_2 + 0x_4 + 0x_5 = 36,000 \tag{1b}$$
$$10x_2 + 1x_4 + 0x_5 = 60,000 \tag{2b}$$
$$2.5x_2 + 0x_4 + 1x_5 = 20,000 \tag{3b}$$

By the linear combination method of Sec. 2-3, the values of x_2, x_4, x_5 which satisfy Eqs. (1b) to (3b) simultaneously are found as follows. Equation (1b) divided by 3 gives

$$1x_2 + 0x_4 + 0x_5 = 12,000 \tag{1c}$$
$$10x_2 + 1x_4 + 0x_5 = 60,000 \tag{2b}$$
$$2.5x_2 + 0x_4 + 1x_5 = 20,000 \tag{3b}$$

Equation (2b) added to Eq. (1c) times -10 gives Eq. (2c). Equation (3b) added to Eq. (1c) times -2.5 gives Eq. (3c).

$$1x_2 + 0x_4 + 0x_5 = 12,000 \tag{1c}$$
$$0x_2 + 1x_4 + 0x_5 = -60,000 \tag{2c}$$
$$0x_2 + 0x_4 + 1x_5 = -10,000 \tag{3c}$$

or

$$x_2 = 12,000 \qquad x_4 = -60,000 \qquad x_5 = -10,000$$

3. To summarize, the values of the variables that satisfy the system of equations (1), (2), (3) when $x_1 = x_3 = 0$ are found to be

$$(x_1, x_2, x_3, x_4, x_5) = (0, 12{,}000, 0, -60{,}000, -10{,}000)$$

Since x_4 and x_5 are negative, the solution is not a feasible solution. We interpret this to mean that if no unit of product I and 12,000 units of product II are produced, the raw material will be used up ($x_3 = 0$), the machine hours will be in short supply by 60,000 hr ($x_4 = -60{,}000$), and the assembly hours will be in short supply by 10,000 hr ($x_5 = -10{,}000$); consequently, the firm could not produce $x_1 = 0$, $x_2 = 12{,}000$. In Exhibit 4-2, the point where the vertical axis meets the raw-material line represents this combination of x_1 and x_2, and, needless to say, it is outside the feasibility region.

Case 3: The solution where $x_1 = x_4 = 0$ and $x_2, x_3, x_5 \neq 0$

1. Since $x_1 = x_4 = 0$, the original equations (1) to (3) are reduced to

$$3x_2 + 1x_3 + 0x_5 = 36{,}000 \tag{1d}$$

$$10x_2 + 0x_3 + 0x_5 = 60{,}000 \tag{2d}$$

$$2.5x_2 + 0x_3 + 1x_5 = 20{,}000 \tag{3d}$$

2. The reader should perform the necessary linear combinations to verify the resulting solution statements

$$0x_2 + 1x_3 + 0x_5 = 18{,}000 \tag{1e}$$

$$1x_2 + 0x_3 + 0x_5 = 6{,}000 \tag{2e}$$

$$0x_2 + 0x_3 + 1x_5 = 5{,}000 \tag{3e}$$

3. In summary, $(x_1, x_2, x_3, x_4, x_5) = (0, 6000, 18{,}000, 0, 5000)$ is a basic feasible solution and is represented by S in Exhibit 4-2.

Case 4: The solution where $x_1 = x_5 = 0$ and $x_2, x_3, x_4 \neq 0$ It is left for the reader to find the values of x_2, x_3, and x_4 which satisfy the three resource constraint equations simultaneously when $x_1 = x_5 = 0$ and show that the solution is nonfeasible because the firm would not have enough machine hours.

Case 5: The solution where $x_2 = x_3 = 0$ and $x_1, x_4, x_5 \neq 0$ Again, the reader should verify that the solution

$$(x_1, x_2, x_3, x_4, x_5) = (9000, 0, 0, 24{,}000, 2000)$$

is a basic feasible solution and is represented by P in Exhibit 4-2.

Cases 6 to 10: For the rest of the candidates for basic feasible solutions, the reader can apply the same procedure (1) to find the values of the variables that satisfy the three resource constraint equations and (2) to check the nonnegativity requirement to determine whether the solution is basic feasible or not. In addition (3) he should be able to interpret each solution and identify its representation in Exhibit 4-2.

Once all the basic feasible solutions are found, the level of attainment of the objective can be computed for each and the best, or optimal, solution identified. As we have seen, the maximum profit in the product-mix example is given by the basic feasible solution, case 5.

SOLVING THE DIET EXAMPLE WITHOUT GRAPHS

The same procedure employed in the profit-maximization product-mix example is applied below (with some minor modification) to identify and evaluate the basic feasible solutions of the cost-minimization diet-mix problem of Example 4-2.

Step 1: Conversion to an equivalent system

Originally formulated

Find the values of x_1 and x_2 that minimize the (cost) objective function

$$C = 4x_1 + 5x_2$$

subject to the dietary constraints

$$40x_1 + 20x_2 \geq 2000 \text{ calories}$$
$$8x_1 + 12x_2 \geq 600 \text{ vitamin units} \qquad x_1, x_2 \geq 0$$

Equivalent formulation

Find the values of x_1, x_2, x_3, and x_4 that minimize the objective function

$$C = 4x_1 + 5x_2 + 0x_3 + 0x_4$$

subject to the dietary constraints

$$40x_1 + 20x_2 - 1x_3 \qquad = 2000 \qquad (1)$$
$$8x_1 + 12x_2 \qquad - 1x_4 = 600 \qquad x_1, x_2, x_3, x_4 \geq 0 \qquad (2)$$

From Exercise 4-5 we know that when the direction of the inequality is $\geq$ instead of $\leq$, a negative number must be added to (or alternatively, a positive number must be deducted from) the left side of the inequality statement in order to convert it into an equivalent equality statement. Since $x_3 \geq 0$ and $x_4 \geq 0$ are stipulated, $-x_3$ and $-x_4$ are negative or 0.

The economic—more accurately, dietary—interpretation of the slack variables x_3 and x_4 is that x_3 represents calories supplied from x_1 units and x_2 units of foods I and II, respectively, in excess of the daily requirement of 2000 calories and x_4 represents vitamin units supplied in excess of the daily requirement of 600 units. Since the excess does not cost any, the cost coefficients of x_3 and x_4 in the objective function are zeros.

Step 2: Identification of basic feasible solutions In the production-mix example, the basic feasible solutions (vertex solutions) were those solutions where two variables were zeros and three had nonzero positive values. How are the basic feasible solutions of the diet example characterized?

In general, whether the problem is that of maximization or minimization, a *basic feasible solution* is a solution where *the number of nonzero (positive) variables is the same as the number of resource constraint equations.* Since there are now two resource constraint equations, the basic feasible solutions are the solutions where two of the four variables are (positive) nonzeros and the remaining two are zeros. The reader should verify that the vertices of the feasible region in Exhibit 4-6 indeed represent the solutions where two of the four variables x_1, x_2, x_3, and x_4 are nonzero positive. There are six different ways in which two out of four variables can be made zero:

Case 1: $[x_1, x_2]$ Case 2: $[x_1, x_3]$

Case 3: $[x_1, x_4]$ Case 4: $[x_2, x_3]$

Case 5: $[x_2, x_4]$ Case 6: $[x_3, x_4]$

Case 1: The solution where $x_1 = x_2 = 0$ and $x_3 \neq 0$, $x_4 \neq 0$ Since $x_1 = x_2 = 0$, Eqs. (1) and (2) are reduced to

$$-1x_3 \qquad = 2000 \qquad \qquad (1a)$$
$$-1x_4 = 600 \qquad \qquad (2a)$$

By multiplying both sides of each equation by -1, Eqs. (1a) and (2a) are converted into the following system:

$$x_3 \qquad = -2000 \qquad \qquad (1b)$$
$$x_4 = -600 \qquad \qquad (2b)$$

In brief, $x_1 = 0$, $x_2 = 0$, $x_3 = -2000$, $x_4 = -600$, satisfies Eqs. (1) and (2) simultaneously, but because $x_3 \not\geq 0$ and $x_4 \not\geq 0$, the solution is not feasible. To interpret: when no foods are bought, the calories supplied are 2000 calories short of the requirement and the vitamin supplied is 600 units short of the requirement. This solution is represented by the origin O in Exhibit 4-6, way outside the feasible region.

Case 2: The solution where $x_1 = x_3 = 0$ and $x_2 \neq 0$, $x_4 \neq 0$ Since $x_1 = x_3 = 0$,

$$20x_2 \qquad = 2000 \qquad \qquad (1c)$$
$$12x_2 - 1x_4 = 600 \qquad \qquad (2c)$$

To find the values of x_2 and x_4 which satisfy the above equations simultaneously, divide both sides of Eq. (1c) by 20 to obtain Eq. (1d), and deduct Eq. (1d) times 12 from Eq. (2c) to obtain (2d):

$$x_2 \qquad = 100 \qquad\qquad\qquad (1d)$$
$$-1x_4 = -600 \qquad\qquad\qquad (2d)$$

or

$$x_2 \qquad = 100 \qquad\qquad\qquad (1d)$$
$$x_4 = 600 \qquad\qquad\qquad (2d)$$

The solution $(x_1, x_2, x_3, x_4) = (0, 100, 0, 600)$ is a basic feasible solution. Point Q in Exhibit 4-6 represents this solution.

Cases 3 to 6 For the rest of the candidates for basic feasible solutions, only the result is summarized in Table 4-2, omitting the process of computation.

Step 3: Cost evaluation of basic feasible solutions Table 4-2 identifies three basic feasible solutions, cases 2, 5, and 6. When the cost for each is computed, case 6 emerges as the minimum-cost solution as in Table 4-3.

Table 4-2 Summary of cases 1 to 6

Case	Solution to Eqs. (1) and (2)	Basic feasible or not	Point in Exhibit 4-6
1	$x_1 = x_2 = 0$ $x_3 = -2000$ $x_4 = -600$	No	O
2	$x_1 = x_3 = 0$ $x_2 = 100$ $x_4 = 600$	Yes	Q
3	$x_1 = x_4 = 0$ $x_2 = 50$ $x_3 = -1000$	No	U
4	$x_2 = x_3 = 0$ $x_1 = 50$ $x_4 = -200$	No	P
5	$x_2 = x_4 = 0$ $x_1 = 75$ $x_3 = 1000$	Yes	V
6	$x_3 = x_4 = 0$ $x_1 = 37.5$ $x_2 = 25$	Yes	W

Table 4-3   Solution costs

Case	Basic feasible solution	Cost
2	$x_1 = x_3 = 0$ $x_2 = 100$ $x_4 = 600$	$C = 4x_1 + 5x_2 + 0x_3 + 0x_4$ $= 4(0) + 5(100) + 0 + 0$ $= 500$
5	$x_2 = x_4 = 0$ $x_1 = 75$ $x_3 = 1000$	$C = 4x_1 + 5x_2 + 0x_3 + 0x_4$ $= 4(75) + 5(0) + 0 + 0$ $= 300$
6	$x_3 = x_4 = 0$ $x_1 = 37.5$ $x_2 = 25$	$C = 4x_1 + 5x_2 + 0x_3 + 0x_4$ $= 4(37.5) + 5(25) + 0 + 0$ $= 150 + 125 = 275$

4-4   SUMMARY AND TRANSITION TO THE NEXT CHAPTER

Starting with an understanding of the general nature of linear-programming problems, this chapter first showed how some simple linear-programming problems can be solved graphically with two hypothetical decision problems, one in maximization and the other in minimization of a specified objective. But the graphic analysis was meant only to enhance intuitive understanding and serve as a springboard to a nongraphic method of solution. Thus, the second task of the chapter was to see how the material in Chap. 2 could be applied to solve linear-programming problems without recourse to graphic aid.

The nongraphic method explained in this chapter consists of the following steps:

1. Conversion of the inequality resource or dietary constraints into the equivalent equality constraints through introducing slack variables
2. Identification of the basic feasible solutions, corresponding to the vertices or extreme corners of the feasible-solution area, which involves finding the values of the variables that satisfy the system of the equivalent resource or dietary equalities and the nonnegativity condition for the variables simultaneously
3. Evaluation of each basic feasible solution in terms of the objective attained through computation by substitution in the objective function
4. The final selection of an optimal solution, a solution that maximizes or minimizes the objective function

Independent though it is from the drawing of graphs, the nongraphic method described in the chapter nonetheless needs improvement to be of practical use. In the product-mix example, there were ten candidates for basic feasible solutions; in other words, the system of three equations had to be solved ten times to identify all the basic feasible solutions.

When the problem involves more than two decision variables and more than three resource constraints, there are many more candidates for basic feasible solutions than in our illustration; consequently, the burden of computation might be too great even for computers. Fortunately, however, mathematicians have devised a way of solving multivariable and multiconstraint linear-programming problems without identifying and evaluating every basic feasible solution. One such method in wide use is the simplex method, which will be studied in the next chapter.

QUESTIONS AND PROBLEMS

1. Give both the mathematical and the economic structure of the linear- and nonlinear-programming problems.

2. In reference to the examples of the chapter, explain what the assumption of linearity means in the decision context.

3. How (or where) would one obtain the information to determine the coefficients of the objective function and of the constraints for the two examples of the chapter?

4. Assume that a municipal government is facing the problem of allocating its funds for the next period to the following types of activities: education, law enforcement, fire department, sanitation-sewage system, and recreational facilities. Formulate the problem in general mathematical statements. What would be the difficulties in applying the linear-programming model to the decision situation?

5. It was stated in the earlier chapters that the essence of mathematical methods is the "if so, then so" kind of logical reasoning. Where in the material of this chapter is this character of mathematical methods evident?

6. Define a feasible solution, the feasible-solution region, a basic feasible solution, a nonbasic feasible solution, an optimal solution, a slack variable, a vertex or extreme-corner solution.

7. What are the differences in the mathematical structure of the minimization or maximization problems of this chapter and that of Chap. 3?

8. (a) Minimize $-\frac{1}{2}x_1 + x_2$ subject to $x_1 + 2x_2 \leq 4$, $x_2 \geq x_1$, and $x_1, x_2 \geq 0$.
(b) Repeat (a) as a maximization problem.

9. Assume that $100 million has been allocated for modification of weapon system A or weapon system B or both. Modification of each unit of A increases the overall strategic capability by 0.004 and that of B by 0.006. Per unit modification of A requires an expenditure of $1 million and 100 hr of engineer's time; that of B requires $2 million and 100 hr of engineer's time. For the modification program no more than 8000 hr of engineer's time may be allocated. There are 200 units of A and 250 units of B.

(a) How many units of A and B should be modified if the objective is to maximize the strategic capability? Solve the problem graphically and mathematically.

(b) Give difficulties and unreasonable assumptions involved in the analysis of the problem.

10. A dog-food canner wishes to minimize the cost of materials required in producing a package of dog food. The package must contain at least 6 oz of protein fiber, at least 4 oz of fat, and at most 1 oz of ash. Two types of meals, I and II, can be used as raw materials. The cost of 1 unit of I is 10 cents, and it yields 0.6 oz of protein, 0.8 oz of fat, and 0.1 oz of ash. The cost of 1 unit of II is 5 cents, and it yields 1.2 oz

of protein, 0.5 oz of fat, and 0.1 oz of ash. What mix of I and II should be used?
Solve the problem graphically and mathematically.

11. An automobile company is organized into four departments, sheet-metal stamping, engine assembly, passenger-car final assembly, and truck final assembly. The capacity of each department in a given planning period is, of course, limited, and the percent of the capacity required per passenger car and truck is as tabulated. Assuming that the

	Percent of capacity required	
Department	Passenger car	Truck
Metal stamping	0.004	0.00286
Engine assembly	0.003	0.006
Passenger-car assembly	0.00444	0
Truck assembly	0	0.00667

selling price of a passenger car is $300 greater than the direct costs (or out-of-pocket costs) and that the selling price of a truck is $250 more than the direct costs, what combination of passenger cars and trucks should the firm produce?[1]

  (a) Formulate the problem in mathematical statements.

  (b) Convert the resource inequalities into the equivalent equalities and interpret the slack variables.

  (c) Solve the problem graphically. Verify that the vertices of the feasible region are the basic feasible solutions.

12. Potato, corn, cattle, and autumn vegetables can be raised on a farm in different mixes. There are four types of limited resources of the farm, the requirements for these resources per unit of each of the farming activities being as tabulated. Which mix of activities should the farm undertake?[2]

	Resource requirement per unit of activity				Total resource available
Resource	Potato	Corn	Cattle	Autumn vegetable	
Spring land, acres	1	2	2	0	60
Autumn land, acres	0	2	2	2	60
Labor:					
I, hr	6.5	12	0	0	1300
II, hr	0	6	0	80	1200
Profit contribution from unit of activity	$80	$90	$70	$650	

---

[1] From R. Dorfman, P. A. Samuelson, and R. M. Solow, "Linear Programming and Economic Analysis," pp. 133–135, McGraw-Hill, New York, 1958.
[2] Adapted from F. V. Waugh and G. L. Burrows, A Short-cut to Linear Programming, *Econometrica*, January 1955, pp. 18–29.

(a) Formulate the problem in mathematical statements.
(b) Convert the resource inequalities into the equivalent equations.
(c) Give any two of the basic feasible solutions and interpret them.
(d) Give any two of nonbasic feasible solutions and interpret.

13. A company's vice president in charge of finances wants to invest a sum of money so as to maximize its yield. He considers the tabulated possibilities but he is not

	Type					
	A_1	A_2	B_1	B_2	C_1	C_2
Yield, %	3	2.5	3.5	4	5	4.5
Invested amount	x_1	x_2	y_1	y_2	z_1	z_2

quite free in his choice because it is the firm's policy that at least 40 percent of the amount be invested in type A and not more than 35 percent in any single one of the other two types.[1] Repeat parts (a) to (d) of Prob. 12.

[1] From S. Vajda, "Readings in Mathematical Programming," p. 46, Wiley, New York, 1962.

5

Linear Programming: Simplex Method and Interpretation

5-0 INTRODUCTION

As noted in the last chapter, the method of solving a linear-programming problem by evaluating all basic feasible solutions is not efficient enough. The present chapter presents the simplex method of solving linear-programming problems, a method which does not ordinarily require evaluation of all basic feasible solutions.

The simplex method, in addition to giving the optimal solution (the optimal mix of the activities), yields the *shadow prices* of the limited resources,[1] information which is very useful for management planning. The chapter discusses the economic meaning of shadow prices as a way of strengthening our understanding of the simplex method and the nature of linear-programming problems and also as a way of suggesting the feasibility of decentralizing the resource-allocation decision.

5-1 THE SIMPLEX METHOD ILLUSTRATED WITH A MAXIMIZATION PROBLEM

The simplex method is illustrated first with reference to the production-mix decision problem of the last chapter (Example 4-1) and in the next

[1] Shadow prices are often called *imputed costs* or *opportunity costs*.

section with reference to the diet problem (Example 4-2). Although the method is most commonly presented in tabular form in textbooks, here it is presented in such a way that its mathematical basis is more apparent. The reader should note that the simplex method is only a slight modification of the method of Chap. 4.

STEP 1: CONVERSION OF INEQUALITIES TO EQUIVALENT EQUATIONS

The first step is the same as in the method given in Chap. 4. Through introduction of slack variables, the original resource constraints in inequalities are converted into the equivalent equations. Then, the problem in its entirety from Sec. 4-3 is to maximize

$$\pi = 5x_1 + 3x_2 + 0x_3 + 0x_4 + 0x_5$$

subject to

$$4x_1 + 3x_2 + 1x_3 + 0x_4 + 0x_5 = 36,000 \tag{1}$$
$$4x_1 + 10x_2 + 0x_3 + 1x_4 + 0x_5 = 60,000 \tag{2}$$
$$2x_1 + 2.5x_2 + 0x_3 + 0x_4 + 0x_5 = 20,000 \tag{3}$$
$$x_1, x_2, x_3, x_4, x_5 \geq 0$$

STEP 2: IDENTIFICATION AND EVALUATION OF THE FIRST BASIC FEASIBLE SOLUTION

The principal difference between the method of the last chapter and the simplex method is that whereas under the former all the basic feasible solutions are identified first and then their profitability is evaluated and compared, under the simplex method, the basic feasible solutions are identified and evaluated *one at a time*. More specifically, starting from the identification of an easiest-to-find basic feasible solution, it is determined whether another basic feasible solution, i.e., the second, would yield a higher profit than the first. If it would, the first is discarded and the second chosen. Then, again, with respect to the second basic feasible solution, it is determined whether there is yet another basic feasible solution, i.e., the third, which would yield a higher profit. If there is, this solution is preferred over the second, and so on, until the basic feasible solution is reached over which no profit improvement is possible by moving to another solution.

What is the easiest-to-find basic feasible solution in our example which provides the start of the above iterative process? Since there are three resource equations, the basic feasible solutions are those solutions where two variables are zeros and three variables nonzeros. From Eqs. (1) to (3) it is readily seen that the easiest to find is the basic fea-

sible solution where x_3, x_4, x_5 are nonzeros and x_1, x_2 are zeros, because
the coefficients of x_3, x_4, x_5 are already in the form

$$\begin{pmatrix} 1 & 0 & 0 \\ 0 & 1 & 0 \\ 0 & 0 & 1 \end{pmatrix}$$

so that the solution can immediately be read off when the x_1 and x_2 terms
are moved to the right-hand side of the equations and set at 0:

$$1x_3 + 0x_4 + 0x_5 = 36{,}000 - 4x_1 - 3x_2 \tag{1a}$$

$$0x_3 + 1x_4 + 0x_5 = 60{,}000 - 4x_1 - 10x_2 \tag{2a}$$

$$0x_3 + 0x_4 + 1x_5 = 20{,}000 - 2x_1 - 2.5x_2 \tag{3a}$$

Since $x_1 = 0$ and $x_2 = 0$, the solution can be read directly from Eqs.
(1a) to (3a) as $x_3 = 36{,}000$, $x_4 = 60{,}000$, and $x_5 = 20{,}000$.

Profit of the first basic feasible solution   By substituting the values of
the solution, $x_1 = 0$, $x_2 = 0$, $x_3 = 36{,}000$, $x_4 = 60{,}000$, and $x_5 = 20{,}000$,
in the objective function, the profit is calculated:

$$\begin{aligned} \pi &= 5x_1 + 3x_2 + 0x_4 + 0x_4 + 0x_5 \\ &= 5(0) + 3(0) + 0(36{,}000) + 0(60{,}000) + 0(20{,}000) \\ &= \$0 \end{aligned}$$

Although it is obvious without further analysis that the zero profit of
this initial solution would be improved through production of some units
of x_1 and x_2, the following formal reasoning is carried out so that it can
be generally applied to less obvious situations.

Investigation of whether another feasible solution would improve profit
In the first basic feasible solution, two variables x_1 and x_2 are zero.
What happens if some quantity of either x_1 or x_2 is produced?   Suppose that 1 unit of the first product is to be produced, namely, $x_1 = 1$,
with x_2 still held at zero.   Since 1 unit of x_1 requires 4 lb of raw material,
4 hr of machine hours, and 2 hr of assembly hours, the quantities of
resources that remain idle now are

$$x_3 = 36{,}000 - 4 = 35{,}996$$

$$x_4 = 60{,}000 - 4 = 59{,}996$$

and

$$x_5 = 20{,}000 - 2 = 19{,}998$$

More formally, by substituting the values of $x_1 = 1$ and $x_2 = 0$, in Eqs. (1a) to (3a) the same result is obtained:

From (1a):
$$1x_3 + 0x_4 + 0x_5 = 36,000 - 4x_1 - 3x_2$$
$$= 36,000 - 4(1) - 3(0)$$
$$= 35,996$$

From (2a):
$$0x_3 + 1x_4 + 0x_5 = 60,000 - 4x_1 - 10x_2$$
$$= 60,000 - 4(1) - 10(0)$$
$$= 59,996$$

From (3a):
$$0x_3 + 0x_4 + 1x_5 = 20,000 - 2x_1 - 2.5x_2$$
$$= 20,000 - 2(1) - 2.5(0)$$
$$= 19,998$$

Incidentally, the reader should note that this new solution,

$$(x_1, x_2, x_3, x_4, x_5) = (1, 0, 35,996, 59,996, 19,998)$$

is a feasible solution but nonbasic. Also note that reductions in the idle capacities, (4 lb, 4 hr, 2 hr), required for bringing into the solution 1 unit of the first product are given mathematically as the coefficients of the x_1 terms in Eqs. (1a) to (3a). In the language of Chap. 2, the coefficients of the x_1 term in these equations give the rates of trade-off or substitution between x_1 and x_3, between x_1 and x_4, and between x_1 and x_5, respectively.

Effect on profit of introducing $x_1 = 1$ What would be the effect on the firm's profit of increasing the production of the first product from $x_1 = 0$ to $x_1 = 1$ as above? According to the coefficient of the x_1 term in the objective function, 1 unit of x_1 brings a \$5 increase in profit, but, as noted above, a 1-unit increase in x_1 requires reductions or sacrifices in x_3, x_4, and x_5 of 4, 4, and 2, respectively. Do these sacrifices necessitated from the change in the solution mean any reduction in profit? The answer is no because the profit coefficients of x_3, x_4, and x_5 in the objective function are all zero. Thus, the \$5 increase in profit is the net gain of the move from the first basic feasible solution,

$$(x_1, x_2, x_3, x_4, x_5) = (0, 0, 36,000, 60,000, 20,000),$$

to a nonbasic feasible solution,

$$(x_1, x_2, x_3, x_4, x_5) = (1, 0, 35,996, 59,996, 19,998).$$

Similarly, for the second product, suppose that its production is increased from $x_2 = 0$ to $x_2 = 1$ while holding x_1 still at zero. Would this change in the production from the first basic feasible solution benefit the firm in net?

Effect on profit of introducing $x_2 = 1$ According to the coefficient of the x_2 term in the objective function, the immediate benefit of the move would be a \$3 increase in profit.   But the move requires reductions in resources remaining idle, x_3, x_4, and x_5, of 3 lb, 10 hr, and 2.5 hr, according to the coefficients of the x_2 terms in Eqs. (1a) to (3a).   Do these reductions in the variables x_3, x_4, and x_5 mean any decrease in profit?   No, because their profit coefficients are zeros.   Thus, the net benefit of moving from the first basic feasible solution,

$$(x_1, x_2, x_3, x_4, x_5) = (0, 0, 36{,}000, 60{,}000, 20{,}000),$$

to a nonbasic feasible solution,

$$(x_1, x_2, x_3, x_4, x_5) = (0, 1, 35{,}997, 59{,}990, 19{,}997.5),$$

is a \$3 increase in profit.

STEP 3: IDENTIFICATION AND EVALUATION OF THE SECOND BASIC FEASIBLE SOLUTION

Now that it is established that the profit could be increased by introducing the production of either x_1 or x_2 into the first basic feasible solution (where there was no production of either), i.e., by changing the value of x_1 or x_2 from zero to a nonzero (positive) value, what would the firm do? First of all, the firm would note that if an increase in x_1 from 0 to 1 unit brings a net profit increase of \$5, the profit increase would be doubled if x_1 were increased to 2 units; consequently, it would wish to increase x_1 as much as it could within the resource constraints.   Likewise, if one unit of x_2 brings a \$3 increase in profit, the firm's profit would be maximized by increasing production of x_2 to maximum.   In order to maximize its profit, then, should the firm increase the production of the first product, x_1, or the second, x_2, or both in some combination?   Although the net profit increase per unit increase in x_1 (\$5) is higher than that for x_2 (\$3), there is no guarantee that the total profit would be higher if x_1 were increased to maximum rather than increasing x_2 to maximum because 1 unit of x_1 might require a lot more of the critical resources than 1 unit of x_2.   But the simplex method usually follows the arbitrary rule that the production of the product which yields the highest per unit benefit is to be increased to maximum.   In accordance with the rule, therefore, it is assumed that the firm would decide to increase the production of the first product to maximum (while still holding x_2 at $x_2 = 0$) in its effort to increase profit over the first basic feasible solution.

Maximum x_1 that could be produced   Although more of x_1 means higher attainment of the objective function, x_1 cannot be increased indefinitely because of the resource limitations. Specifically, as far as the raw-material constraint is concerned, the maximum of x_1 that could be produced is

$$\frac{36,000 \text{ lb}}{4 \text{ lb/unit}} = 9000 \text{ units}$$

As far as the machine-hour constraint is concerned, the maximum of x_1 that could be produced is

$$\frac{60,000 \text{ hr}}{4 \text{ hr/unit}} = 15,000 \text{ units}$$

As far as the assembly-line-hour constraint is concerned, the maximum of x_1 that could be produced is

$$\frac{20,000 \text{ hr}}{2 \text{ hr/unit}} = 10,000 \text{ units}$$

This means that as the firm wishes to increase x_1, it cannot go beyond 9000 units because the firm would run out of its raw-material stock at that volume of production. In notation, $x_3 = 0$. Of course, $x_1 = 9000$ would not exhaust the other two constraints as verified formally below.

Machine hours remaining idle after $x_1 = 9000$ is produced:

Total available hours minus hours used in production

60,000 hr   —   4 hr × 9000

equals hours remaining idle

=   24,000 hr

Assembly hours remaining idle after $x = 9000$ is produced:

Total available hours minus hours used in production

20,000 hr   —   2 hr × 9000

equals hours remaining idle

=   2000 hr

In summary, the result of the decision to produce the first product to maximum is

$x_1 = 9000$ units

$x_2 = 0$ units

$x_3 = 0$ lb

$x_4 = 24,000$ hr

$x_5 = 2000$ hr

Obviously, this is a basic feasible solution—two zero variables and three nonzero positive variables—and constitutes the second basic feasible solution in the iterative process of the simplex method. In other words, to this second basic feasible solution now would be applied the same evaluative criteria as applied to the first in order to determine whether yet another basic feasible solution, i.e., the third, would further improve the firm's profit. Before embarking on the evaluation of the second basic feasible solution, the strictly mathematical method by which the second basic feasible solution could have been obtained is presented.

Mathematical method for identifying the second basic feasible solution
Although the second basic solution has been derived through "economic reasoning," mathematically what is involved is simply solving Eqs. (1) to (3) for the new set of nonzero variables, x_1, x_4, x_5, setting the other two variables, x_2 and x_3, at zero. The solution steps are reproduced below as a review of the linear-combination method of solving a system of equations given in Chap. 2. Recall that the basic idea of the method is to derive the equivalent equations that show the coefficients of the new set of nonzero variables, x_1, x_4, x_5 in the form

$$\begin{pmatrix} 1 & 0 & 0 \\ 0 & 1 & 0 \\ 0 & 0 & 1 \end{pmatrix}$$

so that the values of x_1, x_4, and x_5 can be read off directly. Given

$$4x_1 + 3x_2 + 1x_3 + 0x_4 + 0x_5 = 36{,}000 \tag{1}$$
$$4x_1 + 10x_2 + 0x_3 + 1x_4 + 0x_5 = 60{,}000 \tag{2}$$
$$2x_1 + 2.5x_2 + 0x_3 + 0x_4 + 1x_5 = 20{,}000 \tag{3}$$

Transfer the new zero variables, x_2 and x_3, to the right-hand side:

$$4x_1 + 0x_4 + 0x_5 = 36{,}000 - 3x_2 - 1x_3 \tag{1b}$$
$$4x_1 + 1x_4 + 0x_5 = 60{,}000 - 10x_2 - 0x_3 \tag{2b}$$
$$2x_1 + 0x_4 + 1x_5 = 20{,}000 - 2.5x_2 - 0x_3 \tag{3b}$$

Obtain Eq. (1c) from Eq. (1b) divided by 4:

$$1x_1 + 0x_4 + 0x_5 = 9000 - \tfrac{3}{4}x_2 - \tfrac{1}{4}x_3 \tag{1c}$$
$$4x_1 + 1x_4 + 0x_5 = 60{,}000 - 10x_2 - 0x_3 \tag{2b}$$
$$2x_1 + 0x_4 + 1x_5 = 20{,}000 - 2.5x_2 - 0x_3 \tag{3b}$$

Obtain Eq. (2c) as the difference between Eq. (2b) and 4 times Eq. (1c) and obtain Eq. (3c) as the difference between Eq. (3b) and 2 times Eq. (1c):

$$1x_1 + 0x_4 + 0x_5 = 9000 - \tfrac{3}{4}x_2 - \tfrac{1}{4}x_3 \tag{1c}$$

$$0x_1 + 1x_4 + 0x_5 = 24,000 - 7x_2 + 1x_3 \tag{2c}$$

$$0x_1 + 0x_4 + 1x_5 = 2000 - 1x_2 + \tfrac{1}{2}x_3 \tag{3c}$$

Now, since $x_2 = 0$ and $x_3 = 0$, the x_2, x_3 terms on the right-hand side of each equation are zero, and x_1, x_4, and x_5 are read off from Eqs. (1c) to (3c) as

$$x_1 = 9000$$

$$x_4 = 24,000$$

$$x_3 = 2000$$

In summary, the second basic feasible solution is identified as

$$(x_1, x_2, x_3, x_4, x_5) = (9000, 0, 0, 24,000, 2000).$$

Profit of the second basic feasible solution   By substituting the values of the solution in the objective function, the profit is calculated:

$$\pi = 5x_1 + 3x_2 + 0x_3 + 0x_4 + 0x_5$$
$$= 5(9000) + 3(0) + 0(0) + 0(24,000) + 0(2000)$$
$$= \$45,000$$

Investigation of whether another feasible solution would improve profit
As was done with the first basic feasible solution, the second solution is now evaluated to see whether the firm could improve its profit of $45,000 by bringing into production some units of the variables which are currently zero.   If changing either x_2 or x_3 from the current zero level to some positive level would increase the value of the objective function, then the firm would increase its production as much as possible.   Suppose first that x_2 is increased from zero to $x_2 = 1$ while holding x_3 still at zero.   We know that 1 unit of the second product requires 3 lb of raw material, 10 hr of machine time, and 2.5 hr of assembly-line time.   Where could the firm get them?   As far as the machine and assembly-line times are concerned, the current solution has left plenty of them idle ($x_4 = 24,000$ hr and $x_5 = 2000$ hr), but $x_3 = 0$ in the solution means that there is no unused raw material available.   In order to produce 1 unit of the second product, then, the necessary raw material must be obtained from sacrificing production of the first product; in other words, $x_1 = 9000$ must be reduced to release the raw material.   How many units of x_1 would release the

amount of the raw material required to produce 1 unit of x_2? Inasmuch
as 1 unit of x_1 calls for 4 lb and 1 unit of x_2 calls for 3 lb of the raw
material, the required reduction in x_1 is only $\frac{3}{4}$ unit. With the production
of $x_2 = 1$, all the x_1 that could be produced is now $x_1 = 9000 - \frac{3}{4} = 8999\frac{1}{4}$
units. Mathematically, this trade-off between x_1 and x_2 of $\frac{3}{4}$ unit to 1
unit, of course, appears as the coefficient of the x_2 term in Eq. (1c).
Likewise, the reductions in x_4 and x_5 required for adding 1 unit of x_2 to the
production are given as the coefficients of the x_2 term in Eq. (2c) and
(3c), or -7 and -1.[1]

In summary, the introduction of 1 unit of x_2 into the second basic
feasible solution requires the sacrifices or reductions in the nonzero
variables, x_1, x_4, and x_5 of $\frac{3}{4}$ unit, 7 units, and 1 unit, respectively, and
these trade-off rates are given as the coefficients of the x_2 term in the new
set of equations (1c) to (3c).

Effect on profit of introducing $x_2 = 1$ According to the objective
function, 1 unit of x_2 brings a \$3 increase in the firm's profit. But intro-
duction of 1 unit of x_2, as noted above, requires reductions in x_1, x_4, and
x_5 of $\frac{3}{4}$, 7, and 1. Since the profit coefficients of these variables in the
objective function are \$5, \$0, \$0 (per unit), respectively, the reductions
in the firm's profit from the reductions in these are computed as below:

For x_1: $\$5(\frac{3}{4}) = \$3.75$
For x_4: $0(7) = 0$
For x_5: $0(1) = 0$
                 _____
                      $\$3.75$

The increase of \$3 and the decrease of \$3.75 would mean a net decrease
in profit of \$0.75 (or \$3 $-$ \$3.75 $=$ $-$\$0.75) as the net effect on the
firm's profit of changing the level of x_2 production from the current
$x_2 = 0$ to $x_2 = 1$. If 1 unit of x_2 brings a loss of \$0.75, 2 units would
bring twice as much loss, and so on; consequently, the firm would not
change the second basic feasible solution in the direction of producing
any units of the second product.

Turning next to the other zero variable in the second basic feasible
solution, x_3, Eqs. (1c) to (3c) show that the increase in the level of x_3

[1] As given in the original verbal description of the problem and also in Eqs. (2a) and
(3a) as the coefficients of the x_2 term, 1 unit of x_2 is to require 10 machine hours and
2.5 assembly-line hours. In Eqs. (2c) and (3c), however, the coefficients of the x_2
term which represent the trade-offs between x_2 and x_4 and between x_2 and x_5 are 7
(machine hours) and 1 (assembly-line hour), respectively. This is as it should be
because 1 unit of x_2 requires only 7 *additional* machine hours and 1 *additional* assembly-
line hour *after* the 3 machine hours and 1.5 assembly-line hours that are released by the
reduction of $\frac{3}{4}$ unit of x_1 have been taken into account.

from the current $x_3 = 0$ to $x_3 = 1$ (while holding x_2 still at $x_2 = 0$) would require the reduction in x_1 of $\frac{1}{4}$ unit [because the coefficient of the x_3 term in Eq. (1c) is $-\frac{1}{4}$], the increase in x_4 of 1 unit [because the coefficient of the x_3 term in Eq. (2c) is $+1$], and the increase in x_5 of $\frac{1}{2}$ unit [because the coefficient of the x_3 term in Eq. (3c) is $+\frac{1}{2}$], as verified formally in the following computation:

$$\text{Eq. (1c):} \quad 1x_1 + 0x_4 + 0x_5 = 9000 - 4x_2 - 4x_3$$
$$= 9000 - \tfrac{3}{4}(0) - \tfrac{1}{4}(1)$$
$$= 9000 - \tfrac{1}{4} = 8999.75$$

$$\text{Eq. (2c):} \quad 0x_1 + 1x_4 + 0x_5 = 24{,}000 - 7x_2 + 1x_3$$
$$= 24{,}000 - 7(0) + 1(1)$$
$$= 24{,}000 + 1 = 24{,}001$$

$$\text{Eq. (3c):} \quad 0x_1 + 0x_4 + 1x_5 = 2000 - 1x_2 + \tfrac{1}{2}x_3$$
$$= 2000 - 1(0) + \tfrac{1}{2}(1)$$
$$= 2000 + \tfrac{1}{2} = 2000.5$$

In summary, the nonbasic but feasible solution resulting from the increase in $x_3 = 0$ to $x_3 = 1$ is

$$(x_1, x_2, x_3, x_4, x_5) = (8999.75, 0, 1, 24{,}001, 2000.5)$$

The economic interpretation of the above is that $x_3 = 0$ in the second basic feasible solution means that no idle raw material is available because production of $x_1 = 9000$ uses it all up. Thus, $x_3 = 1$, or to have 1 lb of raw material *idle*, necessitates a reduction of x_1. Since 1 unit of x_1 requires 4 lb of raw material, a reduction of only $\frac{1}{4}$ unit of x_1 is sufficient to obtain 1 lb of idle raw material. This reduction of $\frac{1}{4}$ unit of x_1 releases, in addition to 1 lb of raw material, 1 machine hour and $\frac{1}{2}$ assembly-line hour, which increase the current levels of these resources held idle.

Effect on profit of introducing $x_3 = 1$ Since the profit coefficient of x_3 in the objective function is $0, introduction of $x_3 = 1$ does not increase the firm's profit; however, it necessitates the reduction of x_1 by $\frac{1}{4}$ unit, which in turn reduces the profit of the firm by $1.25 ($5 per unit times $\frac{1}{4}$ unit $= $1.25). The accompanying increase in the idle machine hours x_4 of 1 and in the idle assembly-line hours x_5 of $\frac{1}{2}$ does not entail any change in profit because the coefficients of x_4 and x_5 in the objective function are zero. The net effect, therefore, of increasing x_3 from 0 to 1 would be a loss in profit of $1.25; it does not pay for the firm to increase x_3.

The above investigation demonstrates that bringing into the solution some positive units of either of the two zero variables of the solution, x_2 and x_3, would reduce the profit of the firm. In other words, there is no way the firm could improve its profit by changing the second basic feasible solution;[1] the second basic feasible solution is found to be the optimum solution.

Recapitulation of the simplex method   This exposition of the simplex method for solving linear-programming problems may seem complex; but the essential ideas are not difficult to comprehend (particularly for those who understand the material in Chap. 2 on the solving of systems of equations), and they may be summarized as follows.

1. When the resource constraint inequalities are converted into their equivalent equalities, there emerges a system of equations where the number of variables is more than the number of equations. From Chap. 2 we know that there are many combinations of values of the variables that satisfy such a system of equations, or simply many (feasible) solutions to such system.

2. It can be proved mathematically that of all these many combinations of the variables satisfying the system, the optimal solution—the solution yielding the highest attainment of the objective—will be found only among the basic feasible solutions, namely, the combinations of the variables where the number of nonzero variables is the same as the number of equations. Therefore in our quest for the optimal solution, we need investigate only the basic feasible solutions.

3. The simplex method systematically evaluates the profitability or, more generally, the level of attainment of the objective function, of the basic feasible solutions, one at a time, until it is proved that no improvement in the attainment of the objective is possible from moving to a next basic feasible solution.

4. To begin this iterative evaluative process, any one of the basic feasible solutions may be chosen arbitrarily as the starter, i.e., as the first basic feasible solution, the profitability of which is to be evaluated in order to determine whether or not the move to a second basic feasible solution would pay. Most commonly, the easiest-to-find basic feasible solution is selected as the initial solution. Easiest to find is the one where the variables with zero coefficients in all equations but one and the coefficient of 1 in that last equation constitute the nonzero variables of

---

[1] Although we have examined only the effect of changing the zero variables, x_2 and x_3, to come to this conclusion, it is obvious that changing the nonzero variables, x_1, x_4, and x_5, also would reduce the firm's profit. Any change in one or more of these variables—within the given constraint equations—would mean a reduction of x_1, and when x_1 is reduced, x_2 is inevitably increased. The resulting solution would have more than three nonzero variables, i.e., a nonbasic solution. We have already seen that in order to find an optimum solution we need not worry about nonbasic solutions.

the basic solution. In the above illustration the slack variables provided such nonzero variables.[1]

5. Once the first basic feasible solution is specified, a second basic feasible solution is formed by making one of the nonzero variables of the first solution into a zero variable, which automatically means changing one of the zero variables to a nonzero variable. Which of the nonzero variables will replace which of the zero variables in forming the second basic feasible solution is determined by investigating which zero variable brings the maximum net increase in profit when 1 unit of it is introduced.

6. What is done in step 5 with respect to the first basic feasible solution is repeated with the second, third, . . . , basic feasible solution until no switching of zero with nonzero variables would improve the attainment of the objective.

Exercise 5-1 This exercise is strictly mathematical (i.e., no economic interpretation of the variables is given) to help the reader distinguish between the mathematical and economic aspects of the linear-programming problem and the simplex method of solution.

Maximize

$$z = 4x_1 + 5x_2$$

subject to

$$x_1 + 4x_2 \leq 10 \qquad x_1, x_2 \geq 0$$
$$5x_1 + 3x_2 \leq 16$$

(a) Convert the inequality constraints (except the nonnegativity conditions of the variables) into an equivalent system of equations by introducing two slack variables, x_3 and x_4, which are nonnegative.

(b) Show through examples that there are many feasible solutions to the derived system of equations and the nonnegativity constraints on the variables.

(c) In reference to the derived system of equations only, ignoring the nonnegativity constraints for the variables:

1. Set x_1 and x_2 at $x_1 = 3.2$ and $x_2 = 0$, and solve for x_3 and x_4.
2. Set x_1 and x_2 at $x_1 = 0$ and $x_2 = 5\frac{1}{3}$, and solve for x_3 and x_4.
3. Set x_1 and x_2 at $x_1 = 1\frac{1}{2}$ and $x_2 = 1$, and solve for x_3 and x_4.
4. Set x_1 and x_2 at $x_1 = 0$ and $x_2 = 0$, and solve for x_3 and x_4.
5. Set x_1 and x_3 at $x_1 = 0$ and $x_3 = 0$, and solve for x_2 and x_4.
6. Set x_3 and x_4 at $x_3 = 0$ and $x_4 = 0$, and solve for x_1 and x_2.
7. Set x_3 and x_4 at $x_3 = 2$ and $x_4 = 3$, and solve for x_1 and x_2.

---

[1] Upon conversion of inequalities into equalities, the variables may not show the zero and one coefficients as required to yield the easy-to-find, initial solution. In such cases, the given system of equations would be converted into an equivalent system of equations by introducing some new artificial variables with such coefficients as required. An example of the problem where the introduction of artificial variables is necessary to stipulate the first solution is given later, in the illustration of a cost-miminization problem.

(d) Which of the combinations of x_1, x_2, x_3, x_4 in part (c) satisfy both the original system of inequalities and the nonnegativity constraints of the variables simultaneously?

(e) Which of the combinations of x_1, x_2, x_3, x_4 in part (c) represent basic feasible solutions?

(f) Solve the linear-programming problem by the simplex method.

5-2   THE SIMPLEX METHOD ILLUSTRATED WITH A MINIMIZATION PROBLEM

Solving a cost-minimization problem by the simplex method involves basically the same economic and mathematical reasoning as in the profit-maximization problem illustrated in the preceding section, with some obvious adjustments. As the reader studies the application of the simplex method to the diet problem given in Example 4-2, he should try to identify its similarity to the preceding section, and note (1) the obvious reverse in reasoning when the objective is the minimization of costs rather than the maximization of profit and (2) the introduction of artificial variables in setting up the first basic feasible solution when it is not that easy to find.

Statement of the problem   In Example 4-2, the problem was to find the mix of food I and food II purchased, x_1 and x_2, that would minimize the cost function, $C = 4x_1 + 5x_2$. To restate the problem, minimize

$$C = 4x_1 + 5x_2$$

subject to:

Minimum calorie requirement:	$40x_1 + 20x_2 \geq 2000$	$x_1, x_2 \geq 0$
Minimum vitamin requirement:	$8x_1 + 12x_2 \geq 600$	

STEP 1: CONVERSION OF INEQUALITY CONSTRAINTS TO EQUIVALENT EQUATIONS BY USING SLACK VARIABLES

The first step is exactly the same as in the earlier maximization case except that here the coefficients of the slack variables introduced are -1 instead of $+1$. Thus the first nutritional constraint becomes

$$40x_1 + 20x_2 - x_3 = 2000$$

The coefficient of x_3 must be negative because the direction of the inequality in the current example is $>$ whereas in our earlier example it was $<$ and because we wish to impose the nonnegativity condition on the slack variable, x_3, that is, $x_3 \geq 0$. The slack variable x_3 is interpreted as the number of calories supplied *in excess of* the daily requirement, 2000 calories. An excess is either zero or "something" (positive); hence the nonnegativity restriction, $x_3 \geq 0$.

Likewise, the second nutritional requirement is converted into $8x_1 + 12x_2 - x_4 = 600$, where the slack variable x_4 is interpreted as the number of vitamin units supplied from x_1 and x_2 of food I and food II in excess of the daily requirement of 600 units, and $x_4 \geq 0$.

Since having an excess of calories or vitamin units does not cost any additional money, the cost coefficient (cost per unit) of x_3 and x_4 is $0. The objective function, therefore, is written equivalently as

$$C = 4x_1 + 5x_2 + 0x_3 + 0x_4$$

To recapitulate, solving the original formulation is the same as solving the following equivalent formulation. Minimize

$$C = 4x_1 + 5x_2 + 0x_3 + 0x_4$$

subject to

$$40x_1 + 20x_2 - 1x_3 + 0x_4 = 2000 \tag{1}$$
$$8x_1 + 12x_2 + 0x_3 - 1x_4 = 600 \tag{2}$$
$$x_1, x_2, x_3, x_4 \geq 0$$

STEP 2: IDENTIFICATION AND EVALUATION OF THE FIRST BASIC FEASIBLE SOLUTION

As defined earlier, a basic feasible solution here is a solution where two of the four variables are nonzeros (because the number of constraint equations is two) and the remaining two are zeros. In trying to specify the first basic feasible solution to evaluate, one discovers that no basic feasible solutions can be easily read off from Eqs. (1) and (2). It looks at first glance as though a basic feasible solution might be obtained by setting x_1 and x_2 at zero and solving for the two remaining variables, x_3 and x_4, but the coefficients of these variables are not in the form $\begin{pmatrix} 1 & 0 \\ 0 & 1 \end{pmatrix}$, but in the form $\begin{pmatrix} -1 & 0 \\ 0 & -1 \end{pmatrix}$, and consequently their values when the other two variables are set to zero are $-x_3 = 2000$ and $-x_4 = 600$, or $x_3 = -2000$ and $x_4 = -600$. This is in violation of the nonnegativity conditions of x_3 and x_4. In summary, the ordered 4-tuple

$$(x_1, x_2, x_3, x_4) = (0, 0, -2000, -600)$$

is not even a feasible solution.

Introduction of artificial variables In order to come up with the two variables with the coefficients in the form of

$$\begin{pmatrix} 1 & 0 \\ 0 & 1 \end{pmatrix}$$

two new artificial variables, x_5 and x_6, are introduced to convert the above formulation of the problem to another equivalent formulation. Minimize

$$C = 4x_1 + 5x_2 + 0x_3 + 0x_4 + Mx_5 + Mx_6$$

subject to

$$40x_1 + 20x_2 - 1x_3 + 0x_4 + 1x_5 + 0x_6 = 2000 \qquad (1a)$$

$$8x_1 + 12x_2 + 0x_3 - 1x_4 + 0x_5 + 1x_6 = 600 \qquad (2a)$$

$$x_1,\ x_2,\ x_3,\ x_4,\ x_5,\ x_6 \geq 0$$

Now, Eqs. ($1a$) and (1) are *not equivalent*, as the reader may check through examples, because the combinations of the values of the variables that satisfy the former do not necessarily satisfy the latter, and vice versa, but they will be *equivalent* if and only if x_5 is zero. On the other hand, however, $x_5 = 0$ in the final solution is assured if its cost coefficient in the objective function M is made a "very high number," say 10,000 cents per unit. Since even 1 unit of x_5 is so extremely costly, in the routine application of the simplex method, x_5 would be driven out of the solution, so to speak; i.e., the optimal solution would be a (basic feasible) solution where $x_5 = 0$.

Likewise, Eq. (2) is converted into Eq. ($2a$) through introduction of another artificial variable, x_6, but with the stipulation of a "very high" cost coefficient in the objective function. This high cost coefficient would ensure that in the final optimal solution, x_6 would be zero.

The conclusion is that the same minimum-cost solution of the problem as formulated originally or equivalently with the slack variables x_3 and x_4 would be obtained by solving the new formulation with the artificial variables x_5 and x_6, which are considered to carry an extremely high cost.

Economic interpretation of x_5 and x_6 Imagine two artificial foods, A and B. Suppose that 1 unit of A yields 1 calorie and 0 unit of vitamin, 1 unit of B yields 0 calorie and 1 unit of vitamin, 1 unit of A costs M cents, and 1 unit of B also costs M cents; then x_5 and x_6 can be interpreted respectively as the numbers of units of A and B purchased. Because of its high cost, neither would be purchased in the final solution.

Equations ($1a$) and ($2a$) give two variables, x_5 and x_6, with the coefficients in the form of $\begin{pmatrix} 1 & 0 \\ 0 & 1 \end{pmatrix}$. If the four variables, x_1, x_2, x_3, x_4, are set at zero and Eqs. ($1a$) and ($2a$) are solved for x_5 and x_6, the first basic feasible solution emerges. Formally, by transferring the terms containing the zero variables, x_1, x_2, x_3, x_4, to the right-hand sides of the equations, the following equivalent equations are obtained.

$$1x_5 + 0x_6 = 2000 - 40x_1 - 20x_2 + 1x_3 + 0x_4 \tag{1b}$$
$$0x_5 + 1x_6 = 600 - 8x_1 - 12x_2 + 0x_3 + 1x_4 \tag{2b}$$

When $x_1 = x_2 = x_3 = x_4 = 0$, from Eqs. (1b) and (2b), the values of x_5 and x_6 are obtained as

$$1x_5 + 0x_6 = 2000 - 40(0) - 20(0) + 1(0) + 0(0)$$
or
$$x_5 = 2000$$
and
$$0x_5 + 1x_6 = 600 - 8(0) - 12(0) + 0(0) + 1(0)$$
or
$$x_6 = 600$$

In summary, the first basic feasible solution is identified as

$$(x_1, x_2, x_3, x_4, x_5, x_6) = (0, 0, 0, 0, 2000, 600)$$

The economic interpretation of the solution is that the dietary requirements are met solely from the imaginary foods, A and B.

Cost of the first basic feasible solution   By substituting the values of the solution in the objective function, the cost is calculated:

$$C = 4x_1 + 5x_2 + 0x_3 + 0x_4 + Mx_5 + Mx_6$$
$$= 4(0) + 5(0) + 0(0) + 0(0) + M(2000) + M(600)$$
$$= 2000M + 600M = 2600M$$

The cost of $2600M$ is obviously intolerably high; it pays, therefore, to bring in a new nonzero variable, any one of x_1, x_2, x_3, and x_4, in the second solution.

Investigation of whether another solution would decrease cost   Parallel to the earlier maximization case, the next step is to determine how much net cost decrease there would be if 1 unit of a variable which is currently at zero level were introduced.

Effect on cost of introducing $x_1 = 1$ What would be the effect on cost of increasing the purchase of the first food from $x_1 = 0$ to $x_1 = 1$ while holding x_2, x_3, and x_4 at zero level?

One unit of x_1 purchased would increase the cost by 4 cents, according to its cost coefficient in the objective function. But according to the coefficients of the x_1 term in Eqs. (1b) and (2b), a 1-unit increase of x_1 necessitates reductions in x_5 and x_6 of 40 and 8, respectively. These reductions in x_5 and x_6, namely, reductions in the purchase of the imaginary foods, would bring about a decrease in cost of $40M + 8M = 48M$. The *net* decrease in cost from increasing the purchase of x_1 from $x_1 = 0$ to $x_1 = 1$ is therefore $48M - 4$ cents.

Effect on cost of introducing $x_2 = 1$ Introducing 1 unit of x_2 would increase the cost by 5 cents, but according to the coefficients of the x_2 term in Eqs. (1b) and (2b), it would require reductions in x_5 and x_6 of 20 and 12, respectively, which means the cost saved of $20M + 12M = 32M$ cents. Thus, the *net* decrease in cost from changing the level of purchase of the second food from $x_2 = 0$ to $x_2 = 1$ is $32M - 5$ cents.

Effect on cost of introducing $x_3 = 1$ Introducing 1 unit of x_3 would increase the cost by 0 cents, according to the cost coefficient of the variable. Since the coefficients of the x_3 term in Eqs. (1b) and (2b) of $+1$ and 0 represent the trade-offs between x_3 and x_5 and between x_3 and x_6, respectively, the increase of 1 unit in x_3 would *add* 1 unit of x_5 and leave x_6 unchanged.

The economic interpretation of the above is that a 1-unit increase in the slack variable x_3 means the increase of 1 calorie supplied in excess of the daily requirement, which is acquired from purchasing an additional unit of the imaginary or artificial food, A, yielding 1 calorie/unit.

The additional cost of an increase in x_5 of 1 unit and 0 unit of x_6 (necessitated by a unit increase in x_3) is $1M + 0M = 1M$ cents. Thus, the total *increase* in cost from changing $x_3 = 0$ to $x_3 = 1$ is

$$0 + 1M \text{ cents} = 1M \text{ cents}$$

Alternatively stated, the net decrease in cost from introducing 1 unit of x_3 is $-1M$ cents.

Effect on cost of introducing $x_4 = 1$ A 1-unit increase in x_4 would increase the cost by 0 cents. According to the coefficients of the x_4 term in Eqs. (1b) and (2b), a 1-unit increase in x_4 entails increases in x_5 and x_6 of 0 and 1 unit (completely analogous to the x_3 case above), respectively, or, alternatively, decreases in x_5 and x_6 of 0 and -1 unit, respectively. Multiplying these numbers by the cost coefficients of the variables gives the decrease in cost of $0M + (-1)M = -1M$ cents.

The net effect, therefore, of changing the level of x_4 from $x_4 = 0$ to $x_4 = 1$ is a decrease of $-1M$ cents, i.e., an increase of $1M$ cents, in cost.

The following table summarizes the net effect on cost of bringing 1 unit of each of the variables that are zeros in the first basic feasible solution.

Adding 1 unit of the variable	Net decrease in costs, cents
x_1	$48M - 4$
x_2	$32M - 5$
x_3	$-1M$
x_4	$-1M$

According to the table, x_1 brings the most decrease in cost per unit of all variables. Thus, under the simplex criterion, x_1 (which is zero in the first solution), is to be made one of the two nonzero variables in the second basic feasible solution.

STEP 3: IDENTIFICATION AND EVALUATION OF THE SECOND BASIC FEASIBLE SOLUTION

Which of the nonzero variables, x_5 and x_6, in the first basic feasible solution is to be replaced by the new nonzero variable x_1 and become a zero variable in the second basic feasible solution?

Since 1 unit of x_1 reduces the cost by $48M - 4$ cents, 2 units would double the cost reduction; 3 units would triple the cost reduction; and so on. The decision maker would therefore want to bring in x_1 to the maximum in the second feasible solution. What is the maximum of x_1 that can be introduced within the constraints of Eqs. (1b) and (2b) and the nonnegativity conditions for all the variables? Obviously, x_1 can be increased until either x_5 or x_6 runs out of units to trade for. By dividing $x_5 = 2000$ and $x_6 = 600$ by the trade-off coefficients of 40 and 8 of the x_1 term, which of x_5 and x_6 runs out first is identified:

$$x_5: \quad \tfrac{2000}{40} = 50$$

$$x_6: \quad \tfrac{600}{8} = 75$$

When 50 units of x_1 are introduced, 2000 units of x_5 are exhausted completely, although some units of x_6 still remain. The maximum of x_1 that could be introduced is thus $x_1 = 50$. In the second basic feasible solution, the value of the new nonzero variable, x_1, would be 50, and x_5 would become the new zero variable. In other words, the second basic feasible solution is the solution where x_1 and x_6 are nonzeros, and the rest, x_2, x_3, x_4, and x_5 are zeros.

To determine the values of the nonzero variables, x_1 and x_6, and the trade-offs between them and the zero variables, Eqs. (1a) and (2a) or their equivalents (1b) and (2b), are solved for x_1 and x_6, upon setting x_2, x_3, x_4, and x_5 at zero. In reference to Eqs. (1b) and (2b), by transferring the x_1 terms to the left-hand side and the x_5 terms to the right-hand side, the following equivalent equations are obtained:

$$40x_1 + 0x_6 = 2000 - 20x_2 + 1x_3 + 0x_4 - 1x_5 \qquad (1c)$$
$$8x_1 + 1x_6 = 600 - 12x_2 + 0x_3 + 1x_4 + 0x_5 \qquad (2c)$$

Then through linear combinations, Eqs. (1c) and (2c) are converted into equivalent sets of equations until the coefficients of x_1 and x_6 are in the form $\begin{pmatrix} 1 & 0 \\ 0 & 1 \end{pmatrix}$, so that their values can be read off directly.

Divide Eq. (1c) by 40 to obtain Eq. (1d)

$$1x_1 + 0x_6 = 50 - \tfrac{1}{2}x_2 + \tfrac{1}{40}x_3 + 0x_4 - \tfrac{1}{40}x_5 \qquad (1d)$$
$$8x_1 + 1x_6 = 600 - 12x_2 + 0x_3 + 1x_4 + 0x_5 \qquad (2c)$$

Subtract 8 times Eq. (1d) from Eq. (2c) to obtain Eq. (2d):

$$1x_1 + 0x_6 = 50 - \tfrac{1}{2}x_2 + \tfrac{1}{40}x_3 + 0x_4 - \tfrac{1}{40}x_5 \qquad (1d)$$
$$0x_1 + 1x_6 = 200 - 8x_2 - \tfrac{1}{5}x_3 + 1x_4 + \tfrac{1}{5}x_5 \qquad (2d)$$

From Eqs. (1d) and (2d) the values of x_1 and x_6 when

$$x_2 = x_3 = x_4 = x_5 = 0$$

are determined as

$$x_1 = 50 \qquad x_6 = 200$$

In summary, the second basic feasible solution has been identified as:

$$(x_1,\ x_2,\ x_3,\ x_4,\ x_5,\ x_6) = (50,\ 0,\ 0,\ 0,\ 0,\ 200)$$

Cost of the second basic feasible solution   By substituting the values of the solution in the objective function, the cost is evaluated:

$$C = 4x_1 + 5x_2 + 0x_3 + 0x_4 + Mx_5 + Mx_6$$
$$= 4(50) + 5(0) + 0(0) + 0(0) + M(0) + M(200)$$
$$= 200 + 200M$$

The cost of the second solution still contains an M term. The cost is expected to decrease further by making x_6 a zero variable. Such is indeed proved to be the case as is demonstrated below by the continuous application of the formal simplex evaluation to the second solution.

Table 5-1 Summary of effect on cost

	(1) Cost increase from introduction of 1 unit of x_i; cost coefficient of x_i, cents	*(2)* Cost decrease from reduction of x_1 and x_6 necessitated by introduction of 1 unit of x_i, cents	*(3)* Net cost decrease from introduction of 1 unit of x_i, cents, (2) − (1)
x_2	5	$\frac{1}{2}(4) + 8M = 2 + 8M$	$8M - 3$
x_3	0	$-\frac{1}{40}(4) + \frac{1}{5}M = -\frac{1}{10} + \frac{1}{5}M$	$\frac{1}{5}M - \frac{1}{10}$
x_4	0	$0(4) - 1M = -M$	$-M$
x_5	M	$\frac{1}{40}(4) - \frac{1}{5}M = \frac{1}{10} - \frac{1}{5}M$	$-\frac{6}{5}M + \frac{1}{10}$

Investigation of whether another feasible solution would decrease cost

How much net cost decrease would there be if 1 unit of a variable which is zero in the second solution were introduced to the solution?

Rather than going through the computation variable by variable, as was done for the first solution, we summarize the computation of the decrease in cost from the introduction of a unit of each zero variable in the second solution in Table 5-1.

Although the table is self-explanatory, we explain the process of computation in more detail with an example, the case of x_2. Adding 1 unit of x_2 entails an increase in cost of 5 cents from the cost coefficient (column 1). But the trade-off coefficients of the x_2 term in Eqs. (1d) and (2d) of $\frac{1}{2}$ and 8 represent reductions in x_1 and x_6, respectively, required from the addition of 1 unit of x_2. These reductions would decrease the cost by $\frac{1}{2}(4) + 8M = 2 + 8M$ cents (column 2). (Of course, 4 and M are the cost coefficients of x_1 and x_6, respectively.) Consequently, the net decrease in cost from adding a unit of x_2 is $(2 + 8M) - 5 = 8M - 3$ (column 3). The reader should verify the other computations in the table. In checking, he should be careful in distinguishing the *negative* and *positive* signs of the trade-off coefficients as representing *reductions* in x_1 or x_6 and *increases* in x_1 or x_6, respectively.

According to column 3 of the table, introduction of either x_4 or x_5 would result in a net increase in cost, and introduction of either x_2 or x_3 would result in a net decrease in cost. Since x_2 shows the larger cost saving per unit compared to x_3, it would be chosen as a new nonzero variable in the third basic feasible solution.

STEP 4: IDENTIFICATION AND EVALUATION OF THE THIRD BASIC FEASIBLE SOLUTION

Now that it has been decided that a new nonzero variable in the third solution is to be x_2, which of the nonzero variables, x_1 and x_6, of the second solution is to be replaced by it? Dividing $x_1 = 50$ and $x_6 = 200$

by the trade-off coefficients of $\frac{1}{2}$ and 8 of the x_2 term in Eqs. (1*d*) and (2*d*), we see that the maximum of x_2 that could be introduced is 25 units:

$$x_1: \qquad \frac{50}{\frac{1}{2}} = 100$$

$$x_6: \qquad \frac{200}{8} = 25$$

When 25 units of x_2 are added, x_6 is completely exhausted; that is, $x_6 = 0$, according to Eq. (2*d*).

In summary, the third basic feasible solution consists of the non-zero variables x_1 and x_2 and the zero variables x_3, x_4, x_5, and x_6. Next, in order to determine the values of x_1 and x_2 and the tradeoffs between them and the zero variables, we solve the system of equations (1*d*) and (2*d*) for x_1 and x_2 as follows.

Transfer x_2 terms to the left-hand side and x_6 terms to the right-hand side of Eqs. (1*d*) and (2*d*) to obtain

$$1x_1 + \tfrac{1}{2}x_2 = 50 + \tfrac{1}{40}x_3 + 0x_4 - \tfrac{1}{40}x_5 + 0x_6 \qquad (1e)$$

$$0x_1 + 8x_2 = 200 - \tfrac{1}{5}x_3 + 1x_4 + \tfrac{1}{5}x_5 - 1x_6 \qquad (2e)$$

Multiply Eq. (2*e*) by $\frac{1}{8}$ to obtain (2*f*):

$$1x_1 + \tfrac{1}{2}x_2 = 50 + \tfrac{1}{40}x_3 + 0x_4 - \tfrac{1}{40}x_5 + 0x_6 \qquad (1e)$$

$$0x_1 + 1x_2 = 25 - \tfrac{1}{40}x_3 + \tfrac{1}{8}x_4 + \tfrac{1}{40}x_5 - \tfrac{1}{8}x_6 \qquad (2f)$$

Deduct $\frac{1}{2}$ times Eq. (2*f*) from Eq. (1*e*) to obtain Eq. (1*f*):

$$1x_1 + 0x_2 = 37\tfrac{1}{2} + \tfrac{3}{80}x_3 - \tfrac{1}{16}x_4 - \tfrac{3}{80}x_5 + \tfrac{1}{16}x_6 \qquad (1f)$$

$$0x_1 + 1x_2 = 25 - \tfrac{1}{40}x_3 + \tfrac{1}{8}x_4 + \tfrac{1}{40}x_5 - \tfrac{1}{8}x_6 \qquad (2f)$$

When $x_3 = x_4 = x_5 = x_6 = 0$, $x_1 = 37\tfrac{1}{2}$ and $x_2 = 25$ from Eqs. (1*f*) and (2*f*). The complete description of the third basic feasible solution is

$$(x_1, x_2, x_3, x_4, x_5, x_6) = (37\tfrac{1}{2}, 25, 0, 0, 0, 0)$$

Cost of the third basic feasible solution

$$\begin{aligned}
C &= 4x_1 + 5x_2 + 0x_3 + 0x_4 + Mx_5 + Mx_6 \\
&= 4(37\tfrac{1}{2}) + 5(25) + 0(0) + 0(0) + M(0) + M(0) \\
&= 150 + 125 = 275
\end{aligned}$$

Investigation of whether another feasible solution would decrease cost

By repeating the procedure applied to the first and second solutions the effect on costs of introducing 1 unit of each of the zero variables of the third basic feasible solution is evaluated in Table 5-2.

Table 5-2 Summary of effect on cost

	(1) Cost increase from introduction of 1 unit of x_i; cost coefficient of x_i, cents	(2) Cost decrease from reduction of x_1 and x_2 necessitated by introduction of 1 unit of x_i, cents	(3) Net cost decrease from introduction of 1 unit of x_i, cents, (2) − (1)
x_3	0	$-\frac{3}{80}(4) + \frac{1}{40}(5) = -\frac{1}{40}$	$-\frac{1}{40}$
x_4	0	$\frac{1}{16}(4) - \frac{1}{8}(5) = -\frac{3}{8}$	$-\frac{3}{8}$
x_5	M	$\frac{3}{80}(4) - \frac{1}{40}(5) = \frac{1}{40}$	$\frac{1}{40} - M$
x_6	M	$-\frac{1}{16}(4) + \frac{1}{8}(5) = \frac{3}{8}$	$\frac{3}{8} - M$

Column 3 shows for every zero variable a *negative cost decrease*, or an *increase in cost*. The conclusion, therefore, is that changing the level of none of the zero variables from $x_i = 0$ to $x_i = 1$ would reduce the cost below that of the current solution. The third basic feasible solution has been proved to be the least-cost solution.

To interpret the optimal solution,

$$(x_1, x_2, x_3, x_4, x_5, x_6) = (37\tfrac{1}{2}, 25, 0, 0, 0, 0)$$

the diet or the mix of foods that costs the least does not supply any calorie or vitamin in excess of the minimum daily requirements stipulated, namely, $x_3 = x_4 = 0$, and, as intended originally, the artificial variables x_5 and x_6 are zeros, namely, no purchase of imaginary foods.

The basic ideas behind the simplex procedures are relatively simple, but the actual execution of the necessary computation is another matter. From the above illustration, it is easy to see how unmanageably enormous the required calculation would become when the number of activities and the number of constraints are increased. For most real-world problems, therefore, the simplex computation would have to be performed by the computer. Indeed, computer programs for solving linear-programming problems are readily available. All that the decision analyst has to do is to specify the decision variables, the constants and coefficients in the constraints, and the coefficients of the objective function; the computer does the rest.

5-3 ECONOMIC INTERPRETATION

If the real-world problems that are amenable to linear-programming formulation involve many more decision variables and constraints than are manageable by manual computation, why give such a lengthy explanation of the simplex method through manual computation?   One reason is that it provides a vehicle for appreciating how mathematics can aid in decision analysis; another is that it provides economic insights into the nature of the general problem of allocating limited resources to various activities.   Some of the economic information afforded by the simplex method that is useful for managerial analysis is discussed below.

BOTTLENECK RESOURCES AND IMPUTED RESOURCE VALUES

Recall in the product-mix problem of Example 4-1 that the optimal solution was represented by the ordered quintuple

$$(x_1, x_2, x_3, x_4, x_5) = (9000, 0, 0, 24,000, 2000)$$

There, $x_3 = 0$ meant that upon producing 9000 units of the first product and none of the second product, no idle raw material was available, whereas $x_4 = 24,000$ and $x_5 = 2000$ meant that some of the machine hours and assembly-line hours were still available.   As far as machine hours and assembly-line hours are concerned, the firm could produce more of x_1 and increase its profits further, but because of the *bottleneck* resource, raw material, it could not.   The machine time and assembly-line time were really no constraints on the firm's maneuverability, so to speak.

The simplex method gives more than just the information on which capacities pose bottlenecks and which do not.   It gives, in addition, what would be termed the *imputed value*, or the opportunity cost of each of the resources the firm has under its command.   To illustrate, recall the earlier section where in order to determine whether the solution $(x_1, x_2, x_3, x_4, x_5) = (9000, 0, 0, 24,000, 2000)$ was optimal or not, the effect on the firm's profit of introducing 1 unit of each of the zero variables, that is, x_2 and x_3, was examined.   The result of that examination is reproduced in Table 5-3.

Table 5-3   Effect on profit

	(1) Profit increase from introduction of 1 unit of x_i; profit coeffi- cient of x_i	*(2)* Profit decrease from reduction of x_1 and x_3 necessitated by intro- duction of 1 unit of x_i	*(1)* Net profit increase from introduction of 1 unit of x_i, (1) − (2)
x_2	\$3	$\frac{3}{4}(\$5) + 7(\$0) + 1(\$0)$ $= \$3.75$	$\$3 - 3.75 = \$-0.75$
x_3	\$0	$\frac{1}{4}(\$5) - 1(\$0) - \frac{1}{2}(\$0)$ $= \$1.25$	$\$0 - 1.25 = \$-1.25$

Column 3 gives the net effect on profit of increasing x_3 from $x_3 = 0$ to $x_3 = 1$ as $-\$1.25$; i.e., if the firm wishes to have 1 lb of unused raw material, it must sacrifice \$1.25 of its profit. If the given decision problem is changed so that now the raw material available is 35,999 lb (instead of 36,000 lb as originally stipulated), with all other factors unchanged, the new optimal solution would yield the profit of \$44,998.75 $(= \$45,000 - \$1.25)$. Alternatively, if the bottleneck raw material available is made 36,001 lb, 1 lb more than originally given, the firm's profit could be increased by \$1.25 to \$45,001.25.

This means that the "worth" of 1 "marginal" pound of raw material to the firm is \$1.25, and economists call this the imputed cost (or value), shadow price, or opportunity cost of 1 lb of the raw material. The firm would be willing to pay anything less than \$1.25 for an additional pound of the bottleneck resource because it could make an additional profit of \$1.25 with it. Further, the firm would not channel any of its raw material to any activity other than production of the first product, x_1, unless the contemplated activity brings more than a profit increase of \$1.25. Needless to say, the imputed value or shadow price of the other two nonbottleneck resources is \$0 per unit; the firm would pay nothing for additional units of either resource.

CENTRALIZED VERSUS DECENTRALIZED ALLOCATION DECISION

Economists speak of a very interesting potential use of the imputed values, or shadow prices, of the resources that the simplex method computes. The following brief discussion is intended primarily to gain further insight into the nature of the linear-programming type of problem.

Again in reference to the product-mix example, the management of the firm could solve the resource-allocation problem it faces through two alternative institutional (or organizational) arrangements. One arrangement, which may be called a centralized management system, is to let the top management determine how many units of each product are to be produced on the firm-wide basis. Then, the limited resources will be allocated according to production requirements. Under such an arrangement, the top management, in its decision, would (either explicitly or at an intuitive level) formulate and solve the problem in a manner of linear programming.

The alternative organizational arrangement, which may be referred to as a decentralized management system, is to set up two organizational units headed by two managers, each in charge of one of the two products, and a resource manager who is in charge of managing the firm's resources, and then let the resource manager "sell" his resources to the product managers for "prices," or alternatively, let the product managers "bid" for the resources. In addition, the resource manager and the product managers are told to "maximize" their own departmental profits. Under such an institutional arrangement, the production-mix decision is in effect decentralized to the level of individual product managers, because they would now decide whether or not to produce their products on the basis of the comparison between the selling price of the product and its total costs, including the "prices" they have to pay to the resource manager for the resources they "purchase."

Suppose that the resource manager, in his eagerness to maximize his own profit, decides to charge a high price, say, $3 per pound of raw material, $0 per hour of machine time, and $0 per hour of assembly time. (The probable reason that he charges nothing for machine time and assembly-line time but a high price for raw material is because he is aware that the raw material is the only bottleneck in the situation.) The first product manager would immediately realize that he could not afford to buy the resources at the given prices because while 1 unit of his production would bring in an additional profit to his department of only $5, the resources required for its production would cost $12 as calculated below.

$$\$3/\text{lb} \times 4 \text{ lb} = \$12 \quad \text{for raw material}$$
$$\$0/\text{hr} \times 4 \text{ hr} = \quad 0 \quad \text{for machine hours}$$
$$\$0/\text{hr} \times 2 \text{ hr} = \quad \underline{0} \quad \text{for assembly-line hours}$$
$$\text{Total cost} = \$12$$

Likewise, the second product manager would also refuse to buy any resources because their costs would be more than the additional departmental profit they would bring in.

In order to sell any of his resources, the resource manager must lower his prices. Only when the prices are set at something less than $1.25 per pound, $0 per hour, and $0 per hour for the three resources, would the resources begin to sell. At the exact prices of ($1.25, $0, $0) the costs of producing 1 unit of the first product are computed at $5: ($1.25 $\times$ 4 lb) + ($0 $\times$ 4 hr) + ($0 $\times$ 2 hr) = $5. Inasmuch as the profit contribution is $5 per unit, at resource prices slightly less than (1.25, 0, 0), the product manager of the first product would buy the resources, produce his product, and maximize his profit. The product manager of the second product, however, would still not buy any resources, because at the given price level, the costs of producing 1 unit of his product are $3.75, which is higher than the expected profit contribution of $3, by $0.75.

$$(\$1.25 \times 3 \text{ lb}) + (\$0 \times 10 \text{ hr}) + (\$0 + 2.5 \text{ hr}) = \$3.75$$

The resource manager would have no incentive to lower the prices further, because at the current level the first product manager would buy as much of the bottleneck resource as is available in order to maximize his profit, even though the second product manager demands none.   The result is exactly the same optimal allocation of resources for the firm as under the centralized decision system, the maximum of the first product that could be produced within the availability of the bottleneck resource, $x_1 = 9000$, and none of the second, $x_2 = 0$.

In essence, the latter arrangement is a simulation within a single firm of the free-enterprise–market-price mechanism of the competitive economy.   As the free-enterprise–price system would ensure a reasonable degree of efficiency in allocation of limited resources, so would the simulated price system within a firm achieve a satisfactory degree of efficiency in resource allocation.   Furthermore, the advocates of decentralization claim that it provides much better motivation to the individual managers than centralized management.

Whatever the benefits and pitfalls of decentralization or centralization, if the product-mix decision is to be decentralized to the product manager level, success of the system is critically dependent on the "prices" at which resources are sold to the product managers.   The imputed costs or shadow prices of the resources computed by the simplex method are the "correct" level of the resource prices.[1]

QUESTIONS AND PROBLEMS

1. Explain the concepts and computation steps of the simplex method for solving linear-programming problems.

2. What is the difference between slack variables and artificial variables?

3. Define imputed cost, shadow price, or opportunity cost of a resource and show its relevance to the simplex method and the decentralized allocation of resources.

4. Give any three examples of basic feasible solutions, any three examples of nonbasic feasible solutions, and any one example of nonfeasible solutions for the following systems of mathematical statements:

(a) $3x_1 + 2x_2 + x_3 + 0x_4 = 18$
    $0x_1 + 4x_2 + 0x_3 + 3x_4 = 12$ $x_1, x_2, x_3, x_4 \geq 0$

(b) $2x_1 + x_2 - x_3 = 10$
    $x_1 + 3x_2 - x_4 = 9$ $x_1, x_2, x_3, x_4 \geq 0$

5. Convert the following linear-programming problems into their equivalent forms for the purpose of starting the simplex iteration.

(a) Maximize $x_1 + 4x_2$ subject to
    $3x_1 + 6x_2 \leq 12$
    $-0.1x_1 + 0.2x_2 \leq 0.2$ $x_1, x_2 \geq 0$

(b) Minimize $-\frac{1}{2}x_1 + x_2$ subject to
    $x_1 + 2x_2 \geq 4$
    $x_1 + x_2 \leq 3$ $x_1, x_2 \geq 0$

[1] The formal proof that the *same* optimal solution is obtainable either by the centralized system or by the decentralized system (through shadow-price mechanism) is given by mathematicians under the name *duality theorem*.   For the proof and a more detailed economic-interpretive discussion of duality and shadow prices, see R. Dorfman, P. A. Samuelson, and R. M. Solow, "Linear Programming and Economic Analysis, sec. 4-15 and chap. 7, McGraw-Hill, New York, 1958.

6. For Probs. 8 to 12 of Chap. 4, apply the simplex method to the point where the second basic feasible solution is identified.

7. *A transportation problem*   Suppose that three industrial centers (or supply centers) at three different locations produce a product and supply it to three inventory centers (or demand centers) at three different places.   Although the product shipped is the same, the shipping cost from one particular industrial center is different from the shipping cost from another, perhaps because of the difference in distance and in the carrier employed.   If S_1, S_2, S_3 represent the three industrial (supply) centers, and D_1, D_2, D_3, stand for the three inventory (demand) centers, the different shipping costs per unit from different supply sources to different demand centers are as in the following table.

Shipping cost per unit

Supply source	Demand center		
	D_1	D_2	D_3
S_1	$2.0	$1.0	$2.5
S_2	1.8	1.5	2.0
S_3	1.2	2.0	0.6

The decision problem is to decide how many units of the product are to be shipped from a given supply center S_i to a given demand center D_j so as to minimize the total shipping cost.   The volume of production at the various industrial centers and the volume of demand by the various demand centers are tabulated.

Volume of production		Demand	
Supply center	Units	Demand center	Units
S_1	80	D_1	100
S_1	120	D_2	50
S_3	100	D_3	150
Total	300		300

Since total supply is the same as total demand, all that is produced by S_i's is shipped out to D_j's.

Mathematical formulation of the problem   Before solving the problem, we do not know the units shipped from a particular S_i to a particular D_j.   If we let x_{ij} stand for the number of units to be shipped from S_i to D_j, the numbers of units to be shipped from various S_i's to D_j's are as given in the table.

Number of units to be shipped

	Destination			
Source	D_1	D_2	D_3	Production at S_i
S_1	x_{11}	x_{12}	x_{13}	80
S_2	x_{21}	x_{22}	x_{23}	120
S_3	x_{31}	x_{32}	x_{33}	100
Demand by D_j	100	50	150	300

(a) Formulate the problem mathematically.   The resulting mathematical statements of the problem are somewhat different from the problems discussed so far. They are simpler than the cases of general linear-programming problems in that in the current formulation the coefficients of variables are all either 1s or 0s and the constraints are already in equality statements.   This special class of linear-programming problem is called *transportation problems*, and a special computational method simpler than the general simplex method has been developed to solve them.   This book elects not to give the method.

(b) Give examples of feasible solutions.

8. A manufacturing firm has three groups of general-purpose machines with the tabulated machine hours available for the next planning period.

Machine group	Machine hours available
I	200
II	300
III	200

The firm has received for the next planning period three job orders which can be handled by machines in any group.   The total standard machine hours required by these three orders are:

Job order	Standard machine hours required
1	150
2	250
3	200

No other jobs are planned for the next period which require machining by these three groups of machines. Standard cost per machine hour for a particular job by a machine in a particular group of machines is tabulated. Management wishes to determine how many machine hours from different groups of machines should be used to manufacture each job order. Formulate the problem mathematically.

Standard cost per machine hour

Machine group	Job order 1	Job order 2	Job order 3
I	$20	$12	$16
II	18	15	21
III	15	18	16

6
Decisions under Uncertainty and Probability

6-0 INTRODUCTION

In the examples of the preceding chapters, the models of relations involved were *deterministic* in the sense that once a value for an input variable was specified, the corresponding value for the output variable was assumed to be determined *with certainty*. For instance, in Example 1-1, if the decision variable, i.e., the number of units of output produced, is assigned a particular value, say, 4000, the cost of production is assumed to be $90,000 with certainty. But in real-world problems no outcome of an act would be known with such certainty. If and when 4000 units are indeed produced, the resulting cost may turn out to be $88,400, $91,234 or $95,000, the original prediction of $90,000 notwithstanding.

The assumption of certainty or perfect determination simplifies the models of relations considerably. If the advantage of simplification outweighs the loss in accuracy, the use of certainty models is justified. In the cases, however, where the simplification obtained from assuming certainty is no real gain and the accuracy is regarded as more important, the certainty model must give way to a more realistic model of uncertainty. When a model of relations recognizes explicitly the presence of uncertainty, it is called an *uncertainty model, stochastic model,* or *proba-bilistic model.*

This chapter studies some of the basic concepts and tools that enable us to handle uncertainty models, beginning with the nature of decision making under uncertainty. The discussion of conditional payoff tables, game trees, and the problem of selecting a decision criterion is followed by an introductory study of the concepts and rules of probability.

6-1   DECISIONS UNDER UNCERTAINTY

At the most general level, Exhibit 6-1 and Exhibit 6-2 distinguish decision making under certainty and under uncertainty.

PAYOFF TABLE AND GAME TREE

Although both tables are called *payoff tables*—they present the payoffs or consequences of alternative courses of action—an important difference between Exhibits 6-1 and 6-2 is that whereas in the payoff table under certainty only one possible consequence or outcome is predicted to happen for each act, in the case of uncertainty, a number of possible consequences, that is, m possible outcomes, are listed for each act. The

Act	A_1	A_2	A_3	......	A_{n-1}	A_n
Consequence or outcome	O_1	O_2	O_3	......	O_{n-1}	O_n

Exhibit 6-1   A deterministic decision model.

Event	A_1	A_2	A_3	A_{n-1}	A_n
			Act		
E_1	O_{11}	O_{12}	O_{13}	$\cdots$ $O_{1(n-1)}$	O_{1n}
E_2	O_{21}	O_{22}	O_{23}	$\cdots$ $O_{2(n-2)}$	O_{2n}
E_3	O_{31}	O_{32}	O_{33}	$\cdots$ $O_{3(n-1)}$	O_{3n}
E_{m-1}	$O_{(m-1)1}$	$O_{(m-1)2}$	$O_{(m-1)3}$	$\cdots$ $O_{(m-1)(n-1)}$	$O_{(m-1)n}$
E_m	O_{m1}	O_{m2}	O_{m3}	$\cdots$ $O_{m(n-1)}$	O_{mn}

Exhibit 6-2   An uncertainty decision model: conditional payoff table.

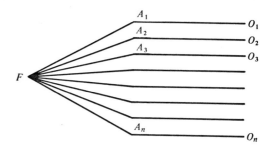

Exhibit 6-3 Game tree for decision under certainty.

table for uncertainty is often referred to as the *conditional payoff table* because the final outcome of a given decision is not only *dependent on*, or *conditional to*, the particular act chosen by the decision maker but is also dependent on, or conditional to, which of the m possible events or states of affairs (E's) chances to happen.   For instance, suppose the decision maker selects the alternative act A_2.   Then one of the m possible outcomes, $O_{12}, O_{22}, O_{32}, \ldots , O_{(m-1)2}, O_{m2}$, will happen depending on which of the m possible events, $E_1, E_2, E_3, \ldots , E_{m-1}, E_m$, happens; and over these the decision maker usually has no control.   To look at the table from another angle, suppose a particular event (or state of affairs), say E_3, has happened.   Then the payoff will be O_{31} if act A_1 is taken, O_{32} if A_2, O_{33} if A_3, and so on.   In general, O_{ij} is said to be the payoff or outcome *conditional to*, or given, the ith event and the jth act.

Another useful way of looking at both the certainty and uncertainty decision models represented by the payoff tables of Exhibits 6-1 and 6-2 is through the so-called *game-tree diagram*.   Exhibits 6-3 and 6-4 give the game-tree representation of the two decision models.

In both game trees, the decision maker is considered to stand at the starting point F, where the fork originates, looking over alternative paths representing alternative acts, one of which he will ultimately decide to select.   In Exhibit 6-3, each alternative act path leads inevitably to one particular outcome, or payoff, but in the uncertainty model of Exhibit 6-4, each alternative act path leads to many possible event paths and consequently to many possible payoffs.   In general, the game tree under uncertainty involves two types of paths: act (path) stage and event (path) stage.   The decision maker has the freedom to influence his destiny only at the act stage; once he reaches the event stage, he has no control over which event fork he will be on and therefore no control over which of the payoffs he will eventually end up with.

EXAMPLE 6-1

It has been decided that a highway authority will build an additional bridge over a river in its jurisdiction in order to divert part of the traffic

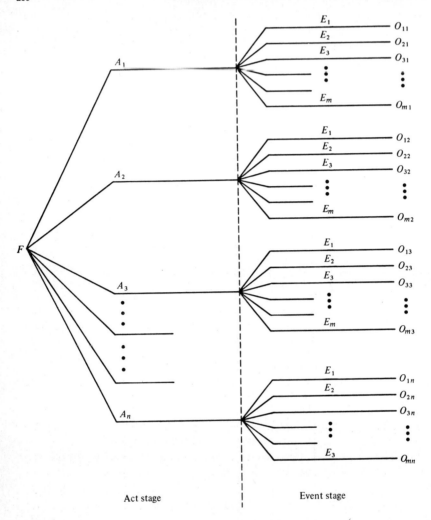

$$A_1 \quad E_1 \to O_{11}, \; E_2 \to O_{21}, \; E_3 \to O_{31}, \; \vdots \; E_m \to O_{m1}$$

$$A_2 \quad E_1 \to O_{12}, \; E_2 \to O_{22}, \; E_3 \to O_{32}, \; \vdots \; E_m \to O_{m2}$$

$$A_3 \quad E_1 \to O_{13}, \; E_2 \to O_{23}, \; E_3 \to O_{33}, \; \vdots \; E_m \to O_{m3}$$

$$A_n \quad E_1 \to O_{1n}, \; E_2 \to O_{2n}, \; E_3 \to O_{3n}, \; \vdots \; E_3 \to O_{mn}$$

Act stage · Event stage

Exhibit 6-4 Game tree for decision under uncertainty.

on the existing bridges and to meet the generally increasing cross-river traffic. The present decision it faces is whether the span should consist of four, six, or eight lanes. If the traffic volume is low, construction of a four-lane bridge would be sufficient; but if the actual volume turns out to be higher *after* the construction of a four-lane bridge, additional lanes must be built at additional cost. A six-lane bridge would be able to handle a medium traffic volume; and eight-lane bridge would be required to accommodate a high traffic volume. If an eight- or six-lane bridge is

	Initial building cost, millions of dollars		
Traffic volume	Four lanes	Six lanes	Eight lanes
Low	$30	$50	$60
Medium	60	50	60
High	80	75	60

Exhibit 6-5 Conditional payoffs for bridge-construction problem.

built in expectation of a high traffic volume but the actual volume proves to be low, the bridge would have an idle, excessive capacity. Exhibit 6-5 gives the estimated conditional payoffs.

Exercise 6-1 (a) Which alternative act should the decision maker follow if it is known with certainty that the actual traffic volume will be medium? If it is known that the volume will be high?

(b) Under the act of initially building a six-lane bridge, why is the cost conditional to the event of low traffic volume the same as the cost conditional to the event of medium traffic volume but different from cost conditional to the event of high traffic volume?

(c) What are some of the assumptions that must have been made implicitly or difficulties involved in estimating the conditional costs?

(d) Draw a game-tree diagram for the decision problem.

In brief, the dilemma of the given decision that stems from uncertainty over the traffic volume may be characterized as that of having to choose one particular act in a situation where one act is preferable to others if certain events happen but another act becomes preferable if other events happen.

Confronted with such a dilemma, what does the decision maker do? Whether at the conscious or the intuitive level, what he does is to rank the three alternative courses of action in the order of preference, net desirability, or *utility*. Since the payoffs are given as costs, the lower its cost, the more preferable the act. But in this problem, the net desirability (or undesirability) of an act depends not only on the magnitude of the conditional cost but also on the chance or likelihood of this cost's actually being realized, or happening. For instance, if the decision maker believes that the traffic volume is *very likely* low, he will tend to rank the first act the best because he will give more weight to the costs shown in the first row of the payoff table than to those of the other rows. In short, the net desirability or utility of an act is a function of two variables, the various possible costs and the likelihood of their happening. More formally, let

U_j = level of utility of a given act A_j

C_i = various possible costs that could happen when that particular act is taken

$P(E_i)$ = degree of likelihood that various possible events E_i will happen

Then

$$U_j = f[C_i, P(E_i)]$$

Since the happening of a particular E_i determines a particular C_i completely, given an act A_j, $P(E_i) = P(C_i)$. Consequently,

$$U_j = f[C_i, P(C_i)]$$

Now the key question is: Can the particular functional relation between utility and costs and their likelihood of happening be quantitatively expressed? Or, to rephrase, can the decision maker's belief in the likelihood of various events happening be quantified, and if so, can the functional form f be specified so as to arrive at a quantitative index of utility? Different decision theorists have different answers to these questions. The reader is introduced briefly to two of many alternative approaches to the problem of constructing the utility index; a fuller discussion is deferred to Chaps. 8 and 9.

MINIMAX DECISION CRITERION

According to some decision theorists, the decision maker would and should use the worst possible outcome of an act that could happen as the index of desirability or utility of that act. Thus, in reference to the payoff table of Exhibit 6-5, the worst possible outcome of the four-lane act is $80 million (when the actual traffic volume turns out high, and consequently the utility—really disutility in this example—of that act is represented by the single cost of $80 million); the worst possible outcome of the six-lane act is $75 million, and consequently its utility is given the cost value of $75 million; the worst possible outcome of the eight-lane act is $60 million, and consequently the utility index assigned to it is $60 million. Since $80 > 75 > 60$, the four-lane act is deemed the least desirable; the six-lane act, the next; and the eight-lane act, the most desirable. The decision maker therefore would and should choose the eight-lane act. Faced with a decision under uncertainty, when a decision maker makes his decision as illustrated above, he is said to follow the *minimax* decision criterion or principle. Representing or summarizing the net desirability of the multiple conditional cost consequences of each act by the single *maximum cost* or *maximum loss* possible under the act, the decision maker chooses that act which carries the least, or *minimum*, of the maximum losses of all alternative acts. In brief, the decision maker acts as though trying to minimize the maximum possible loss; hence the name for the criterion. More formally, the utility of the jth act, U_j, is $U_j = \max C_i$. The likelihood of various events, $P(C_i)$, is considered irrelevant in the determination of the desirability of an act.

To other decision theorists the minimax decision criterion appears singularly unreasonable. Suppose, for example, that in the bridge-construction problem the decision maker believes strongly that the actual traffic volume would very likely be low; then wouldn't he naturally assign to the three alternative acts utilities that are more reflective of the first-row cost figures, namely, $30 million for the four-lane act, $50 million for the six-lane act, and $60 million for the eight-lane act and accordingly prefer the least-cost act, i.e., the four-lane construction, contrary to the dictum of the minimax principle? In general, some of the opponents of the minimax principle believe that a rational decision maker would somehow take into account all possible conditional payoffs (costs in our example)—not only the maximum loss—as well as the likelihoods of these various conditional payoffs in assessing the utility of a given act.

CRITERION OF WEIGHTING POSSIBLE OUTCOMES

By the very nature of the uncertainty present in the decision problem, even when the decision maker believes strongly that a particular event, say the low traffic volume, is very likely to happen, he cannot decide to look at only the first-row cost consequences and ignore the other two rows completely because he would be nagged by the thought: What if the traffic volume turns out to be medium or high? It follows that in assigning a utility to an act, the whole weight cannot be given solely to the cost conditional to the very likely event, low traffic volume, but some weight, small as it may be, must be given to the costs conditional to the other two not very likely events as well. But what relative weights should be assigned to the very likely and not very likely conditional costs? The proponents of the decision criterion that might be called *weighting possible outcomes* believe that a rational decision maker would and should use the relative degrees of likelihood of various events as the relative weights in determining the utility of an act. Deferring to Chaps. 8 and 9 a discussion of the reasonableness of this assertion, we present at a somewhat mechanical level how the utility would be measured under the proposed decision criterion for the alternative acts in the bridge-construction example.

First step Quantify the decision maker's belief in the relative likelihood of various events, i.e., the low, medium and high traffic volumes. In this quantification, the decision maker takes into account all available evidence, e.g., the current and expected traffic pattern in the area, demographic characteristics, and similar past experience. But even if the project is completely novel, the proponents of the criterion insist that the decision maker should and could make explicit his *personal feeling* of which event is more likely and less likely to happen. (If he claimed the task is too difficult, the proponents of the criterion would say that he was avoiding the issue, for a rational decision cannot be made without considering the likelihoods of various traffic volumes.)

Suppose that the decision maker quantified his belief of the likelihoods of various events as below:

Event	Weight
Low traffic volume	4
Medium traffic volume	4
High traffic volume	2

(Perhaps, the above weight assignment had been influenced by the fact that four traffic engineers forecast the low volume, another set of four forecast the medium volume, and another two forecast the high volume.)

Second step   Using these weights, compute the weighted average of all possible costs for each alternative act. The weighted average cost thus calculated would be considered the index of utility (see Table 6-1).

Since the four-lane act yields the least weighted average cost, the decision authority would build four lanes initially. More formally, the weighted average cost or utility of a given act

$$U_j = f[C_i, P(C_i)]$$

where $P(C_i)$ represents the degree of likelihood of C_i happening, is specified as

$$U_j = f[C_i, P(C_i)] = \frac{C_1 P(C_1) + C_2 P(C_2) + C_3 P(C_3)}{P(C_1) + P(C_2) + P(C_3)}$$

$$= \frac{\sum_{i=1}^{3} C_i P(C_i)}{\sum_{i=1}^{3} P(C_i)}$$

Relative weights   The particular *absolute* numerical values of 4, 4, 2, used as weights above are arbitrary in the sense that what is crucial in the

Table 6-1 **Weighted average cost of four-, six-, and eight-lane acts**

Events	Conditional cost	× Weight	=	Weighted cost
Four-lane act				
Low	30	4		120
Medium	60	4		240
High	80	2		160
Total		10		520

Weighted average cost $= \frac{520}{10} = \$52$ million

Six-lane act				
Low	50	4		200
Medium	50	4		200
High	75	2		150
Total		10		550

Weighted average cost $= \frac{550}{10} = \$55$ million

Eight-lane act				
Low	60	4		240
Medium	60	4		240
High	60	2		120
Total		10		600

Weighted average cost $= \frac{600}{10} = \$60$ million

computation of an average is not the absolute weights but the *relative weights*. One could have used any multiple of 4, 4, 2 and still have obtained the same weighted average costs as above. For example, the systems of weights of (8, 8, 4), (2, 2, 1), and (40, 40, 20) would all yield exactly the same answer to the problem because their relative weights are the same. Relative weights are usually (and most conveniently) given in terms of percentages or fractions by dividing the individual absolute weights by the total weights. For illustration, the relative weights corresponding to the system of absolute weights 4, 4, 2 are computed. The total of the absolute weights is 10 (= 4 + 4 + 2). Dividing each weight by the total gives the following relative weights:

$$4 \div 10 = \tfrac{4}{10} = 40\% = 0.4$$
$$4 \div 10 = \tfrac{4}{10} = 40\% = 0.4$$
$$2 \div 10 = \tfrac{2}{10} = 20\% = 0.2$$
$$\text{Total} \quad \tfrac{10}{10} = 100\% = 1.0$$

The reader may verify that the system of weights $(4k, 4k, 2k)$, where k is any real number, would yield the same relative weights as $(4, 4, 2)$.

Inasmuch as the relative weights of all multiples of a given weight system are the same, we can adopt the convention of using relative weights in calculating a weighted average whenever weights represent likelihoods of various events. Under this convention, if the weights are given initially by the decision maker in the form of $(4, 4, 2)$, they would first be converted into the equivalent relative weights $(0.4, 0.4, 0.2)$, and then the weighted average would be computed on the basis of the relative-weight system.

Exercise 6-2 (*a*) Compute the weighted average age of a group of 40 people whose ages are shown in the following:

Age	No. of people
20	5
23	2
28	8
30	10
31	7
33	5
35	3
Total	40

(*b*) What are the relative weights used in the calculation in part (*a*)?

(*c*) Suppose a person is picked at random[1] from the group. What are all possible ages of the person picked? What relative difference is there between the likelihood that the person picked will be twenty-eight years old and thirty-five years old?

(*d*) Suppose a gambler offers you the chance to play the following game. A neutral third man picks a person at random from the group. You guess the age of the person. If your guess is correct, you receive $10 from the gambler; if incorrect, you pay him $1.50. Would you play the game? If yes, which age would you guess under the criterion of weighting possible outcomes? Under the minimax criterion?

(*e*) Draw the decision tree or game tree for part (*d*).

If the relative weights representing the decision maker's belief about the likelihood of occurrence of various outcomes are varied, the weighted average of consequences of alternative acts changes accordingly, and as a

---

[1] Picking a person *at random* means that each and every person in the group (or "population") has an *equal chance* (or probability) of being picked, or the same likelihood of being selected as any other person in the group.

result the decision itself may have to be altered. For example, in the bridge-construction case, assuming that the relative weights are now 0.2, 0.3, and 0.5 for the three events, low, medium, and high volumes of traffic, respectively, the reader may verify that the newly computed weighted average costs of alternative acts would be such that the preferential ranking would change to that of the six-lane act the best, the eight-lane act the second best, and the four-lane act the worst.

Evidently, assignment of "correct" relative weights is critical to a "correct" decision. The remainder of this chapter and the next discusses some of the concepts and rules that will help assign "correct" weights to the various possible outcomes of a decision. These concepts and rules are borrowed directly from the theory of probability developed by mathematicians and statisticians.

Although the ultimate criterion of whether a particular assignment of relative weights to various outcomes is correct may be stated tautologically as that assignment is correct whose particular relative weights lead to correct decisions or decisions that appear reasonable to the reasonable decision maker, there is better assurance that the resulting decision is correct when the formal mathematical rules of probability are followed in assigning relative weights. This is one reason the theory of probability is studied here.

While it is useful in applying the criterion of weighting possible outcomes to a decision, probability theory proves indispensable whenever uncertainty surrounding relations among variables is to be explicitly recognized and investigated. For instance, suppose a biologist establishes the relation between the number of infected cells n and the passage of time (t hr) under certain controlled circumstances as $n = 10 + t^3$. For some purposes it may be sufficient to consider the relation to exist with certainty in the sense that given a t value, n is unequivocally determined; e.g., when $t = 3$, $n = 37$. But for other purposes the biologist may wish to consider explicitly the fact that n may turn out to be 34, 35, 36, 38, 39, 40, etc. (not always 37 exactly) even when t is the same $t = 3$. The questions he might ask are: When $t = 3$, what is the likelihood that $n = 35$? What is the likelihood that $n \geq 39$? Is $n = 35$ more or less likely than $n = 36$? Probability theory facilitates systematic analysis of such questions.

6-2 CONCEPTS AND RULES OF PROBABILITY (AND RELATIVE WEIGHTS)

What is probability? A *direct* definition of probability is difficult, if not impossible, but it can be defined *indirectly* by describing its milieu, attributes and rules, just as chess can be defined in terms of its rules. The following discussion of the rules of probability should enhance our understanding of its very nature; at this point, however, we assert that probability as used in common parlance has close correspondence to, or at least is compatible with, probability as defined by mathematicians and that probability is the numerical relative weights representing the degrees of likelihood of the occurrence of various states of affairs, events, or outcomes of an uncertain phenomenon.

SOME BASIC TERMS AND CONCEPTS

This section defines some of the basic terms and concepts of probability preliminary to the discussion of more concrete rules in the following section.

Random process or experiment　It is often convenient to conceive various events as being the output of an underlying process. Thus we think of the various possible traffic volumes in Example 6-1 as being generated by some process. Such an event-generating process or mechanism is called in formal language a *random process* or *random experiment*. To cite another example, if a die is rolled, the rolling of the die is considered the random experiment which generates six possible events, faces 1, 2, 3, 4, 5, and 6.

Description of events　In Example 6-1, an essential step in constructing the conditional payoff table as an aid for decision was to lay out *all possible courses of action* and *all possible events* (traffic volumes). It is obvious that for a complete and consistent analysis the following rules must be observed in listing alternative acts and events.

Collectively exhaustive description　One cardinal rule that should be followed in laying out events (and alternative acts) in a payoff table is that *all* possible events (and alternative acts) must be covered in the description. Suppose that the description of possible traffic volumes in Example 6-1 were not complete in that another possible volume, say, very high, was left out. For a *rational* decision, then, the consequence of this new possible event would have to be examined for each act; in other words, this new event must be added to the list of events in the payoff table. (Similar reasoning applies when a feasible alternative is omitted from the payoff table.) The description of events must *collectively exhaust* all possible events that could be generated by the random process of concern.

Mutually exclusive description　Another rule that must be obeyed in describing events (and alternative acts) for the payoff table is that they be in a *mutually exclusive* form; i.e., in a manner such that if one event happens, other events cannot happen at the same time (and if one act is chosen, the other acts are not chosen). As an example of an incorrect listing of events, suppose that the traffic volume 1000 cars per hour is included as part of the high volume and at the same time included as part of the medium volume. Then, the description of events (low, medium, high) would *not* be mutually exclusive because when the volume turns out to be 1000 cars per hour, *both* the event medium volume *and* the event high volume would be considered to have happened. For a consistent analysis, the volume of 1000 cars must be classified *either* as part of the medium volume *or* as part of the high volume, making the two events mutually exclusive.

Sample space Sample space is another formal term of the theory of probability. In Chap. 1, a set was defined as a collection of objects (or elements). From the definition, any description or listing of the possible outcomes of a random experiment may be considered as a set. A set whose elements are the various possible events of a random experiment listed in a collectively exhaustive and mutually exclusive manner is called a *sample space* or a sample description space. Thus, the set of various traffic volumes, V = [low, medium, high], is a sample space of the random process which generates these events.

To review the new terms introduced above, another case of an uncertain phenomenon is cited. Suppose that for the purpose of deciding whether to launch a space rocket it is crucial to investigate all the possible types of weather that may be experienced at a given time at a given location. Then, a weather-generating random process may be considered to be at work to determine what particular weather condition shall prevail in the place at the time. (Perhaps, nature is the random process involved.) Suppose now that the possible weathers which the random process might produce are listed as elements of a set,

W = [rainy with wind, rainy without wind, not rainy with wind, not rainy without wind]

If no possible weather that could happen is omitted from the listing and no two weathers listed could occur simultaneously, the events are said to be described in a collectively exhaustive and mutually exclusive way and therefore the set W is a sample space for the random process.

We say *a* sample space rather than *the* sample space because there are other collectively exhaustive and mutually exclusive ways of listing the weather conditions for the same weather-generating random process, namely, other sample spaces. For example, a set of three elements,

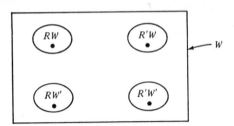

Exhibit 6-6   A sample space of weather-generating process.

T = [rainy with wind, rainy without wind, not rainy], is another collectively exhaustive and mutually exclusive listing of all possible weathers
(at the same specified time and location) and constitutes a sample space
(for the same random process). For some analysis where the distinction
between the two weathers, not rainy with wind and not rainy without
wind, is not critical, the sample space T would suffice. The reader can
verify that U = [rainy, not rainy] is also a sample space for the same
process.

Venn diagram   A useful way of checking whether a description of events
is mutually exclusive and collectively exhaustive and in general of
analyzing relationships among events is provided by Venn diagrams.
Exhibit 6-6 is a Venn diagram for the weather-generating random process.
    In Exhibit 6-6 four points represent the four elements of the set W.
Note that the point designated RW represents the weather rainy with
wind; RW', rainy without wind; $R'W$, not rainy with wind; $R'W'$, not
rainy without wind. The elements of a sample-space set are often
referred to as *sample points*. To emphasize the fact that each point represents a meaningful event and to show that the four events are mutually
exclusive, the points are enclosed by circles that do not overlap one
another. Since each of the four events cannot be broken down into any
more meaningful subevents, it is called an *elementary event*.
    Similarly, the set T, another sample space of the same random pro-
cess defined above, is represented by Exhibit 6-7. The set,

$$T = [RW, RW', R']$$

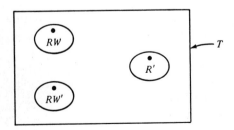

Exhibit 6-7   A sample space of weather-generating process.

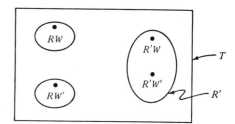

Exhibit 6-8 A sample space of weather-generating process.

has three elements, representing three possible weather conditions, rainy with wind (RW), rainy without wind (RW'), and not rainy (R'). Again, since the three circles representing meaningful events do not overlap one another, they are said to be mutually exclusive. The event R' is not an elementary event because it can be broken down into two meaningful subevents, or two elementary events, not rainy with wind and not rainy without wind. It is called a *unioned event* or a *union* of two events. The *unioned* event R' is considered to have happened if *either* the elementary event $R'W$ *or* the elementary event $R'W'$ happens. To highlight the fact that R' is a union of two component events, $R'W$ and $R'W'$, the set T may be alternatively diagramed as in Exhibit 6-8.

Exhibit 6-9 represents the set U = [rainy, not rainy], another sample space. Two unioned events, R and R', make up the total set. The two circles representing the two events do not overlap each other (do not contain any common points or elementary events) and therefore are mutually exclusive. Further, the two events together cover all four dots; they are collectively exhaustive.

Exhibits 6-10 and 6-11 are given as examples of nonmutually exclusive and noncollectively exhaustive description of events. The sets X and Y represented by the two diagrams are not sample spaces. Exhibit 6-10 demonstrates that the three elements of the set X = [W, R', RW'] are not mutually exclusive because the events W and R', overlap each other, i.e., contain a common point, $R'W$. If the weather happens to be the elementary event $R'W$ (not rainy with wind), then both the event W (wind) and the event R' (not rainy) are considered to have happened.

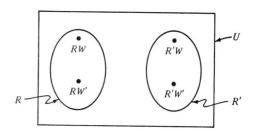

Exhibit 6-9 A sample space of weather-generating process.

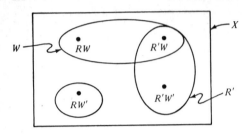

Exhibit 6-10 A description of events which do not represent a sample space.

In other words, that the event W has happened does not preclude the occurrence of the event R', and vice versa.

In Exhibit 6-11 the set Y consists of only two elements, namely, $Y = [W, R']$. The listing of events as in Y omits a possible (elementary) event of the random process on hand, that is, RW', the sample point for which is left uncircled in the diagram. As such, the description is not collectively exhaustive.

Exercise 6-3 Consider a group of 100 people. Of the total 60 are male and 50 are thirty years or older; of the 60 males, 40 percent are younger than thirty years. Supposing a random experiment of picking an individual at random from the group is performed, answer the following.

(a) An obvious sample space for the experiment may be represented by a Venn diagram with 100 sample points. Explain what *event* each of the 100 points represents.

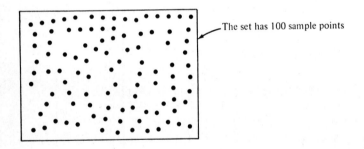

The set has 100 sample points

(b) Draw a circle in the diagram of part (a) binding the sample points that represent the event *male*. Do the same for the event *thirty years or older*. How many sample points are in each circle? How many points are outside either circle?

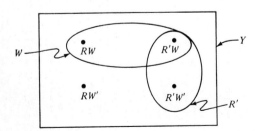

Exhibit 6-11 A description of events which do not represent a sample space.

(c) Parts (a) and (b) would yield a segmentation of the sample space as in the diagram below. Explain what *event* each of the definable segments (or areas) of the Venn diagram represents. How many sample points are in each?

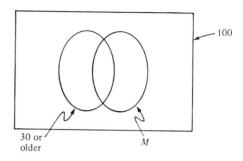

(d) If not already answered as part of (c), define the area which represents the event that the individual picked is male *and at the same time* thirty years or older and the area which represents the event that the individual picked is female *and at the same time* younger than thirty years old. How many elementary sample points are in each area?

(e) If not already answered as part of (c), define the area which represents the event that the individual picked is *either* male *or* thirty years or older and the area which represents the event that the individual picked is *either* female *or* younger than thirty years old. How many elementary sample points are in each area?

BASIC RULES FOR ASSIGNING PROBABILITIES

After alternative acts are listed and possible events are described in a collectively exhaustive and mutually exclusive manner, i.e., a sample space is defined, the next step in decision analysis is to predict conditional consequences—consequences conditional to each act and each event. The result of these steps is the conditional payoff table given earlier. At this point the decision maker may decide to adopt the minimax principle or any other criterion, but should he decide to follow the criterion of weighting possible outcomes, the next task for him is to assign proper weights to various possible outcomes in accordance with the degree of likelihood of these outcomes. In the newly acquired language, he must assign probability weights.

In connection with the bridge-construction–traffic-volume example, we already adopted a *rule*, or convention, of probability assignment, i.e., using relative weights that add up to 1. We restate the rule formally.

Rule 1 The sum of the probabilities or relative weights over a sample space, i.e., assigned to any set of mutually exclusive and collectively exhaustive events, shall be 1. In mathematical notation, $\sum_{i=1}^{n} P(E_i) = 1$, where $P(E_i)$ is the probability of the ith event.

Related to rule 1, and already implicitly followed in the assignment
of relative weights in the traffic volume-example, are the following two
additional rules.

Rule 2   The probability assigned to any one event shall be nonnegative and equal to or less than 1, that is, a number between 0
and 1 (inclusive). In notation,

$$0 \leq P(E_i) \leq 1$$

Rule 3   If two or more mutually exclusive events are *unioned* into a
"compound" event, the probability assigned to this union of events
shall be equal to the sum of the probabilities assigned to the original
component events. In notation, let A and B represent two mutually exclusive events with the probabilities $P(A)$ and $P(B)$, respectively. Then the union of A and B is written as $A \cup B$ and is the
event that *either* A or B happens. Its probability is

$$P(A \cup B) = P(A) + P(B)$$

The reasonableness of rule 3 can be seen in reference to the traffic-
volume example. Recall that the decision maker, upon consideration of
all available information, assigned the probability weights for the three
events low, medium, and high (traffic volumes) as follows: $P(\text{low}) = 0.4$;
$P(\text{medium}) = 0.4$; $P(\text{high}) = 0.2$. If a new event X is defined as a
union of two events medium and high, $X = \text{medium} \cup \text{high}$ means the
event that the traffic volume is *either* medium *or* high. If the weight of
0.4 is given to the event medium and the weight of 0.2 to the event high,
it is only natural that the weight of $0.4 + 0.2 = 0.6$ is assigned to the
unioned event. In notation,

$$P(X) = P(\text{medium} \cup \text{high})$$
$$= P(\text{medium}) + P(\text{high}) = 0.4 + 0.2 = 0.6$$

To repeat, the above rule is applicable only when mutually exclusive
events are compounded to form a union. The rule for assigning the
probability to a union of nonmutually exclusive events will be given later
in the chapter.

One disturbing fact about the three rules given above is that given
a sample space, there exist many alternative assignments of probabilities
that satisfy these rules. For example, in the traffic-volume case, it was

noted that if the evidence and the decision maker's judgment so indicated, the relative weights assigned to the three events might be (0.2, 0.3, 0.5) instead of (0.4, 0.4, 0.2). Neither of these weight systems violates the three rules of probability. In both cases, the weights add up to 1; they are all between 0 and 1; and rule 3 may be applied to determine the probability weight for unions of events. In fact, there are many sets of probability values different from either one of the two that could be assigned without violating the rules; for example, $\frac{1}{3}$ each to the three events. A natural question that comes to mind is: Which system of relative weights or probabilities is correct, (0.4, 0.4, 0.2), (0.2, 0.3, 0.5), or $(\frac{1}{3}, \frac{1}{3}, \frac{1}{3})$? Mathematics cannot help much in answering this fundamental question except perhaps to acknowledge that probability weights should reflect the degree of likelihood of events' happening. Past data on changes in traffic volumes in the vicinity under similar circumstances and ultimately the decision maker's best judgment are the basis for determining this degree of likelihood. But what mathematics can do is to point up internal inconsistencies, if any, in the assignment of probabilities to events derived from the events for which the probabilities are initially specified. For instance, if the decision maker assigns a probability other than 0.6 to the event that the traffic volume is either medium or high while accepting the probability of 0.4 for medium and the probability of 0.2 for high, rule 3 would indicate the inconsistency.

Now to continue developing more rules of probability, consider the case where the decision maker believes that one of the events specified in a sample space would never happen. What weight should be assigned to such event? Since the decision maker believes that the event would not happen, whatever the consequences conditional to or contingent upon that event are, they should be discarded in weighing consequences for decision. If the weight of 0 is assigned to the event, the consequences conditional to that event will have no effect on the weighted average calculation.

The other extreme might be the case where the decision maker believes that a given event is *sure* to happen, or happens always. The probability to be assigned to such an event is 1. This way the weighted average payoff will be the same as the payoff conditional to that sure-to-happen event. Rule 4 restates formally the rules governing these two extreme cases.

Rule 4 If an event will certainly not occur, the probability assigned to the event shall be 0. If an event will certainly occur, the probability assigned to the event shall be 1.

The reader should note that rule 4 is compatible with rules 1 to 3.

EXAMPLE 6-2

Suppose we are offered a chance to play a game which is described as follows. Two fair coins are tossed once. If the outcome is no heads, we receive $12; if one head, we have to pay $6; if two heads, we have to pay $3. Should we play the game?

Two alternative acts available to the decision maker are *play* and *not play*. What are the possible outcomes of the coin-tossing random experiment? One way of describing all possible events would be to write down TT for the event that both coins fall tails, TH for the event that the first coin falls tails *and* the second falls heads, HT if the order of the coins falling tails and heads is reversed, and HH if both coins fall heads. These four events *exhaust* all possible outcomes and are *mutually exclusive*. The set $S_1 = [TT, TH, HT, HH]$ is a sample space of the random experiment.

Another way of describing a sample space for the same random experiment would be to record the number of heads that appear: write 0 if neither coin falls heads; 1 if one falls heads, the other tails; 2 if both fall heads. Then, 0, 1, 2 exhaust all possible outcomes and are mutually exclusive. This set, $S_2 = [0, 1, 2]$, is another sample space. Observe that the element 1 in S_2 corresponds to (or is a union of) two elements, HT and TH, in S_1.

Now the conditional payoff table relevant to the decision can be prepared. Since events can be described in two alternative ways, two alternative payoff tables are shown in Exhibit 6-12.

If we decide not to play the game, we gain nothing regardless of the outcome of the coin tossing; thus the not-play column in both tables shows all zeros. Under play the positive number represents a gain and the negative entry a loss.

	Payoff table (a)			Payoff table (b)		
	Act				Act	
Event	Play	Not play	Event		Play	Not play
TT	$12	$0	0 (heads)		$12	$0
TH	−6	0	1		−6	0
HT	−6	0	2		−3	0
HH	−3	0				

Exhibit 6-12

Suppose that the decision maker elects to follow the principle of weighting possible outcomes. He must now assign weights or probabilities to various possible outcomes according to the degree of likelihood of their occurrence.

First, with respect to the sample space $S_1 = [TT, TH, HT, HH]$, as long as the coins are fair, all four events will be judged equally likely to happen. TT is as likely to happen as TH, HT, and HH. Or, taking a slightly defensive attitude, there is no sufficient reason to believe that one is more likely or less likely to happen than another. Thus, an equal weight would be assigned to each element in the set and a weight of an arbitrary number, say 17, may be assigned to each of the four events. But our self-imposed rules for assigning relative weights or probabilities forbid us to use such numbers as 17.   Under the rules, a weight of $\frac{1}{4}$ must be assigned to each of the four equally likely events.   In notation, let $P(E_i)$ represent the probability of the event E_i; then

$$P(TT) = P(TH) = P(HT) = P(HH) = 0.25$$

Since $0 \leq P(E_i) = 0.25 \leq 1$, rule 2 has been obeyed; also, rule 1 has not been violated:

$$\Sigma P(E_i) = \tfrac{1}{4} + \tfrac{1}{4} + \tfrac{1}{4} + \tfrac{1}{4} = 1$$

Now these probability weights are entered in the payoff table and the weighted average receipt for each act calculated.

On the basis of Table 6-2, the weighted average receipt of each act is computed as in Table 6-3, according to the formula $\Sigma R_i P(E_i)$, where R_i is the receipt conditional to E_i.

Since the weighted average receipt of the act not play, \$0, is higher than that of the act play, $-\$0.75$ (a loss of 75 cents), the decision is not to play the game.

Table 6-2   Modified payoff table (a)

		Act	
Event	Probability or weight	Play	Not play
TT	0.25	\$12	\$0
TH	0.25	-6	0
HT	0.25	-6	0
HH	0.25	-3	0

Table 6-3   Weighted average receipt based on payoff table (a)

Conditional receipts	× Probability =	Weighted receipts
Act: play		
$12	0.25	$ 3
−6	0.25	−1.5
−6	0.25	−1.5
−3	0.25	−0.75
Weighted average receipt of play		$−0.75
Act: not play		
$0	0.25	$0
0	0.25	0
0	0.25	0
0	0.25	0
Weighted average receipt of not play		$0

If the decision analysis is repeated on the basis of payoff table (b) instead of (a), it is expected that the selection of the same act (not play) will be indicated, for the decision problem is still the same.

The sample space of payoff table (b) is $S_2 = [0, 1, 2]$. What weights or probabilities should be assigned to events 0, 1, and 2? Rightly or wrongly, we *might* consider the three events equally likely and assign an equal weight, $\frac{1}{3}$, to each event. In notation, $P(0) = P(1) = P(2) = \frac{1}{3}$, and $P(0) + P(1) + P(2) = 1$. Such an assignment is consistent with rules 1 and 2. With these probabilities, the weighted average receipt of each act is computed in Table 6-4.

Since the weighted average receipt, $1, of act play is higher than the weighted average receipt, $0, of act not play, the decision is to play the game. This decision is at variance from the earlier one based on payoff table (a). Something has gone wrong. It is the same game, with the same experiment of tossing two fair coins, and the same decision principle has been followed; the decision should be the same.

The trouble is of course attributable to the haphazard way in which the probabilities were assigned over the sample space S_2. The assignment of the same $\frac{1}{3}$ weight to each element of S_2 was in fact in violation of rule 3. Event 0 is "no heads," corresponding to event TT in the sample space of S_1. Event 2 is two heads, corresponding to

Table 6-4   Weighted average receipt based on payoff table (*b*)

Conditional receipts	× Probability =	Weighted receipts
Act: play		
$12	$\frac{1}{3}$	$ 4
−6	$\frac{1}{3}$	−2
−3	$\frac{1}{3}$	−1
Weighted average receipt of play		$ 1
Act: not play		
$0	$\frac{1}{3}$	$0
0	$\frac{1}{3}$	0
0	$\frac{1}{3}$	0
Weighted average receipt of not play		$0

event HH of S_1.   But event 1 is one heads; it corresponds to two events, HT and TH, in S_1.   Event 1, in other words, is a union of two mutually exclusive events, HT and TH, each of which carries the probability of $\frac{1}{4}$. The probability of event 1, therefore, should have been the sum of the probabilities of the two elementary events, according to rule 3.   Formally,

$$P(1 \text{ heads}) = P(HT \cup TH) = P(HT) + P(TH)$$
$$= \tfrac{1}{4} + \tfrac{1}{4} = \tfrac{1}{2}$$

The correct assignment of probabilities on the sample space S_2, or the assignment *consistent* with the probability assignment over the sample space S_1, should have been $P(0) = \frac{1}{4}$, $P(1) = \frac{1}{2}$, $P(2) = \frac{1}{4}$.

With these correct probabilities, the same decision will result as when the decision analysis was based on the sample space S_1.   The reader may verify that the weighted average receipt of play on the basis of newly assigned probabilities over S_2 is −$0.75, the same as in the original computation based on S_1.

This discussion highlights the usefulness of studying the mathematical rules of probability.   By applying rule 3, the inconsistency in the initial assignment of probabilities over the sample space S_2 was brought to light.   Here again, we see the general mathematical method (the "if so, then so" kind of reasoning) at work.   If the probabilities assigned over S_1 are accepted as true, then the probability assignment over S_2 *must* be such and such.   The study of additional rules of proba-

Condition	Number
Male:	
Read	185
Not read	365
Female:	
Read	115
Not read	335
Total population	1000

Exhibit 6-13 Survey of magazine readership.

bility in the following section would be beneficial exactly in the same sense.

Exercise 6-4 In reference to Example 6-2, (*a*) draw a game tree for the decision problem.

(*b*) Apply the minimax principle.

(*c*) Application of the criterion of weighting possible outcomes indicates the selection of not play. Supposing the same conditional payoffs as in payoff table (*a*) or (*b*), the decision maker may prefer to play the game if the coin is "crooked" in a certain way. What kind of crookedness of the coin would make the play act more desirable than the not play act?

6-3 DERIVED EVENTS AND FURTHER RULES OF PROBABILITY

Section 6-2 gave a rule by which the probability of a union of mutually exclusive elementary events could be assessed. But *union* is only one of many ways of forming a new derived event from given events. This section illustrates derivations of events other than unions and the general rules for assigning probabilities to them.

EXAMPLE 6-3

The results of a survey of a group of 1000 people by a magazine publisher on whether or not they read a particular magazine are summarized in Exhibit 6-13.

The data of Exhibit 6-13 can be rearranged as in Exhibit 6-14. Now the random experiment of concern is the selection *at random* of 1

	Male	Female	Total
Read	185	115	300
Not read	365	335	700
Total	550	450	1000

Exhibit 6-14 Survey of magazine readership.

person out of this group of 1000 people.[1] The experiment is assumed to consist of only one trial; i.e., the selection process is not repeated. What are the possible outcomes of the experiment? Since every one of the 1000 individuals represents an outcome mutually exclusive to the others, one basic way of describing all possible outcomes is a sample space consisting of 1000 elements representing 1000 individuals. Then, since each element of the sample space has an equal chance of being selected, a same probability, $\frac{1}{1000}$, is assigned to each of the 1000 elements.

What is the probability of event M, the event that the selected person is a male? Since 550 elements out of 1000 represent males (550 balls are marked male in the standard urn), event M is the union of 550 mutually exclusive elementary events. Thus,

$$P(M) = 550(\tfrac{1}{1000}) = 0.550$$

Likewise, the probability of event F, the event that the selected person is a female, is $P(F) = 450 \,(\tfrac{1}{1000}) = 0.450$ (450 elements out of 1000 represent female).

Events M and F are obviously mutually exclusive. (A ball marked male cannot be also marked female at the same time in the standard urn.) Thus, the probability of the union of M and F, that is, the probability of the selected person being *either* a male *or* a female is

$$P(M \cup F) = P(M) + P(F) = 0.550 + 0.450 = 1$$

The probability of 1 means that the event is certain to happen. Indeed, the selected person has to be either a male or a female.

Next, define event R as the event that the person chosen reads the magazine; 300 elements out of 1000 represent people (male or female) reading the magazine. Thus, $P(R) = 300(\tfrac{1}{1000}) = 0.300$. Likewise, the probability of event R', the event that the person selected does not read the magazine, is $P(R') = \tfrac{700}{1000} = 0.700$. Events R and R' are mutually exclusive, and therefore

$$P(R \cup R') = P(R) + P(R') = 0.300 + 0.700 = 1$$

Complementary events When two events are such that if one event happens, the other event cannot happen, but either one or the other must happen for certain, the two events are called *complementary* to each other.

---

[1] The selection at random as required here may be simulated by constructing a *standard urn* which contains 1000 balls, each of which represents a different person in the group of 1000 persons and accordingly is marked to show whether the represented person is male or female and reads the magazine or does not read it. Now mix the balls in the urn well; choose one ball and read what is marked on it. The outcome may be a ball marked male and read, male and not read, female and read, or female and not read.

M and F are *complements;* R and R' are *complements.* From the definition of the complementary events, it follows that

$$P(M) = 1 - P(M') = 1 - P(F) \qquad P(R) = 1 - P(R')$$
$$P(F) = 1 - P(F') = 1 - P(M) \qquad P(R') = 1 - P(R)$$

This is consistent with the earlier rules

$$P(M \cup F) = P(M) + P(F) = 1$$

and

$$P(R \cup R') = P(R) + P(R') = 1$$

Joint event or intersection of two events Given the two events, M (male) and R (reader), the joint event, or intersection, of the two, event A, is defined as the event that *both M and R* happen, i.e., the person selected is a male reader. Formally, the intersection of the events is denoted as $A = M \cap R$. The probability of this joint event is $P(A) = P(M \cap R) = \frac{185}{1000} = 0.185$. (In terms of the standard urn, 185 balls out of 1000 balls in the urn would be marked male and read.) Likewise,

$$P(M \cap R') = \frac{365}{1000} = 0.365$$
$$P(F \cap R) = \frac{115}{1000} = 0.115$$
$$P(F \cap R') = \frac{335}{1000} = 0.335$$

Often, an intersection of events may represent an event that is impossible. For example, the intersection of the two events M and F is impossible (the person selected would have to be both male and female at the same time). Therefore, its probability is $P(M \cap F) = 0$.

Union of nonmutually exclusive events Rule 3 applies only to the union of mutually exclusive events. What is the rule for assigning the probability to the union of events that are not mutually exclusive? For illustration, consider events M and R. The two are not mutually exclusive, because the fact that M has happened does not necessarily mean that R has not happened and vice versa. If the person selected happens to be male and a reader of the magazine, both events M and R are considered to have happened. (Of course, M could happen without R also happening, i.e., the person selected could be male but a nonreader; R could happen without M also happening, i.e., the person could be a reader but female.)

If event B is the union of M and R, B is the event that *either M or R* happens. Formally, $B = M \cup R$. *Either one* of the two events, M and R, is sufficient to qualify as event B. There are three mutually exclusive ways in which B can happen: (1) if the person selected is male and non-reader $(M \cap R')$, B is considered to have happened; (2) if the person selected is female and reader $(F \cap R)$, B is considered to have happened; and (3) if the person selected is male and reader $(M \cap R)$, B is considered to have happened. In other words, B is the union of three mutually exclusive events, $(M \cap R')$, $(F \cap R)$, and $(M \cap R)$. Its probability is therefore

$$P(B) = P(M \cup R) = P(M \cap R') + P(F \cap R) + P(M \cap R)$$
$$= 0.365 + 0.115 + 0.185 = 0.665$$

Alternatively, the probability of the union of M and R can be derived according to the following formula, provided that $P(M)$, $P(R)$ and $P(M \cap R)$ are already known:

$$P(M \cup R) = P(M) + P(R) - P(M \cap R)$$
$$= 0.550 + 0.330 - 0.185 = 0.665$$

$P(M) = 0.550$ includes $P(M \cap R) = 0.185$ once; $P(R) = 0.300$ includes $P(M \cap R) = 0.185$ once again. Thus, the probability of *either* M *or* R is $0.550 + 0.300$ minus that portion counted twice, i.e., 0.185. (In the standard-urn context, 550 balls are marked *male;* 300 balls are marked *read*. But 185 balls marked *male* and *read* are counted as part of male balls and also as part of read balls. Thus, $550 + 300 - 185 = 665$ balls out of 1000 balls in the urn are marked either male or read.) The above formula applies to the union of any two events and may be rewritten as another general rule of probability:

> *Rule 5* The probability of the union of two given events (say, M and R) is the sum of the probabilities of the two events less the probability of the intersection of the two events. Or
>
> $$P(M \cup R) = P(M) + P(R) - P(M \cap R)$$

Note that rules 5 and 3 are perfectly compatible with each other in that rule 3 is but a special case of the more general rule 5. For if two events M and F are mutually exclusive, the probability of their intersection is always zero regardless of the individual probabilities of M and F. Formally, $P(M \cap F) = 0$. Consequently, rule 5 becomes rule 3:

$$P(M \cup F) = P(M) + P(F) - P(M \cap F)$$
$$= P(M) + P(F)$$

Conditional probability A very useful concept in the theory of probability is that of conditional probability. The conditional probability of event

M *given* the occurrence of event R is denoted by $P(M/R)$. The basic idea of the conditional probability is as follows: If the outcome of the random person-selection experiment is known to be event R, given this knowledge that the person selected is a reader, what probability should be assigned to the event that this person is male? Would the probability be different from the probability of event M assigned earlier without the knowledge that event R has happened? In terms of the standard-urn simulation, the knowledge of the occurrence of R means that the ball chosen is known to be one of 300 balls marked read. What is not known is which of these 300 balls is the chosen ball. Since, within the reduced group of 300 balls, each ball has an equal chance of being the chosen ball and 185 balls are marked male, the probability of the chosen ball's being marked male is 185 balls out of 300, or $P(M/R) = \frac{185}{300}$.

The same conditional probability of M given R can be obtained alternatively from the formula

$$P(M/R) = \frac{P(M \cap R)}{P(R)}$$

Since $P(M \cap R) = \frac{185}{1000}$ and $P(R) = \frac{300}{1000}$, the formula yields

$$P(M/R) = \frac{\frac{185}{1000}}{\frac{300}{1000}} = \frac{185}{1000}\frac{1000}{300} = \frac{185}{300}$$

The formula seems reasonable when interpreted as follows.

Event R (readership) can happen in two ways: $M \cap R$ (male and reader) and $F \cap R$ (female and reader). $P(R) = \frac{300}{1000}$, $P(M \cap R) = \frac{185}{1000}$, and $P(F \cap R) = \frac{115}{1000}$ are the probabilities or relative weights stated in relation to the total weight of the original sample space with 1000 elements. The fact that R has happened means that the sample space of concern has been reduced to that with only 300 elements. If $P(R) = \frac{300}{1000}$ is converted to 1 (because in the *reduced sample space* R represents the total space), what are the corresponding changes in $P(M \cap R) = \frac{185}{1000}$ and $P(F \cap R) = \frac{115}{1000}$? To convert $P(R) = \frac{300}{1000}$ to the total weight of 1, $P(R)$ is divided by $P(R)$ itself:

$$\frac{P(R)}{P(R)} = \frac{300}{1000}\frac{1000}{300} = 1$$

To convert $P(M \cap R) = \frac{185}{1000}$ to the same basis, it is divided by the same factor, $P(R)$:

$$\frac{P(M \cap R)}{P(R)} = \frac{185}{1000}\frac{1000}{300} = \frac{185}{300}$$

This is the probability of M given or *conditional to* the knowledge that R has happened, that is, $P(M/R)$. Similarly,

$$P(F/R) = \frac{P(F \cap R)}{P(R)} = \frac{115}{300}$$

Formally the above rule for computing the conditional probability is designated as rule 6:

Rule 6 The conditional probability $P(M/R)$, namely, the probability of event M given the knowledge that event R has happened, is computed as the probability of the intersection of M and R divided by the probability of R, or

$$P(M/R) = \frac{P(M \cap R)}{P(R)}$$

If this expression is true, $P(M \cap R) = P(R) \times P(M/R)$ must be true mathematically; consequently, a corollary of rule 6 is the following rule:

Rule 7 The probability of the intersection of the two events, M and R, is computed as the probability of R multiplied by the conditional probability of M given the knowledge that R has occurred, or

$$P(M \cap R) = P(R) \times P(M/R)$$

For our example, the above rule is verified as

$$P(M \cap R) = \tfrac{300}{1000} \tfrac{185}{300} = \tfrac{185}{1000}$$

Rules 6 and 7 may really be considered one rule instead of two In order to be able to use rule 7 to obtain the probability of $M \cap R$ $P(M/R)$ must be known; i.e., one must go back to rule 6. But in turn in order to obtain $P(M/R)$ by rule 6, the probability of $M \cap R$ is needed There is obviously a vicious circle. It is indeed true that the two rules are of no use if only $P(M)$ and $P(R)$ are known. With these two probabilities alone, there are no rules by which either $P(M/R)$ or $P(M \cap R)$ can be derived.

Finally, the reader should verify and interpret

$$P(R/M) = \frac{P(M \cap R)}{P(M)} = \frac{0.185}{0.550} \approx 0.336$$

Statistical independence and dependence When the knowledge that one event, for example, R, has happened *does not alter* the probability of another event, for example, M (from the one assessed when the knowledge was lacking), then the two events M and R are said to be *statistically independent*. Conversely, when the knowledge that one event (R) has happened *changes* the probability of another event (M), the two events (M and R) are said to be *statistically dependent*.

An obvious example of statistical independence is the case when two events are generated from physically separate experiments as in a toss of two coins. If event 1 is defined as the outcome of the first coin and event 2 as the outcome of the second coin, events 1 and 2 are statistically independent (as well as "physically") because the knowledge of event 1 (say, tails is the outcome) does not affect what happens to the second coin, i.e., event 2, and vice versa. On the other hand, if two events are a major snowstorm and car accidents, the knowledge that a major snowstorm has happened would increase the probability assessed for car accidents. Here the two events are statistically dependent.

Formally, the statistical independence and dependence between two events, M and R, are defined as follows:

If $P(M/R) = P(M)$ and $P(R/M) = P(R)$, M and R are statistically independent.

If $P(M/R) \neq P(M)$ and $P(R/M) \neq P(R)$, M and R are statistically dependent.

It happens that in the readership-survey example, event M (male) and event R (reader) are statistically dependent, as verified below.

$P(M)$, the *unconditional* probability of M (unconditional to whether R happens or not) is $P(M) = \frac{550}{1000} = 0.550$. $P(M/R)$, the conditional probability of M (conditional to R) is $P(M/R) = \frac{185}{300} \approx 0.617$; $P(M) < P(M/R)$. Similarly, $P(R) = 0.300 < P(R/M) \approx 0.336$.

Intuitively, what does the statistical dependence mean in this particular case? Suppose that we were trying to predict whether or not a randomly selected person is a reader of the magazine. If we did not know the sex of the selected individual, we would assign the probability of $P(R) = 0.300$. But if we had the additional information on the selected person that the individual is a male, we would change the assignment of probability to the event that the person is a reader to 0.336. This means that the magazine appeals more to men than women; the information on sex improves the prediction of the magazine readership.[1]

---

[1] If the survey data are changed slightly from those given in Exhibits 6-13 and 6-14 M and R may become statistically independent. For example, if the number of male readers is changed to 165 (from 185) while holding the totals the same but making other necessary changes, M and R would become independent of each other, as the reader may verify.

	Male M	Female F	Marginal or unconditional probability
Read R	$P(M \cap R) = 0.185$	$P(F \cap R) = 0.115$	$P(R) = 0.300$
Not read R'	$P(M \cap R') = 0.365$	$P(F \cap R') = 0.335$	$P(R') = 0.700$
Marginal or unconditional probability	$P(M) = 0.550$	$P(F) = 0.450$	$P(M \cup F)$ or $P(R' \cup R')$ or 1.000

Exhibit 6-15 Magazine-readership probability table.

Observe that when two events are statistically independent, the formula for the probability of the joint event,

$$P(M \cap R) = P(R) \times P(M/R)$$

reduces to $P(M \cap R) = P(R) \times P(M)$, because $P(M/R) = P(M)$. Thus, in the experiment of tossing two coins, the probability of the joint event, say, of both coins falling heads, or $H_1 \cap H_2$ (where the subscripts 1 and 2 refer to the first and second coins, respectively), is

$$P(H_1 \cap H_2) = P(H_1) \times P(H_2/H_1) = P(H_1) \times P(H_2) = \tfrac{1}{2} \times \tfrac{1}{2} = \tfrac{1}{4}$$

Exhibit 6-15 summarizes the probabilities of various events of the magazine-readership example in a useful probability-table form. The probabilities of the intersections of events are often called the *joint probabilities*. The inner four entries in Exhibit 6-15 are joint probabilities. The unconditional probability (often called *marginal probability* in the sense that it is shown in the margin of the probability table) of, say, event M, namely, $P(M)$ is the sum of the joint probabilities, $P(M \cap R)$ = 0.185 and $P(M \cap R') = 0.365$. Note that conditional probabilities such as $P(R/M)$ are not shown in Exhibit 6-15.

6-4 SUMMARY AND TRANSITION

This chapter started out by noting that in many decision situations the effect of uncertainty in the future cannot be ignored. Once it is decided that uncertainty must be explicitly recognized, the task of relating alternative acts to predicted consequences becomes a lot more complicated than in the cases where certainty can be safely assumed. For each alternative act, consequences have to be predicted contingent upon or, conditional to, various possible events. When the result of this task is summarized in tabular form, it is called the conditional payoff table.

According to the conditional payoff table, one act may be preferred to another act if a certain event happens, but the preference ranking of the acts may be reversed if other events occur. Decision theorists provide guides to solve the dilemma. One decision principle suggested is the minimax principle; another, the principle of weighting possible outcomes or, in short, the *expected-value* criterion. This chapter has not attempted to reject or justify these decision principles. More will be said on this subject in Chaps. 8 and 9. At this time it is merely observed that a major part of modern statistical decision theory is based on the principle of weighting possible outcomes.

A crucial step in following the criterion of weighting possible outcomes is the assignment of proper weights to consequences, i.e., to various events. Weights are to be assigned according to the likelihood of occurrence of various events. Weights assigned according to the likelihood are synonymous to probabilities. Herein lies the motivation for studying the theory of probability. Knowing the theorems or rules of probability (as developed by mathematicians) enables us to assign correct weights to events; they provide means by which appropriate weights are assigned to derived events from the events whose weights are already known, and provide checks for internal consistency.

In Chaps. 8 and 9 it will become clearer how probabilities are used in decisions under uncertainty and why such incorporation of probabilities in the decision analysis is reasonable and desirable, but before that, some further technical aspects of probability, i.e., probability assignment to events generated by different types of random experiments or processes, will be studied in Chap. 7.

QUESTIONS AND PROBLEMS

1. (a) Distinguish the assumptions of decision under certainty and decision under uncertainty.

(b) Distinguish the relation under certainty and the relation under uncertainty.

2. Explain and evaluate two of the decision criteria or principles given in this chapter.

3. Define or explain random experiment, sample space, event, probability, mutually exclusive events, collectively exhaustive events, complementary events, union of events, intersection of events, and Venn diagram.

4. Speculate which steps an insurance company would follow in setting insurance premiums for its life insurance policies, automobile collision insurance policies, and group health insurance policies.

5. Discussing next week's demand for a certain tool in a plant, the manager of the tool room makes the following statement. "The chances for no demand are the same as those for the demand for more than five tools, about 1 in 20. I'd give an even chance (fifty-fifty chance) that the demand will be more than three. Further, I believe that there is about 3 in 10 chance of the demand being two or less and a 1 in 5 chance of the demand being more than four. The probability of the demand being two is about the same as that of the demand for five.''

(a) Consistent with the above statement, give the probabilities for the next week's demands.

(b) Compute the weighted average weekly demand or the expected weekly demand.

6. The table shows the results of a survey of 1500 major automobile collision accidents on a certain highway during a given period.

Total major collision accidents	1500
Number of drivers wearing seat belts	825
Total number of drivers fatally injured	483
Number of drivers fatally injured among those wearing seat belts	132

(a) Select a driver at random from the total 1500 accidents surveyed. (1) What is the probability that he has had a fatal injury? (2) What is the probability that he has not suffered a fatal injury? (3) What is the probability that he had a seat belt on?

(b) Suppose that the driver picked in part (a) had his seat belt on. What is the probability that he did not suffer a fatal injury?

(c) What is the probability that a randomly selected driver had his seat belt on and still suffered a fatal injury?

(d) Are the events wearing seat belt and fatal injury statistically dependent on each other? Do seat belts help prevent fatal injuries?

7. In PERT network drawings, if the sequential relations among three tasks, A, B, C, are represented as in the following diagram, it means that A can be performed independently of B and C but C cannot be started until B is completed. When both A and C are finished, the whole job is considered done. Suppose that the possible completion times for A are 10, 11, and 12 days with the probabilities of 0.3, 0.6, and 0.1, respectively; for B, 5, 6, and 7 days with the probabilities of 0.4, 0.3, and 0.3, respectively; for C, 3 and 4 days with the probabilities of 0.5 and 0.5, respectively.

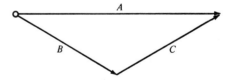

(a) What are the possible completion days for the whole job and the associated probabilities?

(b) What is the probability that the whole job will be completed in 10 days if it is known that B takes more than 5 days?

(c) What is the probability that the job takes less than 8 days?

8. From a lot of 200 parts that contains 5 percent defective units, two items are selected at random for testing.

(a) What is the probability that the first item selected will be defective? Good?

(*b*) What is the probability that the second item selected is defective given the fact that the first item was defective, assuming that the first item has been returned to the lot after testing?

(*c*) Repeat part (*b*) assuming that the first item has not been returned to the lot after testing.

9. Consider a random experiment wherein a red die and a black die are tossed simultaneously. The experiment is assumed to consist of only one trial, i.e., the two dice are thrown only once. One of the many possible ways of listing all possible outcomes is a sample space consisting of the elementary events as described by a set, S

$$S = [(1, 1), (1, 2), (1, 3), (1, 4), (1, 5), (1, 6),$$
$$(2, 1), (2, 2), (2, 3), (2, 4), (2, 5), (2, 6),$$
$$(3, 1), (3, 2), (3, 3), (3, 4), (3, 5), (3, 6),$$
$$(4, 1), (4, 2), (4, 3), (4, 4), (4, 5), (4, 6),$$
$$(5, 1), (5, 2), (5, 3), (5, 4), (5, 5), (5, 6),$$
$$(6, 1), (6, 2), (6, 3), (6, 4), (6, 5), (6, 6)]$$

Each of the 36 elements of the set is an ordered pair of the numbers appearing on the red die and the black die. For example, the element (2, 1) represents a possible outcome of the experiment, namely, 2 on the red die and 1 on the black die. In general, (*r*, *b*) represents the event that the number on the red die is *r* and the number on the black die is *b*. In the Venn diagram representation of the sample space S, its 36 elements are shown as 36 dots; P represents element (4, 5), i.e., the event where 4 on the red die and 5 on the black die appear; Q represents element (3, 2), the event 3 on the red die and 2 on the black die. Both dice are fair.

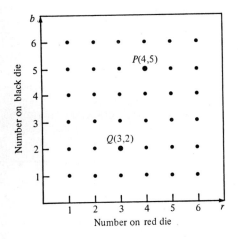

(*a*) Define verbally event A, which consists of (*r*, *b*)'s that satisfy $r + b = 8$.
(*b*) Define verbally event B, which consists of (*r*, *b*)'s that satisfy $r + b = 9$.
(*c*) Define verbally event C, which consists of (*r*, *b*)'s that satisfy either $r + b = 8$ or $r + b = 9$.
(*d*) Define verbally event D, which consists of (*r*, *b*)'s that satisfy both $r + b = 8$ and $r + b = 9$.
(*e*) Show A, B, C, D on the Venn diagram.
(*f*) What are the probabilities of A, B, C, D, A/B, B/A, A/C, $A \cup B$, $A \cap B$, A', and C'?

(*g*) Define verbally and show on the Venn diagram event G, which consists of (r, b)'s satisfying $r + b \geq 8$, and event H, defined as the event that b is either 3 or 4.

(*h*) Define verbally and find the probabilities of $G \cup H$, $G \cap H$, H/G, and G/H.

(*i*) Are H and G statistically independent?

(*j*) Define verbally and find the probabilities of $r = 1$, $r = 1/b = 2$, $b = 3$, and $b = 3/r = 4$.

(*k*) Suppose an option to play or not to play the following gamble is offered to you. If $r + b$ is more than 6, you receive the same dollar amount as the difference between r and b. If $r + b$ is less than 6, you pay the same dollar amount as the difference between r and b. If $r + b = 6$, you neither receive nor pay any. (1) Construct the conditional payoff table that would help you make the decision. (2) What would your decision be under the minimax criterion and under the expected-value criterion (weighting possible outcomes), respectively? Which of the two coincides with your personal, intuitive decision? How would you explain to others that your decision is rational? (3) How much would you pay to play the game (or not to play the game as the case may be)?

7
Probability Functions

7-0 INTRODUCTION

According to the last chapter, a critical element in applying the criterion of weighting possible outcomes, i.e., the expected-value criterion, to decisions under uncertainty is that probabilities are assigned to events or, more formally, *a set of events is related to a set of relative weights or probabilities*. This fits the definition of a function, given in Chap. 1. In other words, given a decision situation involving uncertainty, there exists a specific *probability function* that relates a set of events (or associated consequences) to a set of probabilities. As in Chap. 1, a probability function can be represented in process-diagram form, as in Exhibit 7-1.

For a given event, say E_i, the functional relation (or process or rule of conversion) yields a corresponding probability value which is denoted by $P(E_i)$. A particular functional relation would be determined by the particular nature of the event-generating mechanism or random process particular to the given decision situation. For instance, if payoffs

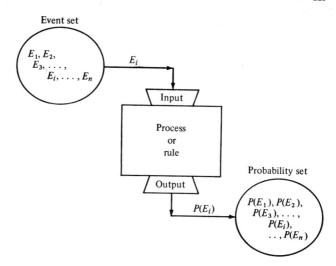

Exhibit 7-1 Process diagram of a probability function.

resulting from a given decision are dependent upon the outcome of a toss of an honest coin, the random process involved is the toss of the coin, and it would generate a set of two possible events, heads and tails, which in turn is related by the particular probability function to a set of probabilities, $\frac{1}{2}$ and $\frac{1}{2}$. If the coin is crooked, the coin-tossing random experiment yields a probability function different from that for an honest coin; e.g., the coin may be so loaded that heads and tails might be associated with the probabilities of, say, $\frac{2}{5}$ and $\frac{3}{5}$, respectively. In notation, the functional relation between events and probabilities may be represented by $P = f(E_i)$ or simply $P = f(E)$, where P, the dependent variable, stands for probability values and E_i or E, the independent variable, for various events.

As in the relations encountered in Chaps. 1 to 3, the relation between probabilities and events may be stated in a specific mathematical statement. Unlike the relations of those chapters, however, in the probability-event relationship not many real-world event-generating processes can be approximated by such simple functional forms as linear and quadratic. Over the centuries, mathematicians and statisticians have studied properties of a number of specific (mostly nonlinear) probability functions that can be used as approximations of the probability-event relations in real-world random phenomena. This chapter introduces some of the probability functions that are used widely in scientific analyses. Specifically, the following *classes* of random processes and associated probability functions will be introduced.

Class of random process	*Class of probability function*
Bernoulli process	Binomial probability function
Poisson process	Poisson probability function (and exponential probability function)
Normal process	Normal probability function

Just as the relation between the total cost of production and the number of units produced can be *modeled* as a linear volume-cost process in a given firm in a given period, a given event-generating mechanism in the real world can be modeled by a *Bernoulli process*. Further, just as $C = a + bx$ refers to the whole class of linear volume-cost situations, the binomial probability-function formula would refer to the whole class of Bernoulli random processes; and just as the definition of the parameters a and b in the linear-function formula would specify a particular linear cost function for a given situation, the definition of the parameters of the binomial probability-function formula would specify a particular binomial function. The same can be said of the other two processes listed above. Although all three processes in the list will be studied, the chapter deals in detail only with the Bernoulli process. Preliminary to its discussion the concepts of what are called random variables and the probability function in general are defined.

7-1 RANDOM VARIABLES AND PROBABILITY FUNCTIONS

Conceptually, variables in a functional relation may represent sets of various *qualitative* descriptions rather than sets of numbers. For example, a set of alternative girls one might marry (Mary, Jane, etc.) and a set of consequences of marrying different girls may be the two variables in a functional relation between alternative acts and predicted consequences. Then, the consequences of marriage are said to be a function of the girl one marries. One can even define some specific pattern of the relationship: if the girl is intelligent, the corresponding consequences are . . . ; if the girl is not intelligent, the corresponding consequences are . . . ; etc. But mathematics cannot be of much help when the decision situation is represented by relations where the alternative acts and consequences, i.e., variables, are qualitative descriptions, not represented by some meaningful numerical values. Thus, an effort is made to characterize different girls by some numerical measurements, i.e., to *quantify*. For instance, it may be meaningful and useful for the selection-of-wife decision problem that different girls are characterized by the number of cavities in their teeth; one of the relevant marital consequences would be dental-care costs. Then mathematics can be of great help in locating the girl with lowest expected dental-care costs. Admittedly, quantitative measures are only a partial and imperfect representation of the qualitative "thing itself" being measured, but in complex situations, they are an indispensable aid to decisions.

In dealing with probability functions, too, when the independent variable, or event, is described qualitatively, such as heads and tails (in the coin-tossing experiment) and clear without wind, rainy with wind, etc. (in the weather case), not much benefit can be expected of mathematical analysis. Attempts therefore are made to represent various possible events by some meaningful numerical values. If it is meaningful to the decision at hand, various weather conditions can be characterized by temperature, or even a composite measure of wind velocity and temperature. Likewise, four possible events, TT, TH, HT, HH, in the experiment of tossing two coins, may be given the numerical representation of 0, 1, 1, 2, according to the number of heads appearing. When various events are given some numerical characterization, the set is called a *random variable*. Formally, a random variable is *a set of numerical values corresponding to the various possible events of a sample space.*

For the same random experiment, there may be alternative ways of defining the random variable. (Just as different girls may be characterized by such alternative quantitative measures as the number of cavities, weight, age, etc.) In the traffic-volume–bridge-construction problem of Example 6-1, the outcomes of the traffic-volume-generating random process may be most naturally quantified by the number of cars per hour, so that the event of low volume is measured by 2000 cars per hour; medium volume by 4000 cars per hour; and high volume by 6000 cars per hour. The set of numbers [2000, 4000, 6000] may be considered a random variable. But another way of defining the random variable in the same situation may be the set of numbers representing the conditional cost consequences of the first act, i.e., the four-lane act, [$30 million, $60 million, $80 million], inasmuch as these numbers also represent the outcomes of the same traffic-volume-generating random process (given the first act). Likewise, given the act of building a six-lane bridge, the outcomes of the same random process may be characterized by a new random variable, [$50 million, $50 million, $75 million]. Another random variable may be the set of [$60 million, $60 million, $60 million], the cost resulting from various traffic volumes conditional to the third act (of building an eight-lane bridge).

Similarly, in reference to the decision situation involving the experiment of tossing two coins in Example 6-2, at least three random variables can be defined. According to payoff table (*b*) of Exhibit 6-12, one random variable is the variable that can assume 0, 1, 2 (according to the

Random variable, number of heads	0	1	2
Probability	0.25	0.50	0.25

Exhibit 7-2a Probability function in table form.

number of heads), corresponding to the four possible events, *TT*, *TH*, *HT*, *HH*. Another random variable is the variable that can take on 12, −6, −3 (dollar payoffs of the act *play*), again corresponding to the four possible events. Still another random variable is the variable that can take on 0, 0, 0 (dollar payoffs of the act *not play*).

Once the random variable is defined as above, the probability function can be considered as the relationship between various events and probabilities or alternatively as the relationship between a random variable and probabilities. Probability functions are sometimes called probability distributions.

WAYS OF REPRESENTING PROBABILITY FUNCTIONS

As in other functions, probability functions may be represented in tabular form, in graphic form, and in mathematical notation. Exhibits 7-2a and 7-2b show the probability function of the random variable, the number of heads in reference to the random experiment of tossing two coins. Simple as the probability function of this example is, it is instructive to observe the following points:

1. The random variable, the number of heads, is a discrete variable, as defined in Chap. 1. The variable can take on only three values, 0, 1, 2. Point Q is not an element of the function.

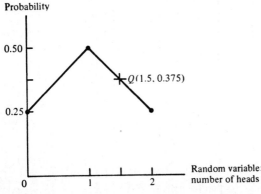

Probability

0.50

$Q(1.5, 0.375)$

0.25

Random variable:
number of heads

0   1   2

Exhibit 7-2b Probability function in graph form.

2. The sum of all probabilities is $0.25 + 0.50 + 0.25 = 1.00$. In any probability function, the sum of all probabilities of all possible values of the random variable should be 1. A *value* of the random variable corresponds to one of the mutually exclusive and collectively exhaustive events (see rule 1 of Chap. 6).

3. There is no prartical *specific* mathematical functional form that can characterize the probability function of this example. Of course, *in general form*, the function could be written $P = f(x)$, where P stands for probability and x for the number of heads.

EXAMPLE 7-1

In Prob. 9 of Chap. 6, the probabilities of various events connected with the event-generating experiment of tossing two fair dice, red and black, were examined. A sample space there consisted of 36 elementary events, (r, b)'s, where r represents an outcome of the red die and b an outcome of the black die. For example, $(2, 5)$ is an outcome where 2 appears on the red die and 5 appears on the black die.

Now, for the same experiment, define another sample space represented by the set $S = [2, 3, 4, 5, 6, 7, 8, 9, 10, 11, 12]$, where each element in the set represents the *sum* of the numbers on two dice. Eleven integers between 2 and 12 (inclusive) exhaust all possible outcomes of the experiment. If 3 is on the red die and 5 on the black die, the sum is 8; if 6 is on the red die and 6 on the black die, the sum is 12; and so on. The sum of the numbers on the two dice is a random variable, inasmuch as the various numerical values the variable can assume correspond to the various outcomes or events of the random experiment. If this random variable is denoted by s, its probability function $P = f(s)$ is specified in tabular form as in Exhibit 7-3a. The graphic representation of the same data is given in Exhibit 7-3b.

Again observe that this particular probability function is discrete and that the sum of all probabilities is 1.

A more formal way of describing the probability function is by mathematical statements such as

$$P = f(s) = \begin{cases} \dfrac{s-1}{36} & \text{for } 2 \le s \le 7 \\[2mm] \dfrac{13-s}{36} & \text{for } 8 \le s \le 12 \qquad s \text{ an integer} \\[2mm] 0 & \text{for all other values of } s \end{cases}$$

The reader may verify that the probability table of Exhibit 7-3a can be reproduced from the above set of mathematical statements of the probability function.

Random variable s, sum of two numbers	2	3	4	5	6	7	8	9	10	11	12
Probability $P = f(s)$	$\frac{1}{36}$	$\frac{2}{36}$	$\frac{3}{36}$	$\frac{4}{36}$	$\frac{5}{36}$	$\frac{6}{36}$	$\frac{5}{36}$	$\frac{4}{36}$	$\frac{3}{36}$	$\frac{2}{36}$	$\frac{1}{36}$

Exhibit 7-3a   Tabular representation of a probability function.

Cumulative distributions   Often an analyst's interest is not in the probability that the random variable is a particular value such as $s = 9$ or $s = 3$ but in the probability that the random variable is less than or greater than a particular value.   In connection with the experiment at hand, the payoffs of alternative acts may depend on whether the sum of the two numbers is less than, say, 5.   (For example, the decision maker may gain \$10 if the sum of the numbers is less than 5 but lose \$6 if not.) Of interest, then, are the probability that the sum of the two numbers is less than 5 and the probability that it is not.

The functional relationship between a random variable and its probability may be stated so that the probability of the random variable being less or greater than a specified value can be more readily obtained. When the function is given in such form, it is called a *cumulative (probability) distribution*.   Exhibit 7-4 gives a cumulative distribution of the random variable s in tabular form.   The probability of the sum s being less than 2 is 0; that is, $P(s < 2) = 0$.   This is so, of course, because

$$P(s < 2) = \sum_{i=0}^{1} P(s = i) = P(s = 0) + P(s = 1) = 0 + 0 = 0$$

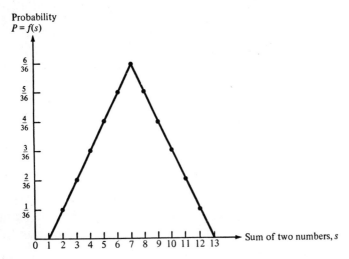

Exhibit 7-3b   Graphic representation of a probability function.

$P(s = 0) = P(s = 1) = 0$ because the lowest possible sum of the numbers on the two dice is 2 (when 1 on the red die and also 1 on the black die).

$P(s < 13) = 1$, because $s < 13$ covers all possible values of s between 2 and 12 inclusive. Probabilities of all possible values of the random variable (or equivalently, of all possible events) should add up to 1.

The probability that the sum of the two numbers is less than 5, namely, $P(s < 5)$, is $\frac{6}{36}$. For,

$$P(s < 5) = \sum_{i=0}^{4} P(s = i)$$

$$= P(s = 0) + P(s = 1) + P(s = 2) + P(s = 3) + P(s = 4)$$

$$= 0 + 0 + \frac{1}{36} + \frac{2}{36} + \frac{3}{36}$$

$$= \frac{6}{36}$$

Note that $s < 5$ does not include $s = 5$; accordingly, $P(s < 5)$ does not include $P(s = 5)$.

Since the probabilities of all possible values of the random variable should always add up to 1, if the probability that the sum of the two numbers is *less than 5* is $\frac{6}{36}$, the probability that the sum of the numbers is *not less than 5* must be $1 - \frac{6}{36}$, namely, $\frac{30}{36}$. The sum of the two numbers is *not less than 5* when it is *either equal to 5 or greater than 5*. Thus, the probability that the sum of the two numbers is *equal to or greater than 5* is $\frac{30}{36}$. Formally,

$$P(s \geq 5) = 1 - P(s < 5) = 1 - \frac{6}{36} = \frac{30}{36}$$

Next, assume a decision situation where the payoffs of alternative acts depend on whether the sum of the two numbers is *equal to or less than 5* rather than simply *less than 5*. For an analysis of the decision, the cumulative distribution of Exhibit 7-4 would have to be slightly modified. The modified distribution is shown in Exhibit 7-5.

The only difference between the two cumulative distributions is that whereas in Exhibit 7-4 probabilities are given in *less-than* form, $P(s < s)$, in Exhibit 7-5 they are in *less-than-or-equal-to* form, $P(s \leq s)$.

Random variable s, sum of two numbers	2	3	4	5	6	7	8	9	10	11	12	13
Probability that s is less than s	$\frac{0}{36}$	$\frac{1}{36}$	$\frac{3}{36}$	$\frac{6}{36}$	$\frac{10}{36}$	$\frac{15}{36}$	$\frac{21}{36}$	$\frac{26}{36}$	$\frac{30}{36}$	$\frac{33}{36}$	$\frac{35}{36}$	$\frac{36}{36}$

Exhibit 7-4 Cumulative distribution of s.

Random variable s, sum of two numbers	2	3	4	5	6	7	8	9	10	11	12
Probability that s is equal to or less than s	$\frac{1}{36}$	$\frac{3}{36}$	$\frac{6}{36}$	$\frac{10}{36}$	$\frac{15}{36}$	$\frac{21}{36}$	$\frac{26}{36}$	$\frac{30}{36}$	$\frac{33}{36}$	$\frac{35}{36}$	$\frac{36}{36}$

Exhibit 7-5 Cumulative distribution of s.

According to Exhibit 7-4,

$$P(s < 5) = \sum_{i=0}^{4} P(s = i) = P(s = 0)$$
$$+ P(s = 1) + P(s = 2) + P(s = 3) + P(s = 4)$$
$$= \tfrac{6}{36}$$

According to Exhibit 7-5,

$$P(s \le 5) = \sum_{i=0}^{5} P(s = i) = P(s = 0) + P(s = 1)$$
$$+ P(s = 2) + P(s = 3) + P(s = 4) + P(s = 5)$$
$$= \tfrac{10}{36}$$

$P(s \le 5)$ includes $P(s = 5)$ in addition to $P(s < 5)$. To restate:

$$P(s \le 5) = P(s < 5) + P(s = 5)$$

The reader should also verify that

$$P(s \le 5) = P(s < 6)$$
$$P(s > 5) = 1 - P(s \le 5)$$
$$P(s \le 5) = 1 - P(s > 5)$$
$$P(s = 5) = P(s < 6) - P(s < 5) = P(s > 4) - P(s > 5)$$
$$P(s < 5) + P(s = 5) + P(s > 5) = 1$$

The graphic representation of the cumulative distribution of Exhibit 7-5 is presented in Exhibit 7-6.

Continuous probability functions Many real-world random processes can be dealt with using discrete random variables, but when the number of possible values that a discrete random variable can assume becomes large, it is difficult to manipulate mathematically. Thus, an analyst prefers that the random variables under investigation can be assumed continuous. For example, consider a teenage girl making a telephone call. What are the possible lengths of her telephone conversation? From what is known about the girl's habits and those of teenagers in

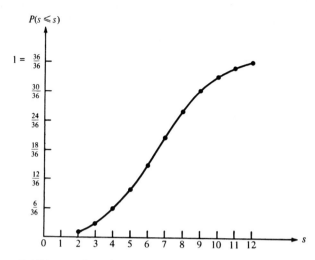

Exhibit 7-6   Cumulative distribution.

general, assume that the conversation is going to last somewhere between 0 and 120 min.   (This is quite an assumption because if she *could* talk for 120 min, there is no reason why she could not talk for 121, 122 min, and so on.   But for simplicity, it is assumed here that she would never talk beyond 120 min.)

If the possible lengths (in minutes) of the telephone conversation are denoted by x, x is a random variable.   How many possible values of x are there? x could be 0 min, it could be 5.65479207 min, provided that there is a watch that can measure 1/100,000,000 min.   *Conceptually,* though not practically, the random variable x may be treated as a continuous variable—in the sense that the interval between any two numbers of x (within the interval of 0 to 120 min) can be segmented into infinitely many infinitely small subintervals.

How are probabilities to these infinitely many possible values of the variable to be assigned?   For example, what is the probability of the talk's lasting exactly 0 min?   What is the probability of its lasting exactly 5.654792071 min in contrast to that of exactly $5.654792071\tfrac{1}{2}$ min?   When one recalls the cardinal rule of probability of Chap. 6 that the sum of the probabilities of all possible outcomes (values of the random variable) must be 1, the difficulty of the task is obvious.   Even if a very small—almost infinitely small—probability is assigned to each possible value, the infinite number of these very small probabilities would add up to more than 1, indeed, an infinitely large number.   (For even if a very small probability of, say, 0.000000000001 is assigned to each possible value, an infinite number of times of this will be infinity.)   Conceptually, therefore, the only way out of the difficulty is to assign an *infinitely small* probability, denoted by 0, to each possible value of the random variable. Then, again conceptually, an infinite number of times this infinitely small probability is seen to add up to 1.

Assignment of 0 probability to each of an infinite number of all possible values of the random variable sounds a bit contrived and makes one feel somewhat uneasy, particularly because it was decided earlier in Chap. 6 to assign a probability of 0 to events that are *certain not to occur*, or impossible to happen. When we assign the probability of zero to a possible event, or a *possible* value of the random variable, say, *exactly* 4 min, are we saying that the event that the telephone talk lasts *exactly* 4 min is certain not to happen? Though the paradox is real, a further conceptual contrivance may get us out of the trouble. What can be done is to agree that although we assign 0 probability to an impossible event, we do not accept the converse; in other words, 0 probability does not necessarily mean that the event is impossible to happen. The event with zero probability is considered *possible*, but with an infinitely small likelihood. (Assignment of zero probability to an event exactly 4 min is not too unreasonable when it is kept in mind that *exactly 4 min* refers not to 4.001 min, not to 4.00000001 min, but to 4.0000000000 . . . , where the dots denote "and so on infinitely without limit."

In the face of these conceptual and practical difficulties in assigning probability to a single, specified value, more meaningful is the assignment of probabilities with regards to the continuous variable in the following sense.

Suppose that it is more likely that the call will last somewhere between 10 and 20 min than that it will last somewhere between 90 and 100 min. Then a higher probability must be assigned to the 10-min *interval* between 10 and 20 min of the random variable than to the 10-min *interval* between 90 and 100 min. In the case of the continuous random variable, some definite probability values make sense only in terms of *intervals* of the random variable. Thus, for the example on hand, specific probabilities may be assigned to specific intervals, as in the probability table on Exhibit 7-7.

Interval	0 to 10	10 to 20	20 to 30	30 to 40	40 to 50	50 to 60	60 to 70	70 to 80	80 to 90	90 to 100	100 to 110	110 to 120
Probability	0.20	0.30	0.20	0.10	0.07	0.05	0.03	0.02	0.01	0.01	0.01	0.00

Exhibit 7-7 Interval probabilities of a continuous variable.

Notes on Exhibit 7-7

1. The probabilities of all intervals add up to 1. In other words, the probability of the call's lasting somewhere between 0 and 120 min is 1.

2. Boundary values of the intervals are included in two adjoining intervals. For instance, the value of the variable 20 (min) is included in the interval 10 to 20 and also in the interval 20 to 30 as the ending and the beginning boundary of the two intervals, respectively. No harm is done by this double inclusion, because $P(x = 20) = 0$. In the continuous case, $\leq$ may be replaced by $<$ and $\geq$ by $>$ at any time. For example, $P(10 \leq x \leq 20) = P(10 < x < 20) = 0.30$.

3. Probabilities of smaller intervals can be added together in order to obtain probabilities of larger intervals. Thus,

$$P(10 \leq x \leq 30) = P(10 \leq x \leq 20)$$
$$+ P(20 \leq x \leq 30) = 0.30 + 0.20 = 0.50$$

Turning now to the graphic representation, in the case of a continuous probability function, a probability value of a given interval is conventionally represented by the *size of an area* shown above that interval. Thus, to represent $P(10 \leq x \leq 20) = 0.30$, a rectangular area is erected above the interval 10 to 20 that has an *area* of 0.30 as in the diagram.

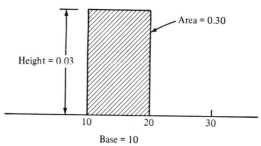

Because the base of the rectangle above is 10 (or $20 - 10$). the height of the rectangle must be 0.03 to make the area 0.30, (Area of rectangle = base × height = 10 × 0.03 = 0.3.) Exhibit 7-8 shows the graph or *histogram* drawn according to this convention.

In Exhibit 7-8, the vertical axis does *not* give the probability values directly as for the discrete probability function. In the continuous case, the vertical axis measures the "height" value, or *the density*, which when multiplied by the width of the interval yields the area of the rectangle erected above the interval, namely, the probability of that interval. Thus, $P(30 \leq x \leq 40)$ can be obtained from Exhibit 7-8 by reading the height value, or density, of the rectangle above the interval $30 \leq x \leq 40$

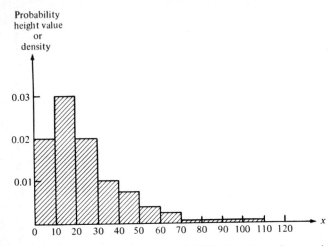

Exhibit 7-8 Histogram of the probability function of a continuous random variable.

on the vertical axis as 0.01 and then multiplying this value, 0.01, by the width of the interval, 10 (or 40 − 30); i.e.,

$$P(30 \leq x \leq 40) = \text{height value} \times \text{width}$$
$$= 0.01(10) = 0.10$$

Since the probabilities of all possible intervals must add up to 1, the sum of all shaded areas in Exhibit 7-8 is 1.

The choice of the size of the interval, 10 min, above was quite arbitrary. The interval chosen for illustration could have been 40, 5, 1 min or any other duration. If the 1-min interval had been chosen, there would have been 120 intervals between 0 and 120, and the graphic representation would have looked like Exhibit 7-9. There are 120 small rectangles; the area of each represents the probability of each 1-min interval. The areas of the 120 rectangles add up to 1.

Conceptually, the interval can be made smaller and smaller. In fact, it is mathematically very convenient to imagine an infinitely small interval. Then, the graphic representation would become something like Exhibit 7-10. Still the total area under the curve between 0 and 120 of x, made up of an *infinite* number of *infinitely* small "rectangular" areas, should be 1. The probability of any interval is represented by the area under the curve above the interval, i.e., the sum of all infinitely small rectangular areas within the specified interval. Thus

$$P(6 \leq x \leq 25) = P(6 < x < 25) = \text{area } A$$
$$P(50 \leq x \leq 70) = P(50 < x < 70) = \text{area } B$$

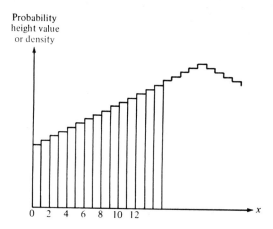

Probability
height value
or density

0   2   4   6   8   10 12   x

Exhibit 7-9   Histogram with 1-min intervals.

To repeat, the height of the curve corresponding to *a particular single value* of x does not represent the probability directly.   The height represents only the density.   In the continuous case, the *area* under the curve over a given interval represents the probability of the interval. If the heights of the curve, or densities, over a certain interval are larger than the heights or densities over some other interval, the probability of the former interval would be larger than the probability of the latter interval if the two are of the same width.

Height, or density, as defined above is obviously a function of the random variable.   When the probability function of a continuous random variable is represented in terms of the density over the random

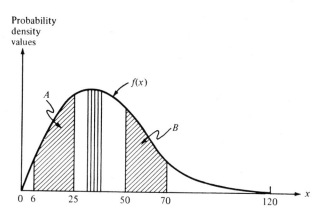

Probability
density
values

$f(x)$

A

B

0   6   25   50   70   120   x

Exhibit 7-10   Histogram for infinitely small intervals or density function.

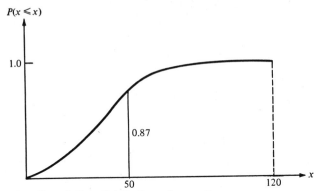

Exhibit 7-11a   Cumulative distribution of a continuous random variable.

variable, it is called the *probability density function* in order to distinguish it from the probability function of a discrete variable, where the height of the curve itself represents the probability of the corresponding value of the random variable and which is often called the *probability mass function.*[1]

As in the case of discrete variables, the cumulative function can be defined for continuous variables.   Exhibits 7-11a and 7-11b show the cumulative distribution derived from the density function of Exhibit 7-10.   The height of the curve of Exhibit 7-11a corresponding to a speci-

[1] Some do not distinguish the two but use the term density function even for discrete cases.

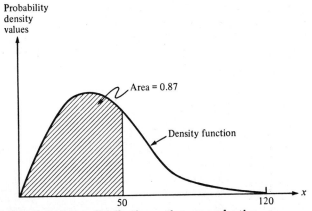

Exhibit 7-11b   Cumulative distribution as the area under the density function.

fied x value represents the cumulative probability. Thus, the cumulative probability, $P(x \leq 50)$ or $P(x < 50)$, is the height of the cumulative curve, 0.87. This value, 0.87, would be shown as the shaded area in the graph of the density function of Exhibit 7-11b.

With this general understanding of the probability function, we proceed to study the three specific classes of random processes and the associated probability functions named earlier. First the Bernoulli random process and its probability function, the binomial probability, are discussed by means of an example.

7-2 BERNOULLI PROCESS AND BINOMIAL PROBABILITY FUNCTION

EXAMPLE 7-2

Five shots are fired at a target from a gun. The probability of each shot's hitting the target, i.e., of being successful, is assumed to be $\frac{1}{6}$. The outcomes (hit or miss, or success or failure) of the five shots are *independent* of one another; i.e., the particular results of earlier shots do not change the probability of hit or miss of successive shots, and vice versa. What is the probability that exactly two out of five shots are successful in hitting the target?

To list some of the possible outcomes of the five shots, let S stand for success (hit), F for failure (miss). Then, $SSFSF$ would denote an event where the first two shots are successes, the third failure, the fourth success, and the fifth failure. This, of course is only one out of a number of cases of three successes out of five shots. Some other cases of three successes are $SSSFF$, i.e., the first three shots successes, the last two failures; $SFFSS$; etc. An extreme event, rather unlikely, is $SSSSS$, all shots resulting in success. The other extreme is the event that all shots miss, or $FFFFF$.

Returning to the events of interest in the problem, how many events are there where exactly two successes out of five shots occur? All possible events of two successes out of five shots are listed below:

$SSFFF$	$FSSFF$	$FFSSF$	$FFFSS$
$SFSFF$	$FSFSF$	$FFSFS$	
$SFFSF$	$FSFFS$		
$SFFFS$			

In all there are ten possible orders in which two successes out of five trials may happen. Since if one of these ten events happens, the other nine events cannot happen, these events are mutually exclusive.

Thus, the probability of two successes out of five shots (regardless of the order in which two successes and three failures appear) is the probability of the *union* of the above ten mutually exclusive events and therefore can be calculated by adding their probabilities (see rule 3 of Chap. 6). The next logical task is to find the probability of each of these ten possible outcomes.

What is the probability of *SSFFF*, the first of these ten? *SSFFF* is considered to have happened if and only if the first shot results in success *and* the second shot in success *and* the third shot in failure *and* the fourth shot in failure *and* the fifth shot in failure. Thus, *SSFFF* is the intersection, or joint event, of these five events. Because these five events are assumed to be independent of one another, the probability of the intersection is, according to rule 7 of Chap. 6,

$$P(SSFFF) = P(S) \times P(S) \times P(F) \times P(F) \times P(F)$$
$$= \tfrac{1}{6} \times \tfrac{1}{6} \times \tfrac{5}{6} \times \tfrac{5}{6} \times \tfrac{5}{6} = (\tfrac{1}{6})^2(\tfrac{5}{6})^3 = \tfrac{125}{7776}$$

Likewise, for the second event,

$$P(SFSFF) = P(S) \times P(F) \times P(S) \times P(F) \times P(F)$$
$$= \tfrac{1}{6} \times \tfrac{5}{6} \times \tfrac{1}{6} \times \tfrac{5}{6} \times \tfrac{5}{6} = (\tfrac{1}{6})^2(\tfrac{5}{6})^3 = \tfrac{125}{7776}$$

Evidently the probability of each of the ten possible cases of two successes out of five trials can be calculated as $(\tfrac{1}{6})^2(\tfrac{5}{6})^3 = \tfrac{125}{7776}$. The probability of the event that two out of five shots are successes, then, can be obtained by adding $\tfrac{125}{7776}$ ten times, i.e., $10(\tfrac{125}{7776}) = \tfrac{1250}{7776}$.

By applying the same process the probability of any given number of successes can be determined. For example, the probability of the event that four out of five shots are successes is computed as follows.

Step 1   List all possible orders in which four successes can occur.

SSSSF   *SFSSS*   *SSFSS*   *SSSFS*   *FSSSS*

There are five possible cases in all.

Step 2   Find the probability of each of all possible cases. For example, find $P(SSSSF)$. *SSSSF* is the joint event of the five independent events, namely, the event that the first shot is a success, the event that the second shot is a success, the event that the third shot is a success, the event that the fourth shot is a success, *and* the event that the fifth is a failure. Thus, its probability is

$$P(SSSSF) = P(S) \times P(S) \times P(S) \times P(S) \times P(F)$$
$$= \tfrac{1}{6} \times \tfrac{1}{6} \times \tfrac{1}{6} \times \tfrac{1}{6} \times \tfrac{5}{6} = (\tfrac{1}{6})^4(\tfrac{5}{6})^1 = \tfrac{5}{7776}$$

Likewise,

$$P(SSFSS) = P(S) \times P(S) \times P(F) \times P(S) \times P(S)$$
$$= (\tfrac{1}{6})^4(\tfrac{5}{6})^1 = \tfrac{5}{7776}$$

Step 3 The probability of four successes out of five shots is obtained by adding $\tfrac{5}{7776}$ five times.

$P(4$ successes out of 5$)$

$$= P(SSSSF) + P(SFSSS) + P(SSFSS) + P(SSSFS) + P(FSSSS)$$
$$= \tfrac{5}{7776}(5) = \tfrac{25}{7776}$$

The following summarizes the probabilities of all possible numbers of successes out of five. Verification of computations is left for the reader as an exercise.

$P(0$ successes out of 5$) = \tfrac{3125}{7776}$

$P(1$ success out of 5$) \quad = \tfrac{3125}{7776}$

$P(2$ successes out of 5$) = \tfrac{1250}{7776}$

$P(3$ successes out of 5$) = \tfrac{250}{7776}$

$P(4$ successes out of 5$) = \tfrac{25}{7776}$

$P(5$ successes out of 5$) = \tfrac{1}{7776}$

These probabilities add up to 1. This is as it should be because 0 hits, 1 hit, 2 hits, 3 hits, 4 hits, 5 hits exhaust all possible outcomes of the random process and in addition are mutually exclusive events.

Furthermore, since the set of numbers [0, 1, 2, 3, 4, 5] in the above description of the sample space represents a meaningful assignment of numerical values to all possible outcomes of a random process, the number of successes can be considered a random variable. This random variable is of course a discrete variable.

Exercise 7-1 (*a*) Present the tabular and graphic representations of the probability (mass) function of the above random variable, the number of successes out of five trials.

(*b*) Define a cumulative probability distribution of the above variable.

In general, given the probability of success (or hit) of each trial (or shot) p (and the probability of failure of $q = 1 - p$), the probability of r successes out of n trials is determined as follows.

Step 1 Count the number of all possible orders in which r successes and $n - r$ failures can occur. In the above example, the number of all possible orders in which $r = 2$ successes and $n - r = 3$ failures can occur was counted as 10. In notation, $\binom{r}{n}$ denotes the number of all possible orders in which r successes out of n trials can occur. Thus, in the above example,

$$\binom{n}{r} = \binom{5}{2} = 10$$

$$\binom{n}{r} = \binom{5}{4} = 5$$

$$\binom{n}{r} = \binom{5}{0} = 1$$

· · · · · · · · · ·

The following is a very convenient formula for computing $\binom{n}{r}$:

$$\binom{n}{r} = \frac{n!}{r!(n - r)!}$$

where $n!$ stands for $1 \times 2 \times 3 \times \cdots \times n$ and is read "n factorial." Thus

$$n! = 1 \times 2 \times 3 \times \cdots \times n$$
$$r! = 1 \times 2 \times 3 \times \cdots \times r$$
$$(n - r)! = 1 \times 2 \times 3 \times \cdots \times (n - r)$$

In the above example when $n = 5$ and $r = 2$,

$$\binom{n}{r} = \binom{5}{2}$$

$$= \frac{5!}{2!(5 - 2)!} = \frac{5!}{2!3!}$$

$$= \frac{1 \times 2 \times 3 \times 4 \times 5}{(1 \times 2)(1 \times 2 \times 3)} = 10$$

Verify that

$$\binom{5}{3} = 10 \qquad \binom{5}{4} = 5 \qquad \binom{5}{1} = 5 \qquad \binom{5}{0} = 1 \qquad \binom{5}{5} = 1$$

The convention that $0! = 1$ must be adopted in calculating the last two cases.

Step 2   Now that the number of all possible ways in which r successes can occur out of n trials has been counted, the next step is to assign an appropriate probability to *each* of these possible ways. The probability of r successes and $n - r$ failures in any given specific order is calculated as

$$\underbrace{(p \times p \times p \times \cdots \times p)}_{r \text{ times}}\underbrace{(q \times q \times q \times \cdots \times q)}_{n - r \text{ times}} = p^r q^{n-r}$$

Thus, in the above example, the probability of each of all 10 possible ways in which $r = 2$ successes and $n - r = 3$ failures can occur was calculated as

$$p^r q^{n-r} = p^2 q^{5-2} = \underbrace{(\tfrac{1}{6} \times \tfrac{1}{6})}_{2 \text{ times}}\underbrace{(\tfrac{5}{6} \times \tfrac{5}{6} \times \tfrac{5}{6})}_{3 \text{ times}} = (\tfrac{1}{6})^2(\tfrac{5}{6})^3$$

Step 3 Multiply the number of possible ways in which r successes can occur by the probability for each of these possible ways to obtain the probability of r successes out of n trials:

$$P(r = r) = \binom{n}{r} p^r q^{n-r}$$

In the above example, $P(r = 2) = \binom{5}{2} p^2 q^3 = 10(\tfrac{1}{6})^2(\tfrac{5}{6})^3$.

When n and p values are specified, as $n = 5$, $p = \tfrac{1}{6}$ were in the above example, the varying probability values for varying r values can be determined from the formula. Complicated as it may seem, the formula is nothing but the mathematical statement of a functional relationship between the random variable r and the dependent variable, probability P. The reader should be able to verify easily that the table and the graph of Exercise 7-1 are equivalent to the notational representation of the probability function, $P(r = r) = \binom{5}{r}(\tfrac{1}{6})^r(\tfrac{5}{6})^{5-r}$.

Binomial probability function Just as any function which has the form of $y = a + bx$ is called the linear function, the probability function which has the general form of $P(r = r) = \binom{n}{r} p^r q^{n-r}$ is called the *binomial probability function*. Also, just as different values for the parameters a and b are specified for the linear function in different decision situations, different values of the parameters n, p, and q would be specified for the binomial probability function in different situations. Thus, the binomial function where $n = 12$, $p = \tfrac{1}{3}$, and $q = 1 - p = \tfrac{2}{3}$ would be specified as $P(r = r) = \binom{12}{r}(\tfrac{1}{3})^r(\tfrac{2}{3})^{12-r}$. This specific form would be appropriate if twelve shots (instead of five) were fired and the probability of success for each of these twelve shots were $\frac{1}{3}$ (instead of $\frac{1}{6}$).

The binomial probability function has a wide application to the real-world event-generating processes. The circumstances under which a random process can be modeled by the binomial probability function are explained below.

Bernoulli processes   Whenever the random variable is generated by a process that can be defined as a Bernoulli process, its probability function is defined as a binomial distribution.   The following characteristics make a random process a Bernoulli process.

1. Events or values of the random variable are generated by a number of *distinct* trials.   That is, n must be a positive integer.   In the above example, five shots fired constitute five distinct trials.   If twelve shots, twelve trials, and so on.
2. The possible outcomes of *each* trial are *only two*.   That is, each and every trial results in *one* or *the other* of the two possible events.   In the above example, each and every shot results either in a hit or a miss, or equivalently, in a success or a failure.
3. The probability p of success and the corresponding probability $q = 1 - p$ of failure from a trial remain *stable* throughout all trials.   No matter how many trials are performed by the process, the probability of success in later trials is the same as the probability of success in earlier trials.   In the above example, the effectiveness of the gun in hitting the target remains unchanged regardless of the number of shots fired.
4. Implied in characteristic 3′, but worth restating, is that the event of one particular trial is independent of the events of all previous and all following trials.   In a manner of speaking, the process does not have "memory."   For instance, if the probability of success is specified as $p = \frac{1}{6}$, even if by some sheer chance the first 20 shots hit the target, the probability of a hit for the twenty-first shot is still $\frac{1}{6}$.

Many real-world random processes may be considered to meet these requirements of an *ideal* Bernoulli process.   No gun retains the same effectiveness after a round of shots; nevertheless, the *model* of the Bernoulli process may be used to represent the real phenomenon of firing of a gun so that the binomial distribution can be used in order to ask and answer readily such questions as: What is the probability of at least one hit if five shots, ten shots, or n shots are fired?   What is the probability of no hit when n shots are fired?   To attain the level of effectiveness of at least one hit with the probability of, say, $\frac{1}{4}$, how many shots should be fired? Some examples of situations where the Bernoulli process can be adopted as a reasonably accurate model of the random process involved follow.

Examples of the Bernoulli process

1. The probability that each strategic bomber (or missile) will successfully penetrate the enemy defense system is given by p. An assumption that must be made to qualify as a Bernoulli process is that this probability of successful penetration does not change from the first bomber sent to the last bomber, although in reality it may improve from the first to the second, to the third, . . . , and to the last. The outcome of a bomber sent is *one* or *the other* of the only two possibilities: successful penetration or no penetration. What is the probability of exactly r successes or of at least r successes out of 100 bombers sent?

2. The reliability of a medical test, or the probability of successfully detecting a particular disease when a person with the disease is subjected to the test, is p. Accordingly, the probability of non-detection when the tested person has the disease is $q = 1 - p$. If 20 carriers of the disease are put through the test, i.e., 20 trials, what is the probability of all being detected or of more than r going undetected?

3. An automatic machine produces a certain part with a known average defective percentage of 20 percent, namely, the probability that an item produced by the machine is defective (or call it "success") is 0.2. Accordingly, the probability that an item is good (call it "failure") is $q = 1 - 0.2 = 0.8$. If the efficiency of the machine is assumed not to change from the production of the first item to the production of the last item in a given run of, say, n pieces, i.e., the probability of success (defective) remains 0.2 throughout the run, what is the probability that more than or less than r units will be defective?

4. The probability that a traveling salesman assigned to a particular territory will succeed in making a sale per customer call is given as p, that of not making a sale is given as $1 - p$. If the salesman makes 20 calls a day, what is the probability of making r sales?

Cumulative binomial distribution In many applications of binomial probabilities, the cumulative distribution is more directly useful than the mass function. $P(r \geq r)$ denotes the cumulative probability of the number of successes r being equal to or greater than a specified number r. In reference to Example 7-2 it is easy to verify the following statements concerning cumulative probabilities.

1. $P(r \geq r) = \displaystyle\sum_{r=r}^{n} P(r) = P(r) + P(r+1) + P(r+2) + \cdots + P(n)$

The probability that the number of successes is *equal to or greater than* r is the sum of the probability of r successes, the probability of $r+1$ successes, the probability of $r+2$ successes, . . . and the probability of n successes. For example,

$$P(r \geq 3) = \sum_{r=3}^{5} P(r) = P(r=3) + P(r=4) + P(r=5)$$

$$= \tfrac{250}{7776} + \tfrac{25}{7776} + \tfrac{1}{7776} = \tfrac{276}{7776}$$

2. $P(r > r) = \displaystyle\sum_{r=r+1}^{n} P(r)$

$$= P(r+1) + P(r+2) + P(r+3) + \cdots + P(n)$$

For example,

$$P(r > 3) = \sum_{r=4}^{5} P(r)$$

$$= P(r=4) + P(r=5) = \tfrac{25}{7776} + \tfrac{1}{7776} = \tfrac{26}{7776}$$

3. $P(r \leq r) = \displaystyle\sum_{r=0}^{r} P(r) = P(0) + P(1) + P(2) + \cdots + P(r)$

For example,

$$P(r \leq 3) = \sum_{r=0}^{3} P(r)$$

$$= P(r=0) + P(r=1) + P(r=2) + P(r=3)$$

$$= \tfrac{3125}{7776} + \tfrac{3125}{7776} + \tfrac{1250}{7776} + \tfrac{250}{7776}$$

$$= \tfrac{7750}{7776}$$

4. $P(r \leq r) = 1 - P(r > r)$ or $P(r > r) = 1 - P(r \leq r)$

For example,

$$P(r \leq 3) = 1 - P(r > 3) = 1 - \tfrac{26}{7776} = \tfrac{7750}{7776}$$

5. $P(r = r)$

The (noncumulative) binomial probability that the number of successes is exactly r, can be obtained from cumulative probabilities. For example,

$P(r = 3)$

$$= P(r \geq 3) - P(r > 3) = P(r \geq 3) - P(r \geq 4)$$

$$= [P(r=3) + P(r=4) + P(r=5)] - [P(r=4) + P(r=5)]$$

$$= \tfrac{276}{7776} - \tfrac{26}{7776} = \tfrac{250}{7776}$$

The result, that is, $P(r = 3) = \frac{250}{7776}$, is the same as that obtained directly from the formula for the noncumulative binomial probability

$$P(r = r) = \binom{n}{r} p^r q^{n-r}$$

$$= \binom{5}{3} (\tfrac{1}{6})^3 (\tfrac{5}{6})^2 = \tfrac{250}{7776}$$

In general,

$$P(r = r) = P(r \geq r) - P(r > r)$$
$$= P(r \geq r) - P(r \geq r + 1)$$

Or similarly,

$$P(r = r) = P(r \leq r) - P(r < r)$$
$$= P(r \leq r) - P(r \leq r - 1)$$

7-3 POISSON PROCESS AND POISSON PROBABILITY FUNCTION

The binomial probability function gives the probability of r successes out of n *distinct* trials. For example, using the binomial function one could assess the probability of $r = 4$ defective units (successes) found in a random sample of $n = 100$ units (trials) selected from a large shipment of a certain product item if the underlying process met the conditions of a Bernoulli process. But of course there are many real-world random phenomena that do not qualify as Bernoulli processes, and consequently the binomial probability model cannot be applied to them. Poisson processes constitute another class of random processes that give rise to a mathematically tractable probability model called *Poisson probability distribution*. The difference between the Bernoulli process (binomial probability model) and the Poisson process (Poisson probability distribution) is that whereas in the former the probability asked is that of r successes out of n distinct, discrete trials, in the latter the probability of concern is that of r successes in a specified, continuous *space* such as time, length, area, volume. For instance, on a given day (a given time space) no ship, one ship, two ships, three ships, . . . , or r ships (successes) may arrive at a dock, and one may be interested in the probability of each of the possible events, 0, 1, 2, 3, . . . , r ship arrivals. Here we have a continuum of time space, a day—instead of n distinct trials as was the case with the Bernoulli process—within which the number of successes is to be observed. The random process described is definitely not a Bernoulli process, but it *may* qualify as a Poisson process. (Qualifications for the Poisson process are given later.) If it qualifies as a Poisson process, the probabilities of various numbers of successes may be represented and computed by the following Poisson function formula:

$$P(r = r) = \frac{\lambda^r e^{-\lambda}}{r!}$$

where r = number of successes, e.g., number of ships arriving

λ = *average intensity* of successes within specified time space, e.g., the long-run average number of ships arriving per day

$e \approx 2.718$

Formidable as it may appear, the formula is no more so than the binomial probability formula. Analogous to n and p in the binomial case, λ is the parameter of the Poisson distribution. For a specific Poisson situation, there is a specified value of λ. For example, different docks at different harbors have different long-run average ship arrivals per day, namely, different λ values. The following are the computations of the probabilities of various numbers of ship arrivals using the Poisson formula under the assumption of the long-run average intensity of ship arrivals of $\lambda = 2$ ships per day.

Event that no ship would arrive at the dock on a given day:

$$P(r = 0) = \frac{\lambda^r e^{-\lambda}}{r!} = \frac{(2)^0 e^{-2}}{0!} = \frac{1 e^{-2}}{1} = \frac{1}{e^2} \approx \frac{1}{2.718^2} \approx 0.135$$

Event that one ship would arrive at the dock on a given day:

$$P(r = 1) = \frac{\lambda^r e^{-\lambda}}{r!} = \frac{2^1 e^{-2}}{1!} = \frac{2 e^{-2}}{1} = \frac{2}{e^2} \approx 0.271$$

Event that two ships would arrive at the dock on a given day:

$$P(r = 2) = \frac{\lambda^r e^{-\lambda}}{r!} = \frac{2^2 e^{-2}}{2!} = \frac{4 e^{-2}}{2} = \frac{2}{e^2} \approx 0.271$$

Event that three ships would arrive at the dock on a given day:

$$P(r = 3) = \frac{\lambda^r e^{-\lambda}}{r!} = \frac{2^3 e^{-2}}{3!} = \frac{8 e^{-2}}{6} = \frac{4}{3e^2} \approx 0.180$$

For the event that four ships would arrive at the dock on a given day the reader should complete the computation

$$P(r = 4) = \frac{\lambda^r e^{-\lambda}}{r!} = ?$$

Since fractions of ship arrivals, e.g., 2.4 ships arriving, are meaningless, the random variable r of the Poisson distribution is allowed to assume only integers; consequently, it is a discrete function, as was the binomial distribution.

The conditions for qualifying a random process as a Poisson process are similar to conditions 3 and 4 of a Bernoulli process, with obvious modifications. First, the intensity of success must be *stable*. In reference to the ship-arrival phenomenon, neither more nor fewer ships should arrive on the average in the early hours of the day than the late hours of the day; in other words, the same intensity of ship arrivals applies to any part of the given time space, a day. Second, what happens in the earlier part of the given space is *independent* of what happens in the later part and vice versa. For example, even if a lot of ships arrive in the first hour of the day, no more and no fewer ships than indicated by the given intensity are deemed likely to arrive in the ensuing hour. Note that the parameter of the process λ, or the intensity of the process, depends on the specified space. Thus, in our ship-arrival example, $\lambda = 2$ ships is the long-run average *per day*. If one is interested in the probabilities of various numbers of ship arrivals in *2 days*, λ in the formula must be increased to $\lambda = 4$ ships per *2 days*, assuming that the stability and independence of the intensity of the process applies to the extended time space of 2 days.

The following are some examples of the real-world random processes for which the function has been successfully used as the model:

1. What are the probabilities of different numbers of customers arriving at the checkout counters at a supermarket in a given time period of a day? Of different numbers of cars arriving at the tollbooths on a turnpike? In general, of different numbers of "customers" demanding a particular product or service?
2. What are the probabilities of different numbers of calls being placed at a central telephone exchange during a given time of a day?

Exponential probability function   Before leaving the Poisson process, the reader is referred to another probability function which has wide application in scientific analyses, namely, the exponential probability function. It is formally represented by

$$P(t) = \alpha e^{-\alpha t}$$

where t is the random variable and α the parameter. The exponential probability function results from the Poisson process when it is looked at from an angle different from that of the Poisson probability model.   In reference to the ship-arrival phenomenon, one might be primarily interested in the passage of time between two ship arrivals.   The questions posed are: What are the probabilities that less than 4 hr, more than 10 hr, between 8 and 9 hr, etc., will elapse between the arrival of the first ship and that of the second ship, between the arrival of the tenth ship and that of the eleventh ship?   The formula above will yield these probabilities after some mathematical manipulation when the parameter α is specified as the long-run average ship arrivals per unit of time, e.g., hour.   The exponential distribution is continuous, and therefore the probabilities are meaningful only for given *intervals* of space, e.g., time, whereas the Poisson distribution is discrete.[1]

7-4 NORMAL PROCESS AND NORMAL PROBABILITY FUNCTION

The normal process constitutes another idealized, mathematically manageable class of random process which may be used as the model of many real-world processes.   For example, suppose an individual is selected at random from a group of people and weighed.   The random process would yield a sample space consisting of various possible weights, or a random variable.   If we denote the different possible weights by x, we may speak of a probability function in general, $P = f(x)$.   The specific form of the relation between P and x, of course, would depend on the kind of the population from which the individual was selected.   It is in the "nature of nature" that the probability function for "typical" population groups can be approximated by the formula

$$P(x) = \frac{1}{\sigma \sqrt{2\pi}} e^{-\frac{1}{2}[(x-\mu)/\sigma]^2}$$

where x is the random variable; μ and σ (the Greek letters mu and sigma) are the parameters.   (Of course, $\pi \approx 3.14$; $e \approx 2.718$.)   A particular given population would determine the particular values of the process parameters μ and σ.   Again, the formula appears complicated but we know by now that $P(x)$ values can be calculated for different values of x once μ and σ values are specified.   For example, suppose that the population is such that $\mu = 150$ and $\sigma = 20$.   Then, for $x = 190$, $P(x)$ is computed as

[1] In this book, discussion of the Poisson process and the normal process (in the next section) is kept at a minimum.   For a more detailed intuitive explanation of the Poisson process and its probability models, i.e., the Poisson distribution, and the normal process and probability, see Robert Schlaifer, "Probability and Statistics for Business Decisions," McGraw-Hill, New York, 1959.

$$P(x) = \frac{1}{\sigma \sqrt{2\pi}} e^{-\frac{1}{2}[(x-\mu)/\sigma]^2}$$

$$= \frac{1}{20\sqrt{2(3.14)}} (2.718^{-\frac{1}{2}[(190-150)/20]^2})$$

$$= \frac{1}{20\sqrt{6.28}} 2.718^{-\frac{1}{2}(4)}$$

$$= \frac{1}{20\sqrt{6.28}} \frac{1}{2.718^2}$$

There is nothing in the formula that restricts the values the random variable x can assume. Indeed, in order to be able to apply the normal probability model to a given situation, the random variable involved must be considered *continuous*. In terms of the weight example on hand, the individual may weigh 182 lb, 182.006 lb, 179.09628, . . . lb. Once we assume continuity of the variable, as noted earlier, probabilities make sense only in terms of given weight intervals. For example, it is meaningful to ask the probability that the individual will weigh between 160 and 175 lb or between 90 and 102 lb but not the probability that he will weigh exactly 160 lb or 162.6 lb. Exhibit 7-12 is a graphic representation of the relation between x and $P(x)$.

Notes on Exhibit 7-12

1. The highest value of $P(x)$ is found at $x = 150$, the value of the parameter μ.
2. The curve is symmetrical in shape with respect to the vertical line $x = 150$.
3. The probability density value decreases further as x increases or decreases further from $x = 150$ but never becomes zero. This means that we must allow the possibility that the individual weighs 1000, 2000 lb, etc., and -100, -5000 lb, etc. Though unrealistic, the assumption does not distort reality much because the probability values for these unrealistic values of x are so small that they can be ignored.
4. The probability that the individual weighs between 160 and 175 lb is represented by the shaded area bound by the curve, the lines $x = 160$ and $x = 175$, and the horizontal axis.
5. The total area under the curve and the horizontal axis is 1. Given the formula of the curve, this fact can be proved mathematically.

In the above, the process parameters were assumed to be $\mu = 150$

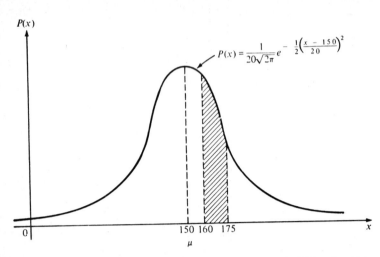

$$P(x) = \frac{1}{20\sqrt{2\pi}} e^{-\frac{1}{2}\left(\frac{x-150}{20}\right)^2}$$

Exhibit 7-12 Graphic representation of a normal probability function.

and $\sigma = 20$. In other groups of population, however, μ and σ values may be different. For example, if a group consists of children, the parameters may take the values, say, $\mu = 53$ lb and $\sigma = 10$ lb. But the normal probability formula is such that even with different values of μ and σ, the graph of the function would have the same general shape as in Exhibit 7-12 except that now the highest value of probability density would be at $x = 53$, the new μ value, and there would be some difference in the flatness or peakedness of the curve, which comes from the fact that the σ value is different. Exhibits 7-13a and 7-13b illustrate what happens to the normal probability curve when the parameter values are changed. Note that μ determines the "location" of the curve given the same σ value (Exhibit 7-13a); σ determines the flatness or peakedness of the curve given a same value of μ (Exhibit 7-13b); i.e., the larger the σ value, the wider the spread of the curve.

The parameter μ is often called the *central tendency* of the normal curve because it determines where the center, that is, peak, of the curve is, and it is the *weighted average* or *expected value* of x's (weights of the individuals). The parameter σ denotes the spread of the curve and is called the *standard deviation* of the distribution. The definitions of the expected value and the standard deviation are given in the next chapter. The following are examples of real-world random phenomena that could fit the model of a normal process.

1. The results of an IQ test of a group of children may be *normally distributed*. This means that if a child is chosen at random, the

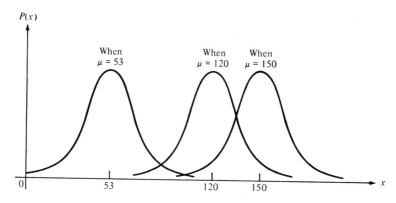

Exhibit 7-13a σ remains the same.

probability that his IQ score is higher or lower than a given figure or falls within a given interval of scores can be represented by the normal probability function. μ would be the weighted average IQ score of the whole group; σ is a measure of spread or scatter of the curve, i.e., a measure of homogeneity or heterogeneity of the group with respect to IQ.

2. An automatic machine is set to produce parts the diameters of which average 3.5 in. in the long run.   It may be appropriate to consider the machine process normal with μ = 3.5 and a specified σ.   One could compute the probability of a part produced by the machine having a diameter larger or smaller than a specified number of inches or within a specified interval.

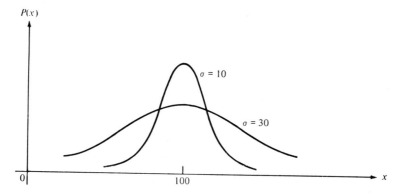

Exhibit 7-13b μ remains the same.

7-5 PROBABILITY AND FREQUENCY DISTRIBUTION

In the discussions of Chap. 6 and the present chapter, a problem of critical importance has been ignored: How in practice are specific probabilities assigned to specific events (or values of a random variable) or, more particularly, how is a random process recognized to be representable by one of the theoretical probability models such as binomial, Poisson, and normal, and once recognized, how are the parameters specified? Recall that in discussing the traffic-volume–bridge-construction example in Chap. 6, the probabilities of various traffic volumes, i.e., low, medium, and high, were simply assumed to be 0.4, 0.4, and 0.2, respectively. Where were these relative weights obtained? What were the bases for such assessment of relative weights or probabilities as indices of likelihood of various traffic volumes happening? In the coin tossing, how can one assert that the reasonable or natural assignment of probabilities according to the likelihood of happening is $\frac{1}{2}$ and $\frac{1}{2}$ for heads and tails?

Frequency distribution and objective probability In many cases, the primary basis for assignment of probabilities to events (or values of a random variable) is the record of actual outcomes observed in the past. Thus, in the ship-arrival example given earlier, the analyst may have ready access to the ship-arrival records of the past for the dock in question. Suppose the actual records of the past 40 weeks are as summarized in Exhibit 7-14. The second column gives the absolute number of days and the third column the *relative frequency*.

Given this historical record of what happened in the past, or the absolute or relative frequency distributions of ship arrivals, how would the analyst assign probabilities to the various events? Whether absolute

Number of ships arriving	Number of days	Relative frequency
0	35	0.125
1	82	0.293
2	78	0.279
3	41	0.146
4	30	0.107
5	12	0.043
6	0	0
7	2	0.007
8	0	0
9 or more	0	0
Total	280	1.000

Exhibit 7-14 Historical ship-arrival data.

(number of days) or relative (fractions), the frequency distribution is a faithful recording of what happened *actually in the past*, whereas the probability distribution refers to *a future happening* which has not occurred yet. In the frequency distribution, the actual outcomes of *many trials* are summarized, and therefore all events listed have occurred at one time or another. In contrast, the probability distribution refers essentially to the outcome of only *one future trial*, and therefore only one of many possible events listed will actually happen (all others will not happen). Yet, if the frequency distribution is presented to a "reasonable" man, he is most likely to make use of the given information in assigning the probability of the future event. In an extreme case, he may not have any other information on the (future) ship-arrival pattern except the (past) frequency distribution reproduced in Exhibit 7-14. Under such an extreme assumption, if he has no reason to believe that the event-generating process, which generates the number of ship arrivals, has changed from the past to the present and will change from now to the future, he will use the *past* "frequencies" of events as the measure of the relative weights representing the likelihood of the *future* happening of the events. Since relative frequencies are in a form compatible with the rules of probability of Chap. 6, they can be used directly as the probability distribution. But, to repeat, such use of the past relative frequency distribution is based on the analyst's judgment that it is the only information available on the random process of concern and that the nature of the process has not changed and will not change in the future. When probability is assigned on the basis of long-run frequencies, it is called *objective probability* as contrasted to *subjective probability*, which will be discussed shortly.

Having decided to use the past record as the basis for probability assignment for future ship arrivals, the analyst next may wish to find out whether one of the theoretical probability models could be applied to the situation, for such application may save a lot of computational and analytical work.[1]

He may note that the ship-arrival process is independent and stable, as defined earlier in connection with the Poisson process, and therefore may wish to see if the Poisson model can be applied. Then, the next step is to compute the average ship arrival per day from the frequency data of Exhibit 7-14. The reader may verify that the weighted average ship arrivals per day from the exhibit is computed as about $\lambda = 2$ ships per day. In order to evaluate the goodness of fit of the Poisson process with $\lambda = 2$ to the actual situation, the analyst would compute the theo-

---

[1] In addition to formulas, most standard texts in statistics give tables of probabilities for Bernoulli, Poisson, and normal processes, which facilitates computations further. See, for example, Schlaifer, op. cit.

Number of ships	Theoretical Poisson probability with $\lambda = 2$	Frequency from Exhibit 7-14
0	0.135	0.125
1	0.271	0.293
2	0.271	0.279
3	0.180	0.146
4	0.090	0.107
5	0.037	0.043
6	0.012	0
7	0.003	0.007
8	0.001	0
9 or more	0.000	0
Total	1.000	1.000

Exhibit 7-15a Tabular comparison of theoretical distribution with frequency distribution.

retical Poisson probabilities from the Poisson formula given earlier, $P(r) = \lambda^r e^{-\lambda}/r!$, or from the Poisson probability table if one is available, and contrast it to the actual frequency distribution of Exhibit 7-14. Exhibit 7-15a shows such comparison in table form; Exhibit 7-15b does the same in graphic form.

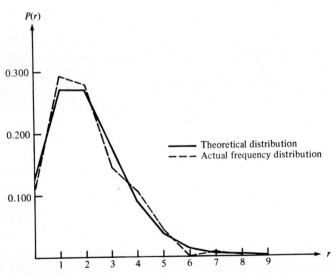

Exhibit 7-15b Graphic comparison of theoretical distribution with frequency distribution.

From the comparison, the analyst may conclude that the fit is good enough and use the Poisson model in his analysis.

Another useful basis for probability assessment is the analysis and study of the nature of the event-generating random process itself. For example, upon examination of the shape of a coin and a die, we may decide that the coin and the die are "fair," and accordingly assign the probability of 0.5 to the outcome heads and the probability of $\frac{1}{6}$ to the outcome of ace. But how does one know that a fair coin or a fair die would call for such probability assignment? Perhaps the answer is that in the past we have observed numerous flippings of numerous fair coins and numerous rolls of numerous fair dice, and from this experience we know that about one-half the time heads appear and one-sixth the time aces appear. If so, the distinction between the two bases of probability assessment— the relative-frequency and the analysis of the process—becomes obscure. Many do not distinguish the two. At any rate, in most practical probability assignments, both kinds of evidence should be taken into account if available.

Uncertainty and subjective probability In many real decision situations under uncertainty, neither frequency distribution nor the knowledge of the event-generating process may be available. Suppose a shipwrecked man drifts onto a desert island and tries to assess probabilities of various weather possibilities for the next day. He has no knowledge of the island whatsoever. Faced with this kind of uncertainty, some theorists may say that he should not even try to assign any probabilities at all. Decision problems involving such uncertainty, according to them, can best be handled by some methods other than the principle of weighting outcomes by probability weights, such as the minimax principle mentioned in Chap. 6. What they claim is that although it may be an interesting mental exercise to speak of the probability, say, 0.20, of the occurrence of the World War III by the year 2000 which would lead to the annihilation of mankind, that kind of probability cannot be of any help to any practical decisions because past patterns of world politics and military technology have no relevance to the happening of World War III.

On the other hand, other theorists insist that rationality dictates that even under such uncertainty as where neither the past observation of the outcomes of the random process in question nor the knowledge of the nature of the process is available, probabilities have to be assigned explicitly. Each alternative course of action may yield different consequences depending on which event happens. Even when there is very little scientific, objective ground on which the probability assignment can be based, if the decision maker ever has some "belief" or "feel" that certain events are more likely to happen than others, no matter how unreliable such belief or feel may be, that is the only rational basis on which he can make decisions. (The topic is discussed further in Chaps. 8 and 9.)

Probabilities assigned not on the basis of objective evidence but on the basis of the decision maker's own personal judgment are called *subjective probabilities;* it is a point of contention among decision theorists whether they should be incorporated in decision analysis or not.

7-6 SUMMARY AND TRANSITION

This chapter has introduced three of the idealized random processes, Bernoulli, Poisson, and normal, which can be adopted as the model of a real-world random process. Although more time has been spent on the discussion of the Bernoulli process and its binomial function than the other two processes, it is not because the Bernoulli process is more important than the others but because discussion of one is directly relevant to the others.

As noted in the beginning of Chap. 6, our main purpose in studying probability theories is to make use of them in decision problems. The next chapter therefore returns to our original concern, namely, decision making under uncertainty, or how probabilities can be incorporated in the analysis for decision under uncertainty.

QUESTIONS AND PROBLEMS

1. Define and explain random variable, continuous and discrete probability function, probability mass function, probability density function, cumulative distribution, and frequency distribution.

2. Distinguish objective probabilities from subjective probabilities.

3. Define and give examples of Bernoulli, Poisson, and normal processes.

4. A given coin is so crooked that the probability of heads is 0.30. Compute the following probabilities:

   (*a*) The probability of 4 or more heads in 7 tosses.
   (*b*) The probability of 3 or more heads in 7 tosses.
   (*c*) The probability of exactly 3 heads in 7 tosses.
   (*d*) The probability of fewer than 3 heads in 7 tosses.
   (*e*) The probability of equal to or fewer than 3 heads in 7 tosses.
   (*f*) The probability of no heads in 7 tosses.

5. An urn contains a total of 100 balls, of which 40 are red and 60 are black. Suppose 20 balls are taken from the urn at random.

   (*a*) What is the probability that fewer than 3 are black under sampling with replacement? Sampling with replacement means that upon selection of each ball, the ball is put back into the urn and thoroughly mixed with other balls before the next ball is selected.

   (*b*) What is the probability that fewer than 3 are black under sampling without replacement, i.e., if after each selection, the ball is not put back into the urn?

(c) What happens to the difference between the probabilities of parts (a) and (b) when the total number of balls in the urn is increased to 1000, 10,000, etc., while holding the relative proportions of red and black balls the same?

6. (a) Change Prob. 5 to the one in the typical opinion-survey context; i.e., considering red balls as those favoring a certain candidate for a political office and black balls as those against him in a given group of voters, restate the wordings of parts (a) to (c) of Prob. 5.

(b) How could you achieve the sampling with replacement in the opinion-survey context?

7. A company purchases large lots of a certain electronic component. The decision to accept these purchased lots or reject them is based upon a sample of 10 items from each lot. If any of the 10 items drawn at random from a lot are defective, the lot is rejected; otherwise, it is accepted.

(a) What is the probability of rejecting a lot that has 5 percent defective?

(b) What is the probability of accepting such a lot?

(c) What is the probability of accepting a lot containing 10 percent defective?

8. The manager of a store wishes to assess the probability of each possible value of demand for a product between 9 and 10 A.M. on a Saturday morning. He believes that the demand is dependent on two variables: (1) how many customers enter the store, and (2) how many of these entering the store buy the product. On the basis of past records the manager assigns the probability for the first variable as follows:

Number of customers entering the store	Probability
0	0
1	0
2	0.2
3	0.3
4	0.4
5	0.1
6 or more	0

For every customer who enters the store, the manager believes that the probability that he buys the product is 0.4.

(a) What is the probability that three customers buy the product given that five enter the store?

(b) What is the probability that the demand for the product between 9 and 10 A.M. on a Saturday morning is 3 or 4?

9. Repeat Prob. 8 under the assumption that the number of customers entering the store is Poisson distributed with the average of three customers.

8

Decision Making under Uncertainty: Expected-value Criterion

8-0 INTRODUCTION

Chapter 6 introduced the concept of payoff tables which summarize the consequences of all alternative courses of action conditional to each possible event and the use of the probabilities of events as weights in the systematic weighting of possible outcomes under one of the decision criteria. This decision principle is more commonly referred to as *the expected-value criterion* or *Bayesian decision criterion,* and much work has been done on it under such titles as *statistical decision theory.* The present chapter discusses the expected-value criterion in more detail, introducing some new concepts useful in decision analyses; in the next chapter, alternative decision theories will be studied. In both chapters the main purpose is to gain insight into the decision-making process under uncertainty in general.

Specifically, this chapter attempts first to see the "reasonableness" of the expected-value criterion through an illustration of a concrete decision problem. The question raised is: How can we say that the decision maker is acting rationally when he follows the expected-value-decision principle? The chapter then introduces some of the decision-analytic concepts such as the *value of perfect information, opportunity cost or loss,* and *cost of uncertainty.* Finally, the chapter concludes with a discussion of a *multistage* decision example, which is more realistic than the *single-stage* decision examples given in the earlier part of the chapter. As an integral part of the discussions of these topics, the chapter also defines the probability-theoretic concepts, the *expected value, variance,* and *standard deviation* of a random variable.

8-1 ADVOCACY OF THE EXPECTED-VALUE CRITERION

In brief, the decision under the criterion of weighting possible outcomes involves the following steps: (1) predict for each act multiple consequences conditional to various possible events; (2) replace the multiple consequences of each act by their weighted average or expected value as the overall index of desirability of the act; and (3) rank alternative acts according to this index of desirability and choose the best act. (In contrast, under the minimax criterion, the multiple consequences of an act are replaced by the worst possible consequence of the act as the index of desirability.) In reference to the traffic-volume–bridge-construction example of Chap. 6, the weighted average cost or expected cost, $52 million, of the four-lane act is deemed to *represent* and *summarize* its underlying multiple (conditional) costs, $30 million, $60 million, and $80 million. Likewise, the expected cost, $55 million, of the six-lane act is considered to *represent* and *summarize* its underlying multiple consequences, $50 million, $50 million, and $75 million; the expected cost, $60 million, of the eight-lane act is a summary utility measure of the multiple cost consequences, $60 million, $60 million, and $60 million. Is the weighted average indeed the "best" overall representation of multiple consequences? Put differently, how can we say that the decision maker is not being "rational" if he does not follow the expected-value criterion? Even if we all agree that the different likelihoods of different consequences within a given set of multiple consequences must be in one way or another taken into account in a rational decision, it is another matter whether one agrees to the proposition that the particular method of weighted average computation yields the utility index which would result in the most "reasonable" decision. There is as a matter of fact no logically irrefutable direct argument to offer in support, but the following is a somewhat feeble, indirect advocacy for the expected-value decision criterion.

EXAMPLE 8-1: INVENTORY DECISION UNDER UNCERTAINTY

Suppose that at the beginning of a particular week, a retailer decides how many units of a particular product to purchase and stock in antici-

Weekly demand D, units	Probability of event P(D)
0	0.10
1	0.25
2	0.30
3	0.20
4	0.10
5	0.05
Total	1.00

Exhibit 8-1 Probability of weekly demand.

pation of an uncertain demand for the item during the coming week. The purchase price per unit is $3; the selling price per unit is $5. Since the product is easily perishable, whatever remains unsold at the end of the week has to be disposed of. The salvage value for an unsold unit is $1. How many units should the retailer stock at the beginning of the week? Assume that the product can be bought only once at the beginning of the week.

The first step in the analysis for decision is to determine the magnitude of the demand during the week. On the basis of the demand in the past and what the decision maker knows about the future market for the product, he assigns the probabilities to the possible numbers of units demanded for the next week as in Exhibit 8-1.

The second step is to construct the conditional payoff table, as in Exhibit 8-2, according to which, six alternative courses of action are available to the retailer. These alternative acts are characterized by the number of units bought and stocked, $Q = 0, 1, 2, 3, 4, 5$. There are six possible events characterized by the six possible values of a random variable, number of units demanded, $D = 0, 1, 2, 3,$

	Alternative acts, stock Q					
Demand D	0	1	2	3	4	5
0	0	−2	−4	−6	−8	−10
1	0	2	0	−2	−4	− 6
2	0	2	4	2	0	− 2
3	0	2	4	6	4	2
4	0	2	4	6	8	6
5	0	2	4	6	8	10

Exhibit 8-2 Conditional payoff table.

4, 5. For each act, i.e., for each specific number Q of units stocked, six possible profit consequences conditional to six possible events are listed. Thus, for the act $Q = 0$, no matter which of the possible events happens, the profit is always 0, because if the retailer does not stock any, he does not pay anything, but at the same time he does not have any revenue, consequently his profit is $0. For the act $Q = 1$, the act of stocking exactly 1 unit, the retailer pays $3 for the purchase of 1 unit, and if there is no demand, namely, if the event is $D = 0$, he receives $1 as the salvage value; the net loss is therefore $3 − $1 = $2; −$2 is shown at the intersection of the $Q = 1$ column and the $D = 0$ row. If the event is $D = 1$, he can sell the unit stocked, thereby generating a revenue of $5; his net profit would be $5 − $3 = $2. This net profit of $2 appears at the intersection of the $Q = 1$ column and the $D = 1$ row. For the events $D = 2$, $D = 3$, $D = 4$, and $D = 5$, because he has stocked only 1 unit, he can sell only 1 unit even if the demand happens to be higher than 1; therefore, the net profit is still $5 − $3 = $2. All the remaining entries in the $Q = 1$ column thus show the same $2. The reader should verify all the entries in the table before proceeding. At the same time he is urged to draw the game-tree diagram for the decision problem.

The third step, according to the expected-value criterion, is to replace the multiple conditional payoffs of each act by one overall index of profitability, namely, the weighted average net profit. In Exhibit 8-3, the weighted average or expected net profit for the act $Q = 3$ is computed. For other acts, the expected net profit is shown in Exhibit 8-4 for verification by the reader.

Inasmuch as act $Q = 2$ yields the largest weighted average of conditional net profits, $2.20, the expected-profit criterion dictates that the retailer stock 2 units for the next week. But what if he decides to stock some other number, say 3 units? Can we brand him as irrational even

Demand D	Probability $P(D)$ $\times$	Conditional profit	Weighted = average net profit
0	0.10	−6	−0.60
1	0.25	−2	−0.50
2	0.30	2	0.60
3	0.20	6	1.20
4	0.10	6	0.60
5	0.05	6	0.30
Weighted average net profit			1.60

Exhibit 8-3   Expected net profit for act $Q = 3$.

Act Q	0	1	2	3	4	5
Weighted average net profit	0	1.60	2.20	1.60	0.20	−1.60

Exhibit 8-4 Expected net profits of alternative acts.

within the assumption that he is a profit maximizer? In support of his act of stocking 3 units instead of 2, he may observe that under the $Q = 3$ act he would make $6 profit if he is lucky to have the actual demand of 3 or more, although if the demand is less than the number of units stocked, he may lose $2 or $6, whereas the luckiest outcome he can hope for under the $Q = 2$ act is only $4, the unluckiest outcome being a loss of $4. For a *one-shot decision for a single week*, there is no direct way of convincing a decision maker that the application of the expected-profit-maximization principle results in the best decision for him. The reasonableness of the decision criterion, however, may be seen indirectly from its reasonableness when applied to the repeatable-decision case, as demonstrated below.

Suppose now that the retailer has to make the same decision over and over every week for, say, 100 weeks. If he follows the expected-value principle every week, and thus stocks 2 units every week, how much total net profit can he expect for the entire 100-week period?

In some of the 100 weeks, the retailer will be unlucky and have no demand for the product, thus ending up with a loss of $4; in other weeks only 1 unit will be demanded, and he ends up with $0 profit; still other weeks will have a demand for 2 or more, and he ends up with $4 profit. What is the sum of these actual profits for 100 weeks?

The fact that the retailer has assigned the probabilities to various demands as in Exhibit 8-1 and that no change in the market condition is expected in the future makes him expect the weekly demand of 0 units for 10 weeks out of the 100 weeks, 1 unit for 25 weeks, 2 units for 30 weeks, 3 units for 20 weeks, 4 units for 10 weeks, and 5 units for 5 weeks. The total expected net profit for the 100-week period would therefore be calculated as in Exhibit 8-5.

According to the exhibit, the total profit for 100 weeks is expected to be $220, and the expected net profit per week in the *long run* of 100 weeks is $2.20, which is the same as the expected net profit for act $Q = 2$ calculated earlier for the single-week decision. This is so because conditional profits are weighted by the same relative weights in both computations.

Likewise, the *long-run* expected weekly net profit for other acts can be verified to be the same as the weighted average net profit given in

$$Weekly\ profit \times \frac{Number\ of}{weeks} = Total\ profit$$

$ -4	10	$ -40
0	25	0
4	30	120
4	20	80
4	10	40
4	5	20

Total expected profit for
100 weeks $ 220

Expected profit per week: $220/100 weeks = $2.20 per week

Exhibit 8-5   Total net profit for 100 weeks of act $Q = 2$.

Exhibit 8-4. As a profit maximizer, the retailer would choose that act which yields the expectation of the highest total net profit in the long run, namely, for 100 weeks, or equivalently, of the highest weekly average net profit. The expected profit-decision criterion sounds reasonable when the same decision is repeated week after week.[1]

Is the criterion as reasonable when the decision is to be made *only once*, for the next week? The answer by many decision theorists—who may be called Bayesian decision theorists—is yes, provided that the conditional net profits in the payoff table are valid measures of desirability of consequences; but the reasonableness is harder to see in one-shot decision cases. Especially when the probabilities assigned to various events (various demands in the above example) are not based on such objective evidence as past observation and knowledge of market conditions and other verifiable evidence but on personal, subjective conviction, many theorists question the wisdom of the Bayesian approach. One of the alternative theories is the minimax criterion, already intro-

[1] Note how the retailer's decision for the 100-week period can be simulated by using a standard urn containing 100 balls marked for possible weekly demands according to the same relative proportions as the probabilities given in Exhibit 8-1: 10 balls marked $D = 0$ units; 25 balls marked $D = 1$ unit; 30 balls marked $D = 2$ units; and so on. Suppose the retailer decides to follow the strategy of stocking $Q = 2$ units every week. The market random process is simulated by drawing a ball from the urn at random. The repeated draw of a ball 100 times is considered to give the weekly demand for 100 weeks. Thus, in the first week of the simulated operation, the ball drawn may be marked $D = 4$ units. Then the act $Q = 2$ and $D = 4$ would yield the simulated profit of $2. And so on. We may likewise simulate the 100-week operation under other acts, $Q = 0$, $Q = 1$, $Q = 3$, . . . , and compare the "actual" simulated profit under different strategies. More will be said about simulation in Chap. 12.

duced in Chap. 6. The next chapter discusses a more refined Bayesian decision theory which purports to cover the cases where the weighted average of monetary values or other "original" measures used in stating the conditional payoffs cannot be considered directly representative of the degree of desirability of alternative acts. In the current chapter, it is assumed that the expected-value decision theory is valid even when the decision is to be made only once and even when the probabilities assigned are the reflection of the decision maker's personal belief in the likelihood of various events' happening, and also that the monetary values or other original measures used as conditional payoffs serve directly as the measure of desirability.

The weighted average or expected value of a random variable obviously occupies a critical place in the Bayesian decision approach, but the concept of expected value as a summary representation of a random variable is essential in any kind of statistical work. In the following we digress to gain a broader understanding of the concepts of expected value and other descriptive measures of a probability function and at the same time tie these general statistical terms to our decision-analytic framework.

8-2 WAYS OF DESCRIBING THE PROBABILITY FUNCTION OF A RANDOM VARIABLE

There are seven random variables in the payoff table of Exhibit 8-2. One of them is the number of units demanded D. Its probability function is specified by the probability $P(D)$ in the table of Exhibit 8-1. The six other random variables are the six sets of the multiple profit figures given under six alternative acts. The profit for each act qualifies as a random variable because it takes on varying numerical values corresponding to various possible events, as in the definition of the random variable given in Chap. 7. When probabilities are assigned to the possible values of each random variable, a probability function emerges. The seven tables of Exhibit 8-6 reproduce the probability functions of the seven random variables given in the payoff table of Exhibit 8-2. Note that the probability function of the random variable, the profit of act $Q = 0$ is trivial: the only possible value of the random variable is seen to be 0 in row (b). The table could be reduced to the form in Table 8-1. Similarly, row (e) could be reduced to an equivalent form, as in Table 8-2.

In all these tables, the probability function of the random variable is *completely described* in that the probabilities of all possible values of the random variable are given. For certain analytical purposes, however, such a complete description of the random variable is not necessary—

(a) Random variable, demand D	0	1	2	3	4	5
Probability, $P(D)$	0.10	0.25	0.30	0.20	0.10	0.05

(b) Random variable, profit of act $Q = 0$	0	0	0	0	0	0
Probability	0.10	0.25	0.30	0.20	0.10	0.05

(c) Random variable, profit of act $Q = 1$	-2	2	2	2	2	2
Probability	0.10	0.25	0.30	0.20	0.10	0.05

(d) Random variable, profit of act $Q = 2$	-4	0	4	4	4	4
Probability	0.10	0.25	0.30	0.20	0.10	0.05

(e) Random variable, profit of act $Q = 3$	-6	-2	2	6	6	6
Probability	0.10	0.25	0.30	0.20	0.10	0.05

(f) Random variable, profit of act $Q = 4$	-8	-4	0	4	8	8
Probability	0.10	0.25	0.30	0.20	0.10	0.05

(g) Random variable, profit of act $Q = 5$	-10	-6	-2	2	6	10
Probability	0.10	0.25	0.30	0.20	0.10	0.05

Exhibit 8-6 Seven random variables of Example 8-1.

Table 8-1 Modification of row (b) of Exhibit 8-6

Random variable profit of act $Q = 0$	0
Probability	1.0

Table 8-2 Modification of row (e) of Exhibit 8-6

Random variable, profit of act $Q = 3$	−6	−2	2	6
Probability	0.10	0.25	0.30	0.35

in fact, it is often downright confusing. Thus, in the inventory-decision problem, application of the Bayesian principle required the reduction of the complete description of the profit random variable (for each alternative act) to an overall index of profitability, a value *representative* of the whole probability function of the random variable. The overall, summary measure of the random variable adopted there was the weighted average or expected value of the variable. In many other areas of statistical analysis, too, it may be sufficient to represent the whole probability function of a random variable by its expected value.

In general, suppose that a random variable is specified or completely described as in Table 8-3. The summary measure, the expected value, of the random variable $E(X_i)$ would be calculated as in Table 8-4.

Other summary measures Although the expected value is the summary measure most often used in statistics, there are other summary measures of a random variable. In some instances, such measures as the *mode* and the *median* may be considered useful as representative of the whole probability function of a random variable. These measures are not discussed in this book except for the following brief discussion of the mode.

The mode is defined as the value of a random variable with the largest associated probability. Thus, in the inventory-decision example,

Table 8-3 Complete description of a random variable

Random variable x_i	x_1	x_2	x_3	$\cdots$	x_n
Probability $P(x_i)$	$P(x_1)$	$P(x_2)$	$P(x_3)$	$\cdots$	$P(x_n)$

Table 8-4   Calculation of expected value

$\begin{array}{c}Value\ of\ the\\random\ variable\end{array}$ $\times$ Probability	= Expected value	
x_1	$P(x_1)$	$x_1 P(x_1)$
x_2	$P(x_2)$	$x_2 P(x_2)$
x_3	$P(x_3)$	$x_3 P(x_3)$
. . . .		
x_n	$P(x_n)$	$x_n P(x_n)$
	$E(x_i)\quad =$	$\displaystyle\sum_{i=1}^{n} x_i P(x_i)$

the mode of the random variable, the profit of act $Q = 5$, is $-\$2$, which carries the probability of 0.30, the largest probability of all. Likewise, the modes for $Q = 0, 1, 2, 3, 4$ are \$0, \$2, \$4, \$2, \$0, respectively. If the retailer adopts the mode as the summary representation of multiple possible profits of each act, the decision would be to stock 2 units, which happens coincidentally to be the same as under the expected-value criterion. But the reader should be able to change the problem so that the mode criterion and the expected-value criterion yield different decisions. He is also urged to speculate why Bayesian decision theorists consider the mode inferior to the expected value as the decision criterion.

Variance and standard deviation   According to the expected-value decision rule, the desirability of act $Q - 1$ and the desirability of act $Q = 3$ are the same because the expected profit is the same, \$1.60, for both acts. But one of the two random variables, the profit of $Q = 1$, varies from -2 to 2 (over a narrow range of 4), whereas the values of the other variable, the profit of $Q = 3$, vary from -6 to 6 (over a wide range of 12). Does the same expected value do justice in representing or summarizing the two different random variables? Bayesian decision theorists would say that for the purpose of decision making the representation is adequate, provided that the monetary payoff is a valid measure of desirability of consequences. Others, however, would maintain that even if the monetary profit is considered a valid measure of utility of consequences, the expected value alone cannot represent the multiple profit values associated with each act. The difference between the two random variables, as well as their similarity in having the same expected profit, they would say, must somehow be recognized.

The variables, to repeat, are different in the range of possible values. In other words, the two are different in their scatteredness around the expected value. Their expected value is the same, but in the $Q = 1$ case, the possible values of the random variable are scattered on either side of the expected value less widely than in the $Q = 3$ case.

The *range* is often used as a measure of scatteredness; it is the difference between the highest and lowest possible values the random variable can assume. But more meaningful, more widely used, and more convenient to operate with mathematically are the *variance* and the *standard deviation* as the measure of scatteredness of a random variable around its expected value.

> Formally, the variance is defined as the weighted average of the squares of the difference between the expected value and all possible values of the random variable, with probabilities used as weights.

For illustration, the variances of the two variables, the profit of act $Q = 1$ and the profit of act $Q = 3$, are calculated.

Variance of the profit of $Q = 1$ According to row (c) of Exhibit 8-6, there are two possible values of the random variable, namely, 2 and -2. Associated with the value 2 is the probability of 0.90; associated with the other value, -2, is the probability of 0.10; the expected value of the random variable has already been calculated as 1.60. The differences between the expected value and possible values are

$$2 - 1.6 = 0.4$$
$$-2 - 1.6 = -3.6$$

The squares of the differences are $(0.4)^2$ and $(-3.6)^2$. The weighted average of the squares is calculated as

$$
\begin{array}{ll}
(0.4)^2(0.90) = & 0.144 \\
(-3.6)^2(0.10) = & \underline{1.296} \\
\text{Variance} & 1.440
\end{array}
$$

Variance of the profit of $Q = 3$ According to row (e) of Exhibit 8-6, all possible values of the random variable and associated probabilities are as shown in Table 8-5.

Table 8-5   Modification of row (e) of Exhibit 8-6

Value of random variable	-6	-2	2	6
Probability	0.10	0.25	0.30	0.35

The expected value has already been calculated as 1.60. The differences between the expected value and possible values are

$$-6 - 1.6 = -7.6$$
$$-2 - 1.6 = -3.6$$
$$2 - 1.6 = 0.4$$
$$6 - 1.6 = 4.4$$

The squares of the differences are

$$(-7.6)^2 = 57.76$$
$$(-3.6)^2 = 12.96$$
$$(0.4)^2 = 0.16$$
$$(4.4)^2 = 19.36$$

The weighted average of these squares is calculated as

$$57.76(0.10) = 5.776$$
$$12.96(0.25) = 3.240$$
$$0.16(0.30) = 0.048$$
$$19.36(0.35) = \underline{6.776}$$
$$\text{Variance} \quad 15.840$$

The variance of the profit of the act $Q = 3$ is more than 10 times as large as the variance of the profit of the act $Q = 1$. The reader should attempt to decide which of the two random variables, i.e., two acts, he would prefer, remembering that the expected value is the same, 1.6, and that the expected value may be interpreted as the long-run average weekly profit if the decision can be repeated.

Formally, the general procedure for computation of the variance of a random variable x_i with the corresponding probability $P(x_i)$ is

$$[x_1 - E(x_i)]^2 P(x_1)$$
$$[x_2 - E(x_i)]^2 P(x_2)$$
$$[x_3 - E(x_i)]^2 P(x_3)$$
$$\cdots \cdots \cdots \cdots$$
$$\underline{[x_n - E(x_i)]^2 P(x_n)}$$
$$\sum_{i=1}^{n} [x_i - E(x_i)]^2 P(x_i)$$

Often the expected value of x_i is denoted by $\bar{x}$ (read "x bar"); the above formula may then be rewritten

$$\text{Variance} = \sum_{i=1}^{n} (x_i - \bar{x})^2 P(x_i)$$

The other measure of the scatter of a random variable, the standard deviation, is simply the square root of the variance:

$$\text{Standard deviation} = \sqrt{\text{variance}}$$

In statistics books, standard deviation is often denoted by σ; variance by σ^2. Formally,

$$\text{Standard deviation} = \sigma = \sqrt{\sum_{i=1}^{n} (x_i - \bar{x})^2 P(x_i)}$$

Exercise 8-1:   You are offered two lotteries each of which consists of a standard urn containing 100 balls marked by varying dollar amounts as in Table 8-6.   You are to choose one of the two urns offered and then pick a ball at random from the chosen urn. You receive the dollar amount marked on the ball picked.   Dollar amounts with the negative sign mean that you must *pay* (instead of receiving) those amounts.

(*a*) Compute the expected payoff for each lottery.   Which lottery would you select if you follow the expected-value criterion?   Does this decision agree with the decision you would reach intuitively?

(*b*) Convert the data in the above tables to graphs of the probability functions and observe which of the two gives wider scatter.

Table 8-6   Lotteries

First urn		Second urn	
Dollar amount on the ball	*Number of balls*	*Dollar amount on the ball*	*Number of balls*
$1	10	$-1.5	2
2	20	-0.5	5
3	40	0.5	8
4	20	1.5	15
5	10	2.5	20
	100	3.5	20
		4.5	15
		5.5	8
		6.5	5
		7.5	2
			100

(c) Explain what this wider scatter means intuitively in terms of chances of different dollar amounts you might receive or lose. How does this affect your decision?

(d) Verify the difference in the scatter between the two functions by computing variances and standard deviations.

Summary measures of discrete random variables   The formulas given above for the expected value, variance, and standard deviation apply only to discrete random variables. It can be shown that according to these formulas, the summary measures of the binomial probability function, $P(r) = \binom{n}{r} p^r q^{n-r}$, are

Expected value $= E(r) = np$

Variance $= npq$

Standard deviation $= \sqrt{npq}$

and those of the Poisson function, $P(r) = \lambda^r e^{-\lambda}/r!$, are

Expected value $= E(r) = \lambda$

Variance $= \lambda$

Standard deviation $= \sqrt{\lambda}$

An obvious payoff from modeling real random variables under investigation by the ideal, mathematical probability functions such as binomial and Poisson is that when in the course of investigation the need arises for the summary measures of the random variable, they can be obtained readily from the parameters of the function (n, p, and λ) without having to go through lengthy computation.

Summary measures of continuous random variables   Though conceptually similar to the case of discrete variables, computation of the summary measures of a continuous random variable requires a new set of formulas. Since the formulas involve integration, this book does not discuss them except to note that they yield for the normal distribution given in Sec. 7-4

Expected value $= E(x) = \mu$

Variance $= \sigma^2$

Standard deviation $= \sigma$

8-3 FURTHER CONCEPTS USEFUL FOR DECISION ANALYSIS

An attempt has been made to show the reasonableness of using a basic statistical-probabilistic concept, expected value (and also variance and standard deviation) in decisions under uncertainty. Of course usually a decision analysis even under the expected-value-decision criterion would require much more than computing expected values. This section discusses further economic-analytic and probabilistic concepts that may prove useful in formal decision analyses.

Concept of perfect information   Whenever uncertainty exists with respect to some crucial element in the decision, an obvious alternative the decision maker (or his analyst) has is to make the decision right away, taking whatever risk accompanies it, but another course of action, time and cost permitting, is to try to reduce the degree of uncertainty by gathering additional information before making the final decision. How the decision maker decides whether to collect additional information or not is the main concern of Chap. 10; here our discussion is on how the maximum amount the decision maker is willing to pay for additional information can be determined.

Returning to Example 8-1, suppose that a *perfect predictor* of events were available to the retailer. In other words, in advance of the retailer's decision, the predictor would supply to him information on which specific event was going to happen, i.e., how many units would be demanded.

If the predictor predicts the demand to be $D = 0$, the rational decision is to stock 0 units ($Q = 0$), because given the event $D = 0$ (given the first row in the payoff table of Exhibit 8-2) the most profit the retailer can attain is $0 under $Q = 0$ column, all other acts resulting in a loss. Should the predictor predict the demand to be $D = 1$, the best the retailer can do is to earn a profit of $2 by taking act $Q = 1$. Likewise, for $D = 2$, the best act is $Q = 2$, with the resulting profit of $4. And so on. Exhibit 8-7 summarizes the results of the best decision with the use of the perfect predictor.

The perfect predictor can predict perfectly, but it cannot control which event, namely, which demand, will occur. If the demand that will occur happens to be 0, the predictor will perfectly, with certainty,

Demand D	Best payoff with perfect predictor
0	$ 0
1	2
2	4
3	6
4	8
5	10

Exhibit 8-7 Conditional payoffs with a perfect predictor.

Table 8-7   Calculation of expected profit with perfect predictor

Conditional profit with perfect predictor	× Probability	= Expected profit
$ 0	0.10	$0
2	0.25	0.50
4	0.30	1.20
6	0.20	1.20
8	0.10	0.80
10	0.05	0.50
Expected profit with perfect predictor		$4.20

predict $D = 0$, *prior to decision;* if the demand that will occur happens to be 1, the predictor will perfectly, with certainty, predict 1; and so on. Thus, even with the perfect predictor, the profit cannot be always $10; it will vary, as in Exhibit 8-7, from $0 to $10. Thus, the profit obtainable with the perfect predictor is also a random variable. Its expected value is calculated in Table 8-7.

If the decision is repeated 100 times over 100 weeks with the help of the perfect predictor, for 10 weeks out of 100 weeks, the demand will be 0 units; the predictor will faithfully predict $D = 0$; the best decision will be $Q = 0$; consequently, the profit will be $0. For 25 weeks out of 100, the demand will be 1; the predictor will faithfully predict 1; the best decision will be $Q = 1$; consequently, the profit will be $2. It follows that the total expected profit for the 100-week period is computed as shown in Table 8-8.

The average weekly expected profit with the perfect predictor would be $420/(100 weeks) = $4.20 per week. The expected profit with the

Table 8-8   Total expected profit for 100 weeks with perfect predictor

Conditional profit with perfect predictor	× Number of weeks	= Profit
$ 0	10	$ 0
2	25	50
4	30	120
6	20	120
8	10	80
10	5	50
Total expected profit for 100 weeks		$420

perfect predictor of $4.20 for a single decision calculated in Table 8-7 may be interpreted intuitively as this long-run average weekly expected profit.

Expected value of perfect information   The expected profit with the perfect predictor is $4.20, whereas the expected profit of the best act, $Q = 2$, *without* the perfect predictor was $2.20 according to Exhibit 8-4.   Or, to rephrase, the expected profit *with perfect information* (PI) is $4.20, but the expected profit of *the best act without perfect information,* or *the best act under uncertainty,* is $2.20.   The difference of $2 is therefore attributable to the availability of perfect information.   Accordingly, this difference of $2 is called the *expected value of perfect information.*   The profit is expected to increase by $2 from $2.20, the best that can be expected under uncertainty, if uncertainty can be removed by the perfect predictor or perfect information.   How much should the decision maker pay for the predictor?   Since the improvement on the expected profit from the best decision under uncertainty (without perfect information) to the decision with perfect information is $2, he should not pay any more than this expected improvement in profit.   If the maximum he would pay for perfect information is $2, for any information less than perfect he naturally would pay something less than $2.   To recapitulate:

1. Expected value of perfect information (EV of PI) equals expected profit with perfect information (EV with PI) minus expected profit of the best act under uncertainty (EV under uncertainty).
2. The decision maker would not pay any more than the expected value of perfect information for any additional information.

Concept of opportunity loss   The expected value of perfect information was calculated above, *first* by determining the expected profit under certainty (or with perfect information) and the expected profit under uncertainty (or without perfect information) and *second* by deducting the latter from the former.   The same expected value of perfect information can also be obtained, *first* by deducting the conditional profits of the best act under uncertainty from the conditional profits under certainty (namely, with perfect information) and *second* by determining the *expected value of the differences* between the conditional profits as calculated in the first step.   This alternative method for calculating the expected value of perfect information is reproduced in Exhibits 8-8 and 8-9.

If the event is $D = 0$, the profit with the predictor is $0, but the profit of the best act ($Q = 2$) without the predictor is $-$4.   Given the event $D = 0$, the best the retailer can do is to make $0 profit by taking the act $Q = 0$, but because he does not have the predictor, he takes the

Demand D, units	Best profit with perfect predictor −	Payoff of best act without perfect predictor Q = 2 =	Difference or opportunity loss
0	$ 0	$ −4	$4
1	2	0	2
2	4	4	0
3	6	4	2
4	8	4	4
5	10	4	6

Exhibit 8-8   Opportunity loss of act $Q = 2$.

act $Q = 2$, the best act without the predictor, and consequently loses $4 when the event turns out to be $D = 0$. The difference of $4, or $0 − $(−4), is therefore attributable to the predictor and is shown on the $D = 0$ row in Exhibit 8-8. If the event is $D = 1$, the profit with the predictor is $2 (from taking $Q = 1$ act), but the profit without the predictor (from taking $Q = 2$ act, the best act under uncertainty), is $0. The additional profit of $2 (or 2 − 0) that could be made if the retailer had the predictor would be lost because he took another act due to the lack of the predictor. The $2 "profit lost" is shown on the $D = 1$ row in Exhibit 8-8. Likewise, all other entries under the last column represent the additional *profit lost* for each event possibility because act $Q = 2$ is taken instead of the act that would be chosen if the predictor accurately predicted the demand *prior to decision*. Looked at in another way, these are the *opportunities for higher profits* forgone—opportunities for lower losses forgone if losses instead of profits are involved, as in the $D = 0$ case—because act $Q = 2$ is taken rather than the best act dictated by the accurate prediction of events by the predictor. These forgone opportunities for higher profits are called the *opportunity losses* of act $Q = 2$.

It should be remembered that the opportunity losses of act $Q = 2$ in Exhibit 8-8 are *conditional opportunity losses*—conditional to various events happening. Thus, the expected opportunity loss can be computed as in Exhibit 8-9. As asserted earlier, the expected opportunity loss (EOL) of act $Q = 2$ of $2 is the same as the expected value of perfect information. To recapitulate:

1. Earlier, the expected value of perfect information was defined as
    EV of PI = expected profit with PI minus expected profit of the best act without PI.

Demand D, units	Probability P(D) ×	Conditional opportunity loss =	Expected opportunity loss
0	0.10	$4	$0.40
1	0.25	2	0.50
2	0.30	0	0.00
3	0.20	2	0.40
4	0.10	4	0.40
5	0.05	6	0.30
			$2.00

Exhibit 8-9 Expected opportunity loss of act $Q = 2$.

2. Now the expected opportunity loss of the best act under uncertainty is calculated as: EOL of the best act under uncertainty = EV of differences between conditional profits with PI and conditional profits of the best act without PI.
3. EV of PI = EOL of best act under uncertainty.

The reader may find it profitable to interpret the concepts of the expected opportunity loss and the expected value of perfect information in reference to the case where the decision can be repeated week after week for 100 weeks.

Cost of irrationality The conditional opportunity losses and the expected opportunity loss were determined for the best act, $Q = 2$. The notion of opportunity losses, however, can be extended to acts other than the best act. Thus, the conditional opportunity losses and the expected opportunity loss of act $Q = 0$ in comparison with the best acts with perfect information are calculated as in Exhibit 8-10.

As in the case of $Q = 2$, the conditional opportunity losses of act $Q = 0$ shown in column 4 of Exhibit 8-10 are calculated by deducting the conditional profits of the act (column 3) from the conditional profits under certainty (column 2). These represent the opportunities for higher profits forgone by selecting $Q = 0$ instead of the best acts under certainty (or with perfect information), given various events.

The expected opportunity loss of $4.20 of $Q = 0$ is higher than that of $2 of $Q = 2$ because $Q = 2$ is the best act under uncertainty (with the highest expected profit), whereas $Q = 0$ is one of the non-best acts under uncertainty. If the decision maker selects $Q = 0$, despite its expected profit lower than that of the best act, $Q = 2$, he is acting irrationally. Thus, the difference between the expected opportunity loss of a non-best act, $Q = 0$, and the expected opportunity loss of the best act, $Q = 2$, namely, $2.20, may be called the *cost of irrationality*. It follows that the

(1)	(2)	(3)	(4)	(5)	(6)
Demand D, units	Conditional profit under certainty	Conditional profit of act Q = 0	Conditional opportunity loss of act Q = 0 (2) − (3)	Probability P(D)	Expected opportunity loss of act Q = 0 (4) × (5)
0	$ 0	$0	$ 0	0.10	$0
1	2	0	2	0.25	0.50
2	4	0	4	0.30	1.20
3	6	0	6	0.20	1.20
4	8	0	8	0.10	0.80
5	10	0	10	0.05	0.50
					$4.20

Exhibit 8-10 Expected opportunity loss of act $Q = 0$.

expected opportunity loss of $4.20 for a non-best act, $Q = 0$, may be viewed as consisting of two elements, i.e., that element attributable to uncertainty or lack of perfect information and that element attributable to irrationality.

Breakdown of the expected opportunity loss of $Q = 0$

Cost of uncertainty, which is the same as the expected opportunity loss of the best act $Q = 2$	$2.00
Cost of irrationality, which arises because a non-best act, instead of the best act, is chosen	2.20
Expected opportunity loss of a non-best act, $Q = 0$	$4.20

The cost of irrationality of the act $Q = 0$ could also have been computed from the expected profits of that act and of the best act $Q = 2$.

Alternative definition of cost of irrationality

Expected profit of the best act $Q = 2$ (see Exhibit 8-4)	$2.20
Expected profit of a non-best act $Q = 0$ (see Exhibit 8-4)	−0
Cost of irrationality	$2.20

By choosing act $Q = 0$, the decision maker is forgoing the expected profit of $2.20 which could be obtained if $Q = 2$ were taken. The cost of taking a "wrong" act is therefore $2.20 − $0 = $2.20. Again, the

| Demand | Act Q | | | | | |
D, units	0	1	2	3	4	5
0	$ 0	$2	$4	$6	$8	$10
1	2	0	2	4	6	8
2	4	2	0	2	4	6
3	6	4	2	0	2	4
4	8	6	4	2	0	2
5	10	8	6	4	2	0

Exhibit 8-11 Conditional opportunity losses.

reader may wish to interpret the expected cost of irrationality, $2.20, in terms of repeated decisions.

Similarly, the conditional and expected opportunity losses can be calculated for acts other than $Q = 0$ and $Q = 2$. Exhibits 8-11 and 8-12 summarize the conditional opportunity losses and the expected opportunity losses, respectively, of all acts. The reader is urged to verify the computations.

As in the case of act $Q = 0$, the expected opportunity loss of each act may be considered to consist of two elements, the (expected) cost of uncertainty and the (expected) cost of irrationality. The cost of uncertainty is $2 for all acts, i.e., the expected opportunity loss of the best act, the most rational act, under uncertainty, in comparison with what the decision maker could expect if the perfect predictor of events were available. The cost of irrationality varies from one possible act to another because the degree of desirability of acts varies. In the extreme case of $Q = 2$, the best act under uncertainty, the cost of irrationality is zero, because choosing that act is the most rational thing to do in the face of uncertainty (lack of perfect information).

So far the concept of the opportunity loss and related concepts have been discussed in reference to the "original" payoff table which shows conditional *profits* of various acts. The concept can be directly extended to the decision problems where the relevant consequences of the decision are expressed as costs rather than profits. For illustration, suppose that the decision situation is characterized by the conditional

Act Q	0	1	2	3	4	5
Expected opportunity loss	$4.20	$2.60	$2.00	$2.60	$4.00	$5.80

Exhibit 8-12 Expected opportunity losses.

Event	Probability $P(E_i)$	Act			
		I	II	III	IV
E_1	0.3	②	4	5	3
E_2	0.5	3	③	4	6
E_3	0.2	5	6	③	4

Exhibit 8-13   A hypothetical cost payoff table.

cost consequences of Exhibit 8-13.   There are four alternative acts, I, II, III, IV, and three possible events, E_1, E_2, E_3, with the probabilities of 0.3, 0.5, 0.2, respectively.   Since the payoffs are stated in costs, the expected-value-decision criterion would dictate the selection of the act with the *least* expected cost.

Without reproducing the process of computation, the expected costs under uncertainty of all acts are summarized in Exhibit 8-14.   The act with the least expected cost is act I; therefore, this is the best act to be selected under uncertainty.   If the decision maker chose any act other than act I, he would be acting irrationally.   The costs of irrationality of the various acts are:

Act I: $3.1 - 3.1 = 0$

Act II: $3.9 - 3.1 = 0.8$

Act III: $4.1 - 3.1 = 1.0$

Act IV: $4.7 - 3.1 = 1.6$

If the perfect predictor or perfect information were available, given each event, the decision maker could take an action such that the cost would be minimum.   The conditional costs for the decision under certainty, therefore, are the circled cost figures in Exhibit 8-13, i.e., the minima of the row entries.   The expected cost under certainty (or the expected cost with perfect information) is

$$2(0.3) + 3(0.5) + 3(0.2) = 2.7$$

Compare this expected cost *under certainty* of $2.7 with that of the best act *under uncertainty* of $3.1.   The difference of $0.40 $(3.1 - 2.7)$

Act	I	II	III	IV
Expected cost	$3.1	$3.9	$4.1	$4.7

Exhibit 8-14   Expected costs.

Event	Probability	Act			
E_i	$P(E_i)$	I	II	III	IV
E_1	0.3	0	2	3	1
E_2	0.5	0	0	1	3
E_3	0.2	2	3	0	1

Exhibit 8-15   Conditional opportunity losses.

is the improvement in the expected cost attributable to the removal of uncertainty (or availability of perfect information) and accordingly is called the expected value of perfect information or, equivalently, the expected cost of uncertainty. The decision maker would pay something less than $0.40 for a perfect predictor.

The conditional opportunity losses of each act are obtained by deducting the conditional costs of the decision *under certainty* from the conditional costs of the act. The conditional opportunity losses of an act represent *the opportunity for lower costs forgone* because that particular act is selected instead of the best act that would be chosen if perfect information were available. The conditional opportunity losses are derived from the cost table of Exhibit 8-13 by deducting the circled cost figure from other cost entries in a given event row. Exhibit 8-15 summarizes the conditional opportunity losses of all acts thus obtained.

Exhibit 8-16 shows the expected opportunity losses computed on the basis of the conditional opportunity losses of Exhibit 8-15.

Without perfect information, i.e., under uncertainty, the best the decision maker can do is to choose act I and expect an opportunity loss of $0.4. Since this expected opportunity loss is unavoidable given uncertainty, it is called the (expected) cost of uncertainty; to eliminate it, i.e., for perfect information, the decision maker would pay an amount less than that. Note that the same cost of uncertainty was obtained earlier as the difference between the expected costs under certainty and under uncertainty.

The expected opportunity losses of non-best acts, II, III, and IV, are higher than the expected opportunity loss of the best act, I, by the

Act	I	II	III	IV
Expected opportunity loss	$0.4	$1.2	$1.4	$2.0

Exhibit 8-16   Expected opportunity losses.

expected costs of irrationality, the costs of taking acts other than the best. Again, these costs are the same as those calculated earlier from comparing expected costs.

Decision with expected opportunity losses   From this study of the relationships between original profits (or costs) and opportunity losses derived from them, it is evident that for a given problem the same decision results regardless of whether the expected profits (or costs) or the expected opportunity losses are used as the criterion for decision.   Stated alternatively, both criteria yield the same ranking of alternative acts in order of preference.

Concept of differential consequences   Although opportunity losses were derived from the profit or cost data in the above illustrations, construction of an opportunity-loss table does not necessarily require construction of profit or cost payoff tables as a prerequisite.   Often it can be directly constructed from the original description of the decision situation. Depending on the decision problem on hand, sometimes profit or cost data for alternative acts are more readily available and manageable than opportunity losses; at other times, opportunity-loss data are more readily available and useful for analytical purposes than profit or costs.

The basis of a rational decision is the explicit recognition of the *differences* in consequences that alternative acts make.   Any part of consequences that is common to all alternative acts is irrelevant to the decision.   What makes the difference in the desirability of alternative acts comes only from the difference in consequences.   Opportunity losses emphasize the *differences* in consequences.   As may be recalled, opportunity losses of alternative acts given a specific event are simply differences in profits or costs as the case may be among alternative acts.

8-4   ANALYSIS OF MULTISTAGE SEQUENTIAL DECISION PROBLEMS

The examples of decision under uncertainty discussed so far may be characterized as *simple single-stage* problems in that in all of them it was assumed that the decision maker makes his decision *only once, at a given time*, without any concern over—or independent of—any other decisions he may make in the future.   But in many real-world problems the decision maker may not be able to make a current decision without regard to what other related decisions he may have to make subsequently.   When a decision problem requires more than one related decision over a period of time, it is called a *multistage, sequential decision*.   The following example is offered to facilitate the understanding of the nature of multistage, sequential decision problems.

EXAMPLE 8-2

A firm must decide whether to prepare and submit a bid for a certain job.
If it decides not to bid for the job, it gains nothing and loses nothing, but
if it decides to make a bid, it expects to incur a cost of $2000 for prepa-
ration of the bid. (Perhaps for building a prototype model and for
estimating costs.) Upon bidding, the firm may or may not be awarded
the contract for the job, the gross receipt of which amounts to $10,000.
Once the contract is awarded to the firm, the job may be performed by
one of the three alternative methods of operations, I, II, III. Method I
is the traditional processing method necessitating total operating costs of
$4000. Method II is a new method which would involve the total oper-
ating costs of only $2500 if it works, but if it does not and consequently
requires an additional corrective work, the total operating costs for the
job would be $6000. Method III is based on purchasing a critical com-
ponent from an outside supplier and costs $3800 for the job.

Exhibit 8-17 is a game-tree representation of the decision problem
summarized above. The problem is multistage because there is more
than one decision or action stage: at the first action stage, the decision
maker decides whether or not to bid; at the second action stage, he
decides on one of the three alternative processing methods. In addition,
the problem is sequential because the first-stage decision cannot be made
without understanding the consequences of the second-stage decision.

Backward analysis of a sequential decision   In reference to the decision
tree of Exhibit 8-17, the decision maker may be considered to be standing, chronologically speaking, at point a, trying to decide whether to take
the path labeled *Bid* or the path labeled *Do not bid*. Obviously, this
present decision cannot be made without analyzing the second-stage decision problem involving the three alternative operating methods. The
following is a backward analytical procedure by which the problem can
be solved.

Step 1   Suppose that the decision maker is at point d. More specifically, this means that the decision maker has already chosen the path
bid *and* the contract has already been awarded, *and* the decision has
already been made to employ the new operating method. Observe that
once point d has been reached, there is no choice for the decision maker
but to accept and live with either of the cost consequences, $2500 (if the
new method proves successful) and $6000 (if it is not).

The decision maker, needless to say, has no control over which of
the two possible costs will be the eventual outcome (this to be determined by the particular random process in the situation), but suppose
that a gambler or an insurance man comes along and offers an option

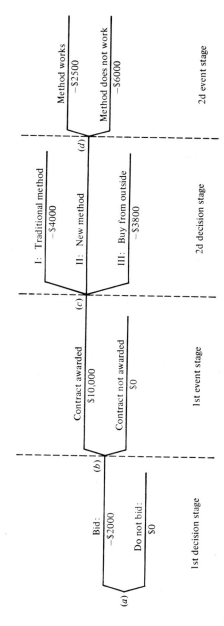

Exhibit 8-17 Game tree for a two-stage sequential decision.

(a)

Bid:
−$2000

Do not bid:
$0

1st decision stage

(b)

Contract awarded
$10,000

Contract not awarded
$0

1st event stage

(c)

I: Traditional method
−$4000

II: New method

III: Buy from outside
−$3800

2d decision stage

(d)

Method works
−$2500

Method does not work
−$6000

2d event stage

279

whereby the decision maker would agree to pay *now* a cash amount *certain*, say $X, to the gambler for his willingness to take over the risk caused by the uncertainty surrounding the cost consequences. In effect, the gambler says to the decision maker, "You and I both know that if you are lucky, your new operating method will work and your outlay will be only $2500, but if you are unlucky, you will be socked with an outlay of $6000. You can, however, eliminate this uncertainty by buying insurance from me under which I assume the responsibility of reimbursing you for whatever the actual operating cost turns out to be, in return for your payment of a fixed sum to me now. How much will you pay me?"

The decision maker, of course, will not buy the insurance if the price is $6000 (or more) because $6000 is the worst that can happen to him if he does not buy the insurance. On the other extreme, the gambler would refuse to write the insurance if the payment offered by the decision maker is $2500 (or less), because $2500 is the best outcome the gambler can attain from the assumption of the risk in the manufacturing operation. It follows that the two could probably agree on the price of the insurance somewhere between the two extremes, $2500 and $6000, say $X. From the decision maker's point of view, this means that if he were to pay any more than X, he would rather take the gamble (between $2500 and $6000 inherent in the original decision problem) himself and that the degree of undesirability (or disutility) of $X with certainty is the same as the degree of undesirability of the uncertainty or gamble between the payment of $2500 and the payment of $6000. In other words, the decision maker is *indifferent* between the certain payment of $X and the uncertain payment of either $2500 or $6000, or, alternatively, the *cash certainty equivalent* of the gamble between $2500 and $6000 is $X.

Determination of the exact amount of X, the cash certainty equivalent, is dependent at least on the decision maker's belief in the relative likelihood of $2500 and $6000 happening and on his subjective like or dislike—utility or disutility—of the payment of $2500, $6000, and $X. If the decision maker is a believer in the expected-value-decision criterion, the expected cost would serve as the index of disutility of the uncertain cost outcomes, i.e., the gamble involving two possible costs. In order to apply the expected-value criterion, then, probabilities must be assigned to the events *new method works* and *new method does not work*. Assume, for the purpose of illustration, that the probabilities are 0.7 and 0.3, respectively. The expected cost is computed as

$$\$2500(0.7) + \$6000(0.3) = \$3550$$

On the other hand, the expected value of certain cash payment of $3550 is $3550(1.0) = $3550.

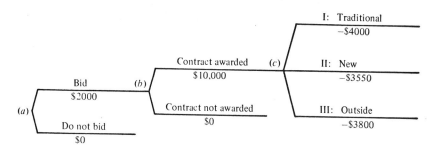

Exhibit 8-18   Game tree equivalent to the original game tree.

Inasmuch as the worth of the gamble the decision maker faces at point d has been determined to be the same as the worth of the certain cash payment of $3550, the two-branch fork starting at d can be replaced by a single branch carrying the certain amount of $3550 without altering the nature of the decision problem.   Exhibit 8-18 shows the result of such a modification at point d.

Step 2   Now, in reference to the tree of Exhibit 8-18, suppose that the decision maker is at point c.   The three alternative-act branches emanating from c represent three alternative cash payments with certainty.   Unlike the case at point d above, point c represents an action stage controllable by the decision maker, and therefore he would naturally choose the branch with the minimum payment.   Such a branch is act II, with the cash equivalent payment of $3550.   This means that the undesirability of the tree at point c to the decision maker can be replaced by this least cost of $3550.   The tree of Exhibit 8-19 incorporates this modification.

Step 3   Next, supposing that the decision maker is at point b in the tree of Exhibit 8-19, the same kind of analytical reasoning as in step 1 is repeated.   If and when the decision maker is at b, it is beyond his control whether or not the contract will be awarded to him.   If he is lucky, he will get the contract and the net monetary consequence will be a $6450 gain; if he is unlucky, he will not be awarded the contract and con-

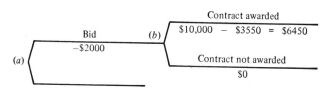

Exhibit 8-19   Game tree equivalent to the original game tree.

sequently will have no additional receipt nor payment. For what amount of *certain cash receipt* would the decision maker trade this gamble option? Since the worst that could happen to him if he chose to stick to the gamble is $0 when no contract is awarded, he would ask the would-be insurer to pay him something more than $0. On the other hand, since the best outcome of the gamble that could happen is a net gain of $6450, the insurer would not pay to the decision maker any more than $6450 for the privilege of buying the gamble from him. When the insurer and the decision maker agree on the cash payment certain of, say Y, in trade for the uncertainty option, Y can be used to replace the desirability of the game at point b.

Again, if the decision maker follows the expected-value criterion, the cash receipt certainty equivalent of the gamble between the possible receipt of $6450 and the possible receipt of $0 is the expected value of the two amounts. Assuming the probabilities of both events, contract awarded and contract not awarded, as 0.5, the expected monetary gain at point b is computed as

$$\$6450(0.5) + \$0(0.5) = \$3225$$

Substituting this expected value of $3225 as the cash certainty equivalent at point b, a new equivalent game tree is obtained as in Exhibit 8-20.

Step 4 Finally, if the decision maker must choose between two action branches in Exhibit 8-20, he would take the upper branch with $1225 gain over the lower with $0.

The successive steps 1 to 4 which the decision maker follows guarantee that all the consequences of the decisions subsequent to the initial decision at point a are taken into account in deciding on the path at the original point a.

A special case of multistage sequential decisions arises in connection with the decision maker's desire to obtain additional information about the nature of the random process which is the source of uncertainty in a given decision problem. If the decision maker, for instance, wishes to delay the action of introducing a new product to some future time in

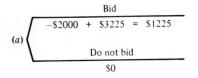

Bid

−$2000 + $3225 = $1225

(a)

Do not bid

$0

Exhibit 8-20 Game tree equivalent to the original game tree.

order to assemble more information about the uncertain market condition, the decision problem may be defined as a multistage one because
he makes two-stage decisions: one now whether to delay the action or
not and subsequently whether to introduce the new product or not.   In
addition, the decision is sequential because the second-stage decision is
dependent upon the result of the first-stage decision, and vice versa.
This kind of sequential decision is the subject of Chap. 10.

8-5 SUMMARY AND TRANSITION

This chapter has tried to demonstrate the reasonableness of the expected-
value-decision criterion, under which the utility or cash certainty equivalent of a set of multiple possible consequences of an alternative act is
represented by the expected (monetary) value.   The rationality of the
criterion is easier to see in connection with a repeatable decision than for
a one-shot decision, but there are situations where application of the
expected-value criterion may lead to decisions that are patently unreasonable to most reasonable men.   The next chapter deals with such
situations and alternative decision criteria suggested for them.   This
chapter, in addition, has discussed some other economic and statistical
concepts useful in decision analyses.

QUESTIONS AND PROBLEMS

1. Discuss the expected value, mode, and worst outcome as the cash certainty equivalent or utility index of multiple outcomes of a single-shot decision and of a repeatable
decision.

2. Two mutually exclusive investment proposals, A and B, have been made, each
requiring an initial outlay of $1 million.   The rate of return could vary between
−5 to 30 percent for A and between 0 to 20 percent for B with the probabilities
as tabulated.

	Probability	
Rate of return, %	A	B
−5	0.10	0
0	0.10	0.15
5	0.15	0.20
10	0.15	0.30
15	0.20	0.20
20	0.15	0.15
25	0.10	0
30	0.05	0

(a) Which project would be chosen under the expected-value criterion? Under the mode criterion? Under the minimax criterion?

(b) Compute the variances. What is the implication of the difference in variance on the decision?

(c) What additional information would help the decision maker?

3. *Break-even analysis under uncertainty* A machine shop is considering whether to purchase machine A or machine B for production of a certain product. Machine A requires an outlay of a fixed cost of \$500 a year and a variable cost of \$2.50 per unit; machine B requires a fixed cost of \$800 and a variable cost of \$1.50 per unit. The product is to be produced in a minimum production run of 100 units. The future annual production requirement may vary between 0 and 500 inclusive with probabilities as in the following table. Supposing that the minimization of the annual

Demand X units	0	100	200	300	400	500
Probability $P(X)$	0	0.15	0.20	0.30	0.30	0.05

operating costs is the objective, the machine shop must ultimately decide which machine to buy. There are three random variables of interest in this problem, demand X; C_{ai}, the annual operating cost of machine A; and C_{bi}, the annual operating cost of machine B. The operating costs of A and B are functions of the number of units demanded X_i:

$$C_{ai} = f(X_i) = 500 + 2.5X_i$$
$$C_{bi} = g(X_i) = 800 + 1.5X_i$$

(a) Give the cost payoff table of two alternative acts and represent the same graphically. What is the break-even volume?

(b) Compute the expected values, variances, and standard deviations of the three random variables, X_i, C_{ai}, C_{bi}.

(c) Which machine would be bought under the expected-value criterion? Under the mode criterion? Under the minimax criterion? Would the variances make any difference in decision making?

(d) Construct the opportunity-loss table and compute the expected opportunity losses. Which machine is better?

(e) How much would the machine-shop management pay for perfect information?

(f) What is the cost of uncertainty?

(g) What is the cost of irrationality?

(h) In general, the expected value of $a + bX_i$ can be computed by the formula $E(a + bX_i) = a + bE(X_i)$. Demonstrate the validity of the formula by computing the $E(C_{ai})$ and $E(C_{bi})$ in two alternative ways.

(i) In general, the variance of $a + bX_i$ is

$$\sum_{i=1}^{n} [(a + bX_i) - E(a + bX_i)]^2 P(X_i) = b^2 \sum_{i=1}^{n} (X_i - EX_i)^2 P(X_i)$$

Demonstrate the validity of the above formula by computing var C_{ai} and var C_{bi} in two alternative ways.

4. Demand for a certain perishable product is modeled by a Poisson process with the average of 2 units/day. The product sells for $8 and costs $6; if not sold on the day stocked, it is discarded with no salvage value.

(a) Construct the conditional-profit table for the decision of how many units to stock per day.

(b) How many units would be stocked under the expected-value criterion? Under the minimax? Under the mode criterion?

(c) Compute the expected opportunity loss and the cost of irrationality of each alternative act.

(d) Compute the cost of uncertainty.

(e) Demonstrate that the expected value of a random variable r is λ if r is Poisson distributed, namely, $P(r) = \lambda^r e^{-\lambda}/r!$, by computing the daily expected demand.

5. An urn contains 10 balls, 6 of which are marked heads and 4 marked tails. You are offered an option to play a game wherein 5 balls are sampled at random with replacement and if fewer than 2 balls are marked heads, you receive $2 multiplied by the difference between the number of balls marked heads and 2.

(a) Would you play the game?

(b) How much would you pay for the privilege of playing the game?

(c) Demonstrate that the expected value of a binomial random variable is np, where n is the number of trials, and p the probability of success, by computing the expected number of heads out of 5 balls drawn.

6. A hotel chain is considering whether to build a new hotel on a given site. It may go ahead and build one on the basis of information available currently, or it may undertake a more extensive market survey prior to the decision. If the survey indicates a favorable demand, the new hotel will be built; otherwise, the proposal will be rejected. Even if the survey result is favorable, there is no guarantee that the hotel will be profitable; in particular, it may be a very profitable, moderately profitable, or loss operation.

(a) Draw the decision tree. Identify event and action stages.

(b) Would the probabilities for very profitable, moderately profitable, and loss operation events without the market survey be different from those with the market survey?

(c) Explain the steps necessary in the backward analysis for the decision.

(d) How could the decision tree be expanded in order to make it more realistic?

9
Decision Making under Uncertainty: Expected-utility Criterion

9-0 INTRODUCTION

The expected-value-decision criterion, or Bayesian decision theory, constitutes the mainstay of modern statistical decision theory. To the extent that the relative weights to be used in weighting outcomes (in the process of constructing the desirability index of each act under the criterion) represent the degree of likelihood of occurrence of these outcomes, they correspond closely to the probabilities of these outcomes. We were thus motivated to learn the theory of probability, or the rules of probability, as a means of improving our ability to assign probabilities in a logically consistent manner. In particular, Chap. 7 introduced some of the mathematically manageable probability functions, i.e., the binomial, the Poisson, and the normal, knowledge of which proves useful in assigning and analyzing the probabilities of events generated by some of the more commonly observable real-world random processes. Chapter 8 attempted to justify the reasonableness of the expected-value criterion, mostly by way of interpreting the weighted consequences, namely, the expected value of consequences, in terms of the long-run average consequences expected if the same decision could be repeated many times.

But there are situations where the decision according to the expected-value criterion is either infeasible or unreasonable in the sense that the result is unacceptable to most reasonable men. The present chapter examines some of the decision circumstances in which the application of the expected-value principle appears unreasonable and proposes alternative criteria to overcome them.

Basically, two major sources of difficulty in using the expected-value-decision criterion may be identified: (1) In some decision situations neither the decision maker nor his analyst has any objective basis for specific probability assignment over the possible outcomes of relevance, and accordingly he may refuse to make such an assignment. Inasmuch as the probabilities of the outcomes are an essential ingredient in the computation of the expected value, the expected-value criterion falls apart. (2) Even when meaningful probabilities can be assigned to uncertain events, in some situations the expected value of consequences simply does not seem *reasonable* as the basis for comparing the desirability of alternative acts.

One of the decision theories suggested to deal with the first case, where no meaningful probability assignment is available, is the minimax principle, already introduced. It will be discussed in more detail in the first part of this chapter. An expansion or refinement of the expected-value criterion, known as expected-utility theory, intended to handle the second difficulty is presented in the latter part of the chapter.

9-1 DECISION UNDER UNCERTAINTY WITHOUT PROBABILITY ASSIGNMENT

Imagine a firm contemplating introduction of a new product to the market. For various planning purposes such as decisions involving investment, manpower, production run, inventory level, etc., the company is of course vitally interested in how well the new product will sell next year. Obviously, many levels of sales are possible, but there is no way of predicting with certainty.

Faced with the uncertainty, the analyst may first attempt to derive probabilities for the various possible levels of sales through analyzing past records of the sales of similar products when they were introduced. If the new product is considered similar enough to these other past new products, their actual sales records would serve as the starting point for a meaningful assignment of probabilities for the various levels of sales of the product. Then the decision can be made according to the expected-value criterion using these probabilities. If, however, the new product cannot be considered sufficiently similar to any of the past new products, the actual sales records of these products are of no help in assessing probabilities of various sales levels of the new product; in short, no *objective* probabilities are available.

Failing to produce the objective probabilities, the analyst's next step may be to ask top management to give its best judgment on the likelihood of various possible levels of the future sales of the new product. Not all decision makers can express their "feel" about, or "belief" in, the relative likelihood of events in accordance with the rules of probabilities studied in Chaps. 6 and 7, but the analyst can help them convert personal feeling and belief into probabilities conforming to the rules, thus assuring some consistency in the assignment. The resulting *subjective probabilities* would then serve as the basis for application of the expected-value criterion.

Granting that the Bayesian expected-value criterion gives an acceptable solution to the decision problems where either objective or subjective probabilities are available, what if problems are under "true" uncertainty, where no meaningful probabilities are forthcoming? The hard-core Bayesian decision theorists answer that inasmuch as the choice of acts depends on which particular possible event happens, the likelihood of events *cannot* be ignored in rational decision making; therefore, the decision maker *should be forced* to express his *best conviction* as to the likelihood of events no matter how crude it may be. Probabilities based on such conviction are personal and subjective but would be used as weights in weighting various consequences under the expected-value principle. Bayesian theorists claim that especially with the expansion or refinement of the theory to be discussed in the latter part of the chapter, the Bayesian theory yields the most reasonable decision under all circumstances.

Other theorists, however, maintain that there are situations where available information is so scanty that no sensible assignment of probabilities (to various possible events) is possible and the decision maker is justified in refusing to make decisions on the basis of probabilities as weights. The minimax, one of the principles offered by these theorists as applicable in decision making under true or complete uncertainty where the probability distribution is unknown, is discussed below.

EXAMPLE 9-1

Suppose that the payoff table of a hypothetical decision problem is as in Exhibit 9-1. The various events on which the consequences of alternative acts depend are represented by S_i's, where $i = 1, 2, 3, 4$; and alternative acts are represented by A_j's, where $j = 1, 2, 3, 4$. The conditional consequences given in the table are assumed to be *desirable* consequences. Thus, the figures represent such indices of desirability as

	Act			
Event	A_1	A_2	A_3	A_4
S_1	3	8	1	6
S_2	3	6	3	3
S_3	3	4	6	9
S_4	3	1	8	0

Exhibit 9-1 Payoff table for a hypothetical decision.

profits in business decisions and effectiveness in government decisions; consequently, the higher the number, the more preferable. In the following discussion, these numbers are assumed to be dollar profits.

As seen in Chap. 6, according to the maximin or minimax decision rule, the decision maker would choose that act whose *worst possible consequence* is the best (or the most desirable or the least undesirable) of the worst possible consequences of all acts. Since the relevant consequences in the payoff table are assumed to be profits, the decision is made so as to *maximize the minimum possible profits.* Hence the name, *maximin principle.* If the relevant consequences were something undesirable, i.e., sacrifices or costs, the decision would be made so as to *minimize the maximum possible sacrifices,* costs or losses. Hence, the name *minimax principle.*

In the given profit payoff table, the worst possible consequence, or the minimum profit, of each act is as summarized below:

Act	A_1	A_2	A_3	A_4
Worst consequence, minimum possible profit	\$3	\$1	\$1	\$0

If A_1 is chosen, no matter what happens, a minimum profit of \$3 is *guaranteed,* while if other acts are chosen and if the decision maker is unlucky, the resulting profit could be as low as 1, 1, and 0, for A_2, A_3, and A_4, respectively. The choice of A_1 will guarantee the attainment of the highest level of *security,* i.e., minimum possible profit, \$3.

The maximin principle (or minimax principle if payoffs are stated in costs) is essentially conservative, pessimistic, and unadventurous. Adherence to it means forgoing chances of making higher profits. The luckiest outcome from selecting the maximin act A_1 is only \$3, whereas if other acts (A_2, A_3, or A_4), are chosen and the decision maker is lucky (or luckier than the worst anyway), he will make a profit higher than \$3.

Does the maximin principle seem *reasonable* to *reasonable* men? In other words, does the higher *security* or insurance level attained under the principle justify the entailing sacrifice of opportunity for higher profits? Although the reader should attempt to judge the reasonableness of the principle on his own, at least the following three factors should be considered.

1. Suppose that the decision maker believes that the event S_3 is the *most likely* to happen and the event S_4 *very unlikely* to happen. Would the decision maker still follow the maximin principle and choose the act A_1? Or would he switch to the act A_4 because if S_4 is very unlikely and S_3 is very likely, he is very likely to obtain the profit of \$9 if A_4 is taken as opposed to \$3 profit, the best that could be hoped for if A_1 is chosen? The answer evidently depends crucially on *how* very likely and unlikely the decision maker believes S_3 and S_4 to be. If the degree of likelihood is of such crucial importance, the Bayesian decision theorists contend, the decision maker's belief in it should be made explicit. Refusing to do so would be merely to avoid what must be done. The crudest assignment of probabilities is better than none even under complete ignorance of the nature of the event-generating random process. To them, the decision without explicit consideration of the relative likelihood of events is irrational and unacceptable.

2. Supposing that the decision maker cannot (or refuses to) assess meaningful probabilities, would he switch from the maximin decision if some of the conditional profit figures were different? For illustration, change the decision problem such that the conditional profits of A_2 now are \$800 for the event S_1, \$600 for S_2, \$400 for S_3, and \$1 for S_4. Even with the changed conditional profits, the minimum possible profit of A_2 is \$1, and therefore, in comparison to A_1 whose minimum possible profit is still \$3, A_2 is inferior according to the maximin decision rule. Would most reasonable men choose A_1 over A_2 for the difference in the minimum possible profit of only \$2 $(3 - 1)$, forgoing the possibility or opportunity of making \$800, \$600, \$400? We guess not! Most reasonable men would choose A_2 over A_1.

3. Suppose that the event-generating process which produces S_1, S_2, S_3, or S_4 is not neutral but malevolent, i.e., it is *willed* by an "enemy" who wishes us ill. If S_i's are weather conditions, the event-generating process is nature, and there is no reason to believe that nature would deliberately generate weather conditions so that we would fare badly. But if S_i's are the various possible enemy strategies in a battle situation, the enemy would *try* to choose its strategy so as to inflict the most damage to us or allow us the least gain. In such situation, we take the view that the uncertainty, or the S_i-generating process, is controlled by a *willful, intelligent* being.

When uncertainty in a decision situation is caused by an intelligent being, the situation is often referred to as a *game*,[1] and a great deal of theoretical work has been done recently under the name of the game theory on how rational decisions can be made in game situations.[2] Although this book does not discuss game theory in detail, the maximin-minimax principle will be shown to be the most reasonable approach to a special type of the game situation, namely, *strictly competitive games*.

Suppose in Exhibit 9-1 that S_i's are the alternative strategies available to the enemy rather than the events generated by a neutral mother nature and that A_j's are the alternative strategies available to *our* decision maker. Then, further assume that the numbers in the payoff table represent the number of square miles gained by us in the battle, contingent on each of our strategies and each of the enemy's strategies. Since the territory gained by us is the territory lost by the enemy, the same payoff table can be regarded as the payoff table for the enemy as well as for us. The enemy is in an unenviable position because he will lose always or gain nothing at best. The game situation is a *perfectly* or *strictly competitive one* in that what we gain is what the opponent loses and vice versa.

If we assume that the enemy is as intelligent as we are and therefore knows all the information contained in the payoff table, as we do, what decision should we make? One approach is to follow the Bayesian theory and choose that strategy which gives us the highest expected gain in square miles. The probability that the enemy would choose a particular strategy can be obtained from what we know about past enemy behavior, other available information, and subjective judgment. Suppose, for illustration, A_2 is the best act under the Bayesian rule (presumably because we have assigned high probabilities to S_1 and S_2).

In a perfectly competitive game, however, the expected-value criterion does not give us an equilibrium solution. Since the enemy is assumed to be intelligent, we have to worry about the enemy trying to outguess or outsmart us. The enemy might reason as follows: "They [we, that is] would follow the Bayesian theory and consequently choose A_2. If so, we should choose S_4 so that we would allow them only 1 mi². "

But we are also intelligent and therefore would try to outsmart our enemy as follows: "If the enemy chooses S_4 on the basis that we might

---

[1] The reader should note that the term game here is used in a more restrictive sense than in earlier chapters, where the same term was used rather loosely to refer to any decision situation where uncertainty is involved, as when we spoke of game trees, in which the random processes are not controlled by intelligent beings.

[2] The interested reader is referred to the pioneering work by J. von Neumann and Oskar Morgenstern, "Theory of Games and Economic Behavior," 2d ed., Princeton, Princeton, N.J., 1947, or an easier exposition by R. D. Luce and Howard Raiffa, "Games and Decisions," Wiley, New York, 1957.

select A_2 according to the Bayesian decision rule, then we should discard the Bayesian rule and switch to A_3 so that we gain 8 mi²." The outguessing game would go on and on, for now the enemy would switch to S_1, which is his best counterstrategy against our strategy A_3; then we would switch our strategy to . . . ; and so on. One reasonable way out of this endless circle of indecision is the maximin-minimax principle which would assure us some minimum gain regardless of what the enemy might do. Thus, we look at the worst possible outcome associated with each of our available strategies and choose that act which has the maximal minimum gain. The maximin act is, of course, A_1. This act guarantees us the gain of 3 mi² regardless of what the enemy may do.

There are many other decision theories suggested by various theorists intended to apply to decisions where probability assignment is not available, but this book does not discuss them except to observe that each has its own shortcomings. Given a particular criterion, it is not difficult to conceive of plausible decision situations where its application would result in a patently unreasonable decision.

9-2 DECISION UNDER UNCERTAINTY: EXPECTED-UTILITY CRITERION

The following example illustrates a situation where the expected-value criterion yields a choice of an act which is contrary to the best intuitive judgment of most reasonable men.

EXAMPLE 9-2

Suppose that we are confronted with an option between receiving $10,000 for certain, and flipping a fair coin and receiving $20,100 if heads and nothing if tails. Exhibit 9-2 represents the decision problem on hand more formally.

Act A_1 represents the option of receiving $10,000 with certainty; act A_2 represents the gamble option of receiving $20,100 if heads and $0 if tails. The expected monetary values of A_1 and A_2 are

$$EV(A_1) = 0.5(10,000) + 0.5(10,000) = \$10,000$$
$$EV(A_2) = 0.5(20,100) + 0.5(0) = \$10,050$$

| | | Act | |
Event	Probability	A_1	A_2
Heads	0.5	$10,000	$20,100
Tails	0.5	10,000	0

Exhibit 9-2 Payoff table for Example 9-2.

Since the expected receipt of A_2 is larger than that of A_1, we *should* choose A_2 according to the expected-value criterion. But is the choice reasonable? Would we indeed select A_2 in reality? Most of us, we suspect, would prefer A_1 to A_2.

To state explicitly what is an obvious notion, if we choose A_1 instead of A_2, contrary to what is indicated by the expected-value criterion, we do so because the desirability or *utility* to the decision maker of the certainty of receiving \$10,000 is larger than the desirability or *utility* of the gamble of receiving \$20,100 with a half chance and receiving nothing with the other half chance. In symbols, $U(A_1) > U(A_2)$.

The desirability or utility referred to above is strictly a personal and subjective concept. Depending on the individual's values, some may prefer A_2 to A_1; in other words, they put a higher utility on A_2 than on A_1, whereas most of us would not. To be specific, imagine a rich man with some gambling instinct faced with the same decision situation. Such a man might well prefer to choose A_2, a gamble which *might* bring a payoff of \$20,100, over A_1, a certainty of receiving \$10,000. And if he indeed chooses A_2, we cannot say that he is being any less rational than we who prefer A_1. In the following discussion of utility we should keep in mind this personal nature of utility. Utility is meaningful only in reference to a specific decision maker and a specific decision situation.

Now suppose that the decision maker is not that much of a gambler and therefore prefers A_1 to A_2. Would he still prefer the certainty of a specified sum of money to the gamble option when that specified certain sum of money is reduced to, say, \$9000? Again the answer depends on what the individual decision maker's predilection for gambling is. For the sake of discussion, however, assuming that the decision maker still prefers the certainty of \$9000 to the gamble, we could, of course, go on to reduce the sum of money to be received with certainty further to \$8000, \$7200, \$7000, \$6000, . . . , and confront the decision maker with a series of decisions involving the option of the certain receipt of a sum of money and the option of the gamble between \$20,100 and \$0 with fifty-fifty chances. If the sum of money to be received with certainty is reduced to \$0, of course, any economic decision maker would prefer the gamble between \$20,100 and \$0 to the certainty of the receipt of \$0. Even if the sum of money to be received with certainty is raised to \$50, most of us would prefer the gamble to the certain receipt.

Cash certainty equivalent When the sum of money to be received for certain is somewhere between \$9000 and \$50, we expect the decision maker to switch his preference from the certainty option to the gamble option. Suppose that such switching of preference occurs at \$1200.

That is, suppose that the decision maker would prefer any certain sum higher than $1200 to the fifty-fifty gamble between $20,100 and $0, that he would prefer the gamble to the certain sum if the certain sum is less than $1200, and that if the certain sum is exactly $1200, he would be indifferent between the certainty option and the gamble option, namely, he would not care if someone else chose for him one or the other act arbitrarily. Then this critical amount, $1200, is called the *cash certainty equivalent* of the gamble. If the certainty option of receiving $1200 is added to the original payoff table as act A_3, the new payoff table is as shown in Exhibit 9-3. The ranking of the acts can be formally stated as

$$U(A_1) > U(A_2)$$
$$U(A_2) = U(A_3)$$

and obviously

$$U(A_1) > U(A_3)$$

(For most people would prefer the certain $10,000 to the certain $1200.)

Expected utility To recapitulate, $U(A_1)$ is simply the utility to the decision maker of receiving $10,000, $U(A_1) = U(\$10,000)$. Likewise, the utility of A_3 is the utility of receiving $1200 with certainty, expressed as $U(A_3) = U(\$1200)$.

But the utility of A_2, the gambling option, is of a somewhat different nature. It depends on three elements: $20,100, the conditional receipt if heads; $0, the conditional receipt if tails; and the probabilities of the contingencies or events, i.e., heads and tails. Inasmuch as the outcomes of the flip of a coin, heads or tails, occur independently of conditional payoffs associated with them, we can meaningfully define the utility (or desirability) of $20,100 and of $0 independently of the probabilities of events. We can then consider the utility of A_2, the gamble option, as dependent on the *utilities* of the conditional payoffs of $20,100 and $0 and the *probabilities* of heads and tails. Thus, the one holistic

		Act		
Event	Probability	A_1	A_2	A_3
Heads	0.5	$10,000	$20,100	$1200
Tails	0.5	10,000	0	1200

Exhibit 9-3   Modified payoff table for Example 9-2.

gamble option is decomposed into two constituent elements: utilities of monetary sums when their receipt becomes certain and the probabilities of receiving them.

Now representing the utility of \$20,100 by $U(20,100)$ and the utility of \$0 by $U(0)$, the expected utility (weighted average utility) of A_2 is defined as

$$EU(A_2) = P(H)U(20,100) + P(T)U(0)$$

Where $P(H)$ and $P(T)$ are the probabilities of heads and tails, respectively. Since $P(H) = P(T) = \frac{1}{2}$,

$$EU(A_2) = \frac{1}{2}[U(20,100)] + \frac{1}{2}[U(0)]$$

Could this $EU(A_2)$ be considered equivalent to the utility of the whole gamble option, $U(A_2)$? Alternatively, is it reasonable to say that since $U(A_2) = EU(A_2)$, $EU(A_2)$ can be compared with $U(A_1)$ and $U(A_3)$ in deciding whether the gamble option, A_2, is preferable to the certainty options, A_1 and A_3? The answer is yes *if* utility values for the certainty amounts of money involved (\$0, \$20,100, \$10,000, \$1200) are correctly assigned. More precisely, the theorists say that the indices of the decision maker's utilities for various dollar amounts to be received with certainty can be so constructed that the expected utilities may be used as representing the desirabilities of alternative acts regardless of whether the acts were gambles or certainty options.[1]

In particular, the (conditional) monetary receipts shown in the payoff table of Exhibit 9-3 (to be received with certainty given an event and an act) can be converted into *utility measures* such that the expected utilities may serve as the indicators of the desirabilities of various acts. Conceptually, the original monetary payoff table of Exhibit 9-3 would be converted into the equivalent utility payoff table of Exhibit 9-4.

[1] What is being asserted here is, in effect, that the numbers 0, 20,100, 10,000, and 1200 do not correctly reflect the relative degrees of utility of the (certain) receipts of \$0, \$20,100, \$10,000, \$1200, respectively, that the decision maker assigns, and this is why the expected monetary value cannot be used as the basis for decision, but if correct utility values are found, the expected-value criterion will again be valid.

		Act		
Event	*Probability*	A_1	A_2	A_3
Heads	0.5	$U(10,000)$	$U(20,100)$	$U(1200)$
Tails	0.5	$U(10,000)$	$U(0)$	$U(1200)$

Exhibit 9-4 Utility payoff table.

On the basis of the newly constructed utility payoff table, the three acts A_1, A_2, and A_3 are ranked in order of preference according to the *expected utility* of each act as defined below:

$$EU(A_1) = P(H)U(10,000) + P(T)U(10,000)$$
$$EU(A_2) = P(H)U(20,100) + P(T)U(0)$$
$$EU(A_3) = P(H)U(1200) + P(T)U(1200)$$

Now the crucial question is: What utility values can we assign to the certain monetary receipts of \$0, \$1200, \$10,000, and \$20,100 such that the expected utility can be used as the criterion of choice between A_1, A_2, and A_3, the consequences of which involve these sums? Decision theorists following von Neumann and Morgenstern assert that the expected utility would be the reasonable basis for decision if the following procedure is followed in assigning utility values to various monetary payoffs.

Procedures for constructing utility index

Step 1 Find the best, i.e., most desirable, and the worst, i.e., least desirable conditional consequences from the payoff table representing the decision problem. In our example, the best consequence is the receipt of \$20,100 conditional to the event heads and the alternative act A_2; the worst consequence is the receipt of \$0 conditional to the event tails and the alternative act A_2.

Step 2 Assign a completely arbitrary number, say 100, to the best consequence of the payoff table as the index of its utility; i.e.,

$$U(20,100) = 100$$

Next assign another completely arbitrary number, say -100, to the worst consequence of the payoff table as its index of utility except that the arbitrary number assigned to the worst consequence must be smaller than the number assigned to the best consequence. Thus,

$$U(0) = -100$$

The two numbers 100 and -100 assigned as indices of utility for the receipt of \$20,100 and the receipt of \$0, respectively, are completely arbitrary except that the index for the best consequence is higher than that for the worst consequence. This restriction is natural because the utility of the best consequence is greater than the utility of the worst consequence. Although the particular numbers 100 and -100 were chosen for illustration here, any other pairs of numbers that satisfy the condition given above could have been used; e.g., 1100 and −50, 1 and 0, or 5 and 2.   Conventionally, however, 1 and 0, 1 for the best consequence and 0 for the worst consequence, are most often used.

Step 3 Design a *standard gamble* (or reference gamble) which involves the best and worst conditional payoffs, i.e., $20,100 and $0, such that if the decision maker plays it, he will receive $20,100 with a specific probability of p and $0 with the probability of $1 − p$.   The standard gamble can best be understood by imagining a *standard urn* containing 1000 balls, each of which is marked either $20,100 or $0 and has an equal chance of being chosen when a ball is selected at random.   The gamble is that from this standard urn a ball is selected at random, and if the selected ball is marked $20,100, the decision maker receives $20,100; if it is marked $0, he receives $0.   The proportion of the number of balls marked $20,100 in the urn to the total number of balls in the urn is p; the remainder of the balls, $1 − p$, are marked $0.

Step 4 The desirability, or utility, of the standard gamble to the decision maker varies as the probability p of winning $20,100 is varied, i.e., when the proportion or the mix of the balls marked $20,100 and $0 is varied.   Thus, the more balls there are marked $20,100, the more preferable the gamble.

For example, compare the standard gamble A where the probability of winning $20,100 is $p = 0.2$ (out of the total 1000 balls, the number of balls marked $20,100 is 200) and the standard gamble B where the probability of winning $20,100 is $p = 0.6$ (the number of balls marked $20,100 is 600).   Clearly, B is preferred to A in this situation. In symbols,

$$U(\text{standard gamble } A) < U(\text{standard gamble } B)$$

If the rule is adopted that the *utility of the standard gamble* is to be represented by its *expected utility*, the expected utility of a standard gamble is calculated as

$$EU(\text{standard gamble}) = p[U(20,100)] + (1 − p)[U(0)]$$

Specifically, for A and B, the expected utilities are

$$EU(\text{standard gamble } A) = 0.2(100) + 0.8(−100) = −60$$
$$EU(\text{standard gamble } B) = 0.6(100) + 0.4(−100) = 20$$

The expected utility of standard gamble B is obviously higher than the expected utility of standard gamble A.   The ranking between the two gambles on the basis of expected utility is the same as the ranking that would be made on the basis of the knowledge of the difference in the number of balls marked $20,100, i.e., the probability of winning the amount.

Step 5   The expected utility was chosen as the index of the desirability of various standard gambles in step 4 so that it in turn could be used (in step 6) as the yardstick in assigning utility values to the various conditional monetary values of the payoff table in Exhibit 9-3.   But let us first compute the expected utilities of some other standard gambles besides the two given in step 4.

For the standard gamble with $p = 1$ (all balls marked $20,100):

$$EU(\text{standard gamble, } p = 1) = 1(100) + 0(-100) = 100$$

For the standard gamble with $p = 0.9$ (900 balls marked $20,100):

$$EU(\text{standard gamble, } p = 0.9) = 0.9(100) + 0.1(-100) = 80$$

For the standard gamble with $p = 0.8$ (800 balls marked $20,100):

$$EU(\text{standard gamble, } p = 0.8) = 0.8(100) + 0.2(-100) = 60$$

For the standard gamble with $p = 0.3$ (300 balls marked $20,100):

$$EU(\text{standard gamble, } p = 0.3) = 0.3(100) + 0.7(-100) = -40$$

For the standard gamble with $p = 0$ (all balls marked $0):

$$EU(\text{standard gamble, } p = 0) = 0(100) + 1(-100) = -100$$

Step 6   Now the conditional monetary receipts of Exhibit 9-3 are replaced by their equivalent utility indices, as laid out in Exhibit 9-4.

Utility of $20,100   *When and if* the decision maker chooses A_2 and the coin falls heads, he is entitled to receive $20,100 with certainty. Supposing that this eventuality has taken place, would he be willing to trade this certainty of receiving $20,100 for one of the alternative gambles defined in steps 4 and 5?   If he is a rational man, he would not trade the certain receipt of $20,100 unless $p = 1$ in the standard gamble. In other words, he would be indifferent between *the standard gamble with* $p = 1$ and the certainty of $20,100.   In symbols

$$U(20,100) = U(\text{standard gamble, } p = 1)$$

Since

$$U(\text{standard gamble, } p = 1) = EU(\text{standard gamble, } p = 1)$$
$$= 100$$

according to steps 4 and 5,

$$U(20,100) = 100$$

To repeat, the utility of \$20,100 is considered the same as the utility of the standard gamble with $p = 1$. Since the utility of the standard gamble with $p = 1$ is measured by its expected utility 100, \$20,100 to be received for certain when and if the decision maker chooses A_2 and the coin falls heads is given the same utility index of 100.

Utility of \$10,000   *When and if* the decision maker chooses A_1 and the coin falls heads, or *when and if* the decision maker chooses A_1 and the coin falls tails, he is entitled to receive \$10,000 with certainty. Supposing that such an eventuality has actually taken place, would he be willing to trade this certain \$10,000 for one of the alternative standard gambles? If he is a rational man, he would be willing to trade the certain \$10,000 for the standard gamble with $p = 1$, which brings \$20,100 for certain.

As to the next alternative standard gamble shown in step 5, i.e., the standard gamble with $p = 0.9$, whether to trade \$10,000 (certain) for it would depend on the decision maker's degree of pessimism or optimism—is he willing to go for the chance of receiving \$20,100 with the probability of 0.9 instead of the certain receipt of \$10,000? Suppose the answer is yes. Then, this means that to the decision maker

$$U(10,000) < U(\text{standard gamble, } p = 0.9)$$

Since

$$U(\text{standard gamble, } p = 0.9) = EU(\text{standard gamble, } p = 0.9)$$
$$= 80$$

$$U(10,000) < 80$$

As the probability p of winning \$20,100 in the standard gamble is successively lowered, it is expected that at some value of p the decision maker will be indifferent between the certain prospect of \$10,000 and the standard gamble. For the purpose of discussion, assume that when $p = 0.85$, the decision maker is indifferent between the standard gamble and the certain \$10,000. Then

$$U(10,000) = U(\text{standard gamble, } p = 0.85)$$
$$= EU(\text{standard gamble, } p = 0.85)$$
$$= 0.85(100) + 0.15(-100)$$
$$= 70$$

For the values of p lower than 0.85

$$U(10,000) > U(\text{standard gamble}, p = p)$$
$$= EU(\text{standard gamble}, p = p)$$

Utility of $1200 *When and if* the decision maker chooses A_3 and the coin falls heads, or *when and if* the decision maker chooses A_3 and the coin falls tails, the decision maker is entitled to receive $1200 with certainty.

At which value of p, the probability of winning $20,100 in the standard gamble, would the decision maker be indifferent between the standard gamble and the certainty of receiving $1200? If $p = 0$, a rational decision maker, of course, would state

$$U(1200) > U(\text{standard gamble}, p = 0)$$

Recall the earlier discussion comparing A_2 and A_3, where the nature of the decision maker is assumed to be such that he would be indifferent between the certain $1200 and the gamble between $20,100 and $0 with fifty-fifty chances. Since the amounts of $20,100 and $0 in the gamble in the earlier discussion are the same as the ones involved in the standard gamble, to be consistent, the same decision maker must be assumed indifferent between the certain $1200 and the standard gamble with $p = 0.5$. Formally,

$$U(1200) = U(\text{standard gamble}, p = 0.5)$$
$$= EU(\text{standard gamble}, p = 0.5)$$
$$= 0.5(100) + 0.5(-100)$$
$$= 0$$

Utility of $0 *When and if* the decision maker chooses A_2 and the coin falls tails, the decision maker is entitled to receive $0 with certainty. Supposing that this eventuality has happened, when (namely, at what value of p) would he be indifferent whether he trades the $0 certain prospect with the standard gamble?

If p is anything larger than 0, the decision maker would prefer the standard gamble to the certain $0. When $p = 0$, he will be indifferent between the standard gamble and the certain $0. Thus

$$U(0) = U(\text{standard gamble}, p = 0)$$
$$= EU(\text{standard gamble}, p = 0)$$
$$= 0(100) + 1.0(-100)$$
$$= -100$$

When these concrete utility values are substituted in Exhibit 9-4, the new equivalent utility payoff table (Exhibit 9-5) is obtained.

		Act		
		---	---	---
Event	Probability	A_1	A_2	A_3
Heads	0.5	70	100	0
Tails	0.5	70	−100	0

Exhibit 9-5 Utility payoff table.

Step 7 Now as the final step in the decision, the expected utilities of alternative acts are computed:

$$EU(A_1) = 0.5(70) + 0.5(70) = 70$$
$$EU(A_2) = 0.5(100) + 0.5(-100) = 0$$
$$EU(A_3) = 0.5(0) + 0.5(0) = 0$$

Since $EU(A_1) > EU(A_2) = EU(A_3)$, according to the expected-utility criterion, the decision maker should be indifferent between A_2 and A_3 and should prefer A_1 to either A_2 or A_3. At least in this instance, the expected-utility criterion yields a more reasonable ranking among various acts than the expected-monetary-value criterion.

An informal proof of the reasonableness of the expected-utility criterion
It was asserted that if the particular method of assigning utility equivalents to conditional monetary payoffs is employed, the expected-utility criterion will yield the decision that is reasonable to a rational decision maker. But is the assertion valid?

What was done above in assigning utilities to the various conditional monetary amounts was in effect to replace each consequence in the original payoff table of Exhibit 9-3 with its equivalent standard gamble involving two sums of money, $20,100 and $0. Thus, because the decision maker is indifferent between the certain sum of $10,000 and the standard gamble with probability of winning $20,100 of 0.85, the 10,000 entry in the original conditional payoff table could be replaced by the standard gamble with $p = 0.85$ without changing the essence of the decision problem. Similarly, because the decision maker is indifferent between the certain sum of cash, $20,100, and the standard gamble with the probability of winning $20,100 of $p = 1$, the $20,100 entry in the original conditional payoff table could be replaced by the standard gamble with $p = 1$. And so on for $0 and $1200. Exhibit 9-6 lays out explicitly the conditional standard gambles replacing the original conditional monetary receipts.

According to Exhibit 9-6, if the decision maker takes the act A_1 and if the event is heads, he will be entitled to the standard gamble with

Event	Probability	Act		
		A_1	A_2	A_3
Heads	0.5	Standard gamble with $p = 0.85$	Standard gamble with $p = 1.0$	Standard gamble with $p = 0.50$
Tails	0.5	Standard gamble with $p = 0.85$	Standard gamble with $p = 0$	Standard gamble with $p = 0.50$

Exhibit 9-6 Conditional payoffs in equivalent standard gamble.

$p = 0.85$; then, if the ball drawn at random from the standard urn (with 85 percent of the balls marked $20,100 and the remaining 15 percent marked $0) happens to be marked $20,100, he will receive $20,100, and if marked $0, he will receive $0.   If the decision maker takes the same act A_1 but the event is tails, he will be entitled to the same standard gamble.

If, however, the decision maker takes act A_2, there are two possible outcomes: (1) If the event is heads, the decision maker will be entitled to the standard gamble with $p = 1$; then, if the ball drawn at random from the standard urn (with 100 percent of the balls marked $20,100 and none marked $0) happens to be one marked $20,100 (which it always will be), then he receives $20,100.   (2) If the event is tails, the decision maker will be entitled to the standard gamble with $p = 0$; and so on.

Exhibit 9-7 represents the same decision example in the game-tree form.   Originating from point a are three branches, A_1, A_2, A_3, one of

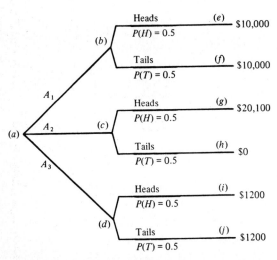

Exhibit 9-7 Game-tree representation of the original decision problem.

which the decision maker ultimately chooses. If he takes, say A_2, and, further, if the coin falls heads, he will end up at point g, one of the terminal points of the tree, and be entitled to $20,100. The reader should be able to interpret the path to each of the terminal points e to j.

Now the decision problem on hand may be viewed as that of comparing the desirabilities of the pair of possible terminal values at e and f associated with A_1, the pair of possible terminal values at g and h associated with A_2, and the pair of possible terminal values at i and j associated with A_3. The trouble in this comparison is that these terminal points represent different monetary amounts, the magnitudes of which are not directly indicative of their "true" relative desirabilities. One way of overcoming the difficulty is to replace the different monetary values at various terminal points by the equivalent standard gambles involving the *same* two amounts of money, as in the game tree of Exhibit 9-8.

The reader should observe that the two trees in Exhibits 9-7 and 9-8 are identical from the origin at point a to points e to j. The only

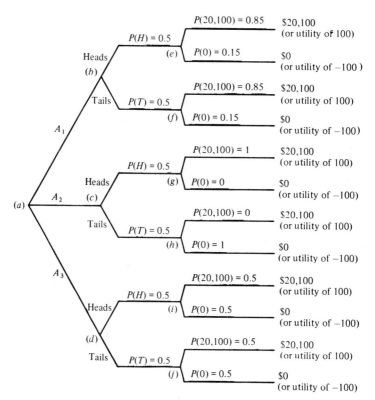

Exhibit 9-8 Game tree equivalent to that of Exhibit 9-7.

difference between the two is that in the former, points e to j constitute the terminal points with the specified terminal monetary values to be received with certainty by the decision maker when and if he reaches these points, whereas in the latter, these certain sums have been replaced by their equivalent standard gambles involving $20,100 and $0. For example, in the game tree of Exhibit 9-7, when and if the decision maker reaches point e, he receives $10,000 with certainty, but in the game tree of Exhibit 9-8, when and if the decision maker reaches point e, he is entitled to a *gamble* between $20,100 and $0 with the probability of winning $20,100 of 0.85. The assurance that such replacement at each of points e to j does not change the nature of the decision problem comes from the fact that earlier the decision maker stated his indifference between the certain monetary sums and the gamble options.

In terms of the new equivalent game tree of Exhibit 9-8, we observe that the critical question to be asked is: Which of the three points b, c, and d does the decision maker prefer most to be at? Upon taking one of the three alternative acts, A_1, A_2, A_3, the decision maker will find himself at either point b or point c or point d, namely, the time point just before the coin is tossed. Once he reaches this time point, the rest is up to chance, which is uncontrollable by him; i.e., it depends on the outcome of the toss of the coin first and then the outcome of the standard gamble. Although the future outlooks at points b, c, and d are all different, they are in comparable terms because all three involve eventually only the same two possible outcomes: $20,100 (with the arbitrarily assigned utility index of 100) and $0 (with the arbitrarily assigned utility index of -100). The difference in the outlook at these points is merely in the degree of chance or probability of winning $20,100 and its complement, the probability of winning $0. The problem of comparing the relative desirabilities of points b, c, and d is then equivalent to that of comparing the probabilities of winning $20,100 at points b, c, and d.

Which of points b, c, and d offers the highest probability of winning $20,100 (or alternatively the lowest probability of winning $0)? To put it differently, which of the three alternative acts, A_1, A_2, and A_3, offers the highest probability of winning $20,100 before the coin is flipped?

For point b or alternatively for act A_1 According to the game tree of Exhibit 9-8, $20,100 will be won either (1) if the coin falls heads and also the ball chosen from the standard urn is marked $20,100 or (2) if the coin falls tails and also the ball drawn from the standard urn is marked $20,100. (The reader should identify the two paths representing eventualities 1 and 2.) Event 1 is the joint event or the intersection of two events, the coin falling heads and the ball being marked $20,100, and event 2 is the joint event or the intersection of two events, the coin falling tails and the ball being marked \$20,100. The probability of joint event 1 therefore is computed as

$$P(H)P(20,100/H) = 0.5(0.85) = 0.425$$

The probability of the joint event 2 is computed as

$$P(T)P(20,100/T) = 0.5(0.85) = 0.425$$

The probability of winning \$20,100 is the probability of the union of event 1 and event 2, or the probability of either event 1 or event 2. Thus, the probability of winning \$20,100 at point b or given A_1 is

$$P(20,100/b) = P(20,100/A_1) = P(H)P(20,100/H)$$
$$+ P(T)P(20,100/T)$$
$$= 0.425 + 0.425$$
$$= 0.85$$

It follows that the probability of winning \$0 at b or given A_1 is the complement of $P(20,100/b)$ or $P(20,100/A_1)$:

$$P(0/b) = P(0/A_1) = 1 - P(20,100/A_1) = 1 - 0.85 = 0.15$$

For point c or for act A_2   Similarly, \$20,100 will be won either (3) if the coin falls heads and also the ball chosen from the urn is marked \$20,100 or (4) if the coin falls tails and also the ball chosen is marked \$20,100. The probability of joint event 3 is computed as

$$P(H)P(20,100/H) = 0.5(1) = 0.5$$

The probability of joint event 4 is computed as

$$P(T)P(20,100/T) = 0.5(0) = 0$$

Consequently, the probability of winning \$20,100 at point c or given act A_2 is the probability of the union of the events 3 and 4:

$$P(20,100/c) = P(20,100/A_2) = P(H)P(20,100/H)$$
$$+ P(T)P(20,100/T)$$
$$= 0.5 + 0$$
$$= 0.5$$

The probability of winning \$0 at point c or given A_2 is

$$P(0/c) = P(0/A_2) = 1 - P(20,100/A_2) = 1 - 0.5 = 0.5$$

For point d or for act A_3　Likewise,

$$P(H)P(20,100/H) = 0.5(0.5) = 0.25$$

$$P(T)P(20,100/T) = 0.5(0.5) = 0.25$$

$$P(20,100/d) = P(20,100/A_3) = P(H)P(20,100/H)$$
$$+ P(T)P(20,100/T)$$

$$= 0.25 + 0.25$$

$$= 0.50$$

$$P(0/d) = P(0/A_3) = 1 - P(20,100/A_3) = 0.50$$

Exhibit 9-9 summarizes the results of the above computations ni a game-tree form equivalent to Exhibit 9-8.

The decision problem represented by the new game tree is considerably simpler than the original decision problem represented in Exhibit 9-7. The problem now has been reduced to that of choosing between three alternative acts each one of which involves the same possible payoffs, $20,100 and $0, but with different probabilities of winning them. According to the tree, the probabilities of winning these same amounts are the same for A_2 and A_3; the desirability of the two acts are therefore the same. A_1, on the other hand, shows a higher probability of winning $20,100 (consequently, a lower probability of winning $0) than A_2 or A_3; A_1 therefore is preferred to A_2 or A_3.

In addition to the dollar payoff, Exhibits 9-8 and 9-9 show the utility indices, i.e., 100 for the best outcome ($20,100) and -100 for the worst outcome ($0), as assigned earlier. That the arbitrariness in selecting the utility indices makes no difference in the decision can be seen readily from the fact that the decision, or preferential ranking of the alternative acts, hinges critically upon the probabilities of winning the best and worst payoffs but not upon the magnitudes of payoffs themselves. Thus, even if the utility indices are changed to, say 1 and 0, for

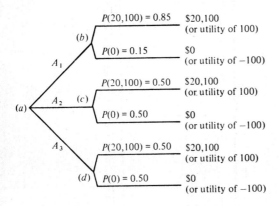

Exhibit 9-9 Game tree equivalent to that of Exhibit 9-8.

$20,100 and $0, respectively, the choice of A_1 as the best act remains unaltered, as the probability of winning the best payoff (or the utility of 1 for that act) is still 0.85, the highest of all acts.

Exhibit 9-9 makes it clear that the following three seemingly different alternative decision rules are essentially the same thing and therefore would yield the same decision:

1. The higher the probability of winning the best outcome ($0, or utility of 100) in the standard gamble, the better the act.
2. The lower the probability of winning the worst outcome ($0, or utility of -100) in the standard gamble, the better the act.
3. The higher the expected utility of the standard gamble, the better the act.

The expected utility of A_1 is the expected utility of the standard gamble with the probability of winning $20,100 (or utility of 100) of 0.85 and the probability of winning $0 (or utility of -100) of 0.15:

$$EU(A_1) = 0.85(100) + 0.15(-100)$$

Likewise for A_2 and A_3,

$$EU(A_2) = 0.5(100) + 0.5(-100)$$

and

$$EU(A_3) = 0.5(100) + 0.5(-100)$$

The EU of the acts increases as the probability associated with winning $20,100 increases; the ranking of the acts under the third rule is necessarily the same as under the first or the second rule.

The decision by the probabilities of winning the best (or worst) outcome in the standard gamble really lies at the core of the earlier decision based on the expected utilities computed from Exhibit 9-5. To demonstrate this point, first recall how the expected utilities of alternative acts were calculated in step 7:

$$EU(A_1) = 0.5(70) + 0.5(70) = 70 \tag{1}$$
$$EU(A_2) = 0.5(100) + 0.5(-100) = 0 \tag{2}$$
$$EU(A_3) = 0.5(0) + 0.5(0) = 0 \tag{3}$$

The conditional utility payoffs used in the above calculation, 70, 100, -100, 0, were obtained from Exhibit 9-5. But to recall further, these utility payoffs were in turn calculated as the expected utilities of the standard gambles equivalent to the certain monetary payoffs. Thus, for example, the conditional utility of 70 for A_1 entered in Exhibit 9-5 was obtained earlier by the computation

$$EU(\text{standard gamble}, p = 0.85) = 0.85(100)$$
$$+ 0.15(-100) = 70 \quad (4)$$

Substituting Eq. (4) in Eq. (1) for $EU(A_1)$, we get

$$EU(A_1) = 0.5(70) + 0.5(70) = 0.5[EU(\text{standard gamble}, p = 0.85)]$$
$$+ 0.5[EU(\text{standard gamble}, p = 0.85)]$$

$$= 0.5[0.85(100) + 0.15(-100)]$$
$$+ 0.5[0.85(100) + 0.15(-100)]$$

$$- 0.5[0.85(100)] + 0.5[0.85(100)] + 0.5[0.15(-100)]$$
$$+ 0.5[0.15(-100)]$$

$$= [0.5(0.85) + 0.5(0.85)](100)$$
$$+ [0.5(0.15) + 0.5(0.15)](-100)$$

$$= 0.85(100) + 0.15(-100)$$

This demonstrates that calculating the expected utility from the utility payoff table of Exhibit 9-5 for act A_1 is equivalent to calculating the expected utility from Exhibit 9-9.

Likewise, for other acts

$$EU(A_2) = 0.5(100) + 0.5(-100) = 0.5(100) + 0.5(-100)$$
$$EU(A_3) = 0.5(0) + 0.5(0) = 0.5(100) + 0.5(-100)$$

Utility function   Exhibit 9-10 summarizes the utilities of various monetary receipts as determined above. Formally, the monetary receipts constitute one set and the utilities another. Further, each element of one set is associated with a corresponding element of the other set. In short, utility is a function of monetary receipt. From the way the utility values are assigned it is clear that the utility function would vary among individual decision makers and according to the particular decision situation. To be more specific, it depends on whether the decision maker is adventurous or conservative and how consequential given additional

Money received with certainty	Utility assigned
$ 0	−100
1,200	0
10,000	70
20,100	100

Exhibit 9-10   Utility function.

Dollar amount received with certainty	Utility assigned
$200	0.2
400	0.7
600	0.9

Exhibit 9-11   Utility function.

monetary receipts are to the decision maker's welfare in a given decision situation.

Attitudes of risk preference and risk aversion   How is the utility function of a conservative person different from that of an adventurous person? The concepts of risk preference and risk aversion are more precisely defined in the discussion that follows.

Suppose that a decision maker assigns the utilities of 0.2, 0.7, and 0.9 to the certain receipts of money of $200, $400, and $600, respectively, according to the procedure explained earlier. The resulting utility function consisting of three ordered pairs is given in tabular form in Exhibit 9-11 and in graphic form in Exhibit 9-12.

In the graph, the three points P, Q, and R represent the three combinations of *certain* cash amounts and utility values. These three points are linked by a curve for easier visualization.

When a decision maker has a utility function as in the above, he is considered a risk averter within the given range of cash amounts, $200 to

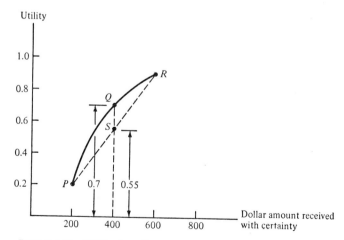

Exhibit 9-12   Utility function.

$600, in the following sense. Suppose that the decision maker is given an opportunity to gamble between $200 and $600 with the 0.5 probability of winning $600 and the 0.5 probability of winning $200. The utility of the gamble is then calculated as

$$U(\text{gamble}) = EU(\text{gamble}) = 0.5[U(600)] + 0.5[U(200)]$$
$$= 0.5(0.9) + 0.5(0.2)$$
$$= 0.55$$

(as represented by the height of point S in Exhibit 9-12). Now, on the other hand, the expected monetary value of the same gamble is

$$EMV(\text{gamble}) = 0.5(600) + 0.5(200)$$
$$= \$400$$

Suppose this $400 is offered to the decision maker with certainty. Then, from the utility function, it is already known that $U(400) = 0.7$ (as represented by the height of point Q).

The utility of $400 certain of 0.7 is higher than the utility of the gamble between $600 and $200 with fifty-fifty chances, i.e., 0.55. To the decision maker, the certainty of $400 is preferable to the gamble which yields the expected monetary value of the same $400. When a decision maker prefers the certainty of receiving a given sum of money to a gamble with the expected monetary value of the same amount, he is said to be a risk averter within the range of $200 to $600. Formally, the condition of risk aversion is stated as

$$EU(\text{gamble}) < U(\text{certainty of EMV of the same gamble})$$

or

$$p[U(M)] + (1 - p)[U(L)] < U[p(M) + (1 - p)(L)]$$

where M = highest amount of gamble = $600

L = lowest amount of gamble = $200

p = probability of winning amount M

Although p was specified as $p = 0.5$ in the above illustration, the same definition applies even when p is some other value. For example, if $p = 0.8$, the expected monetary value of the gamble, $EMV(\text{gamble})$, is

$$EMV(\text{gamble}) = p(M) + (1 - p)(L)$$
$$= 0.8(600) + 0.2(200)$$
$$= 520$$

If this amount of \$520 is offered to the decision maker *with certainty*, he would assign some specific utility of $U(520)$.

Now the expected utility of the same gamble is defined as

$$EU(\text{gamble}) = p[U(M)] + (1 - p)[U(L)]$$
$$= 0.8(0.9) + 0.2(0.2)$$
$$= 0.76$$

According to the definition, the decision maker is a risk averter if the utility he assigns to the certainty of \$520 is higher than this 0.76, the expected utility of the gamble which has the expected monetary value of \$520. That is, $U(520) > 0.76$ is the condition of risk aversion.

Conversely, if the decision maker assigns a utility to the certainty of \$520 that is lower than the expected utility of the gamble, he is said to be a risk taker. In general, the decision maker is considered to be adventurous, to prefer risk, if the following condition holds:

$$EU(\text{gamble}) > U(\text{certainty of EMV of the same gamble})$$

or

$$p[U(M)] + (1 - p)[U(L)] > U[p(M) + (1 - p)(L)]$$

At the conceptual level, the expected utility can handle the decision situations where the expected monetary value (or the expected value of the primary or original measures of consequences other than monetary measure) cannot be regarded as indicating the level of desirability of alternative acts. But at the practical level, can the expected utility be applied meaningfully? Many doubt that it can. One of the difficulties is that utility indices assigned are subjective and depend on the particular decision context. Utility assignment varies among different people and according to different decision situations even for the same individual decision maker. Whose utilities should be used as the basis for decision in an organization? The decision maker's staff analyst's or that of the organization as a whole to which the decision maker belongs?

Another source of difficulty is that it is extremely difficult for anyone to articulate preference or indifference between payoffs with certainty and gambles. For instance, suppose the standard gamble is between \$2000 gain and \$1000 loss and the decision maker is asked at what value of probability of winning \$2000 in the gamble he would be *just willing* to trade the certainty of receiving, say, \$500 for the privilege of undertaking the gamble. Can he meaningfully answer such question? Advocates of the expected-utility theory would agree that the task is difficult, but at the same time they maintain that the alternative to facing the difficulty squarely is to escape from rationality. They claim that the questions involving the standard gamble and one amount of certainty at a time are a lot easier to answer than making decisions in any rational sense without answering them from the original payoffs "in the raw."

9-3 A CONCLUDING REMARK

This chapter has studied the decision situations where the application of the expected-value decision criterion to the raw payoff measures—for example, dollar measures—seems unreasonable, and two of the decision theories suggested to deal with such situations, namely, the minimax and the expected utility. At least at the conceptual level, the expected-utility criterion based on the personal preferences of a given decision maker can be seen to yield "correct" decisions in all conceivable decision situations. But, of course, many doubt its usefulness in practical applications. Whatever our judgment is concerning the immediate practical usefulness of the decision criteria we studied in this chapter and in Chap. 8, it is hoped that the discussion has sharpened our insight into the nature of decision making under uncertainty in general.

QUESTIONS AND PROBLEMS

1. A decision maker is indifferent between a project which yields a profit of $40,000 with certainty and a project which yields a profit of $100,000 with a probability of 0.8 or a loss of $75,000 with a probability of 0.2.

(a) What utility value does the decision maker assign to the project which offers a profit of $40,000 with certainty if a utility of 1 is given to a profit of $100,000 and a utility of 0 to a loss of $75,000?

(b) Is the decision maker a risk taker or a risk averter?

2. A commander faces a battle situation characterized by the following payoff table. He has three feasible alternative tactics, T_1, T_2, T_3. The outcomes of each tactic depend on the three possible weather conditions (or enemy tactics), W_1, W_2, W_3. Positive entries in the table represent gains and negative entries represent losses (in square miles). Sacrifices in manpower and equipment are ignored.

Mileage payoff table

		Tactic		
Event	Probability	T_1	T_2	T_3
W_1	0.6	2000	200	400
W_2	0.3	−1200	600	400
W_3	0.1	−1600	1200	400

(a) Rank the alternative tactics under the expected-value criterion.

(b) Rank the alternative tactics under the expected-utility criterion assuming the following utility function of the commander:

Square miles gained with certainty	Utility assigned
2000	1
1200	0.9
600	0.7
400	0.6
200	0.5
−1200	0.15
−1600	0

(c) Demonstrate that the utility values assigned to various square-mileage gains in the utility function are the same as the probabilities themselves of winning the best outcome, 2000-mi^2 gain, in the standard gamble only because a utility of 1 is assigned to the best outcome, the certainty of 2000 mi^2, and a utility of 0 to the worst outcome, the certainty of −1600 mi^2.

(d) Is the commander a risk taker or risk averter?

3. Assume that you are on a TV program, confronted with three alternative deals, a_1, a_2, a_3, the payoffs of which depend on the outcome of a flip of an honest coin, as in the table.

Event	Probability	Act a_1	Act a_2	Act a_3
Heads	0.5	$5000	$1500	$3600
Tails	0.5	0	2000	600

(a) On the TV program you must choose one deal on the basis of quick intuitive judgment. Which deal would you choose?

(b) Suppose you were allowed some time to analyze the problem before making the decision. (1) Choose the best act under the expected-monetary-value criterion and under the minimax criterion. (2) Choose the best act under the expected-utility criterion. In the process of following the expected-utility criterion, you would have to compare the utility of the *certain* receipt of a sum of money with the utility of a standard gamble. Consider your own financial position, family situation, etc., in such a comparison.

(c) Is the intuitive decision under part (a) consistent with the decision under (2) of part (b)? If not, which one is better for you?

4. Referring to the two-stage decision problem of Example 8-2, explain the steps of the backward decision analysis under the expected-utility criterion.

10
Use of Additional or Sample Information

INTRODUCTION

So far we have assumed implicitly that the decision must be made *right away*, but this may not be a realistic assumption. In many decision situations, the decision maker may wish and be able to delay his decision to obtain additional information which can serve to reduce the degree of uncertainty. For instance, a politician may decide to run for an office today, or he may delay his decision and take a poll of voters' preference among potential candidates in the field. A business firm thinking of marketing a new product may decide to embark on its development and production immediately, or it may decide to delay the final decision until it obtains additional information on the uncertainty in the level of demand for the product through small-scale market testing. To cite still more examples, when a shipment of parts is received, the decision to accept or reject it may be postponed until the result of testing a sample of items chosen from the shipment is observed; or a team of surgeons faced with the decision whether to perform major surgery on a patient may conduct a series of additional tests first.

Obviously, all these decisions are multistage, sequential decisions as defined in Chap. 8 because the decision comprises at least two stages of decision: (1) whether to make the "final" decision "now" on the basis of information currently available or to delay it in order to gather more information and (2) whether or not to take the final action on the basis of the additional information obtained. The present chapter investigates the particular class of multistage, sequential decisions where the first-stage decision concerns whether or not to attempt collecting additional information.

On the quantifiable level, reduction of uncertainty from additional information means a change or revision of probabilities of various possible events generated by the source of uncertainty of concern. Thus, if the politician cited above had assigned the probability 0.6 of his being elected *prior to* undertaking the poll, he might revise his chance for election to something higher or lower than 0.6 on the basis of a favorable or unfavorable poll result. For the business firm trying to decide on the new product, a favorable or unfavorable market-test result may force revision in the probability of the event that the annual demand will be more than a specified level, say $1 million. This chapter begins with a discussion of the systematic way in which additional information, once it has been obtained, is incorporated into the revision of originally assigned probabilities and the analysis for the final decision. The latter part of the chapter explains how the first stage of the multistage decision, i.e., whether to delay the final decision in order to obtain additional information, should be made.

EXAMPLE 10-1

The decision maker is presented with a coin and is told that it may be fair with the probability of heads of $\frac{1}{2}$ or so loaded that the probability of heads is 0.1. Thus the two possible kinds of coin can be characterized by the probability of heads p. The fair coin is represented by $p = 0.5$, and the loaded one by $p = 0.1$. As may be recalled from the discussion of the binomial probability in Chap. 7, the probability of heads p is the *process parameter* of the coin-tossing experiment, a Bernoulli process.

The decision in this problem involves two alternative courses of action: (1) guess that the coin presented is a fair one with the process parameter $p = 0.5$ and (2) guess that the coin presented is a loaded one with the process parameter $p = 0.1$. If the decision maker calls the coin fair and is correct, he receives $15; if wrong, he has to pay $5. If he calls the coin loaded and is correct, he receives $15; if wrong, he has to pay $8. The payoff table for the decision is given in Exhibit 10-1a.

The notation $C(p = 0.5)$ stands for the event that the coin is fair, i.e., the process parameter $p = 0.5$; the notation $A(p = 0.5)$ stands for

Event	Act	
	$A(p = 0.5)$	$A(p = 0.1)$
$C(p = 0.5)$	$15	$-8
$C(p = 0.1)$	-5	15

Exhibit 10-1a Payoff table.

the act of the decision maker calling the coin fair; and similarly for the others. The monetary receipts and payments are assumed to be the indicators of their inherent utility to the decision maker.

The first step in deciding which of the two acts, $A(p = 0.5)$ or $A(p = 0.1)$, to choose is to assess the likelihood of the coins being fair and being loaded. The task is not easy, but through physical inspection of the coin and from the knowledge of the character of the man who presented the coin, the decision maker has a feeling that the coin may be fair. Yet he is not sure because the coin might actually be loaded but made to look like a fair one. In the end, he decides that there is no reason to believe that the event that the coin is fair is more likely or less likely than the event that the coin is loaded. Consequently, he assigns $\frac{1}{2}$ probability to the event that the coin is fair and the same $\frac{1}{2}$ probability to the event that the coin is loaded.

In Exhibit 10-1b these probabilities are added to the payoff table of Exhibit 10-1a.

Decision without additional information As in Chap. 8, the decision maker can apply the expected-value criterion on the basis of the sub-

Event	Probability	Act	
		$A(p = 0.5)$	$A(p = 0.1)$
$C(p = 0.5)$	0.5	$15	$-8
$C(p = 0.1)$	0.5	-5	15

Exhibit 10-1b Payoff table.

jective probabilities assigned to the two events. The expected monetary values of the two acts $A(p = 0.5)$ and $A(p = 0.1)$ are calculated as

$$\text{EMV}[A(p = 0.5)] = 0.5(15) + 0.5(-5) = 5.0$$
$$\text{EMV}[A(p = 0.1)] = 0.5(-8) + 0.5(15) = 3.5$$

The decision would be to call the coin fair.

Decision with additional information The decision maker realizes that the probability of $\frac{1}{2}$ assigned to the event $C(p = 0.5)$ and the event $C(p = 0.1)$ is very tentative, though the best under the circumstances. Thus, if possible, he would like to find out more about the coin before deciding. One way is to flip the coin a number of times and observe the outcomes. The pattern in which heads and tails turn up in these trials may provide a clue to the nature of the coin. For instance, suppose the coin is flipped 10 times and 9 out of the 10 trials result in tails. With this new information on the nature of the coin, would the decision maker stick to his original assessment of probabilities or would he change it by giving a higher probability to the event $C(p = 0.1)$ than the event $C(p = 0.5)$? Would it not be more likely to have 9 tails out of 10 trials when the coin is loaded than when it is fair? Most of us would indeed revise the original probabilities in light of the new information. But by how much? A systematic approach to the revision of probabilities on the basis of new information follows.

10-1 REVISION OF PROBABILITIES: BAYES' THEOREM

The discussion begins with a simple case where only one toss of the coin is allowed. The question is: How does one change the original probabilities upon observing tails from one toss of the coin? The concepts of conditional, joint, and marginal probabilities defined and studied in Chap. 6 are used in answering the question.

We recapitulate all the givens in symbols before proceeding.

Probability that coin is fair $= P[C(p = 0.5)] = 0.5$

Probability that the coin is loaded $= P[C(p = 0.1)] = 0.5$

Probability of heads from one toss of the coin *given a fair coin*
$$= P[H/C(p = 0.5)] = 0.5$$

Probability of tails from one toss of the coin *given a fair coin*
$$= P[T/C(p = 0.5)] = 1 - P[H/C(p = 0.5)] = 0.5$$

Probability of heads from one toss of the coin *given a loaded coin*
$$= P[H/C(p = 0.1)] = 0.1$$

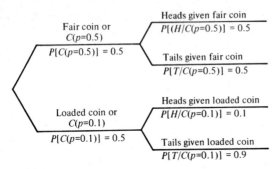

Exhibit 10-2a   Game tree for flipping the coin.

Probability of tails from one toss of the coin *given a loaded coin*
$$= P[T/C(p = 0.1)] = 1 - P[H/C(p = 0.1)] = 0.9$$

These probabilities can be summarized in a game or probability tree as in Exhibit 10-2*a*.

     Now the task is to assign new (revised) probabilities for the event fair coin, $[C(p = 0.5)]$ and the event loaded coin, $[C(p = 0.1)]$, *upon observing* or *given* tails from one toss of the coin. In symbols,

$$P[C(p = 0.5)/T] = ?$$
$$P[C(p = 0.1)/T] = ?$$

     As the first step to finding these probabilities, the probability tree of Exhibit 10-2*a* is completed by determining the joint probabilities of the joint events represented by the four terminal branches in the tree.

     The four joint events are:

1. The event that the coin is fair *and* the flip of the coin results in heads; $C(p = 0.5) \cap H$.
2. The event that the coin is fair *and* the flip of the coin results in tails; $C(p = 0.5) \cap T$.
3. The event that the coin is loaded *and* the flip of the coin results in heads; $C(p = 0.1) \cap H$.
4. The event that the coin is loaded *and* the flip of the coin results in tails; $C(p = 0.1) \cap T$.

The probabilities of these four joint events are

     Event 1: $P[C(p = 0.5) \cap H] = P[C(p = 0.5)]P[H/C(p = 0.5)]$
$$= 0.5(0.5)$$
$$= 0.25$$

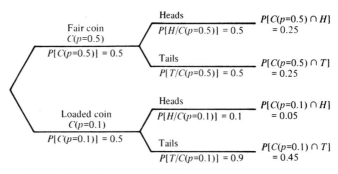

Exhibit 10-2b   Game tree for flipping the coin.

Event 2: $P[C(p = 0.5) \cap T] = P[C(p = 0.5)]P[T/C(p = 0.5)]$
$$= 0.5(0.5)$$
$$= 0.25$$

Event 3: $P[C(p = 0.1) \cap H] = P[C(p = 0.1)]P[H/C(p = 0.1)]$
$$= 0.5(0.1)$$
$$= 0.05$$

Event 4: $P[C(p = 0.1) \cap T] = P[C(p = 0.1)]P[T/C(p = 0.1)]$
$$= 0.5(0.9)$$
$$= 0.45$$

Exhibit 10-2*b* is the result of entering these joint probabilities in the probability tree.

The same data in the probability tree of Exhibit 10-2*b* can be presented in table form as in Exhibit 10-3.

Outcome of a toss of the coin	Fair coin, $C(p = 0.5)$	Loaded coin, $C(p = 0.1)$	Marginal or conditional probabilities
Heads	$P[C(p = 0.5) \cap H]$ $= 0.25$	$P[C(p = 0.1) \cap H]$ $= 0.05$	$P(H) = 0.30$
Tails	$P[C(p = 0.5) \cap T]$ $= 0.25$	$P[C(p = 0.1) \cap T]$ $= 0.45$	$P(T) = 0.70$
Marginal or unconditional probabilities	$P[C(p = 0.5)] = 0.5$	$P[C(p = 0.1)] = 0.5$	1.0

Exhibit 10-3   Probability table.

Either from the probability tree of Exhibit 10-2b or from the probability table, note that the event heads happens when *either* the joint event $C(p = 0.5) \cap H$ *or* the joint event $C(p = 0.1) \cap H$ happens. That is, the event heads is the union of $C(p = 0.5) \cap H$ and $C(p = 0.1) \cap H$. Therefore, the probability of the event heads $P(H)$, namely, the unconditional (or marginal) probability of the event heads, is

$$P(H) = P[C(p = 0.5) \cap H] + P[C(p = 0.1) \cap H]$$
$$= 0.25 + 0.05$$
$$= 0.30$$

This probability $P(H)$ of heads, is simply the probability that the toss of the coin results in heads—without any reference to whether the coin is fair or loaded.

Similarly, the event tails happens when *either* the joint event $C(p = 0.5) \cap T$ *or* the joint event $C(p = 0.1) \cap T$ happens; i.e., it is the union of $C(p = 0.5) \cap T$ and $C(p = 0.1) \cap T$. Therefore, the probability $P(T)$ of the event tails, namely, the unconditional (or marginal) probability of the event tails is

$$P(T) = P[C(p = 0.5) \cap T] + P[C(p = 0.1) \cap T]$$
$$= 0.25 + 0.45$$
$$= 0.70$$

Now, returning to the original question: What is the probability of the coin's being fair, conditional to (or given) the observation of the event tails? *Conditional to the event tails*, means that, in the language of Chap. 6, the sample space is reduced to the row labeled tails in the probability table of Exhibit 10-3. Within that reduced sample space are two events, fair coin and loaded coin. If the probability weight of 1 is assigned to the reduced sample space, namely, the event tails, what probability weight should be given to the event fair coin within this reduced space? Since the probability weight of the event fair coin was 0.25 when the probability weight of the event tails was 0.7, the relative weight of the event fair coin must be converted from 0.25 to $0.25/0.70 \approx 0.357$ if the weight of the event tails is converted to 1 (from 0.70). In symbols,

$$P[C(p = 0.5)/T] = \frac{P[C(p = 0.5) \cap T]}{P(T)}$$

$$= \frac{0.25}{0.70} \approx 0.357$$

Since $P(T) = P[C(p = 0.5) \cap T] + P[C(p = 0.1) \cap T]$, the formula for $P[C(p = 0.5)/T]$ can be restated as

$$P[C(p = 0.5)/T] = \frac{P[C(p = 0.5) \cap T]}{P[C(p = 0.5) \cap T] + P[C(p = 0.1) \cap T]}$$

$$= \frac{0.25}{0.25 + 0.45} = \frac{0.25}{0.70} \approx 0.357$$

Similarly, for $P[C(p = 0.1)/T]$ within the same reduced sample space as above represented by the row labeled tails in Exhibit 10-3, if the probability of 1 is assigned to the event tails, the probability of the event loaded coin must be changed from 0.45 to $0.45/0.70 \approx 0.643$:

$$P[C(p = 0.1)/T] = \frac{P[C(p = 0.1) \cap T]}{P(T)}$$

or

$$= \frac{P[C(p = 0.1) \cap T]}{P[C(p = 0.5) \cap T] + P[C(p = 0.1) \cap T]}$$

$$= \frac{0.45}{0.25 + 0.45} = \frac{0.45}{0.70} \approx 0.643$$

Exhibit 10-4 summarizes the process for revision of probabilities based on additional information.

Original probabilities (column 2) are often called *prior probabilities;* revised probabilities (column 6) are often called *posterior probabilities.* The formula used in this computation of posterior, or revised, proba-

(1) Event	(2) Original probability $P[C(p = p_i)]$	(3) Conditional probability $P[T/C(p = p_i)]$	(4) Joint probability $P[C(p = p_i) \cap T]$ (2) $\times$ (3)	(5) $P(T)$	(6) Revised probability $P[C(p = p_i)/T]$ (4) $\div$ (5)
Fair coin $C(p = 0.5)$	0.5	0.5	0.25		0.357
Loaded coin $C(p = 0.1)$	0.5	0.9	0.45		0.643
				0.70	1.000

Exhibit 10-4 Computation of revised probabilities.

bilities, known as *Bayes' formula* or *Bayes' theorem*, plays a central role in modern statistical analysis.

Based on the new probabilities, the expected monetary values of the two acts $A(p = 0.5)$ and $A(p = 0.1)$ are calculated as

$$\text{EMV}[A(p = 0.5)] = 0.357(15) + 0.643(-5) = 2.14$$
$$\text{EMV}[A(p = 0.1)] = 0.357(-8) + 0.643(15) = 6.79$$

The act of calling the coin loaded is preferred to the act of calling it fair. This switch in the decision attributable to the new evidence is intuitively reasonable: the experimental flip of the coin falling tails tends to reinforce our belief that the coin is loaded in favor of tails.

EXAMPLE 10-2

In a given population of 10,000, 0.1 percent carries a certain disease. If a carrier of the disease is subjected to a special medical test, the result of the test will turn out positive about 90 percent of the time and the rest negative. If a noncarrier of the disease is subjected to the same test, the result of the test will be negative about 99 percent of the time and the rest positive.

A man chosen at random from the population is given the test and the result proves positive. What is the probability that he is indeed a carrier of the disease?

The following summarizes the information already given.

1. The probability that a person selected at random from the given population is a carrier of the disease is $P(D) = 0.001$ where D represents the event that a person selected at random is a carrier. This probability is, of course, unconditional to the test result, in other words, without the benefit of the test, or prior to the test.
2. Since a person is either a carrier or a noncarrier of the disease, the probability of the event that a person selected at random is a noncarrier prior to the test is

$$P(D') = 1 - P(D) = 1 - 0.001 = 0.999$$

where D' represents the event that a person is a noncarrier.
3. Given a carrier, the probability of the event that the test result is positive is

$$P(T/D) = 0.90$$

4. It follows then that the conditional probability of the test result being negative given a carrier is

$$P(T'/D) = 0.10$$

5. Given a noncarrier, the probability of the event that the test result is negative is

$$P(T'/D') = 0.99$$

6. Given a noncarrier, the probability of the event that the test result is positive is

$$P(T/D') = 0.01$$

These known probabilities can be summarized in a probability tree as in Exhibit 10-5.

The question Without knowing the test result, the probability of a selected person's being a carrier is determined to be $P(D) = 0.001$, but once the positive test result of a person is observed, a probability higher than 0.001 would be assigned to the event that he is a carrier of the disease. What is this revised probability? Or what is $P(D/T)$, the conditional probability that a person is a carrier of the disease given the positive test result?

Analysis If a person is selected from the population and given the test, the following four elementary events are possible:

1. The person is indeed a carrier *and* shows positive on the test; $D \cap T$.
2. The person is indeed a carrier *and* shows negative on the test; $D \cap T'$.
3. The person is not a carrier *and* shows positive on the test; $D' \cap T$.
4. The person is not a carrier *and* shows negative on the test; $D' \cap T'$.

If one of the above four is the case, none of the other three can happen; since there are no other possibilities than the given four, the four events listed represent a sample space. They are shown as the four terminal branches in the probability tree of Exhibit 10-5. From the unconditional and the conditional probabilities of various events given in the exhibit, the probabilities of these joint events can be computed:

Event 1: $\quad P(D \cap T) = P(D)[P(T/D)] = 0.001(0.90) = 0.0009$

Event 2: $\quad P(D \cap T') = P(D)[P(T'/D)] = 0.001(0.10) = 0.0001$

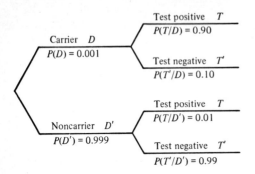

Exhibit 10-5 Probability tree.

Event 3: $P(D' \cap T) = P(D')[P(T/D')]$
$$= 0.999(0.01) = 0.00999$$

Event 4: $P(D' \cap T') = P(D')[P(T'/D')]$
$$= 0.999(0.99) = 0.98901$$

The sum of the four probabilities is 1 as expected because the four events are mutually exclusive and collectively exhaustive.

In terms of these four elementary events, the event that a person is a carrier can happen in two ways: *either* event 1, $D \cap T$, *or* event 2, $D \cap T'$. That is, D is the union of the two events. Formally,

$$D = (D \cap T) \cup (D \cap T'),$$

and consequently,

$$P(D) = P(D \cap T) + P(D \cap T')$$
$$= 0.0009 + 0.0001 = 0.001$$

Similarly, the probability that the test performed on a person selected at random would be positive is

$$P(T) = P(D \cap T) + P(D' \cap T)$$
$$= 0.0009 + 0.00999 = 0.01089$$

Alternatively,

$$P(T) = P(D)[P(T/D)] + P(D')[P(T/D')]$$
$$= 0.001(0.90) + 0.999(0.01)$$
$$= 0.0009 + 0.00999 = 0.01089$$

Likewise, the unconditional probability that the person is not a carrier $P(D')$ and the unconditional probability that the person would show negative on the test $P(T')$ are easily computed. The results are summarized in Exhibit 10-6.

Answer to the question   Finally, what is the probability that a person selected at random with the positive test result is indeed a carrier of the disease?   (In symbols, $P(D/T) = $?)

In terms of the sample space described by the four elementary events, the knowledge that the test result was positive reduces the sample space.   The reduced sample space consists of two elements, $D \cap T$ and $D' \cap T$, and is represented in the probability table of Exhibit 10-6 by the row labeled test positive T.   Within this reduced sample space, the two events $D \cap T$ and $D' \cap T$ have the relative probability weights of 0.0009 and 0.00999, respectively, which add up to $\varGamma(T) = 0.01089$. If the probability of 1 is assigned to the reduced sample space (instead of 0.01089), then the probabilities of the two constituent events should be revised upward according to the 0.01089:1 ratio.   Thus, the probability of D given T is

$$P(D/T) = \frac{0.0009}{0.01089} \approx 0.082$$

and that of D' given T is

$$P(D'/T) = \frac{0.00999}{0.01089} \approx 0.918$$

	Event		Marginal or unconditional probability
Event	Carrier D	Noncarrier D'	
Test positive T	$P(D \cap T) = 0.0009$	$P(D' \cap T) = 0.00999$	$P(T) = 0.01089$
Test negative T'	$P(D \cap T') = 0.0001$	$P(D' \cap T') = 0.98901$	$P(T') = 0.98911$
Marginal or unconditional probability	$P(D) = 0.0010$	$P(D') = 0.99900$	1.00000

Exhibit 10-6 Probability table.

Since the probabilities 0.0009, 0.00999, and 0.01089 used above are $P(D \cap T)$, $P(D' \cap T)$, and $P(T) = P(D \cap T) + P(D' \cap T)$, respectively, the general formulas for $P(D/T)$ and $P(D'/T)$ are

$$P(D/T) = \frac{P(D \cap T)}{P(T)}$$

$$= \frac{P(D \cap T)}{P(D \cap T) + P(D' \cap T)}$$

$$= \frac{P(D)[P(T/D)]}{P(D)[P(T/D)] + P(D')[P(T/D')]}$$

$$P(D'/T) = \frac{P(D' \cap T)}{P(T)}$$

$$= \frac{P(D' \cap T)}{P(D \cap T) + P(D' \cap T)}$$

$$= \frac{P(D')[P(T/D')]}{P(D)[P(T/D)] + P(D')[P(T/D')]}$$

Both examples discussed above involved only two possible events and two possibilities of additional information. In particular, in Example 10-1, there were only two possible events, i.e., a fair coin with $p = 0.5$ and a loaded coin with $p = 0.1$, and only two possible outcomes of a flip of the coin, i.e., heads and tails. In Example 10-2, the only possible events were two: the person selected being a carrier of the disease and the person being a noncarrier; the only two possible observations of additional evidence were positive and negative on the test.

Many real decision situations involve more than just two possible events or two possible additional kinds of evidence. For instance, in the coin-gamble example, in addition to the two possibilities of the coin, $C(p = 0.5)$ and $C(p = 0.1)$, we may conceive of such other "loadedness" of the coin as $C(p = 0.2)$ and $C(p = 0.8)$. On the possibilities of additional information, if the coin is flipped three times instead of once, the possible outcomes would include HHH, HTH, HTT, THH, etc., more than just two. The cases with more than two possibilities of events and additional information are fundamentally no different from the two-by-two cases as seen in the following example.

EXAMPLE 10-3

A factory buys one of its parts, number 236, from three sources. Source 1 sets its quality control at $p = 0.12$, the level of defective units (the parts obtained from source 1 contain, on the average, about 12 percent defective units); source 2 has a more stringent quality control at $p = 0.06$, and source 3 has the most stringent at $p = 0.02$. Recently the factory had a bad flood in its storeroom, and as a result the labels on the boxes identifying different supply sources became illegible.

Suppose the center needs a box of number 236 parts for a purpose for which the optimum level of quality is $p = 0.06$. To use the box with the quality level of $p = 0.02$ for this purpose would be wasteful, and yet to use the box with the quality level of $p = 0.12$ would involve a great deal of additional corrective work. At any rate, suppose that the management of the factory needs to assess the probabilities that a particular box at hand belongs to one of the various quality levels. The three possible events are:

1. E_1, the event that the box is from source 1, with the quality level of $p = 0.12$
2. E_2, the event that the box is from source 2, with the quality level of $p = 0.06$
3. E_3, the event that the box is from source 3, with the quality level of $p = 0.02$

From the knowledge of the relative proportions of the boxes with $p = 0.12$, $p = 0.06$, and $p = 0.02$ that were in the storeroom right before the flooding, the management assigns the prior probabilities shown in Table 10-1.

The management may make its decision—whatever it is—on the basis of these prior probabilities, or it may wish to take a couple of samples from the box at random, test whether they are good or defective, and revise the prior probabilities if called for, and then make the final decision on the basis of the revised probabilities. Suppose the management decides to take a sample of two from the box before making the

Table 10-1 Prior probabilites

Event	Probability of event $P(E_i)$
E_1 (or $p = 0.12$)	0.6
E_2 (or $p = 0.06$)	0.3
E_3 (or $p = 0.02$)	0.1
	1.0

final decision.   The sampling is done *with replacement*.[1]   The possible
outcomes of the two parts selected are:

1. S_0, the event that both samples are good, nondefective; (zero subscript for none defective)
2. S_1, the event that one sample is good, one defective[2]
3. S_2, the event that both samples are defective

Given a particular quality level of p for the box, the probability
of the first item's being defective is p, and the probability of the second
item's being defective is also the same p, because the sampling is done
with replacement.   In short, the sampling procedure gives rise to a
Bernoulli process.

Suppose that the quality level of the box is $p = 0.12$, that is,
E_1 has happened.   Then what are the probabilities of no defective,
one defective, and two defectives in the two samples (conditional to E_1)?
From the binomial probability formula of Chap. 7, the probability of
the event that both samples are good given the box of $p = 0.12$ is

$$P(S_0/E_1) = \binom{2}{0} (0.12)^0 (0.88)^2 = 0.7744$$

Alternatively, the same probability of 0.7744 could be calculated as
follows:

1. The probability of drawing a good (nondefective) unit in the first
   sample is $q = 1 - p = 1 - 0.12 = 0.88$.
2. The probability of drawing a good unit in the second sample is also
   the same 0.88.
3. Since the outcomes of the two samples are independent, the probability of the joint event that both result in good units is

$$q \times q = 0.88(0.88) = 0.7744.$$

The probability of the event that one sample results in a good unit and
the other in a defective unit, given the box characterized by $p = 0.12$ is

$$P(S_1/E_1) = \binom{2}{1} (0.12)^1 (0.88)^1 = 0.2112$$

---

[1] Sampling with replacement is possible only if testing does not destroy the item tested.
Even under sampling without replacement, however, the analysis that follows is
valid except that the binomial probability function can no longer be used in assigning
probabilities.   See Prob. 5 of Chap. 7.
[2] The event that one is good and one defective can further be broken down into two
events: the first good, the second defective, and the first defective, the second good;
but for the decision on hand, the distinction is not necessary.

Again, alternatively, the same probability could be calculated as follows:

1. S_1 happens *either* if the first sample result is a good unit G and the second a defective unit D *or* if the first sample result is a defective unit D and the second a good unit G.
2. Thus, the probability of S_1 is

$$P(S_1) = P(GD) + P(DG)$$

3. Since the first and second samples are independent of each other, the probability of GD is

$$P(GD) = P(G)[P(D)]$$
$$= q \times p = 0.88(0.12) = 0.1056$$

Likewise,

$$P(DG) = P(D)[P(G)] = 0.12(0.88) = 0.1056$$

4. Therefore, $P(S_1) = 0.1056 + 0.1056 = 0.2112$.

The probability of the event that both samples result in defective units given the box with $p = 0.12$ is

$$P(S_2/E_1) = \binom{2}{2} (0.12)^2(0.88)^0 = 0.0144$$

Similarly, the probabilities of S_0, S_1, S_2 conditional to E_2 and E_3 can be determined. Given E_2, that is, given the box with $p = 0.06$,

$$P(S_0/E_2) = \binom{2}{0} (0.06)^0(0.94)^2 - 0.8836$$

$$P(S_1/E_2) = \binom{2}{1} (0.06)^1(0.94)^1 = 0.1128$$

$$P(S_2/E_2) = \binom{2}{2} (0.06)^2(0.94)^0 = 0.0036$$

Given E_3, that is, given the box with $p = 0.02$,

$$P(S_0/E_3) = \binom{2}{0} (0.02)^0(0.98)^2 = 0.9604$$

$$P(S_1/E_3) = \binom{2}{1} (0.02)^1(0.98)^1 = 0.0392$$

$$P(S_2/E_3) = \binom{2}{2} (0.02)^2(0.98)^0 = 0.0004$$

Exhibit 10-7, a tree representation of the sampling, shows these probabilities. The probabilities entered at the terminal points of the

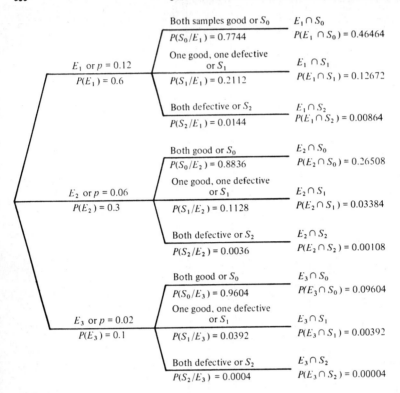

Exhibit 10-7 Game tree for sampling.

tree are the probabilities of the joint events $E_i \cap S_j$, the event that
a particular box has happened and also that a particular sampling result
is observed. They are calculated by multiplying $P(E_i)$ by $P(S_j/E_i)$,
that is, $P(E_i \cap S_j) = P(E_i)[P(S_j/E_i)]$.

Exhibit 10-8 shows the probability data contained in the probability tree in table form. Note that the unconditional probabilities of
S_j's are calculated as

$$P(S_j) = P(E_1 \cap S_j) + P(E_2 \cap S_j) + P(E_3 \cap S_j)$$
$$= \sum_{i=1}^{3} P(E_i \cap S_j)$$
$$= P(E_1)[P(S_j/E_1)] + P(E_2)[P(S_j/E_2)] + P(E_3)[P(S_j/E_3)]$$
$$= \sum_{i=1}^{3} P(E_i)[P(S_j/E_i)]$$

Now suppose that both items in the sample are actually observed
to be good units; that is, S_0 has happened. In terms of Exhibit 10-8,

	Supply sources E_i			
Sample results S_j	Box with $p = 0.12$ or E_1	Box with $p = 0.06$ or E_2	Box with $p = 0.02$ or E_3	Marginal or unconditional probabilities
Both good S_0	$P(E_1 \cap S_0)$ $= 0.46464$	$P(E_2 \cap S_0)$ $= 0.26508$	$P(E_3 \cap S_0)$ $= 0.09604$	$P(S_0) = 0.82576$
One good, one defective S_1	$P(E_1 \cap S_1)$ $= 0.12672$	$P(E_2 \cap S_1)$ $= 0.03384$	$P(E_3 \cap S_1)$ $= 0.00392$	$P(S_1) = 0.16448$
Both defective S_2	$P(E_1 \cap S_2)$ $= 0.00864$	$P(E_2 \cap S_2)$ $= 0.00108$	$P(E_3 \cap S_2)$ $= 0.00004$	$P(S_2) = 0.00976$
Marginal or unconditional probabilities	$P(E_1)$ $= 0.60000$	$P(E_2)$ $= 0.30000$	$P(E_3)$ $= 0.10000$	$\sum_1^3 P(E_i)$ $= \sum_0^2 P(S_j)$ $= 1.0$

Exhibit 10-8 Probability table for sampling.

this means that one of the three events on the first row (S_0 row) has actually happened.

With the knowledge that one of the three joint events on the first row has happened, what is the probability of each particular joint event's being the one that has happened? The three joint events are $E_1 \cap S_0$, $E_2 \cap S_0$, and $E_3 \cap S_0$; and since it is known that one of them has happened, the sum of the probabilities of the three should add up to 1. But the total of the joint probabilities shown on the first row in the table is only $P(S_0) = 0.82576$ because the joint probabilities are the relative weights of these joint events in relation to the original unreduced sample space. In order to make the three joint probabilities add up to 1, each of the three joint probabilities must be divided by their sum, $P(S_0) = 0.82576$. Thus,

$$P(E_1/S_0) = \frac{P(E_1 \cap S_0)}{P(S_0)} = \frac{0.46464}{0.82576} = 0.563$$

$$P(E_2/S_0) = \frac{P(E_2 \cap S_0)}{P(S_0)} = \frac{0.26508}{0.82576} = 0.321$$

$$P(E_3/S_0) = \frac{P(E_3 \cap S_0)}{P(S_0)} = \frac{0.09604}{0.82576} = 0.116$$

Since

$$P(S_0) = P(E_1 \cap S_0) + P(E_2 \cap S_0) + P(E_3 \cap S_0)$$

the formula

$$P(E_1/S_0) = \frac{P(E_1 \cap S_0)}{P(S_0)}$$

may be rewritten

$$P(E_1/S_0) = \frac{P(E_1 \cap S_0)}{P(E_1 \cap S_0) + P(E_2 \cap S_0) + P(E_3 \cap S_0)}$$

Since $P(E_i \cap S_0) = P(E_i)[P(S_0/E_i)]$, the above may be further written

$$P(E_1/S_0) = \frac{P(E_1)[P(S_0/E_1)]}{P(E_1)[P(S_0/E_1)] + P(E_2)[P(S_0/E_2)] + P(E_3)[P(S_0/E_3)]}$$

Likewise

$$P(E_2/S_0) = \frac{P(E_2)[P(S_0/E_2)]}{P(E_1)[P(S_0/E_1)] + P(E_2)[P(S_0/E_2)] + P(E_3)[P(S_0/E_3)]}$$

$$P(E_3/S_0) = \frac{P(E_3)[P(S_0/E_3)]}{P(E_1)[P(S_0/E_1)] + P(E_2)[P(S_0/E_2)] + P(E_3)[P(S_0/E_3)]}$$

Or, in general,

$$P(E_i/S_0) = \frac{P(E_i)[P(S_0/E_i)]}{P(E_1)[P(S_0/E_1)] + P(E_2)[P(S_0/E_2)] + P(E_3)[P(S_0/E_3)]}$$

These are the Bayes' formulas when the number of possible events is 3.

Exercise 10-1 (a) Suppose the actual sample observation is S_1 (one good, one defective). Compute the revised probabilities of E_1, E_2, E_3, namely, the box being of the quality level $p = 0.12$, $p = 0.06$, and $p = 0.02$, respectively. Write out the formulas for $P(E_i/S_1)$.

(b) Suppose the actual sample observation is S_2 (both defective). Compute the revised probabilities of E_1, E_2, and E_3, given the sample information. Write out the formulas for $P(E_i/S_2)$.

10-2   DECISION WHETHER TO SAMPLE

The discussion so far has avoided the question of how to decide whether the decision should be made at once on the basis of prior probabilities or be delayed until new information has been obtained and probabilities have been revised. Additional information (or sample information) reduces uncertainty in the decision, but it is rarely without cost. Thus, before deciding to take a sample, i.e., obtain additional information, the decision maker must compare the benefit of reduction in the degree of uncertainty from additional information with the cost of obtaining it. If the cost outweighs the benefit, he will most likely decide against getting additional information. The remainder of the chapter discusses how such an analysis is carried out.

EXAMPLE 10-4

As a variation of Example 10-3, consider a factory contemplating the use of an unlabeled box of number 236 parts in the manufacture of its product. Because of the recent flood in the storeroom the labels on the boxes containing the parts have become illegible, and therefore there is uncertainty whether the box of parts is at the quality level of $p = 0.12$ or of $p = 0.02$, p being the average fraction of defectives in the box. For simplicity, only two quality levels are assumed to be possible in this example. The box contains 1000 units.

The alternative courses of action available are assumed to be using the parts in the box in manufacturing without inspecting individual parts (act A), and inspecting all 1000 parts individually and correcting all the defective units before putting them into the production line (act B). If act A is chosen (the parts are accepted without inspection), the parts, defective as well as nondefective, are put into the production line, but after inspection of the individual finished products, those with defective parts must be corrected by a special machining operation costing $2 per unit. If act B is chosen, the inspection of 1000 parts will cost $170. In addition to the inspection cost, defective units found from inspection will have to be corrected by a simple operation costing 10 cents per unit. The payoff table incorporating the above facts is given as Exhibit 10-9.

To explain the entries in the payoff table: the conditional cost of $240, given act A (accepting without inspection) and given that the box is the box with quality level of $p = 0.12$, or event $E_{0.12}$, is computed by multiplying the number of defectives expected in the box of 120 units (1000 units $\times$ 0.12) by the $2 extra cost per unit to correct the defects found after production of the finished product. The conditional cost of $182 given act B (inspecting all 1000 units prior to production) and

Event	Probability $P(E_i)$	Act A	B
$p = 0.12$ or $E_{0.12}$	0.6	$240	$182
$p = 0.02$ or $E_{0.02}$	0.4	40	172

Exhibit 10-9 Payoff table.

given $E_{0.12}$ consists of two elements: the flat cost of inspecting 1000 units at \$170 and the cost for correcting the expected 120 defective parts before they are put in the production of \$12 (\$0.10 $\times$ 120). The reader should verify the other two cost entries. The probabilities of $P(E_{0.12}) = 0.6$ and $P(E_{0.02}) = 0.4$, are the prior probabilities.

Should the management take the sample of, say, 2 units from the box before making the decision whether to accept the box of parts without inspection or to inspect all 1000 individual units in the box, or make the decision immediately without the benefit of sampling? To answer the question according to the expected-value criterion, the expected costs must be computed for the two alternatives: making the decision without sampling, alternative I, or taking a sample of two and then making the decision, alternative II.

Alternative I: Expected cost of making decision without sampling Without additional information from sample observations, the prior probabilities as assigned in the payoff table of Exhibit 10-9 are the best assessment of the likelihoods of two possible outcomes of the box. On the basis of these prior probabilities, the expected costs of act A (accepting the box without inspection) and of act B (inspection of all 1000 units before production) are calculated as

$$EC(A) = 0.6(240) + 0.4(40) = \$160$$
$$EC(B) = 0.6(182) + 0.4(172) = \$178$$

If and when the decision maker decides to make the decision on whether to accept A or B without sampling, he will choose A because it gives the minimum expected cost. Thus, the best he can do if and when he decides to make the decision without sampling is this minimum expected cost of \$160 of act A. It can be said, therefore, that the minimum of the expected costs of *all* acts (A and B) represents the expected cost of the alternative I itself. That is, the expected cost of the act of *deciding to make the decision* (on A or B) without sampling is the expected cost of A, \$160. In symbols, $EC(I) = EC(A) = \$160$.

Alternative II: Expected cost of taking a sample of two and then making the decision *If and when* the decision maker samples 2 units, he observes one of the following possible outcomes:

1. Both good, S_0
2. One good, one defective S_1
3. Both defective, S_2

Under Alternative II, the decision maker will decide on A or B after observing one of the above sample outcomes.

Table 10-2 Revision of probabilities in the light of S_0

(1)	(2)	(3)	(4)	(5)	(6)
			Joint		*Conditional or revised*
	Prior	*Conditional*	*probability*	*Marginal*	*probability*
Event	*probability*	*probability*	$P(E_i \cap S_0)$	*probability*	$P(E_i/S_0)$
E_i	$P(E_i)$	$P(S_0/E_i)$	(2) × (3)	S_0	(4) ÷ (5)
$E_{0.12}$	0.6	0.7744	0.46464		0.547
$E_{0.02}$	0.4	0.9604	0.38416		0.453
				0.84880	

Outcome 1   If and when the decision maker takes the sample and observes the particular outcome S_0, he will revise the probabilities on the basis of the sample observation and choose between A and B according to the expected costs calculated on the basis of revised probabilities (Table 10-2).

The expected costs based on revised probabilities are

$$EC(A) = 0.547(240) + 0.453(40) = \$149$$
$$EC(B) = 0.547(182) + 0.453(172) = \$177$$

Thus, if and when the decision maker observes S_0 as a result of sampling, he will choose A because it gives a lower expected cost than B.

Outcome 2   Likewise, if and when the decision maker takes the sample and observes S_1 (one good, one defective), he will revise the probabilities and choose A or B on the basis of these revised probabilities as in the analysis in Table 10-3.   Computation of expected costs based on

Table 10-3 Revision of probabilities in the light of S_1

(1)	(2)	(3)	(4)	(5)	(6)
			Joint		*Conditional or revised*
	Prior	*Conditional*	*probability*	*Marginal*	*probability*
Event	*probability*	*probability*	$P(E_i \cap S_1)$	*probability*	$P(E_i/S_1)$
E_i	$P(E_i)$	$P(S_1/E_i)$	(2) × (3)	$P(S_1)$	(4) ÷ (5)
$E_{0.12}$	0.6	0.2112	0.12672		0.89
$E_{0.02}$	0.4	0.0392	0.01568		0.11
				0.14240	

revised probabilities are

$$EC(A) = 0.89(240) + 0.11(40) = \$218$$
$$EC(B) = 0.89(182) + 0.11(172) = \$181$$

The decision maker will choose B because it gives a lower expected cost than A.

Outcome 3   Similarly, *if and when* the decision maker takes two samples and observes both samples defective, S_2, he will revise the probabilities as in the analysis in Table 10-4 and choose B on the basis of the expected costs as below.

$$EC(A) = 0.982(240) + 0.018(40) = \$236$$
$$EC(B) = 0.982(182) + 0.018(172) = \$182$$

Game tree   The results of these analyses can also be represented in game-tree form as in Exhibit 10-10. It shows four chronological stages. In stage 1, the decision maker decides whether or not to take the sample. In stage 2, one of the three possible events, or the three possible outcomes of the sampling, will happen. Next, in stage 3, if S_0 has been observed in stage 2, choose A or B based on the probabilities revised in the light of S_0; if S_1 has been observed in stage 2, choose A or B based on the probabilities revised in the light of S_1; if S_2 has been observed in stage 2, choose A or B based on the probabilities in the light of S_2. And finally, in stage 4, the box turns out either to be $E_{0.12}$ or $E_{0.02}$, and the decision maker will incur the corresponding cost consequences. Stages 1 and 3 represent an act stage, where decisions are made by the decision maker, and stages 2 and 4 represent an event stage, where events happen over which the decision maker has no control. The decision is multistage and sequential.

Table 10-4   Revision of probabilities in the light of S_2

(1)	(2)	(3)	(4)	(5)	(6)
			Joint		*Conditional or revised*
	Prior	*Conditional*	*probability*	*Marginal*	*probability*
Event	*probability*	*probability*	$P(E_i \cap S_2)$	*probability*	$P(E_i/S_2)$
E_i	$P(E_i)$	$P(S_2/E_i)$	*(2)* $\times$ *(3)*	$P(S_2)$	*(4)* $\div$ *(5)*
$E_{0.12}$	0.6	0.0144	0.00864		0.982
$E_{0.02}$	0.4	0.0004	0.00016		0.018
				0.00880	

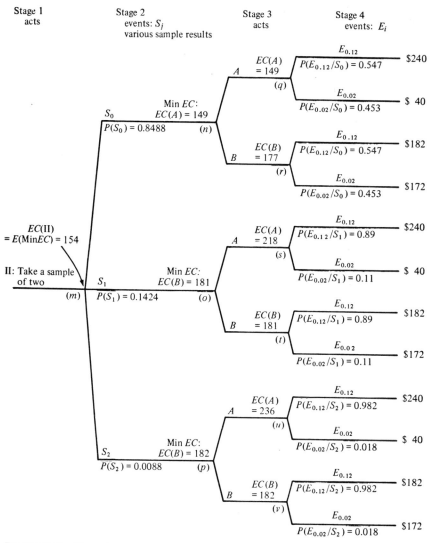

Exhibit 10-10 Game tree.

Further interpretation of the decision tree

1. If and when the decision maker in fact decides to sample two items, observes the sample result S_0, and takes act A, he will be at point q in the tree. The expected cost at q is \$149, computed on the basis of revised probabilities. After the observation of S_0, if and when act B is chosen, the decision maker will be at point r. The expected cost at r

is \$177. Thus, the decision maker would rather be at q than r when he is looking ahead standing at point n. Point n represents the point right after the observation of S_0. Thus, at n, the decision maker would choose act A with the expected cost of \$149. This expected cost of A is then entered at n as the expected cost to the decision maker when and if he is ever at that point. The notation, min EC at point n indicates that it is the minimum of the expected costs of A and B, that is, at points q and r.

2. If and when the decision maker in fact takes the sample and observes S_1, he is at point o, where the expected cost is the minimum of the expected costs of A and B, that is, the expected costs at points s and t. EC at $o = \text{EC}(B) = \$181$.

3. If and when the decision maker in fact takes the sample and observes S_2, he is at point p, where the expected cost is

$$\text{EC at } p = \text{EC}(B) = \$182$$

4. But what is the expected cost at m, that is, *before* the observation of the sample outcomes? At point m, the decision maker is uncertain whether he will be at point n, with an EC of \$149, at point o, with an EC of \$181, or at point p, with an EC of \$182. The unconditional or marginal probabilities of S_0, S_1, and S_2 happening from the sampling are

$$P(S_0) = 0.8488$$
$$P(S_1) = 0.1424$$
$$P(S_2) = 0.0088$$

Thus the expected cost before observing the actual sample result, i.e., the expected cost of the decision to sample, alternative II, is the expected value of the expected costs at points n, o, and p:

$$\begin{aligned}
\text{EC(II)} &= P(S_0)[\text{EC}(n)] + P(S_1)[\text{EC}(o)] + P(S_2)[\text{EC}(p)] \\
&= 0.8488(149) + 0.1424(181) + 0.0088(182) \\
&= 154
\end{aligned}$$

To return to the main train of analysis, recall that the expected cost of the alternative decision to choose between A and B *without sampling* (on the basis of prior probabilities) was determined to be the minimum of the expected costs of two acts, $\text{EC}(A) = \$160$ and $\text{EC}(B) = \$178$, namely, $\text{EC(I)} = \$160$. Since this expected cost is higher than the expected cost of deciding to sample $[\text{EC(II)} = \$154]$, the expected cost at point m in the decision tree of Exhibit 10-10, the decision now is to sample rather than choose between A and B immediately on the basis of prior probabilities without sampling.

Cost of sampling Sampling or gathering additional information usually costs the decision maker time and money. For instance, sampling may involve destruction of the items sampled, as in the case of bullets (to determine whether a bullet is good or bad it must be fired). If additional information is obtained by polling people from a given population, as in testing the marketability of a new product, the cost of constructing questionnaires, conducting interviews, and tallying results is considerable. Finally, delay in the decision necessitated by the time required to gain some additional information, though intangible in some cases, may be the most critical cost of sampling in others.

When additional information requires cost, the improvement in decision from taking samples must, of course, be weighed against the cost of sampling. Thus, in reference to the above sample, the saving in the expected cost from sampling, that is,

$$EC(I) - EC(II) = \$160 - \$154 = \$6$$

is the maximum limit the decision maker would spend for taking the sample of two. Alternatively, in deciding whether to sample or not, the expected cost of the decision to sample should include the cost of sampling, because this cost will not be incurred if sampling is not undertaken.

Sample size Our discussion has dealt with the question of how the decision maker would choose between two alternatives, namely, make the decision between A and B without sampling, alternative I, and take a sample of two items, alternative II, and then make the decision between A and B. But the number of items in the sample, two, was picked completely arbitrarily. Why not a sample of one, three, or ten?

At least at the conceptual level, the optimal sample size can be determined from comparing the expected costs (including the cost of sampling) for taking samples of various sizes. It is obvious that for even a relatively simple decision problem, the amount of computation required in this trial-and-error method of finding the right sample size would be substantial. Modern statistical-decision theorists have developed a number of mathematically manageable models which reduce the amount of computation greatly, especially when the prior probability function is normal and the cost function linear. These models are not discussed in this book.

QUESTIONS AND PROBLEMS

1. Explain the concepts of prior and posterior (or revised) probabilities.

2. A college student has a girl friend of long standing. On about 60 percent of all his dates with her in the past he found her happy. He also found that she wears a colorful

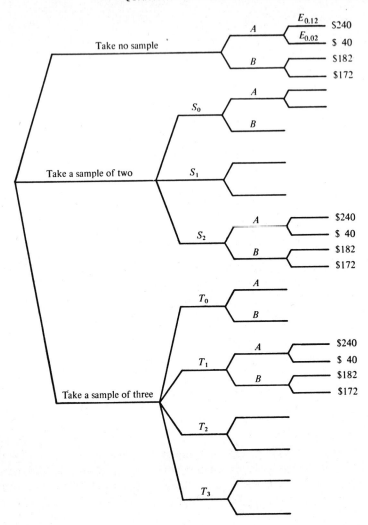

Fig. Prob. 10-4

dress about 80 percent of the times when she is happy and about 30 percent of the times when she is not happy.

(a) What is the probability that his girl friend is happy on a given date?

(b) What is the probability that his girl friend is happy on a given date when she wears a colorful dress? A noncolorful dress?

3. A customer asks a bank for an unsecured commercial loan of $100,000 payable in 90 days at an annual interest rate of 8 percent. The loan officer at the bank must decide whether to grant the loan immediately on the basis of information in the loan application or order a special credit investigation before making the final decision. The special investigation will cost the bank $300. According to the analysis of similar loans in the past, 95 percent of the loans are repaid on time; 4 percent are eventually collected but with an additional collection expense averaging 1 percent of the loan amount; 1 percent are uncollectible (both interest and principle). There is no reason to believe that the present loan applicant is any different from the past applicants of similar loans. The special credit investigation would indicate either a favorable or an unfavorable result. In the past, it used to be the bank's practice to order the special investigation on every application for similar loans. Experience showed that about 80 percent of the investigations turned out favorable and 20 percent unfavorable. Of the loans granted on the basis of the favorable investigation result, 97.5 percent were collected on time; 2 percent were eventually collected but with an additional expense of 1 percent of the loan amount; 0.5 percent were uncollectible. Practically all applications with unfavorable investigation results were rejected. The current bank practice is to give discretion to the loan officer whether or not to order the special investigation.

(a) What should the loan officer's decision be on the loan application?

(b) What would you do to test the soundness of the current bank practice of rejecting all applications when the special investigation returns an unfavorable result?

4. In reference to Example 10-4:

(a) Determine the expected cost of the decision to sample three items and then make the decision between A and B.

(b) Complete the decision tree on the facing page by entering the various probabilities and expected costs and interpret.

(c) T_0, T_1, T_2, T_3 represent four possible outcomes of the sample result, the subscript denoting the number of defective units. State at the conceptual level what additional steps are necessary for the decision maker to decide whether to sample before selecting A or B and how many items to include in the sample if and when he decides to sample.

(d) What modifications should be made in the decision analysis if the expected utility criterion is adopted?

11
Inventory Decision Models

11-0 INTRODUCTION

There are at least two approaches to studying mathematical-statistical methods for managerial decision making. One is to organize the learning in terms of mathematical-statistical topics first and then see what types of managerial problems the various formal methods apply to. The other is to organize it first in terms of types of common managerial problems and then learn whatever mathematical-statistical methods would help solve them. So far in this book, by and large, the first approach has been taken, presenting mathematical-statistical topics in order and bringing in decision examples primarily to facilitate understanding of these topics. In this and the next chapters the second approach is adopted. Certain recurring managerial decision areas are first identified, and then whatever mathematical-statistical methods are necessary to solve them are introduced. This chapter discusses inventory decisions; the next, the queuing problems. The first part of the present chapter presents certainty, or deterministic, inventory models; the second part, uncertainty, or probabilistic, models.

11-1 NATURE OF INVENTORY PROBLEMS AND CERTAINTY MODELS

Broadly defined, inventory is a stock of any economic resources remaining idle at a given point of time, including such nonphysical inventories as level of cash, inventory of accounts receivable, and inventory of human talents, as well as more familiar inventories of physical goods and materials. Although the following discussion deals only with examples involving physical goods and materials, the same concepts and techniques can be modified to apply to other kinds of inventories.

Nature of inventory problems At the most basic level, the relationship between alternative acts and consequences in an inventory decision problem is visualized as in the following schematic diagram:

Alternative acts, or decisions, determine the level of inventory, and the level of inventory in turn determines the consequences. More specifically, in most inventory problems alternative acts may be characterized by alternative decisions on two factors: (1) how much or how many units of an inventory item are replenished each time it is replenished and (2) when the item is to be replenished. As will be seen in subsequent discussions, these two factors controllable by the decision maker determine the level of inventory, given a set of noncontrollable (environmental) factors; associated with the varying level of inventory, in turn, are the varying consequences. In most inventory problems, costs—all inventory-related costs—may be taken as relevant consequences. In general notation, therefore, an inventory decision model may be expressed as $T = f(Q, R)$, where T denotes the total inventory related costs for a given planning period, Q is the quantity replenished or ordered each time the inventory in question is replenished or ordered, and R is the timing of the replenishment. The decision is to find the values of the decision variables Q and R which minimize the total cost T.

Situations which call for an inventory decision are diverse, but they all boil down to this general description of the decision problem. As specific inventory situations are discussed in this chapter, the reader should be aware that the specific models correspond to the general model, with only the specification of the function f varying from one situation to another.

SITUATION I

Assume the following inventory situation.

1. The total demand of the item for the next period, or year, is known with certainty to be $D = 2000$ units.

2. The cost for carrying 1 unit of inventory for 1 year is known to be $k_c = \$0.10$. The inventory carrying cost includes such costs as those relating to storage space, capital tied up in the inventory, insurance, record keeping, deterioration and obsolescence, etc.

3. The known cost of ordering for replenishment is *per order* $k_s = \$5$ regardless of the size of the order. This means that each time inventory is replenished, such costs as cost for requisitioning or ordering (cost of preparing purchase orders if purchased items, cost of machine setup if internally produced items) and costs of trucking, receiving, recording, etc., amount to $5.

4. There is no *lead time;* i.e., when an order for replenishment is placed, the shipment for the entire quantity ordered is received instantaneously without any delay.

5. The rate of use of the inventory item over time is uniform. If there are 365 days in a year, the same $\frac{2000}{365}$ units are demanded of the item every day.

The decision is to determine (1) how many units of the item Q are to be ordered per each replenishment order and (2) when to place an order for replenishment R.

Determination of the order quantity Q At one extreme, the entire requirement for the year of 2000 units may be ordered in one single replenishment order; at the other extreme, only 1 unit each may be ordered every time an order is placed. In between the two extremes, any quantity may be ordered per order. To determine the best quantity to order the decision maker must evaluate the consequences of choosing to order various quantities.

It is obvious that the larger the quantity ordered at a time, the fewer the number of times the replenishment order is placed. For example, if all 2000 units are ordered in one single replenishment, only one ordering is required for the entire period. If a small quantity is ordered each time a replenishment is ordered, the number of times the replenishment order is placed becomes many. For example, if only 100 units are ordered at a time, to meet the total requirement of 2000 units, 20 replenishment orders must be placed in 1 year. As far as the cost of ordering is concerned, the larger the quantity ordered in each order, the less the cost for a given period. More specifically, the variation in the ordering cost according to the variation in order quantity is given in Exhibit 11-1a.

(1) Order quantity, decision variable Q, units	(2) Number of times ordered in 1 year, $N = 2000/Q$	(3) Ordering cost for 1 year $C_s = \$5(2000/Q)$
1	2000	$10,000
100	20	100
250	8	40
400	5	25
500	4	20
1000	2	10
2000	1	5

Exhibit 11-1a   Inventory ordering cost.

Formally, the number of times a replenishment order is placed is $N = 2000/Q$. Column 2 of Exhibit 11-1a gives the N values corresponding to various order quantities. Since it costs $5 per order, the total ordering cost for the year is $C_s = 5N = 5(2000/Q)$. The varying total ordering cost thus obtained for the varying order quantity is given in column 3. As far as the ordering cost is concerned, the best decision is to order 2000 units per order, $Q = 2000$.

But the ordering cost is not the only cost involved in the decision. Associated with different order quantities are different levels of inventory, and different levels of inventory in turn entail different inventory carrying costs. As we shall see, the larger the order quantity, the higher the average inventory level and therefore the higher the inventory carrying cost.

Suppose that the decision maker decides to order 2000 units in one single order at the beginning of the year for the entire year's requirement. The level of inventory at different times of the year can then be visualized as in the graph of Exhibit 11-1b.

At the time point 0 when the shipment on the order is received, the level of inventory is the highest, 2000, but as the item is consumed throughout the year, the level of inventory decreases, reaching finally the 0-unit level at the end of the year. Since the rate of use is assumed uniform throughout the year, the rate of decrease in the level of inventory is uniform and consequently the line representing the level of inventory is a straight line and decreasing. Thus, when one-half of the year is over, the level of inventory is one-half that of the beginning inventory of 2000 units.

What is the total annual inventory carrying cost when the level of inventory varies as in Exhibit 11-1b? If a given level of inventory,

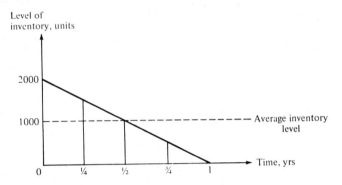

Exhibit 11-1b   Inventory level over time when $Q = 2000$.

say I, is maintained from the beginning to the end of the year, the total carrying cost would be calculated by multiplying the known carrying cost of $0.10 per unit per year by I.   But the problem here is somewhat complicated because from the beginning to the end of the year the level of inventory does not remain the same but decreases.   Under certain circumstances, however, the cost of carrying the decreasing level of inventory as in Exhibit 11-1b may be considered approximately the same as the cost of carrying the *average* inventory—the average of the beginning and ending inventories—throughout the year.   Since the beginning inventory is 2000 units and the ending inventory 0 unit, the average is $(2000 + 0)/2$ or 1000 units.   The inventory carrying cost for the year is $0.10(1000) = $100.

If the order quantity is in general any number Q, then the level of inventory at different times in the year is as in Exhibit 11-1c.   There

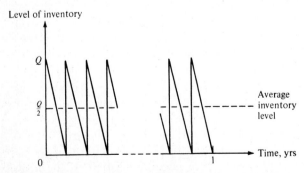

Exhibit 11-1c   Inventory level over time when $Q = Q$.

(1) Decision variable, order quantity Q, units	(2) Average inventory Q/2	(3) Carrying cost per year, 0.10(Q/2)
1	0.5	$ 0.05
100	50	5
250	125	12.5
400	200	20
500	250	25
1000	500	50
2000	1000	100

Exhibit 11-1d Inventory carrying cost.

are $N = 2000/Q$ sawteeth, each tooth representing the same cycle of variation in the level of inventory. Specifically, within each cycle, the level varies from a maximum of Q units to a minimum of 0 unit. The average level of inventory for each cycle and also for the whole year is $(Q + 0)/2 = Q/2$. Approximating the cost of carrying the cyclically varying levels of inventory of Exhibit 11-1c by the cost of carrying $Q/2$ units uniformly throughout the year, the annual inventory carrying cost is computed: $C_c = \$0.10(Q/2)$. Exhibit 11-1d reproduces the annual carrying costs for various Q values.

As expected, the larger the order quantity per order, the larger the average inventory and therefore the larger the inventory carrying cost.

When the inventory order cost for the year (Exhibit 11-1a) and the inventory carrying cost for the year (Exhibit 11-1d) are combined, the total inventory-related costs for the year are obtained as in Exhibit 11-2. The total inventory-related cost per year T is extremely high if the decision is to order 1 unit *at a time* because even though the total annual inventory carrying cost is only $0.05 on account of a negligible inventory level of $\frac{1}{2}$ unit, the annual ordering cost is prohibitively high since 2000 orders must be placed during the year. Then, as the order quantity per order is increased, the annual ordering cost decreases because the number of orders placed decreases but the annual carrying cost increases as the size of the average inventory increases. The decrease in ordering cost and the increase in carrying cost somewhat offset each other's effect on total inventory-related cost, but in the initial stage (of increase in order quantity) the decrease in ordering cost is larger than the increase in carrying cost, the net effect being to decrease the total cost. After a certain point, however, the magnitude of decrease and the

(1) Order quantity: decision variable Q, units	(2) No. of orders per year N 2000/Q	(3) Order cost per year $C_s = \$5(N)$	(4) Average inventory Q/2, units	(5) Carrying cost per year $C_s = \$0.10(Q/2)$	(6) Total inventory cost per year $T = C_s + C_c$ or (3) + (5)
1	2000	$10,000	0.5	$ 0.05	$10,000.05
100	20	100	50	5	105
250	8	40	125	12.5	52.5
400	5	25	200	20	45
500	4	20	250	25	45
1000	2	10	500	50	60
2000	1	5	1000	100	105

Exhibit 11-2   Total inventory cost.

magnitude of increase reverse themselves, and the total cost begins to increase as the order quantity is increased further.

According to Exhibit 11-2, the total cost attains a minimum of $45 at $Q = 400$ and $Q = 500$. This implies that somewhere between the two is an order quantity which yields the minimum total cost (less than $45).

The same relationships between order quantity and costs represented in Exhibit 11-2 are summarized in mathematical statements as follows. The total annual inventory related cost is

$$T = C_s + C_c$$

where the annual cost C_s is

$$C_s = k_s N = k_s \frac{D}{Q}$$

and the annual carrying cost C_c is

$$C_c = k_c \frac{Q}{2}$$

Thus

$$T = C_s + C_c$$
$$= \frac{k_s D}{Q} + \frac{k_c Q}{2}$$

Since the cost of ordering per order is $k_s = \$5$, the carrying cost per unit per year is $k_c = \$0.10$, and the total annual requirement for the item D is $D = 2000$,

$$T = \frac{k_s D}{Q} + \frac{k_c Q}{2}$$

becomes

$$T = \frac{10{,}000}{Q} + \frac{0.10Q}{2}$$

Graphically the same relationships are as represented in Exhibit 11-3. The reader should verify that the heights of the three curves indeed represent the order costs, carrying costs, and the sum of the two, the total costs, respectively, at various order quantities measured on the horizontal axis.

Once the mathematical model of the relationships is defined, the model can be "exercised" by varying the decision variable in order to observe the behavior of the model. Thus, the total costs corresponding to a number of alternative order quantities can be computed (as in Exhibit 11-2) until the minimum-cost order quantity is identified. But a more precise and efficient way of locating the best solution is provided by using calculus, presented in Chap. 3 (see Table 11-1).

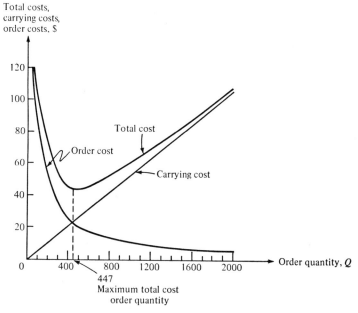

Exhibit 11-3   Order quantity and inventory-related costs.

Table 11-1 Finding Q with the minimum total cost

With general form	*With specified form*
$T = \dfrac{k_s D}{Q} + \dfrac{k_c Q}{2}$	$T = \dfrac{10,000}{Q} + \dfrac{0.10Q}{2}$
$\dfrac{dT}{dQ} = -\dfrac{k_s D}{Q^2} + \dfrac{k_c}{2}$	$\dfrac{dT}{dQ} = -\dfrac{10,000}{Q^2} + \dfrac{0.10}{2}$
Find Q where $\dfrac{dT}{dQ} = 0$	Find Q where $\dfrac{dT}{dQ} = 0$
$0 = -\dfrac{k_s D}{Q^2} + \dfrac{k_c}{2}$	$0 = -\dfrac{10,000}{Q^2} + \dfrac{0.10}{2}$
$\dfrac{k_s D}{Q^2} = \dfrac{k_c}{2}$	$\dfrac{10,000}{Q^2} = \dfrac{0.10}{2}$
$Q^2 = \dfrac{2k_s D}{k_c}$	$0.10Q^2 = 20,000$
$Q = \sqrt{\dfrac{2k_s D}{k_c}}$	$Q^2 = \dfrac{20,000}{0.10}$
	$Q = \sqrt{200,000}$
	$Q = 447$

The minimum-cost order quantity is found in general by the formula derived above, $Q = \sqrt{2k_s D / k_c}$, commonly called the *economic-order-quantity* formula. Although it is based on a number of restrictive assumptions, it has a wide application in real-world inventory management.

Note that with k_s and D remaining the same, if the inventory carrying cost k_c increases, the economic order quantity Q decreases. This is understandable intuitively. Even though a decrease in Q means an increase in the ordering cost, if the inventory carrying cost is made higher, it pays to reduce the order quantity so as to lessen the effect of the increased carrying cost on the total cost. The reader can also see the reasonableness of increasing the order quantity if the ordering cost per order is increased while the carrying cost and demand remain the same.

Sensitivity analysis   In real-world inventory problems, estimation of the ordering cost per order k_s and the carrying cost per unit per year k_c is a hazardous task. Since accounting records do not supply these costs routinely, a lot of guesswork is involved in estimating them. Under such circumstances, the analyst may assign alternative values to k_s and k_c and observe how the resulting economic order quantity varies.

If the order quantity varies widely from a small variation in k_s (or k_c), it is said to be *sensitive* to k_s (or k_c); if not, insensitive. The formula for the economic order quantity makes it obvious that it should be rather insensitive to variation in k_s or k_c. The radical sign in the formula dampens the effect of the parametric variation on the economic order quantity, as the reader may verify by observing the percentage change in Q as k_s or k_c is varied by a certain percentage. Mistakes in estimating the parameters k_s or k_c are not too serious in terms of their effect on the decision of how many units to order in a replenishment order.

Determination of reorder point R   It was stated earlier that an inventory-decision problem involves two decision variables, order quantity Q and reorder point R, or when to place an order. The optimal value of the second variable, R, is determined as follows.

With the assumption of no lead time between placement of the order and receipt of the shipment, an order for Q should be placed whenever the level of inventory falls to zero.[1] In other words, the *reorder point*, R, or level of inventory at which a replenishment order is placed is zero. If the reorder point is set at any level higher than zero, the new replenishment would be received before the existing stock is completely exhausted; consequently, the inventory carrying cost would be higher with no offsetting benefit.

Summary of decision for situation I   The total inventory-related costs per year are minimized if an order for replenishment of $Q = \sqrt{2k_sD/k_c}$ is placed whenever the level of inventory reaches zero, that is, $R = 0$.

SITUATION II

An assumption in situation I was that the shipment on a reorder was received right at the time when the level of inventory reaches zero. This is equivalent to the assumption that no back ordering is allowed. In some situations, however, if no stock is available when a request for the inventory item is received, it may be back-ordered for later shipment to the customer. Situation II is the same as situation I except for the assumption on back ordering.

An obvious benefit of back ordering is that it lowers the average level of inventory. If, for instance, $Q = 400$ units have been ordered, and if a back order of 50 units has been allowed to accumulate, when the shipment of 400 units is received, 50 units in back order would be *immediately* fulfilled so that the maximum inventory right after the receipt of 400 units is only 350 units ($= 400 - 50$), not 400. In the extreme, all customer demand may be back-ordered, and whenever a shipment is

[1] This is true only if no back ordering is permitted. See situation II.

received, the whole shipment may be instantaneously distributed to fill the back orders. The average inventory would be zero, and consequently the inventory carrying cost would be zero. Of course, this cannot be done because back ordering is not free, but costs sales and customer goodwill. When a customer's demand is back-ordered, he may simply turn to other sellers or at least be irritated. Thus, in deciding how many units to back order, the benefit of savings in the inventory carrying cost must be weighed against the costs of back ordering.

The total annual inventory-related cost T of the new inventory situation consists of three classes of costs: ordering costs C_s, carrying costs C_c, and stockout or back-ordering costs C_o. Then the total inventory-related cost T varies as the order quantity Q and the maximum number of units of stockout allowed S are varied. The decision is to find that order quantity and that maximum level of stockout quantity which entail the minimum total cost. The new situation involves two decision variables, Q and S. The problem of reorder point is as trivial as in situation I because zero lead time is still assumed.

Annual ordering costs Precisely as in situation I, the annual ordering costs are

$$C_s = k_s N = k_s \frac{D}{Q}$$

Level of inventory Exhibit 11-4 shows the pattern of variation in the level of inventory and stockout for situation II. The maximum level of inventory is $Q - S$ when the order quantity is Q, because when the

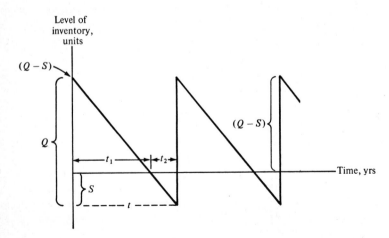

Exhibit 11-4 Variation in the level of inventory and backlog.

shipment of Q units is received, S units in back order are sent out to the customers instantly. Then this maximum inventory is reduced gradually to meet the regular demand until it is depleted. Contrary to the assumption in situation I, no replenishment order is placed in situation II when the level of inventory reaches zero. As the demand for the item continues to come in, it is back-ordered until the backlog reaches the maximum allowable level of S units. Only then is a reorder for Q units placed, and the complete shipment is received instantaneously.

In preparation for mathematical formulation of the cost models for decision, let t_1 stand for the time (a fraction of a year) it takes for the inventory to be depleted from the maximum of $Q - S$ units to zero and t_2 for the time it takes for the level of back order to reach the maximum of S units from the time when the inventory level reaches zero. Then, $t_1 + t_2 = t$ is the time from the placement of one order to the placement of the next. This is the time (a fraction of a year) required for completion of one sawtooth, or one *inventory cycle*. In addition, we let k_o stand for the stockout cost for 1 unit carried in backorder for an entire year.

Carrying cost per cycle Within an inventory cycle, the maximum inventory is $Q - S$; the lowest is zero (not considering the back order as the negative inventory). The average inventory therefore is $(Q - S)/2$. Since this average inventory is considered to be carried for a period of t_1 per cycle, the carrying cost per cycle is

$$\text{Carrying cost per cycle} = k_c \frac{Q - S}{2} t_1$$

Now, t_1 is a fraction of t. From the fact that in the triangle representing an inventory cycle of Exhibit 11-4 t corresponds to Q and t_1 corresponds to $Q - S$, the fraction is determined as $(Q - S)/Q$; namely, $t_1 = t(Q - S)/Q$.* Therefore,

$$\text{Carrying cost per cycle} = k_c \frac{Q - S}{2} t_1$$

$$= k_c \frac{Q - S}{2} \frac{t(Q - S)}{Q} = \frac{(Q - S)^2}{2Q} k_c t$$

Since there are N cycles in 1 year,

$$\text{Annual carrying cost} = \text{carrying cost per cycle} \times N$$

$$= \frac{(Q - S)^2}{2Q} k_c t N$$

---

* The reader may verify the relationship between t_1 and t, that is, $t_1 = t(Q - S)/Q$, by assuming a specific demand rate, a specific Q value, and a specific S value and computing the resulting t_1 and t values.

Because there are N t's in 1 year, $tN = 1$. Thus, the annual carrying cost may be restated as

$$C_c = \frac{(Q - S)^2}{2Q} k_c tN = \frac{(Q - S)^2}{2Q} k_c$$

Stockout cost per cycle The average stockout level is $S/2$. Within each inventory cycle, this average stockout level is carried for a period of t_2. Thus, the stockout cost per cycle is

$$\text{Stockout cost per cycle} = k_o \frac{S}{2} t_2$$

As t_1 was a fraction of t, t_2 is a fraction of t, namely, $t_2 = t(S/Q)$. (Note that since

$$t_1 = t\frac{(Q - S)}{Q} \qquad \text{and} \qquad t_2 = t\frac{S}{Q}$$

$$t_1 + t_2 = t\frac{(Q - S)}{Q} + t\frac{S}{Q} = t\frac{Q - S + S}{Q} = t\frac{Q}{Q} = t$$

that is, $t_1 + t_2 = t$.)

Thus

$$\text{Stockout cost per cycle} = k_o \frac{S}{2} t_2 = k_o \frac{S}{2} \frac{tS}{Q} = \frac{S^2}{2Q} k_o t$$

Since there are N cycles in 1 year,

$$\text{Annual stockout cost} = C_o = \frac{S^2}{2Q} k_o tN$$

As stated earlier, tN is 1 year; therefore, C_o can be rewritten as

$$C_o = \frac{S^2}{2Q} k_o tN = \frac{S^2}{2Q} k_o$$

To summarize, the total inventory-related costs for situation II are

$$T = C_s + C_c + C_o$$

$$= \frac{k_s D}{Q} + \frac{k_c(Q - S)^2}{2Q} + \frac{k_o S^2}{2Q}$$

When $S = 0$, that is, where no back ordering is allowed,

$$T = \frac{k_s D}{Q} + \frac{k_c(Q - S)^2}{2Q} + \frac{k_o S^2}{2Q}$$

$$= \frac{k_s D}{Q} + \frac{k_c Q^2}{2Q} + 0$$

$$= \frac{k_s D}{Q} + \frac{k_c Q}{2}$$

This is the same total cost function as in situation I. Thus, situation I can be said to be a special case of situation II, the case when $S = 0$.

Since there are two decision variables, Q and S, the formulas for Q and S which would yield the minimum total costs are not as easily derived as in situation I, but by applying the concepts of partial derivatives of Sec. 3-4, the optimal values of Q and S can be determined. Specifically, the reader should be able to show that the value of Q which satisfies the condition $\partial T/\partial Q = 0$ is

$$Q = \sqrt{\frac{2k_s D + (k_c + k_o)S^2}{k_c}}$$

and that the value of S which satisfies $\partial T/\partial S = 0$ is

$$S = \frac{k_c Q}{k_c + k_o}$$

The first formula yields the economic order quantity given a particular policy on the (maximum) level of back order allowed; the second yields the best policy on back order given a particular order quantity. The values of Q and S which satisfy both conditions simultaneously will give the minimum inventory-related costs. Though of no import, the reader may, as an exercise, solve the two equations for Q and S to obtain the formulas for the optimal inventory policy.

11-2 INVENTORY MODELS UNDER UNCERTAINTY: REORDER POINT

In situations I and II, the total demand, the rate of demand, and the lead time—the time lapse between ordering and receiving the shipment—were all assumed known with certainty. But, of course, uncertainty in a given situation may be such that certainty models have to be abandoned. This section will illustrate how the concepts of probability and expected value can be explicitly brought into inventory decision analyses. The discussion starts from relaxing the certainty assumption on the lead time.

If the lead time is known with certainty to be L units of time, e.g., 4 days, and if the demand rate per unit of time, e.g., daily use, is known with certainty to be r units, e.g., 10 units, a reorder should be placed whenever the level of inventory reaches $R = rL$ units, e.g., 10 units times 4 days = 40 units, assuming that no backordering is allowed. Then, by the end of L units of time (4 days), R units (40 units) will have been used up; the level of inventory will fall to zero, and a new shipment on order will be received. But if there is uncertainty surrounding the length of lead time and/or the demand rate during the lead time, the question of reorder point cannot be answered so easily.

For illustration, suppose that the expected demand for an inventory item during a lead time is 40 units. When should a reorder be placed? The first inclination of the decision maker might be to place a reorder whenever the level of inventory reaches 40 units. Such a reorder policy, however, should be adopted only upon understanding its full implications. Although on the average a demand of 40 units is expected, what if there should be a demand higher than the available 40 units before the replenishment arrives? This question obviously cannot be answered without taking into account the consequences of being out of stock when an item is demanded. If the consequences of not being able to meet the demand are considered grave, namely, if the cost of stockout is high, the decision maker may wish to provide some cushion in setting the reorder point. Thus, a replenishment may be ordered whenever the level of stock on hand reaches, say 45 units, a level higher than the average demand. Then the difference between the reorder point of 45 units and the expected demand of 40 units, i.e., 5 units, is viewed as a buffer or a cushion against stockout. This cushion is called the *buffer stock* or *safety stock*.

Needless to say, the larger the safety stock, the higher the inventory carrying cost. In establishing the "right" amount of buffer, therefore, both its benefit (reduction in stockout cost) and its cost (increase in inventory carrying cost) must be taken into consideration. Such is the essence of the decision on the buffer stock, or alternatively, on the reorder point, when there is uncertainty surrounding the demand during the lead time. Formally, if R denotes the level of stock at which a reorder is placed, B is the number of units in the safety stock, and $\bar{U}$ is the expected demand or use during the lead time, then $R - \bar{U} = B$, or $R = B + \bar{U}$. The following discussion illustrates how the decision on R or alternatively on B is made.

SITUATION III

Assume the following inventory situation:

1. The total annual demand or use is known with certainty to be $D = 2000$ units.
2. The known cost for carrying 1 unit of inventory for 1 year is $k_c = \$1$.
3. The known cost of ordering per order is $k_s = \$5$. Under these assumptions the economic order quantity is determined as

$$Q = \sqrt{\frac{2k_s D}{k_c}} = \sqrt{\frac{2(5)(2000)}{1}} = \sqrt{20,000} \approx 141 \text{ units}$$

Now (unlike situation I) the following assumption is made on the demand during the lead time.

Number of units demanded during lead time U_i, units	Probability $P(U_i)$
37	0.05
38	0.15
39	0.18
40	0.25
41	0.20
42	0.10
43	0.05
44	0.02
	1.00

Exhibit 11-5 Probability of demand during lead time.

4. The number of units demanded during the lead time varies according to the probability distribution in Exhibit 11-5.

As the reader may verify, this probability distribution yields the expected number of units demanded during the lead time as

$$\overline{U} = \Sigma U_i P(U_i) = 40 \text{ units}$$

The reorder point R can be set at any possible value of U_i: at the level of $\overline{U} = 40$, at a level higher than $\overline{U}$, or at a level lower than $\overline{U}$. If R is set at the level of the expected use, i.e., 40, and if the actual use during the lead time is equal to or less than 40, namely, if $U_i \leq 40$, no stockout occurs; but if $U_i > 40$, a stockout occurs. Further, the probability of stockout, or *service failure*, in a given lead time when the reorder point is set at $R = 40$ is $P(U_i > 40) = \sum_{i=41}^{44} P(U_i) = 0.37$. To interpret, if there are 10 inventory cycles in 1 year (or, alternatively, if the number of times ordered is $N = 10$), with $R = 40$ the inventory center is expected to be out of stock in 3.7 lead times out of the total 10 lead times in 1 year.

Similarly if R is set at $R = 42$, the probability of stockout in a given lead time is $P(U_i > 42) = \sum_{i=43}^{44} P(U_i) = 0.07$. If there are 10 lead times in 1 year, a stockout is expected in less than one lead time in 1 year.

Management specification of service level A practical approach to solving the problem of where to set the reorder level suggests itself. Management may specify its tolerance for stockout in terms of the maximum probability of stockout or service failure for a given lead time or, equivalently, in terms of the maximum number of lead times a stockout is

Decision variable, reorder point R, units	Buffer stock $B = R - \bar{U}$ $= R - 40$	Probability of stockout $P(U_i > R)$	Level of service $P(U_i \leq R)$
37	-3	0.95	0.05
38	-2	0.80	0.20
39	-1	0.62	0.38
40	0	0.37	0.63
41	1	0.17	0.83
42	2	0.07	0.93
43	3	0.02	0.98
44	4	0.00	1.00

Exhibit 11-6 Probability of stockout or level of service during lead time.

allowed in a year. Thus, if management professes that its policy is to keep the probability of stockout at 0.17 at most, the level of R can be found such that $P(U_i > R) = 0.17$. From the probability distribution of Exhibit 11-5, it is found that when $R = 41$, $P(U_i > R) = 0.17$. The decision, therefore, would be to reorder whenever the level of inventory reaches 41 units.

Crucial in such a somewhat informal approach is the probability of stockout, used as an index of level of service failure. Thus, a table showing the probability of stockout at various possible levels of R can be prepared and presented to management. Exhibit 11-6 is such a table. The probability of stockout in the exhibit is merely the cumulative probability distribution derived from the probability distribution of use during a lead time of Exhibit 11-5.

To explain Exhibit 11-6 further, consider the reorder level of 39. A stockout will occur if the actual use during the lead time is either 40, 41, 42, 43, or 44 (or in short, if $U_i > 39$). Adding the probabilities of all these events gives the probability of being out of stock in a given lead time as $P(U_i > R = 39) = 0.62$. On the other hand, with $R = 39$, the inventory center will be able to meet the demand with the probability of $P(U_i \leq R = 39) = 1 - P(U_i > R = 39) = 1 - 0.62 = 0.38$, which may be used as the index of level of service. Note that there will never be a stockout (100 percent service level) if $R = 44$; a stockout will always occur if $R = 36$. Exhibit 11-6 also gives the level of safety stock associated with each reorder level.

Trade-off between stockout and excess inventory As stated earlier, management will not always set R at a level high enough to make the probability of stockout zero or some minimum probability because the higher the reorder point (or the larger the buffer stock) the higher the additional inventory carrying cost. Management, in setting the level of R, cannot evaluate the probability of stockout alone but must evaluate it against the additional inventory carrying cost incurred from maintaining a buffer stock. Exhibit 11-7 contrasts explicitly the probability of stockout against the additional inventory carrying cost for various R and B values.

If management does not wish to provide any cushion against uncertainty, it may set the reorder point at the expected use, $\bar{U} = 40$. Then, during a given year, there will be stockouts in some inventory cycles, i.e., lead times, because the actual demand exceeds the expected demand, but in other cycles, there will be excess or idle inventory when a replenishment is received because the actual demand is less than the expected demand. The effects of stockouts and excess inventories (in different inventory cycles) on the average level of inventory would largely offset each other in the course of a long enough period of time, and as a result, no *additional* inventory carrying cost is *expected* to be incurred for the year—additional to the carrying cost when the demand during the lead time is known with certainty and no stockout is allowed (as in situation I). In this sense, Exhibit 11-7 shows the additional inventory carrying cost for the reorder policy of $R = 40$ to be $0.

But if the reorder level is set at anything higher than the expected use of 40 units, it cannot be expected that the effects of stockouts and excess inventories cancel each other out over a long enough period of time. In particular, when $R > \bar{U}$, it is expected on the average that the average inventory will be higher by $R - \bar{U} = B$, the buffer stock, than the level of average inventory when the demand during the lead time is known with certainty. Column 2 of Exhibit 11-7 gives the excess average inventory, i.e., the buffer stock, that is expected to be carried at

(1) Reorder level R	(2) Buffer stock $B = R - 40$	(3) Additional carrying cost per year k_cB	(4) Probability of stockout per lead time $P(U_i > R)$
40	0	$0	0.37
41	1	1	0.17
42	2	2	0.07
43	3	3	0.02
44	4	4	0.00

Exhibit 11-7 Evaluation of various reorder points.

different levels of reorder point.   Column 3 gives the expected additional
cost associated with the excess average inventory of column 2 and is
obtained by multiplying column 2 by the per unit carrying cost, k_c = \$1.

Exhibit 11-7 does not give the reorder level below the expected
use of 40 units.   Theoretically speaking, however, the reorder point could
be set at a level lower than the expected demand.   Then $R - \bar{U} = B$
would be negative, a negative buffer stock.   The reader may expand the
table of Exhibit 11-7 to include the cases where $R < \bar{U}$ and interpret the
result.   For the present discussion, however, it is assumed that management has ruled out the possibility of setting R at a level lower than the
expected demand.

Presented with Exhibit 11-7, management may ask: "If the reorder
point is raised from 40 units to 41 units, the probability of stockout or
service failure is improved from 0.37 to 0.17, but the inventory carrying
cost is increased by \$1.   Is this a worthwhile trade-off?"   "If the reorder
point is raised from 41 units to 42 units, the probability of stockout is
improved from . . . ?"   Exhibit 11-7 does not provide means to answer
these questions.   Although the approach represented in Exhibit 11-7
is a considerable refinement over the earlier approach, which considered
only the service-failure probabilities but not the additional inventory
carrying cost, still it leaves much to be desired because it does not
explicitly consider the magnitude of consequences of stockout, nor does
it differentiate between stockout of a large number of units and that of
only a few.   The costs of stockouts are taken into account more explicitly
next.

SITUATION IV

In addition to the assumptions of situation III, in situation IV it is
assumed that the cost of stockout per unit per lead time is h_o = \$2.   To
summarize all assumptions of the new situation:

1. Annual demand is D = 2000 units.
2. Order cost per order is k_s = \$5.
3. Carrying cost per unit per year is k_c = \$1.
4. Cost of stockout per unit per lead time is h_o = \$2.
5. Probabilities of various possible demands are as given in Exhibit 11-5.
6. Economic order quantity = $Q = \sqrt{2k_s D/k_c} = \sqrt{2(5)(2000)/1} \approx 141$
   units.
7. Accordingly, the number of times ordered, or number of inventory
   cycles in 1 year, is

$$N = \frac{D}{Q} = \frac{2000}{141} = 14.1 \text{ times}$$

Actual use during lead time U	No. of stockout units	$\times$	Per unit stockout cost h_o	$=$	Conditional stockout cost
≤ 40	0		$\$2$		$\$0$
41	1		2		2
42	2		2		4
43	3		2		6
44	4		2		8

Exhibit 11-8 Conditional stockout costs for $R = 40$.

8. Additional inventory carrying costs per year attributable to the buffer stock are as in column 3 of Exhibit 11-7.

Ultimately the total annual cost of stockout must be calculated so as to compare it with the annual additional inventory carrying cost already determined, but as the first step, the cost of stockout *per lead time* (or per inventory cycle) must be identified. The cost per lead time is then multiplied by the number of lead times in 1 year to obtain the annual stockout cost.

Stockout cost per lead time Suppose that the reorder point is set at $R = 40$. Whenever the actual use is less than or equal to 40 units, namely, $U \leq 40$,[1] there will be no stockout, but when $U = 41$, there will be a stockout of 1 unit; when $U = 42$, a stockout of 2 units; when $U = 43$, a stockout of 3 units; when $U = 44$, a stockout of 4 units. Based on the stockout cost of $h_o = \$2$ per unit per lead time, the conditional stockout costs of $R = 40$ are computed in Exhibit 11-8.

Likewise, the conditional stockout costs for all other possible reorder points can be computed. The cost payoff table of Exhibit 11-9 reproduces the results of such computation.

On the basis of the conditional costs of Exhibit 11-9, the expected stockout cost of each possible reorder point is next calculated. Columns 5 and 6 of Exhibit 11-10 show two alternative ways of computing the expected cost of act $R = 40$. The computation of column 6 makes it obvious that the formula for expected stockout cost can take an alternative form:

$$\text{Expected stockout cost} = \Sigma h_o(U - R)P(U)$$
$$= h_o\Sigma(U - R)P(U)$$
$$= h_o E(U - R)$$

[1] From here on, the subscript i in U_i will be omitted to avoid a cluttered appearance. Thus ΣU stands for ΣU_i.

Actual use	Probability	Reorder point R				
U	P(U)	40	41	42	43	44
≤40	0.63	$0	$0	$0	$0	$0
41	0.20	2	0	0	0	0
42	0.10	4	2	0	0	0
43	0.05	6	4	2	0	0
44	0.02	8	6	4	2	0
	1.00					

Exhibit 11-9 Conditional stockout cost table per lead time.

where $E(U - R) = \Sigma(U - R)P(U)$ is the expected number of units of stockout. (Note that when $U \leq R$, there is 0 stockout. Therefore, for $U \leq R$, $U - R$ is considered 0 in the computation.)

Similarly, the expected stockout costs per lead time for other possible values of R can be determined. Column 2 of Exhibit 11-11 summarizes the results of such computation. When these expected costs per lead time are multiplied by the number of lead times in 1 year, namely, $N = D/Q = 14.1$, the annual expected stockout costs as in Column 3 of the same exhibit are obtained.

Exhibit 11-12 combines the annual expected stockout costs computed in Exhibit 11-11 with the annual expected excess inventory carrying costs computed in Exhibit 11-7 in order to evaluate the total buffer-stock-related costs. There are two kinds of costs related to the buffer

(1)	(2)	(3)	(4)	(5)	(6)
	No. of		Conditional	Expected stockout cost	
Actual use	stockout units	Probability	stockout cost	Method 1:	Method 2:
U	U − R	P(U) or P(U − R)	$h_o \times$ (2)	(4) × (3)	$h_o \times$ (2) × (3)
≤40	0	0.63	$0	$0 × 0.63 = 0	$2 × (0 × 0.63) = 0
41	1	0.20	2	2 × 0.20 = 0.4	2 × (1 × 0.20) = 0.4
42	2	0.10	4	4 × 0.10 = 0.4	2 × (2 × 0.10) = 0.4
43	3	0.05	6	6 × 0.05 = 0.3	2 × (3 × 0.05) = 0.3
44	4	0.02	8	8 × 0.02 = 0.16	2 × (4 × 0.02) = 0.16
		1.00		$1.26	2 × E(U − R) = $1.26

Exhibit 11-10   Expected stockout cost for $R = 40$.

(1)	(2)	(3)
		Annual expected
Reorder point	Expected stockout	stockout cost
R	cost per lead time	(2) × 14.1
40	$1.26	$17.8
41	0.52	7.3
42	0.18	2.5
43	0.04	0.6
44	0	0

Exhibit 11-11 Annual expected stockout cost.

stock: the excess inventory carrying costs and the costs of being out of stock. The expected excess inventory carrying costs increase as the size of the safety stock increases, namely, as the reorder point is raised, while the other costs, the expected costs of stockout, decrease. The optimal level of the buffer stock or the reorder point is the level which gives the minimum of the sum of these two costs related to the buffer stock. In the table of Exhibit 11-12 this level is located at $R = 43$, or $B = 3$.

It is easy to speculate how the minimum-cost level of R or B would vary if the carrying cost k_c or the stockout cost h_o were increased or decreased. Other things being equal, a higher k_c dictates a lower reorder point, and a higher h_o dictates a higher reorder point.

Summary of cost model for situation IV

Total annual buffer-stock-related costs

= additional inventory carrying costs + stockout costs

$$= k_c(R - \bar{U}) + Nh_o \sum_{i=R+1}^{44} (U - R)P(U)$$

The reader should note that in Exhibit 11-12, $k_c(R - \bar{U})$ is given in column 3 as the annual additional carrying costs, and

$$Nh_o \sum_{i=R+1}^{44} (U - R)P(U)$$

is given in column 5 as the annual stockout costs.

Since $N = D/Q$, the above formula for total annual buffer-stock-related costs can be restated as

$$k_c(R - \bar{U}) + \frac{D}{Q} h_o \sum_{i=R+1}^{44} (U - R)P(U)$$

(1)	(2)	(3)	(4)	(5)	(6)
Reorder point R	Buffer stock R − Ū	Annual additional carrying cost $k_c \times (2)$ or $k_c \times (R - \bar{U})$	Stockout cost per lead time $h_o \times (U - R)P(U)$	Annual stockout cost $(4) \times N$	Total annual buffer stock related costs $(3) + (5)$
40	0	$0	$1.26	$17.8	$17.8
41	1	1	0.52	7.3	8.3
42	2	2	0.18	2.5	4.5
43	3	3	0.04	0.6	3.6
44	4	4	0	0	4

Exhibit 11-12   Evaluation of reorder points or buffer stock.

An overall inventory cost model   The above analysis has been concerned only with the buffer stock. Since in addition to the buffer stock, the regular cycle stock is also carried, the *total* inventory-related costs should include both the buffer-stock-related costs and the cycle-stock-related costs.

Total inventory-related costs

$$= \text{cycle-stock-related costs} + \text{buffer-stock-related costs}$$

$$= \left(\frac{D}{Q}k_s + \frac{Q}{2}k_c\right) + \left[k_c(R - \bar{U}) + \frac{D}{Q}h_o\Sigma(U - R)P(U)\right]$$

$$= \frac{D}{Q}k_s + k_c\left[\frac{Q}{2} + (R - \bar{U})\right] + \left[\frac{D}{Q}h_o\Sigma(U - R)P(U)\right]$$

$$= \text{order costs} + \text{carrying costs} + \text{stockout costs}$$

With this overall model of inventory costs, the decision is to determine the values of two decision variables, Q and R, which yield the minimum total costs.

   In determining the optimal values of Q and R, the procedure followed above was to determine the optimal value of Q *first* from only the cycle-stock cost model of $(D/Q)k_s + (Q/2)k_c$ without consideration of the buffer-stock costs, and *then*, on the basis of the optimum value of Q thus determined, the best R value was derived from only the buffer-stock-cost model of $k_c(R - \bar{U}) + (D/Q)h_o\Sigma(U - R)P(U)$ without consideration of the cycle-stock costs. Strictly speaking, this approach would yield an inaccurate choice of Q and R values in the sense that Q and R values thus chosen may not yield the minimum total costs. This is so because the choice of one of Q and R affects the choice of the other. Strictly speaking, therefore, the economic order quantity and the optimum reorder point must be determined simultaneously from the total-cost model. But in many situations, the approximate method of determining Q and R by first obtaining the best Q value, ignoring the buffer-stock costs, and then using this Q value in determining the level of R is sufficiently accurate.

The discussion so far on inventory decision models under uncertainty has been in reference to the decision on reorder point, but the same concepts and techniques apply directly to inventory situations where the decision is not that of setting the reorder point. The following inventory situation demonstrates the general applicability of these concepts and techniques and serves as a vehicle for review.

SITUATION V

A man has leased a concession stand in a county fair. He assesses the following probability distribution of the demand for one of the products he plans to sell at the stand. The selling price per unit is $10. The purchase cost per unit is $2, but in addition to the purchase cost, if the item is sold, an additional cost of $3 per unit has to be incurred. If not sold, no costs except the purchase cost are incurred, but because there is no salvage value to an unsold unit, the purchase cost of $2 is completely lost. How many units of the product should the man stock for the fair?

Demand units	Probability of demand
0	0.05
1	0.10
2	0.20
3	0.30
4	0.25
5	0.10
6 or more	0.00
	1.00

For each unit sold, the merchant makes a net profit of $5 [$10 − ($2 + $3)]. For each unit stocked but unsold, a loss of $2 is incurred. Exhibit 11-13 is a payoff table based on this financial information. As a way of illustrating how the entries in the payoff table are determined,

Events: demand U	Probability of demand $P(U)$	Acts: stock B_j units					
		0	1	2	3	4	5
0	0.05	(0)	−2	−4	−6	−8	−10
1	0.10	0	(5)	3	1	−1	−3
2	0.20	0	5	(10)	8	6	4
3	0.30	0	5	10	(15)	13	11
4	0.25	0	5	10	15	(20)	18
5	0.10	0	5	10	15	20	(25)

Exhibit 11-13   Payoff table.

the computation of the payoff of $8 conditional to the act of stocking 3 units and conditional to the event of the demand being 2 units is shown.

Since there is a demand for 2 units, the gross revenue is

$$\$10(2) = \$20$$

The costs are

Purchase cost of $2(3) = $6
Additional cost for 2 units sold: $3(2) = $6
$12

Gross revenue $20 less total cost $12 is a net profit of $8. The reader should be able to verify all the entries in the table. In addition, he should derive a formula for determining the net profit, namely, specify the functional relationship between the dependent variable, net profit, and the two independent variables, demand and act.

To apply the expected-value criterion, the expected net profit of each act is computed, and that act with the highest expectation of net profit is chosen. It is, however, illuminating to look at the problem alternatively in terms of opportunity losses, as suggested in Chap. 8. As the reader may recall, the opportunity loss is the profit that could have been made if the decision maker had known the actual demand and chosen the best act for the known demand but was lost because another act was chosen. The opportunity-loss table for the problem is given in Exhibit 11-14. It is constructed from Exhibit 11-13 by first circling the best net profit for a given demand and then deducting from the circled net profit the other profit entries in the same demand row.

For illustration, consider the entries in the row for the demand of 2. If the decision maker knew that the actual demand would be 2 units, he

Events: demand U	Probability P(U)	Acts: stock B_j					
		0	1	2	3	4	5
0	0.05	0	2	4	6	8	10
1	0.10	5	0	2	4	6	8
2	0.20	10	5	0	2	4	6
3	0.30	15	10	5	0	2	4
4	0.25	20	15	10	5	0	2
5	0.10	25	20	15	10	5	0

Exhibit 11-14   Opportunity-loss table.

would stock 2 units and make $10 profit because that is the highest profit that could be made for the demand of 2. Thus, for the act of stocking 2 units, the opportunity loss is zero. But if the decision maker chooses other acts, he will be making less profit than if he chooses the best act. Thus, for the act of stocking 0 unit, the opportunity lost is the highest profit that could have been made of $10 less the profit made from act 0, or $10. For act 4, the opportunity lost is the highest profit that could have been made of $10 less the profit from act 4 of $6, namely, $4, and so on.

It is left for the reader to verify that the act of stocking 4 units gives the minimum expected opportunity loss of $2.90 and would therefore be the choice under the expected-value criterion.

Costs of understocking and overstocking   Opportunity losses are incurred when *more* units or *less* units than the actual demand are stocked. Again in reference to the demand-2 row, because the best act is act 2, if act 1 is taken, the opportunity loss of $5 results from stocking 1 *unit less* than the demand. If act 0 is taken, the opportunity loss of $10 results from stocking 2 *units less* than the demand. Thus these opportunity losses can be considered the *cost of understocking.* For each unit understocked the cost is $5.

In the opposite direction, if act 3 is taken, the opportunity loss of $2 results from stocking 1 *unit more* than the actual demand of 2. If act 4 is taken, the opportunity loss of $4 results from stocking 2 *units more* than the actual demand. If act 5 is taken, the opportunity loss of $6 results from stocking 3 *units more* than the actual demand. These opportunity losses therefore can be considered the *cost of overstocking.* The cost of overstocking by 1 unit is $2.

Formally, let B_j and U stand for the number of units stocked and the number of units demanded, respectively. Then, when $U < B_j$, an overstock is $B_j - U$. When $U > B_j$, an understock is $U - B_j$. For each unit overstocked, the cost of overstocking is $C_o = 2$. For each unit understocked, the cost of understocking is $C_u = \$5$.

There is a complete analogy between this situation and situation IV. B_j of this situation corresponds to the various levels of R or B, the reorder point or buffer stock in situation IV. C_o and C_u of this situation correspond to the excess inventory carrying cost k_c and the stockout cost h_o of the last situation, respectively. Thus, whatever is concluded here is adaptable to the reorder case, and vice versa. In particular, an alternative decision rule for the current inventory problem (developed below) utilizes the concepts of costs of understocking and overstocking and is equally applicable to the earlier reorder problem.

An incremental analysis Rather than considering the problem in one single shot, i.e., making one single decision on the basis of the completely laid-out payoff table or opportunity-loss table as above, the same problem can be solved by making a number of sequential decisions as follows:

1. Make the decision on whether to stock the first unit or not.
2. If the decision is made to stock the first unit, make the decision on whether the second unit is to be added to the stock.
3. If the decision is made to add the second unit, make the decision on whether the third unit is to be added to the stock.
4. Continue until the decision on whether to add the jth unit to the stock becomes negative. Then, the overall decision on the whole problem is to stock $j - 1$ units.

This sequence of unit-by-unit decisions is illustrated below.

Decision on the first unit The payoff table for the decision on whether to stock the first unit or not is given in Table 11-2. Two

Table 11-2 Payoff table for decision on first unit

Demand	Probability	Stock the first unit	Do not stock the first unit
No demand for first unit: $U = 0$	0.05	$2	$0
Demand for first unit: $U > 0$	0.95	$0	$5

Table 11-3 Expected costs for decision on first unit

Stock the first unit	Do not stock the first unit
$2P(U \leq 0)$ $2(0.05) \quad = 0.10$ $0P(U > 0)$ $0(0.95) \quad = 0$ $\overline{\quad\quad 0.10}$	$0P(U \leq 0)$ $0(0.05) \quad = 0$ $5P(U > 0)$ $5(0.95) \quad = 4.75$ $\overline{\quad\quad 4.75}$

relevant events are the event that there is no demand for the first unit and the event that there is a demand for the first unit. There is no demand for the first unit if the actual demand is exactly zero. Thus, the probability of no demand for the first unit is the probability of the demand's being zero, $P(U \leq 0) = P(U = 0) = 0.05$. There is a demand for the first unit if the actual demand is 1, 2, 3, 4, or 5, namely, if $U > 0$. Thus, the probability of the demand for the first unit is

$$P(U > 0) = \sum_{i=1}^{5} P(U) = 0.95$$

If the first unit is stocked, and if the event is no demand for the first unit, there will be a stock overage cost of $2. If the first unit is not stocked, and if the event is no demand for the first unit, the decision is correct and therefore there is no overage or underage cost.

If there is a demand for the first unit, the correct decision is to stock the first unit; then there is no overage or underage cost. But if the first unit is not stocked, there is a stock-underage cost of $5.

The expected costs of the two acts are calculated in Table 11-3. Since the expected cost of stocking the first unit, $0.10, is less than the expected cost of not stocking the first unit, $4.75, the decision is to stock the first unit. Formally,

EC of stocking 1st unit $<$ EC of not stocking 1st unit

$$\$2P(U \leq 0) < \$5P(U > 0)$$

$$\$2(0.05) < \$5(0.95)$$

$$\$0.10 < \$4.75$$

Decision on the second unit Now that it has been decided to stock the first unit, should the second unit be stocked? The payoff table for this decision is given in Table 11-4.

Table 11-4 Payoff table for decision on second unit

Demand	Proba- bility	Stock second unit Condi- tional	Stock second unit Expected	Do not stock second unit Condi- tional	Do not stock second unit Expected
No demand for second unit $U \leq 1$	$P(U \leq 1)$ = 0.15	$2	$2P(U \leq 1)$ = 2(0.15) = 0.30	$0	$0P(U \leq 1)$ = 0(0.15) = 0
Demand for second unit $U > 1$	$P(U > 1)$ = 0.85	0	$0P(U > 1)$ = 0(0.85) = 0	5	$5P(U > 1)$ = 5(0.85) = 4.25
				$0.30		$4.25

The events relevant to the decision whether to stock the second unit or not are *no demand* for the second unit and *a demand* for the second unit. There will be no demand for the second unit if the actual demand is 1 or less, $U \leq 1$. The probability of the event is $P(U \leq 1) = 0.15$. There will be a demand for the second unit if the actual demand is more than 1, $U > 1$. The probability of the event is $P(U > 1) = 0.85$.

Again, the expected cost of the act to stock the incremental unit is less than the expected cost of the act not to stock it. Formally,

EC of stocking 2d unit < EC of not stocking 2d unit
$$\$2P(U \leq 1) < \$5P(U > 1)$$
$$\$2(0.15) < \$5(0.85)$$
$$\$0.30 < \$4.25$$

The decision is to stock the second unit.

Decision on the third unit

EC of stocking 3d unit < EC of not stocking 3d unit
$$\$2P(U \leq 2) < \$5P(U > 2)$$
$$\$2(0.35) < \$5(0.65)$$
$$\$0.70 < \$3.25$$

The decision is to add the third unit (see Table 11-5).

Decision on the fourth unit The payoff table is omitted, but the reader should be able to tie the following to the table which is not reproduced here.

EC of stocking 4th unit < EC of not stocking 4th unit

$$\$2P(U \leq 3) < \$5P(U > 3)$$
$$\$2(0.65) < \$5(0.35)$$
$$\$1.30 < \$1.75$$

The decision is to add the fourth unit.

Decision on the fifth unit The expected cost of stocking the fifth unit is seen to be larger than the expected cost of not stocking the fifth unit as in the following:

EC of stocking 5th unit > EC of not stocking 5th unit

$$\$2P(U \leq 4) > \$5P(U > 4)$$
$$\$2(0.90) > \$5(0.10)$$
$$\$1.80 > \$0.50$$

The decision is *not* to add the fifth unit.

The decision on the overall problem, therefore, is to stock 4 units.

As a recapitulation, this incremental reasoning process is repeated for the decision in general on whether to add another unit to a given level of stock, j units.

Decision whether to increase the stock from j to $j + 1$ units The two relevant events are no demand for the $(j + 1)$st unit and a demand for the $(j + 1)$st unit. If $U \leq j$, there is no demand for the $(j + 1)$st unit; if $U > j$, there is a demand for the $(j + 1)$st unit. The expected cost of stocking the $(j + 1)$st unit is $\$2P(U \leq j)$. The expected cost of not stocking the $(j + 1)$st unit is $\$5P(U > j)$.

Table 11-5 Payoff table for decision on third unit

Demand	Proba-bility	Stock third unit Condi-tional	Expected	Do not stock third unit Condi-tional	Expected
No demand for third unit $U \leq 2$	$P(U \leq 2)$ = 0.35	$2	$2P(U \leq 2)$ = 2(0.35) = 0.70	$0	$0P(U \leq 2)$ = 0(0.35) = 0
Demand for third unit $U > 2$	$P(U > 2)$ = 0.65	0	$0P(U > 2)$ = 0(0.65) = 0	5	$5P(U > 2)$ = 5(0.65) = 3.25
			$0.70		$3.25

If $\$2P(U \leq j) < \$5P(U > j)$, the decision is to stock the $(j+1)$st unit; if $\$2P(U \leq j) > \$5P(U > j)$, the decision is not to add the $(j+1)$st unit. Since $P(U > j) = 1 - P(U \leq j)$, $2P(U \leq j) < 5P(U > j)$ is rewritten

$$2P(U \leq j) < 5[1 - P(U \leq j)]$$
$$2P(U \leq j) < 5 - 5P(U \leq j)$$
$$2P(U \leq j) + 5P(U \leq j) < 5$$
$$(2 + 5)P(U \leq j) < 5$$
$$P(U \leq j) < \frac{5}{2 + 5}$$

As long as the cumulative probability of the demand's being less than or equal to the level of stock being evaluated is smaller than the ratio $5/(2 + 5)$, the decision is to add another unit. Since $\$2 = C_o$ and $\$5 = C_u$, the criterion for the inventory decision in general is

$$P(U \leq j) < \frac{C_u}{C_o + C_u}$$

$C_u/C_o + C_u$ is often called the critical ratio.

11-3   CONCLUSION

The problems of inventory control have been discussed in this chapter through solving a number of specific inventory situations. What is important is not the specific solution formulas applying to specific situations but the general approach. At the most general level, the approach in all situations is to construct the model of total inventory-related costs, namely, establish the relationships between the costs and the decision variables, and find the optimum values of the decision variables that will minimize the total costs. In this process, all costs that vary according to variations in decision variables must be included as inventory-related costs.

In every inventory decision problem, there are at least two decision variables, i.e., how much to order per order (the order quantity) and when to order (the reorder point). The approach to inventory management in which the economic order quantity is ordered whenever the level of inventory falls to a predetermined reorder point is often referred to as the *fixed-order-quantity system*. Under this system the time interval between two orders may vary, because depending on the rate of demand, the reorder point may be reached sooner or later than expected.

Though not discussed in this chapter, there is another approach to inventory control, the *periodic-review system*, under which the inventory level is reviewed periodically at predetermined time intervals, and the quantity to be ordered at each review varies according to the use since the last review. Although literature on it is scarcer than on the fixed-order-quantity system, such a system is popular when a permanent record is kept of the fluctuations in the level of inventory, when tighter control is needed because of the importance of the inventory item, when the supplier's production demands advance planning, and/or when the benefit from combining the order for the item with orders on other inventory items is great. Observe that the periodic-review system still involves the two decision variables: when to order and how much to order.

Besides the two decision variables, the total-cost model includes such nondecision variables as demand and the costs of inventory carrying, stockout, and ordering. Estimation of demand and various costs is an extremely important and difficult task. The analyst can never be sure of its reliability. One way of handling the problem of estimation is to evaluate the effect of errors in the estimates of these parameters on the decision through sensitivity analyses.

In the situations discussed in this chapter, the total annual demand has been assumed to be known with certainty. In many problems, the demand may be considered known with certainty without detracting from the validity of the decision, but in some situations, the probability distribution of the annual demand may have to be explicitly considered. In such situations, the solution by strictly mathematical methods, namely, derivation of formulas for the decision variables, may be difficult and complex. Under such circumstances, simulation techniques explained in the next chapter may be applied profitably.

QUESTIONS AND PROBLEMS

1. What costs are included in the inventory carrying costs, in the stockout costs, in the inventory ordering costs?

2. Define the safety or buffer stock.

3. Explain the sensitivity analysis in reference to inventory problems.

4. Explain the difference between the two inventory-control systems, the fixed-order-quantity system and the periodic-review system.

5. Suppose a known demand for an inventory item for the next year of 2000 units, a purchase price per unit of $2, and a known lead time of 7 working days. The cost of carrying 1 unit of inventory for 1 year is 10 percent of the value of the item, and each ordering process costs $10.

    (a) Give the total inventory-related costs for the year as a function of order quantity.

    (b) What should the order quantity be?

    (c) What should the reorder point be?

(d) How much are the total annual inventory-related costs when the order quantity and the reorder point are as determined in parts (b) and (c)?

6. One of the assumptions made in situation I is that the complete shipment of all units ordered is received whenever a shipment is received. This assumption of the receipt at one time of all units ordered may be applicable to the cases when the inventory item is purchased from outside vendors, but it may not be applicable when the inventory item is manufactured internally over a period of time after a requisition is placed. Then manufacturing goes on at the same time the item is demanded by its users. Assume the following inventory situation.

1. The total requirement for the item for 1 year is $D = 2000$.
2. The known cost for carrying 1 unit of inventory for 1 year is $k_c = \$0.10$.
3. The known cost of ordering per order is $k_s = \$5$. If the item is internally manu-
   factured, the ordering cost may include machine setup costs, requisition costs,
   etc.
4. The rate of demand for the item is uniform throughout the year. More specifically, suppose the rate of demand is expressed as the number of units
   demanded per unit of time, $d = 10$ units.
5. Instead of the assumption in situation I of receiving the complete shipment of all
   units once an order is placed, it is assumed here that once an order is placed for
   Q units, the order is manufactured over a period of time at a rate of production
   of $m = 50$ units per unit of time.

    (a) Show in graphic form the variation in the level of inventory over time when the order quantity is 200 units. What is the maximum inventory?

    (b) What is the maximum inventory when the order quantity is Q units?

    (c) Give the total inventory-related costs as a function of order quantity.

    (d) What is the economic order quantity? Derive the general formula as well as giving the specific answer.

7. The total annual demand for the inventory item in question is 2000 units. The inventory carrying cost per dollar purchase value of inventory per year is 10 cents; the order cost per order is $5. The purchase price of the inventory consists of two elements, $2 per unit and $40 fixed charge per order.

    (a) Prepare a table showing the annual order costs, carrying costs, purchase costs, and the total inventory-related costs for some selected values of Q.

    (b) Determine the economic order quantity. How many orders are placed in 1 year if the economic order quantity is indeed ordered per order?

    (c) What is the difference in total annual costs when the economic order quantity is actually ordered and when 100 more units than the economic order quantity are ordered per order?

8. (a) Apply the critical-ratio criterion to solve the inventory problem of Example 8-1.

    (b) Solve the same problem through incremental analysis.

12

Waiting-line Control and Monte Carlo Simulation

12-0 INTRODUCTION

The inventory problems of the last chapter may be characterized by the dilemma between carrying too much inventory and carrying too little. When too much is carried, the costs from understocking—from not being able to meet the demand when it arises—are minimized, while the costs of maintaining inventory become high.   When too little is carried, the costs from understocking become high, although the costs of maintaining inventory are minimized.   The way out of this dilemma is of course to minimize the total costs, the sum of two opposing costs.

There is a class of decision problems in the real world, called *waiting-line* or *queuing problems*, which are conceptually very similar to inventory problems.   In the beginning part of this chapter the nature of the queuing problems and the general approach to solving them will be presented. The latter part of the chapter discusses one widely used solution method, the Monte Carlo method.   It is a simulation method which is frequently applied to many problems other than waiting-line problems.   In addition to applying the method to the queuing problems, its general applicability will be noted by demonstrating how it can be used to analyze other problem areas such as inventory problems.

12-1 NATURE OF QUEUING PROBLEMS

Waiting is an unavoidable phenomenon in this world: people wait at restaurants to be served; wait at the ticket booth to buy tickets; wait for overseas telephone lines to open; wait at the post office to buy stamps; wait at the doctor's office; wait at the supermarket checkout counter; wait for teller service at the bank; and so on. To cite further examples, airplanes must wait for runways to be clear; trucks, trains, and ships wait for loading and unloading sidings or docks to be free; broken-down machines wait for repairmen to be available; and so on.

Hypothetically, in a given situation, the waiting can be entirely (more accurately, almost) eliminated. Thus, the number of tables and waiters can be increased in a restaurant; telephone trunk lines can be added; the number of checkout counters can be increased. Likewise, the number of runways in an airport can be enlarged; more repairmen can be added. The reason that waiting cannot be eliminated, of course, is because adding more service facilities—checkout counters, tellers, runways, docks, etc.—involves additional costs, costs of installation, operation, and maintenance. Yet, waiting is unpleasant and irritating and in many cases involves some tangible dollar costs. The crux of a decision problem characterized as a waiting-line problem is to decide on the optimal number of service facilities by balancing the two opposing costs, namely, the costs of maintaining the facilities and the cost of waiting necessitated by the inadequacy of the facilities. In this sense, waiting-line problems are similar to inventory problems. As there is demand for inventory items in an inventory problem, there is demand for service facilities in a queuing problem. As there is a level of inventory to maintain in an inventory problem, there is a capacity of service facilities to maintain. As there are the opposing costs of understocking and overstocking, there are the opposing costs of too little and too much service capacity. As the inventory decision involves finding the optimal level of inventory which minimizes the total costs, so the waiting-line decision involves finding the optimal level of service capacity which minimizes the total costs. Exhibit 12-1 illustrates the general nature of both classes of problems without specifying the underlying cost functions. One type of cost, i.e., the service-failure costs, decreases as the level of service facilities (or inventory) is increased; the other type, i.e., the costs of maintaining service facilities, increases as the level of service facilities (or inventory) is increased; consequently, the total costs first decrease but

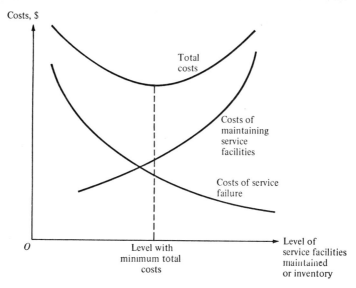

Exhibit 12-1   Relation between costs and service facilities.

soon start to increase as the level of service facilities (or inventory) is increased.

Keeping the similarity between the two classes of decision problems in perspective will clarify the following discussion, but one should also be aware of the difference between the two.   Whereas in inventory problems whatever is unsold or unused in previous periods can be carried over and sold or used in the ensuing periods, in queuing problems, the service capacity that is unused in previous periods is forever lost and cannot be used in the following periods.   Because of this difference, the solution method for inventory problems cannot be applied directly to queuing problems.

If the demand for service comes in, or arrives, with a known regularity and the time required for service per customer is also known with certainty, the problem of deciding the capacity of service facilities is rather trivial.   For instance, if trucks (customers) arrive at the warehouse for service, namely, for unloading or loading, regularly every 20 min, and the unloading or loading per truck always takes precisely 60 min, the number of loading docks (the capacity of service facilities) to be built is obviously three.   If more than three docks are built, some docks will always be idle.   If fewer than three docks are built, the warehouse will get choked, in the sense that the number of trucks waiting to be serviced and the time an incoming truck has to wait for service becomes greater and greater without limit as time goes on.

But in reality, the trouble is that demand seldom arrives regularly (in particular, trucks do not arrive every 20 min) and service time per customer may not be uniform from one customer to another (in particular, the loading time per truck may not be fixed precisely at 60 min for every truck). Even when the average or expected interval between truck arrivals is 20 min, sometimes trucks will arrive in intervals shorter than 20 min; at other times, they will arrive in intervals longer than 20 min. By the same token, loading may take longer or shorter than the expected loading time of 60 min. How many docks should be built under the assumption of random variations in the arrival and service times? An obvious candidate for the answer would be to extend the certainty case and calculate the number of docks to be built as follows:

$$\frac{\text{Expected service time}}{\text{Expected interval between arrivals}} = \frac{60}{20} = 3$$

Typically, this answer will not do. If three docks are built, the service facilities will get choked in the same sense as above. The line of waiting trucks will get longer, and the waiting time for a given truck will get longer, as time passes. To visualize how the system gets choked, suppose that in a given hour trucks arrive in 30-min intervals, in other words, only two trucks arrive in 1 hour. Then, only two docks would be needed to handle the two trucks, one dock remaining idle. Suppose further that in the ensuing hour trucks arrive in 15-min intervals, namely, four trucks arrive. Then, because there are only three docks, one truck would have to wait; three docks can handle three trucks in 1 hour. One idle dock hour of the previous hour when demand for service was below expectation cannot be used in the current hour when demand is higher than expectation. Thus, whenever dock hours are lost, they are lost for good, but whenever there is shortage in dock hours, the shortage accumulates over periods. In queuing problems, service time available must be greater than the expected demand for service time.

Even when the total service time available is greater than the expected service time demanded, there is no guarantee that trucks or customers in general will not wait. As a matter of fact, even when total capacity exceeds total expected demand, a typical or average truck or customer can expect to wait *for some time* upon arrival before being serviced. In other words, at a given point of time, a number of trucks or customers are expected to wait for docks or service facilities in general to clear.

Inasmuch as the expected or average waiting time for an incoming customer and the expected length of waiting customers at a given time are the determinants of the *costs of waiting*, which are eventually compared with the opposing *costs of maintaining a level of service capacity* in the final stage of decision, the major part of analytical effort with respect to a queuing problem concerns determination of these expected quantities and the related probability distributions around them. In skeleton, the analytical process for a waiting-line problem may be represented by the following diagram.

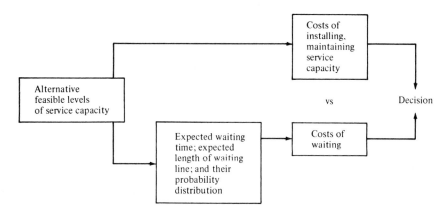

Alternative levels of service capacity entail different costs of installing, operating, and maintaining the capacity; alternative levels of service capacity entail different expected waiting times, lengths of waiting lines, and their probability distributions, which in turn determine the expected costs of waiting. The decision is made such that the total costs, namely, the sum of these two costs, are minimized.

In establishing the relationship between the alternative feasible levels of service capacity and the expected waiting time and waiting line, the former may be considered the decision input variable and the latter as the dependent consequence variables. Then, besides the decision input variable, there are other noncontrollable input variables which together with the decision variable determine the output variables. There are at least three input variables of critical importance other than the alternative levels of service capacity: pattern of arrival of customers, pattern of service-time variation, and what is called *queue discipline* or *priority rule*.

Queue discipline or priority rule refers to the rule by which waiting customers are picked or selected for attention as service channels become open. A most obvious rule, of course, would be the first come, first served basis, but there are other rules, such as ladies first, most important first, shortest service customer first, nearest first, and even take at random.

In many situations, the choice of the priority rule may largely be a matter of the decision maker's control, and therefore it may be considered a decision variable. Problems of queue discipline will not be discussed further except for a comment about the shortest-service-customer-first rule. If there are two groups of customers, one requiring a long servicing time and the other requiring a short servicing time, in general, the *total waiting time*—the sum of the waiting times of the short- and long-service customers—is minimized if the customers requiring shorter service time are serviced first. This is intuitively understandable and can be shown to be true formally. In support of the conclusion, we see express counters in supermarkets, exact-change lanes at tollgates, etc., and we see that broken-down machines that can be repaired quickly are repaired first and put to work first.

In solving waiting-line problems, a considerable amount of thought must be given to finding the patterns of variation in customer arrivals for service and service times required. In many real waiting-line situations, the patterns of random variation in customer arrivals and service times can be represented by the Poisson process. Once it is determined that the real pattern of variation is that of the Poisson process, the results of mathematicians' and statisticians' work on the Poisson probability distribution and the related exponential probability distribution can be applied directly to the determination of the expected waiting time and waiting line and their probability distributions. Because of the heavy mathematics involved, this book omits the analytical derivation of these formulas from the known Poisson and exponential probability (or frequency) distributions of customer arrival and service time.

But an alternative powerful mode of solution, the Monte Carlo method, will be presented by way of an illustrative example. The Monte Carlo method can be applied even to problems where formulas for solution can be derived mathematically. In such cases, solution by the Monte Carlo method may have an advantage over solution by mathematical manipulation in that the rationale of the Monte Carlo method is much better understood by nonmathematician decision makers than the strictly mathematical method. In problems which mathematical analysis cannot cope with successfully because of the complexity involved, the Monte Carlo method is the only method of solution available at present.

EXAMPLE 12-1

A plant has a group of 40 similar machines. These machines break down at random, and breakdowns are independent of one another. (Equivalently, the fact that a particular machine has broken down does not change the likelihood of another machine's breaking down.) When a machine breaks down, it has to be taken out of production until it is repaired. The production lost from a machine's being idle for 1 hour costs the plant $50 (from lost sales). The decision to be made is how many repairmen should be assigned to service the machine breakdowns. Suppose a repairman costs $5 an hour.

The first task for the decision analyst is to find the pattern of random variation in machine breakdowns. Suppose that the analyst, relying on the past relative frequencies of breakdowns, assigns the following probabilities for the various possible numbers of breakdowns that may occur in any given hour:

No. of breakdowns per hour	Probability
0	0.900
1	0.085
2	0.012
3	0.003
	1.000

Then, likewise, the analyst, relying on past observations, assigns the following probabilities to the various possible numbers of hours required for any given breakdown:

No. of hours required for repair per breakdown	Probability
1	0.100
2	0.240
3	0.450
4	0.165
5	0.040
6	0.005
	1.000

The expected number of breakdowns per hour and the expected repair time required per breakdown are computed as follows:

Expected breakdowns per hour = 0(0.900) + 1(0.085) + 2(0.012) + 3(0.003) = 0.118 machine breakdowns per hour

Expected repair time = 1(0.100) + 2(0.240) + 3(0.450) + 4(0.165) + 5(0.040) + 6(0.005) = 2.82 hr

The expected repair time per breakdown of 2.82 hr is easy to understand intuitively, but the expected number of breakdowns per hour of 0.118

may make more sense if it is converted into the expected time between breakdowns as follows:

$$\text{Expected interval between breakdowns} = \frac{1}{0.118} \approx 8.47 \text{ hr}$$

Since a machine breaks down every 8.47 hr and it takes only 2.82 hr to repair it, if there is one repairman, it might appear that he could handle the situation easily. This, however, is not the case, because these figures are only *expectations;* under certain circumstances, e.g., the actual interval between arrivals of two broken-down machines is less than 8.47 hr and the actual service time required is more than 2.82 hr per machine, the machines may have to wait.

What is the average time a broken-down machine must wait until a repairman can get to the machine when there is one repairman, two repairmen, three repairmen? The Monte Carlo solution to the question follows.

12-2 MONTE CARLO METHOD—SOLUTION BY SIMULATION

An approach, impractical as it is, that could be used in analyzing the problem would be the trial-and-error method. Thus, the decision maker may operate the plant *actually* with one repairman over a period of time observing such factors as how many hours broken-down machines actually wait for repair, how long they wait when they do, how many machine hours are lost in total from waiting, etc. After recording these observations for a "long enough" period of time, the plant will be operated with two repairmen, and again observations will be made of the same factors as in the one-repairman operation. Then the plant will be switched to three-repairmen operation for observation, and so on. By comparing the varying waiting patterns thus observed and the associated costs, the decision maker would be able to arrive at the optimal number of repairmen to assign to the servicing of the machines for future operations.

Such an experimentation is obviously too costly. As a cheaper substitute, the decision maker may make use of the Monte Carlo simulation. In brief, what the method does is to *simulate on paper* actual operations period after period so that the simulated waiting behavior can be observed.

Beginning from the simulation of the first hour period, the initial question asked is: Would there be any machine breakdowns in the first hour if the plant were actually operated? The question is answered by adopting the following procedure.

Step 1 Construct a standard urn containing 1000 balls (see Chap. 6 for the definition of a standard urn).

Step 2   Mark each ball in the urn "no breakdown," "one break-down," "two breakdowns," or "three breakdowns," in the following proportion:

Breakdowns	Number of balls
0	900
1	85
2	12
3	3
	1000

This proportion of balls is the same as that of the probabilities of various numbers of breakdowns per hour.

Step 3   Mix all the balls thoroughly in the urn and draw a ball from the urn at random.

Step 4   The number of breakdowns marked on the ball thus drawn is considered to represent what would actually happen in the first hour.

Suppose that the ball drawn were marked no breakdown; then it would be concluded that in the first hour, no machine would break down and the repairman would be idle.   If the ball drawn were marked one breakdown, it would be concluded that in the first hour there would be one machine breaking down and requiring the service of the repairman. But how many hours would the repair take?   In order to answer this question, the same mechanism as that used for simulating the machine breakdown is adopted.

Step 1   Construct a standard urn containing 1000 balls marked as tabulated.   The proportion of balls marked with different service hours

Hours of service time	Number of balls
1	100
2	240
3	450
4	165
5	40
6	5
	1000

required is the same as that of the probabilities of various service hours required per breakdown.

Step 2   Mix the balls thoroughly and draw a ball at random.

Step 3   The number of service hours marked on the ball drawn is considered to represent the actual service time required for the broken-down machine as simulated by the first urn above.

Suppose the ball drawn from the first urn were marked two breakdowns representing two machine breakdowns in the first hour.   The next step is to find out how many hours would be required for repairing each of these two machines.   This is done by drawing *twice* from the second urn with replacement.   That is, draw a ball from the urn, record the number of hours marked on the ball as the repair time required for the first of the two machines, and put the ball back.   Then, after mixing the balls thoroughly again, draw a ball for the second time.   The number of service hours marked on this ball represents the repair time for the second machine.   If there is only one repairman, one of the two machines will have to wait until the repair of the other is completed.   The number of hours that one of these machines must wait is duly recorded.

After simulating the first hour period, the second hour is simulated exactly in the same way.   A ball is drawn from the first urn; the number on the ball is recorded as the number of machine breakdowns in the second hour.   Then, for each of the machine breakdowns, a ball is drawn from the second urn to determine the service time required.   After taking into account whatever broken-down machines carried over from the first hour, the number of hours each of the machines has to wait for repair is determined.   The same procedure is repeated to simulate the third hour, the fourth hour, and so on.

Since the use of standard urns as the simulators of random processes is impractical and inefficient, we must look for a more efficient, practical simulators.   *Random digits* provide the answer.

Random digits   A table of random digits (Appendix A) is simply a list of digits from 0 through 9 arranged in such a way that the digits appear in no particular order but in the long run each of the 10 digits occurs with an equal relative frequency of $\frac{1}{10}$.   For an intuitive understanding of the nature of these digits, they may be considered to have been generated by the following random process.

Step 1   Suppose a standard urn with 10 balls marked with 10 different numbers or digits from 0 through 9.

Step 2   Mix the balls in the urn thoroughly and draw a ball at random so that each of the 10 balls has an equal chance of being drawn. Record the number on the ball in the first position in the table.

Step 3 Put the ball back in the urn, mix the balls thoroughly, and draw a ball at random again. Record the number on the ball in the second position in the table, namely, next to the first position.

Step 4 Put the ball back again in the urn, mix the balls thoroughly, and draw a ball at random. Record the number on the ball in the third position in the table.

Step 5 Put the ball back, ...

If the process is repeated 10,000 times, the result is a table of 10,000 random digits; 20,000 repetitions give 20,000 random digits.

If a digit is drawn at random from the table of random digits, the digits from 0 through 9 represent the 10 possible outcomes with equal probabilities. Thus, the probability that any given number, say 6, will appear in a random draw of a digit from the table is $\frac{1}{10}$. If two digits are drawn at the same time at random from the table, there are 100 possible outcomes represented by two-digit numbers from 00 through 99, each outcome with an equal probability of $\frac{1}{100}$. Thus, the probability that any two-digit number, say 72, will appear in a random draw of two digits from the table is $\frac{1}{100}$. Similarly, the probability that any three-digit number, say 386, will appear in a random draw of three digits is $\frac{1}{1000}$. Further, it follows that the probability that *either one* of any two three-digit numbers, say 012 and 248, will appear in a random draw of three digits from the table is $\frac{2}{1000}$. Likewise, the probability that any one of the three-digit numbers from 000 through 250 will appear in a random draw of three digits from the table is $\frac{251}{1000}$.

This suggests a way of simulating the real random process which generates machine breakdowns in a given hour. For instance, the real random process produces no breakdown with the probability of 0.900. This can be simulated by assigning arbitrarily any 900 three-digit numbers (out of the total possible 1000 numbers from 000 through 999) to the event of no breakdown and considering the event to have happened whenever a random draw of three digits from the table of random numbers results in any one of these 900 three-digit numbers. If the draw results in any three-digit number other than those 900 assigned to the no-breakdown event, one of the events other than no breakdown is considered to have happened, namely, one, two, or three breakdowns.

Specifically, the total 1000 possible three-digit numbers are assigned to the four possible machine-breakdown events as shown in Table 12-1. Three digits are then drawn at random from the table of random digits. If the three digits form one of the 900 three-digit numbers between 000 and 899 (including 000 and 899), no breakdown is considered to have taken place in the period being simulated, if the three digits drawn form one of the 85 three-digit numbers between 900 and 984, one break-

Table 12-1   Assignment of numbers to breakdowns

Number of breakdowns per hour	Assignment of total 1000 three-digit numbers	
	Range	Total number
0	000–899	900
1	900–984	85
2	985–996	12
3	997–999	3
		1000

down is considered to have taken place; if the three digits drawn form one of the 12 three-digit numbers between 985 and 996, two break-downs are considered to have taken place; if the three digits drawn form one of the 3 three-digit numbers between 997 and 999, three breakdowns are considered to have taken place. The drawing of three digits can be repeated to simulate the machine breakdowns of different hours. Exhibit 12-2 reproduces the results of 50 draws simulating the machine break-downs of 50 hourly periods.

The first column in the exhibit gives the time period simulated; the second column gives the three digits drawn from the table of random digits of Appendix A; and the third column gives the number of machine breakdowns corresponding to the three-digit number drawn for the period. Note that the three digits are drawn beginning from the upper left-hand corner of the table. The drawing, however, could have begun from any position in the table. Such is the nature of the table.

There are 10 breakdowns during a 50-hr period. The average number of breakdowns per hour, therefore, is 0.2 ($= 10/50$), which is higher than the expected breakdowns of 0.118 calculated earlier with the original probability distribution. The discrepancy between the two should not bother us because 50 hr is only five 10-hr days. If the simulation is continued for 100, 500, 1000 hr, the average breakdowns per hour is expected to approach 0.118.

To simulate the repair hours required for each of the 10 machine breakdowns, the total 1000 possible three-digit numbers are assigned to various possible repair hours required per breakdown according to the same proportion as the probabilities given earlier. This is shown in Table 12-2.

With the assignment of three-digit numbers, 10 drawings of three digits are made from the random-digit table in simulation of the required

Hour	Three digits drawn	No. of breakdowns	Hour	Three digits drawn	No. of breakdowns
1	100	0	26	611	0
2	375	0	27	154	0
3	084	0	28	945	1
4	990	2	29	424	0
5	128	0	30	235	0
6	660	0	31	044	0
7	310	0	32	005	0
8	852	0	33	359	0
9	635	0	34	598	0
10	737	0	35	460	0
11	985	2	36	321	0
12	118	0	37	692	0
13	834	0	38	195	0
14	886	0	39	451	0
15	995	2	40	948	1
16	654	0	41	980	1
17	801	0	42	331	0
18	743	0	43	809	0
19	699	0	44	797	0
20	098	0	45	186	0
21	914	1	46	740	0
22	803	0	47	541	0
23	441	0	48	116	0
24	125	0	49	483	0
25	636	0	50	690	0
		7			3

Total breakdowns for 50 hr = 7 + 3 − 10

Exhibit 12-2 Simulation of machine breakdowns for 50-hr period.

repair times for the 10 broken-down machines. The results of the simulation are shown in Exhibit 12-3. (Note that the drawing is begun from the upper left-hand corner of the second columnar grouping of Appendix A.) The 10 breakdowns are identified by the letters a to j.

The average repair time per machine breakdown in the 50-hr period simulated is 2.2 hr (22/10), in contrast to the expected repair time calculated earlier of 2.82 hr.

The total repair time of 22 hr in the 50-hr period means that even if there is only one repairman, he would be idle 28 hr out of the 50-hr he is on the job. Yet, as can be seen shortly, some broken-down machines must wait for the repairman to become free.

Table 12-2   Assignment of numbers to repair-hour requirements

Service time required per breakdown, hr	Probability	1000 possible three-digit random numbers assigned	
		Range	Total number
1	0.100	000–099	100
2	0.240	100–339	240
3	0.450	340–789	450
4	0.165	790–954	165
5	0.040	955–994	40
6	0.005	995–999	5
			1000

The total repair time of 22 hr also is the machine time lost because of repairing itself not including time lost from waiting. If one machine hour lost costs $50, the minimum of $50(22) = $1100 is lost in the 50-hr period due to machine breakdowns, even if every broken-down machine is repaired without waiting. This is only the minimum, however, because in addition, more machine time is expected to be lost from waiting; $1100 represents the cost that cannot be reduced from increasing the number of repairmen.

The next step in the analysis is to investigate what happens to the waiting time and the waiting cost when the number of repairmen is

Hour	Machine breakdown	Three digits drawn	Repair time required, hr
4	a	765	3
	b	648	3
11	c	196	2
	d	093	1
15	e	801	4
	f	340	3
21	g	455	3
28	h	020	1
40	i	053	1
41	j	035	1
Total repair hours for 50-hr period			22

Exhibit 12-3   Simulation of repair time required for 10 machine breakdowns.

varied.   In the following discussion the operations are simulated first
with one repairman and then with two.

Waiting time with one repairman   From the first hour through the third
hour the repairman remains idle because there are no breakdowns in this
period.   Then, in the fourth hour, two machine breakdowns, a and b,
occur.   Assuming that a occurs at the beginning of the fourth hour and
b occurs at the midpoint of the fourth hour, the repairman will begin
repairing a at the beginning of the fourth hour.   Since repairing a takes
3 hr according to Exhibit 12-3, when breakdown b occurs $\frac{1}{2}$ hr later, b has
to wait for $2\frac{1}{2}$ hr until the repairman becomes free from a.   Then, until
the repair of b is finished, no new machine breakdowns arrive; therefore,
no additional waiting time is involved.   (Note the arbitrariness of the
assumption that b arrives $\frac{1}{2}$ hr later than a.)

The next breakdowns, c and d, occur in the eleventh hour.   Assum-
ing that c occurs at the beginning of the period and d $\frac{1}{2}$ hr later, d has to
wait for its repair for $1\frac{1}{2}$ hr until the repair on c is completed.   Then, in
the fifteenth hour, two more breakdowns, e and f, take place.   Again
assuming that e happens at the beginning of the hour and f, $\frac{1}{2}$ hr later,
f must wait $3\frac{1}{2}$ hr because e's repair takes 4 hr.   After the fifteenth hour,
although breakdowns, g to j, take place, no more waiting is involved.

In summary, the total waiting time during the 50-hr period with one
repairman is:

Machines	Waiting time, hr
b	$2\frac{1}{2}$
d	$1\frac{1}{2}$
f	$3\frac{1}{2}$
Total	$7\frac{1}{2}$

Since the cost of one idle machine hour is $50, for the idle machine time
of $7\frac{1}{2}$ hr due to waiting, the total cost of waiting with one repairman is

$$\$50(7.5) = \$375$$

Waiting time with two repairmen   If a second repairman is added, it is
clear from examining the data in Exhibit 12-3 that none of the 10 machine
breakdowns has to wait.   But since the total repair time required is still
the same 22 hr, out of the total repairman hours available of 100 hr
(50 hr $\times$ 2), 78 hr would be idle.   Costwise, however, the additional
repairman costs only $5(50) = $250 extra, whereas the cost of waiting
saved is the entire $375 ($50 $\times$ 7.5).   The decision, therefore, would be
to operate the plant with two repairmen.

The Monte Carlo method is a very versatile technique. For instance, it can take care of probability distributions which may not be amenable to theoretical manipulation. It can take care of real-world complications that mathematics cannot handle. For example, suppose that individual machines have different probability distributions of breakdowns. The Monte Carlo method can simulate the breakdown for each machine, according to its own probability function, for each period.

Furthermore, random digits can be generated by computers at high speeds, and thus a simulation of thousands of periods can be performed in a matter of few hours, calculating the expected waiting time, waiting line, idle service-facility time, and associated probabilities.

12-3 MONTE CARLO APPLICATION TO OTHER PROBLEM AREAS

The Monte Carlo is a general method that can be applied to many problems other than queuing problems. For example, it can be used in investigating how far neutrons travel through various shielding substances. It can also be applied to inventory problems. The remainder of this chapter presents its application to a hypothetical inventory problem.

EXAMPLE 12-2

Suppose that the weekly demand is a random variable with the probability distribution as in Table 12-3. The last column is the assignment of random numbers between 00 and 99 in the same proportion as that of the probability distribution.

The lead time is also a random variable, and its probability distribution and the corresponding random numbers assigned are given in Table 12-4.

As observed in Chap. 11, two decision variables in the inventory problem of this type are the order quantity Q and the reorder point R, and the decision maker's task is to find the combination of Q and R

Table 12-3 Probability of weekly demand

Weekly demand, units	Probability	Assignment of random numbers
8	0.20	00–19
9	0.25	20–44
10	0.30	45–74
11	0.15	75–89
12	0.10	90–99

Table 12-4 Probability of lead time

Lead time, weeks	Probability	Assignment of random numbers
1	0.20	00–19
2	0.50	20–69
3	0.30	70–99

values which will minimize the total inventory-related costs, namely, the sum of carrying costs, stockout costs, and ordering costs.

The problem can be solved by applying formulas, as in the last chapter, but, alternatively, the Monte Carlo method of simulation can be used. Exhibit 12-4 reproduces the result of the simulation with one particular alternative inventory policy of $Q = 50$ and $R = 15$. Column 1 designates each of the 20 weeks for which the simulation was conducted. Column 2 shows the level of inventory at the beginning of each week. For the first week the beginning inventory of 30 units was assumed. Column 3 lists the random numbers drawn from the random-digit table of Appendix A for generation of weekly demands. (Note that the drawing of two digits started from the extreme southeast corner of the table, moving upward.) Since the number 38 drawn for the first week corresponds to the demand of 9 units according to the demand-probability table given above, column 4 for the first week gives 9 units. Then the beginning inventory, 30 units, less the use during the week of 9 units leaves an inventory of 21 units at the end of the first week. This figure is shown under column 6. Since the ending inventory of the first week is the beginning inventory of the second week, column 2 for the second week is the same 21 units as the entry in column 6 for the first week. For simulation of the second week's demand, the number 94 is a weekly demand of 12 units, and accordingly, 12 is entered in column 4 for the second week. The ending inventory for the second week then is the beginning inventory of 21 units less the demand during the week of 12, namely, 9 units (column 6). This means that some time during the second week, the level of inventory must have reached the reorder point level, $R = 15$, in other words, an order for $Q = 50$ must have been placed during the week. Now the lead time for the order must be simulated. The random number drawn for this purpose turns out to be 69, which is entered in column 7. (Drawing of random numbers for lead times starts from the extreme southwest corner of the random-digit table.) According to the lead-time table given earlier, 69 corresponds to 2 weeks; this 2 weeks is recorded in column 8. The receipt of 50 units on this order is acknowledged in the fourth-week line, 2 weeks from ordering, in column 5. The reader should satisfy himself as to all other entries in

(1)	(2)	(3)	(4)	(5)	(6)	(7)	(8)
Week	Beginning inventory, units	Random number for demand	Demand, units	Receipt, units	Ending inventory, units	Random number for lead time	Lead time, weeks
1	30	38	9		21		
2	21	94	12		9	69	2
3	9	56	10		−1		
4	−1	24	9	50	40		
5	40	48	10		30		
6	30	36	9		21		
7	21	79	11		10	48	2
8	10	71	10		0		
9	0	43	9	50	41		
10	41	80	11		30		
11	30	76	11		19		
12	19	41	9		10	11	1
13	10	07	8	50	52		
14	52	38	9		43		
15	43	38	9		34		
16	34	41	9		25		
17	25	06	8		17		
18	17	33	9		8	54	2
19	8	29	9		−1		
20	−1	72	10	50	39		

Exhibit 12-4 Simulation of inventory and demand for $Q = 50$, $R = 15$.

the exhibit. One final observation on the exhibit is in order, however: negative entries for the ending inventory (column 6) are stockouts. Thus, in the third week the firm would experience a stockout of 1 unit. There are only two weeks when a stockout occurs in the simulated 50-week period.

Now the decision analyst can compute the costs of inventory carrying based on the simulated beginning and ending inventories, perhaps on the basis of the average of the two if justifiable; he can compute the costs of stockouts on the basis of the simulated stockouts; he can compute the costs of ordering on the basis of the simulated number of times the order is placed.

The decision analyst would repeat the simulation for alternative inventory policies, i.e., different combinations of Q and R values. From comparison of the simulated total inventory-related costs associated with the alternative policies, the decision maker can choose the best course of action.

12-4 CONCLUSION

The reader should distinguish two parts of this chapter. One is an attempt at understanding the nature of waiting-line problems; the other introduces a solution technique called the Monte Carlo method. It is important to recognize that the formal solution technique is much more general than the examples of decision problems used in introducing it.

As a matter of fact, the same conclusion applies to the materials throughout the book. Rigorous observation, analysis, and understanding of a given decision problem situation, which must precede application of solution techniques, is, at the conceptual level, independent of formal, scientific-quantitative methods. The applicability of the mathematical-statistical concepts and methods given in the book is much more general than the vehicles of their exposition, namely, the examples used.

QUESTIONS AND PROBLEMS

1. Explain the nature of queuing problems and compare it with that of the inventory problems of Chap. 11.

2. Explain the Monte Carlo method.

3. The flow of trucks to a central warehouse seems to have increased recently. Currently, there are nine loading docks, but management wonders whether more docks should be built. The structure of the warehouse is such that no more than six docks can be added. Addition of each dock requires an investment of $15,000. In order to establish the truck traffic pattern, management has conducted a 2-month survey of the pattern of truck arrivals, and the pattern of loading. The relative frequencies of the number of trucks arriving in every $\frac{1}{2}$ hr and of the loading time obtained from the survey are as follows:

Number of trucks arriving per $\frac{1}{2}$ hr	Relative frequency	Time required for loading or unloading a truck, min	Relative frequency
0	0.01	15	0.55
1	0.08	30	0.25
2	0.11	45	0.10
3	0.25	60	0.05
4	0.20	75	0.03
5	0.15	90	0.02
6	0.10		1.00
7	0.07		
8	0.03		
	1.00		

(a) Employing the Monte Carlo method, simulate the truck traffic patterns for two 8-hr days and analyze what happens if three or six additional docks are constructed.

(b) What additional information would you need in order to make the decision? How would you obtain it?

appendix A

Random Digits[1]

10	09	73	25	33	76	52	01	35	86	34	67	35	48	76	80	95	90	91	17	39	29	27	49	45
37	54	20	48	05	64	89	47	42	96	24	80	52	40	37	20	63	61	01	02	00	82	29	16	65
08	42	26	89	53	19	64	50	93	03	23	20	90	25	60	15	95	33	47	64	35	08	03	36	06
99	01	90	25	29	09	37	67	07	15	38	31	13	11	65	88	67	67	43	97	04	43	62	76	59
12	80	79	90	70	80	15	73	61	47	64	03	23	66	53	98	95	11	68	77	12	17	17	68	33
66	06	57	47	17	34	07	27	68	50	36	69	73	61	70	65	81	33	98	85	11	19	92	91	70
31	06	01	08	05	45	57	18	24	06	35	30	34	26	14	86	79	90	74	39	23	40	30	97	32
85	26	97	76	02	02	05	16	56	92	68	66	57	48	18	73	05	38	52	47	18	62	38	85	79
63	57	33	21	35	05	32	54	70	48	90	55	35	75	48	28	46	82	87	09	83	49	12	56	24
73	79	64	57	53	03	52	96	47	78	35	80	83	42	82	60	93	52	08	44	35	27	38	84	35
98	52	01	77	07	14	90	56	86	07	22	10	94	05	58	60	97	09	34	33	50	50	07	39	98
11	80	50	54	31	39	80	82	77	32	50	72	56	82	48	29	40	52	42	01	52	77	56	78	51
83	45	29	96	34	06	28	89	80	83	13	74	67	00	78	18	47	54	06	10	68	71	17	78	17
88	68	54	02	00	86	50	75	84	01	36	76	66	79	51	90	36	47	64	93	29	60	91	10	62
99	59	46	73	48	87	51	76	49	69	91	82	60	89	28	93	78	56	13	68	23	47	83	41	13
65	48	11	76	74	17	46	85	09	50	58	04	77	69	74	73	03	95	71	86	40	21	81	65	44
80	12	43	56	35	17	72	70	80	15	45	31	82	23	74	21	11	57	82	53	14	38	55	37	63
74	35	09	98	17	77	40	27	72	14	43	23	60	02	10	45	52	16	42	37	96	28	60	26	55
69	91	62	68	03	66	25	22	91	48	36	93	68	72	03	76	62	11	39	90	94	40	05	64	18
09	89	32	05	05	14	22	56	85	14	46	42	75	67	88	96	29	77	88	22	54	38	21	45	98
91	49	91	45	23	68	47	92	76	86	46	16	28	35	54	94	75	08	99	23	37	08	92	00	48
80	33	69	45	98	20	94	03	68	58	70	29	73	41	35	53	14	03	38	40	42	05	08	23	41
44	10	48	19	49	85	15	74	79	54	32	97	92	65	75	57	60	04	08	81	22	22	20	64	13
12	55	07	37	42	11	10	00	20	40	12	86	07	46	97	96	64	48	94	39	28	70	72	58	15
63	60	64	93	29	16	50	53	44	84	40	21	95	25	63	43	65	17	70	82	07	20	73	17	90
61	19	69	04	46	26	45	74	77	74	51	92	43	37	29	65	39	45	95	93	42	58	26	05	27
15	47	44	52	66	95	27	07	99	53	59	36	78	38	48	82	39	61	01	18	33	21	15	94	66
94	55	72	85	73	67	89	75	43	87	54	62	24	44	31	91	19	04	25	92	92	92	74	59	73
42	48	11	62	13	97	34	40	87	21	16	86	84	87	67	03	07	11	20	59	25	70	14	66	70
23	52	37	83	17	73	20	88	98	37	68	93	59	14	16	26	25	22	96	63	05	52	28	25	62
04	49	35	24	94	75	24	03	38	24	45	86	25	10	25	61	96	27	93	35	65	33	71	24	72
00	54	99	76	54	64	05	18	81	59	96	11	96	38	96	54	69	28	23	91	23	28	72	95	29
35	96	31	53	07	26	80	80	93	54	33	35	13	54	62	77	97	45	00	24	90	10	33	93	33
59	80	80	83	91	45	42	72	68	42	83	60	94	97	00	18	02	12	48	92	78	56	52	01	06
46	05	88	52	36	01	39	09	22	86	77	28	14	40	77	93	91	08	36	47	70	61	74	29	41
32	17	90	05	97	87	37	92	52	41	05	56	70	70	07	86	74	31	71	57	85	39	41	18	38
69	23	46	14	06	20	11	74	52	04	15	95	66	00	00	18	74	39	24	23	97	11	89	63	38
19	56	54	14	30	01	75	87	53	79	40	41	92	15	85	66	67	43	68	06	84	96	28	52	07
45	15	51	49	38	19	47	60	72	46	43	66	79	45	43	59	04	79	00	33	20	82	66	95	41
94	86	43	19	94	36	16	81	08	51	34	88	88	15	53	01	54	03	54	56	05	01	45	11	76
98	08	62	48	26	45	24	02	84	04	44	99	90	88	96	39	09	47	34	07	35	44	13	18	80
33	18	51	62	32	41	94	15	09	49	89	43	54	85	81	88	69	54	19	94	37	54	87	30	43
80	95	10	04	06	96	38	27	07	74	20	15	12	33	87	25	01	62	52	98	94	62	46	11	71
79	75	24	91	40	71	96	12	82	96	69	86	10	25	91	74	85	22	05	39	00	38	75	95	79
18	63	33	25	37	98	14	50	65	71	31	01	02	46	74	05	45	56	14	27	77	93	89	19	36
74	02	94	39	02	77	55	73	22	70	97	79	01	71	19	52	52	75	80	21	80	81	45	17	48
54	17	84	56	11	80	90	33	71	43	05	33	51	29	69	56	12	71	92	55	36	04	09	03	24
11	66	44	98	83	52	07	98	48	27	59	38	17	15	39	09	97	33	34	40	88	46	12	33	56
48	32	47	79	28	31	24	96	47	10	02	29	53	68	70	32	30	75	75	46	15	02	00	99	94
69	07	49	41	38	87	63	79	19	76	35	58	40	44	01	10	51	82	16	15	01	84	87	69	38

[1] Reproduced by permission from The RAND Corporation, "A Million Random Digits," Free Press, Glencoe, Ill., 1955.

Index

Index

Models:
mathematical, 29
probabilistic, statistical, stochastic, or uncertainty, 33, 183–193
of random process (*see* Random experiment or process)
Monte Carlo method, 380, 382
for inventory control, 390–392
for waiting-line control, 380–389
Multistage sequential decision, 277–278
backward analysis, 278–283

Normal process, normal probability function (*see* Probability function; Random experiment or process)
Number:
absolute value of, 98*n*.
fractions, integers, 21
imaginary, rational, real, 21
irrational, 9
real-number line, 24

Objective function (*see* Linear programming)
Open statement, 23
Opportunity cost or loss, 49, 270–271, 276
expected, 271, 276
as related to expected value of perfect information, 272
(*See also* Imputed cost)
Order quantity (*see* Inventory control)
Ordered pairs, triples, *n*-tuples, 7, 11*n*., 28, 50, 54

Parameters, 40–41
of linear and quadratic function, 40–41

Parameters:
of probability function and random process, 237, 242–244, 246, 315
Partial derivative (*see* Derivative or derivative function)
Payoff table, 184–187, 202
Perfect information, 268
expected value of, 270, 276
Poisson process, Poisson probability function (*see* Random experiment or process)
Present value, 84–87
Probability:
Bayes' theorem (or revision of), 317–332
conditional, 209–211
definition of, 193
joint, 211, 213
marginal or unconditional, 213
objective, subjective, 248–252, 288, 317
prior, posterior, 321
(*See also* Events; Probability function)
Probability function:
binomial, 220, 237–241
continuous, 226–229
density of, 229, 232
graph of, 230–232
cumulative, 224–226
exponential, 243–244
and frequency distribution, 248–251
histogram of, 229–230
mass function, 232
normal, 220, 244–247
Poisson, 220, 242–243, 249–251
process diagram of, 219
random variable and, 222
(*See also* Random experiment or process; Random variable)
Probability tree (*see* Game tree)

Quantitative methods, 30–32
  (*See also* Mathematical methods)
Queuing (*see* Waiting-line control)

Random digits, 384–385
  table, 394
Random experiment or process,
  194
  Bernoulli, 220, 233–239
  normal, 220, 244–247
  parameters of (*see* Parameters)
  Poisson, 220, 241–243
  (*See also* Probability function)
Random sampling (*see* Sampling,
  random)
Random variable, 220–221, 260
  summary measure: of continu-
    ous variable, 267
  of discrete variable, 267
  expected value, 262
  median, mode, 262–263
  range, 263
  standard deviation, 264–266
  variance, 264–266
  (*See also* Probability function)
Rate of change:
  derivative as instantaneous,
    89–99
  geometric representation in
    graph of, 43–45, 72
  as gradient or slope, 72
  of linear function, 41–47
  as opportunity cost, 49
  of quadratic function, 41–45
  (*See also* Derivative or deriva-
    tive function)
Rational number (*see* Number)
Real number (*see* Number)
Relation:
  in decision making, 1, 6–10
  distinction between function
    and, 9*n*., 34

Relation:
  linear and nonlinear, 33, 38
  in mathematical statements, 9
  in mathematics and other
    sciences, 10–11
  as points in cartesian diagram,
    or graphing of, 8, 15, 21
  in process diagram, 9, 16
  set-theoretic definition of, 7
  tabular representation of, 6
  (*See also* Function and func-
    tional relation)
Relative weights (*see* Weighted
  average)
Reorder point (*see* Inventory
  control)

Safety stock (*see* Inventory
  control)
Sample, decision whether to,
  332–339
Sample points, 195
Sample size, 339
Sample space, 195–196
  reduced, 210
Sampling, random, 192*n*., 206
  cost of, 339
  with and without replace-
    ment, 252, 328
  use of information gained
    from, 322
  (*See also* Sample, decision
    whether to)
Scientific methods, 30–32
  (*See also* Mathematical methods)
Sensitivity analysis (*see* Inventory
  control)
Service failure:
  in inventory control, 357–358
  in waiting-line control, 375–380
Set, 7–13
  or ordered pairs, 7